Achieving Consistency in Sentencing

Achieving Consistency in Sentencing

LYNDON HARRIS
Barrister, Gray's Inn
6KBW College Hill

OXFORD
UNIVERSITY PRESS

Great Clarendon Street, Oxford, OX2 6DP,
United Kingdom

Oxford University Press is a department of the University of Oxford.
It furthers the University's objective of excellence in research, scholarship,
and education by publishing worldwide. Oxford is a registered trade mark of
Oxford University Press in the UK and in certain other countries

© Lyndon Harris 2022

The moral rights of the author have been asserted

First Edition published in 2022

Impression: 1

All rights reserved. No part of this publication may be reproduced, stored in
a retrieval system, or transmitted, in any form or by any means, without the
prior permission in writing of Oxford University Press, or as expressly permitted
by law, by licence or under terms agreed with the appropriate reprographics
rights organization. Enquiries concerning reproduction outside the scope of the
above should be sent to the Rights Department, Oxford University Press, at the
address above

You must not circulate this work in any other form
and you must impose this same condition on any acquirer

Public sector information reproduced under Open Government Licence v3.0
(http://www.nationalarchives.gov.uk/doc/open-government-licence/open-government-licence.htm)

Published in the United States of America by Oxford University Press
198 Madison Avenue, New York, NY 10016, United States of America

British Library Cataloguing in Publication Data

Data available

Library of Congress Control Number: 2022940735

ISBN 978–0–19–285926–6

DOI: 10.1093/oso/9780192859266.001.0001

Printed and bound in the UK by
TJ Books Limited

Links to third party websites are provided by Oxford in good faith and
for information only. Oxford disclaims any responsibility for the materials
contained in any third party website referenced in this work.

For Mum and Dad x

Preface

This text began as a conversation with Professor Julian Roberts, then the academic member of the Sentencing Council for England and Wales, in a coffee shop opposite the Royal Courts of Justice in London. I enthusiastically (over-confidently?) proffered views as to how the Council could improve its guidelines and the search for consistency in sentencing. Professor Roberts grinned and said words to the effect of 'you should come and do a DPhil and tell me how to make them better'. Without that disarming and characteristic humility, my ideas would have remained in the Fleet Street Press Coffee Shop.

I was so very fortunate that both Julian and Professor Andrew Ashworth agreed to supervise my doctorate. Their wisdom, encouragement, and constructive criticism (eg 'that's a novel view, Lyndon'!) made for a thoroughly enjoyable period of research, reflection, and professional development. I learned so much and I am immensely grateful to them both.

And so to this text. It has its origins in my doctoral thesis. It is intended to straddle both the academic and the practical; to consider the concept of consistency in sentencing from a theoretical standpoint, but with a keen eye on what would be workable in practice. Although there is a clear domestic focus, I hope this text will be of interest to those working in the field of sentencing internationally. Although the sentencing scheme in England and Wales has its quirks and peculiarities, it has at its core many features and principles that are present throughout sentencing around the world. As such, the examination of consistency, judicial discretion, and individualized justice should—I hope—resonate far beyond this jurisdiction. Similarly, the focus on the way in which the Westminster parliament, the England and Wales Court of Appeal (Criminal Division), and the Sentencing Council for England and Wales acts (and has acted) to structure sentencing discretion provides discrete lessons for this jurisdiction, but I hope that it also provides lessons to be learned further afield.

I would like to think that this is a useful contribution to the debate surrounding consistency, sentencers' discretion, and the approach of sentencing guidelines. But there is so much more to be said, domestically and internationally, on the topic.

Finally, I wish to thank OUP—specifically Luise Wilde and Ella Capel-Smith—for their hard work in bringing this to press.

Lyndon Harris
May 2022

Contents

Table of Cases   xv
Table of Statutes   xix
Other Authorities   xxiii
List of Abbreviations   xxv

Introduction   1

1. Sentencing in England and Wales   3
   Introduction   3
   The overarching principle   5
   The tension between principles and the 'real world'   9
   Conclusion   10

2. Conceptualizing consistency in sentencing   13
   Introduction   13
      The need for, and importance of, consistency in sentencing   13
      The basic concept   15
      The structure of this chapter   17
   The scope of the basic concept   18
      Are consistency and disparity interchangeable terms?   18
      Permissible range of sentences and the pursuit of
         principled sentencing   21
   Treating like cases alike   22
   The nature of consistency in sentencing   25
      A consistent approach or a consistent outcome?   25
      Is consistency a procedural or substantive concept?   32
   Conclusion   34
      A credible account of consistency   34
      A revised definition   38

3. Dangers of discretion: Empirical evidence of inconsistency   43
   Introduction   43
   The critical framework   44
   Empirical literature on consistency in sentencing   46
      Introduction   46
      Methodological challenges   48

x CONTENTS

Geographical differences and 'local justice'	51
The 'human' element	57
Sex/Gender	62
Race/Ethnicity	68
Intersectionality	73
Conclusion	75

4. Are individualized justice and consistency incompatible? ... 77
   Introduction ... 77
   Individualized justice ... 78
       The basic concept and its importance ... 78
       The offence, the offender, or both? ... 80
       Individualized justice: Structured discretion or carte blanche? ... 85
       Judicial discretion ... 96
   A permissible range of sentencing decisions ... 99
       A permissible range of sentences and the pursuit of principled sentencing ... 100
   The apparent tension between individualized justice and the concept of consistency ... 104
   Conclusion ... 107

5. When is a sentencing decision 'discretionary' and how should that discretion be structured? ... 109
   Introduction ... 109
   What is judicial discretion? ... 110
       Introduction ... 110
       The scope of the endeavour ... 112
       Summary of argument ... 115
       Identifying the existence of judicial discretion ... 116
       The manner in which the discretionary power must be exercised ... 124
       Conclusion ... 131
   The case for structured judicial discretion ... 133
       Methods of structuring discretion: Limiting or guiding? ... 134
       Limiting measures ... 137
       Guiding measures ... 139
   Conclusion ... 141

6. Statutory methods of structuring judicial discretion at sentencing ... 143
   Introduction ... 143
   Parliament's role in providing structured discretion at sentencing ... 144
       Legislatively structured judicial discretion ... 144

Politics	148
Parliament's role in structuring discretion	149
Provisions of general application	151
General	151
Principles underpinning the sentencing scheme in England and Wales	153
Which sentences may be imposed for which offences?	158
The maximum sentence available for particular offences	159
Availability of sentencing orders	163
Tests for imposing sentencing orders	166
Aggravation and mitigation	170
Other factors operating to reduce the severity of a sentence	174
Assisting the prosecution	175
Guilty plea	176
Totality and multiple offences	177
Minimum and mandatory sentences	179
Minimum sentences	179
Mandatory sentences	183
Conclusion	186
The extent to which judicial discretion is structured by Parliament in England and Wales	186
Parliament's role in structuring discretion	187
Lessons to be learned	188
7. Structuring judicial discretion through the Court of Appeal (Criminal Division)	**189**
Introduction	189
History	190
Legislative history of a criminal appellate court	190
The types of guidance given by the Court of Appeal (Criminal Division)	195
The power of precedent	195
Principles of sentencing and other general concepts	200
Offences: Guidance on the approach to sentencing	203
Offences: Reviewing sentences in specific cases	206
Offences: Traditional guideline judgment	213
Interpretation: Terms in sentencing guidelines	215
Interpretation: Statutory provisions	219
Sentencing procedure	226
Limitations on the CACD's ability to provide guidance and structure	228
Conclusion	231

8. Structuring discretion through sentencing guidelines: Do the Sentencing Council's guidelines promote greater consistency? — 235
   - Introduction — 235
   - The Sentencing Council's guidelines — 236
     - Background — 236
   - The constituent elements of sentencing guidance — 238
   - The Sentencing Council's offence-specific guidelines — 242
     - General — 242
     - Interpreting offence-specific guidelines — 247
     - Robbery Offences Definitive Guideline (2016) — 253
   - Conclusion — 258
   - The Sentencing Council's overarching guidelines — 258
     - The need for substantive guidance — 258
     - Interpretation of overarching guidelines — 261
     - Reduction in Sentence for a Guilty plea Definitive Guideline (2017) — 262
     - Do the Sentencing Council's guidelines contain substantive guidance? — 268
   - The degree of constraint provided by the guidelines regime — 268
     - Duty to 'follow' sentencing guidelines — 268
     - Offence range versus Category range — 273
   - Empirical literature — 274
   - Conclusion — 277

9. Achieving consistency in sentencing — 281
   - Introduction — 281
   - What is consistency in sentencing and what theoretical and practical problems does it pose? — 282
   - Can consistency be reconciled with the concept of individualized justice? — 283
   - What is a discretionary sentencing decision and how may such decisions be structured? — 284
   - How effectively does the system in England and Wales promote consistency? — 285
     - The extent of the structure currently provided — 285
     - The division of labour — 288
   - How could the current regime in England and Wales be improved upon? — 292
     - Insufficient flexibility — 292
     - More substantive guidance — 293
     - What role for the CACD? — 294

Lessons for other jurisdictions	295
The need for a clear principle/principles	295
The need for further guidance in addition to the legislative scheme	296
Each institution giving guidance must know its role	297
Combining limiting and guiding measures	298
Combining offence-specific and overarching guidance	298
Consistency of approach and consistency of outcome	299
A cautious use of language	299
Constraint is not the enemy of discretion, inappropriate constraint is	300
Guidance must be substantive	300
Bibliography	301
Index	313

Table of Cases

Attorney General's Reference (No.16 of 2014) (R. v Gill) [2014]
  EWCA Crim 956 210–11
Attorney General's Reference (No.4 of 1989) (1989)
  11 Cr. App. R. (S.) 517 .... 99–100, 209
Attorney General's Reference (Nos.26 and 27 of 2016) [2016]
  EWCA Crim 613; [2014] 2 Cr.App.R.(S.) 45 99
Attorney General's Reference (R. v Singh) [2021] EWCA Crim 1426 156–57
Attorney General's Reference (No.27 of 2013) (R. v Burinskas)
  [2014] EWCA Crim 334; [2014] 2 Cr.App.R. (S.) 45 .... 26–27, 184–85
Attorney General's Reference (No.53 of 2013) [2013] EWCA Crim 2544;
  [2014] 2 Cr. App. R. (S.) 1 173
Attorney General's Reference (No.96 of 2009) (R. v F) [2010]
  EWCA Crim 350 228
Attorney General's Reference (Nos.21 and 22 of 2003) [2003]
  EWCA Crim 3089 261
Attorney General's Reference (R. v Agolini and Others) [2017]
  EWCA Crim 173 269–70
Attorney General's Reference (R. v Kahar); R. v Ziamani [2016]
  EWCA Crim 568; [2016] 2 Cr.App.R. (S.) 32 .... 214, 275, 289–90,
Attorney General's Reference (R. v NC) [2016] EWCA Crim 1141 275
Attorney General's Reference (R. v Parish) [2017] EWCA Crim 2064 224
Attorney General's Reference (R. v Youngman) [2016] EWCA Crim 2224 157–58
Bugmy v The Queen [2013] HCA 37 83–84
Helvering v Hallock (1940) 309 U. S. 106 196–97
Ivey v Genting Casinos UK Ltd (t/a Crockfords Club) [2017] UKSC 67;
  [2018] A.C. 391 197
Kable v DPP (NSW) (1995) 36 NSWLR 374 78–79
Lewis v Attorney General of Jamaica [2001] 2 A.C. 50; [2000]
  3 W.L.R. 1785 196–97
Liversidge v Anderson [1942] A.C. 206 200–1
Lowe v The Queen [1984] H.C.A. 46 .... 13, 23–24, 103
Markarian v The Queen [2005] H.C.A. 25; (2005) 228 CLR 357 160–61
Muldrock v The Queen [2011] HCA 39; (2011) 244 CLR 120 .... 93, 159–60
Payne v Tennessee (1991) 501 U.S. 808 196–97
R. (Gibson) v Secretary of State for Justice [2018] UKSC 2; [2018]
  1 W.L.R. 629 155–56
R. v A [1999] 1 Cr.App.R.(S.) 52 175
R. v AP [2018] EWCA Crim 1701 210–11
R. v Avis [1998] 2 Cr. App. R.(S.) 178 225
R. v Bailey [2011] EWCA Crim 1585 36
R. v Ball [2019] EWCA Crim 1260 267–68

R. v Beaumont [2015] EWCA Crim 2334; [2016] 1 Cr. App. R. (S.) 58. 217
R. v Blackshaw [2011] EWCA Crim 2312; [2012] 1 Cr. App. R. (S.) 114 . . . . 13–14, 29
R. v Boateng [2011] EWCA Crim 861; [2011] 2 Cr. App. R. (S.) 104. 224
R. v Bond [2013] EWCA Crim 2713; [2014] 2 Cr App R (S) 3. 16–17
R. v Bondzie [2016] EWCA Crim 552; [2016] 1 W.L.R. 3004 . . . . 201, 202–3
R. v Bourke [2017] EWCA Crim 2150; [2018] 1 Cr. App. R. (S.) 42 . . . . . . 169–70, 228
R. v Butcher (1989) 11 Cr.App.R. (S.) 104, CA (Crim Div) 36
R. v Caley [2012] EWCA Crim 2821; [2013] 2 Cr App R (S) 47 14–15
R. v Carter [2021] EWCA Crim 667. 267–68
R. v Chin-Charles [2019] EWCA Crim 1140; [2020] 1 Cr. App. R. (S.) 6 228
R. v Creathorne [2014] EWCA Crim 500; [2014] 2 Cr. App. R.(S.) 48 267–68
R. v Dalton [2021] EWCA Crim 160 267–68
R. v Dart [2014] EWCA Crim 2158 99
R. v Dillon [2015] EWCA Crim 3; [2015] 1 Cr. App. R. (S.) 62 221
R. v Edwards [2006] EWCA Crim 2833; [2007] 1 Cr App R (S) 111. 224
R. v Erskine [2009] EWCA Crim 1425; [2009] 2 Cr. App. R. 29. 29
R. v Forbes [2016] EWCA Crim 1388; [2017] 1 W.L.R. 53 . . . . 196–97, 216
R. v Foster [2015] EWCA Crim 916; [2015] 2 Cr. App. R. (S.) 45 212
R. v Freeman (1989) 11 Cr. App. R. (S.) 398. 210–11
R. v Ghosh [1982] Q.B. 1053 197
R. v Gibson [2004] EWCA Crim 593; [2004] 2 Cr. App. R. (S.) 84 79–80
R. v Gladue [1999] 1 S.C.R. 688. 83–84
R. v Glover [2010] EWCA Crim 1714. 79–80
R. v Gomes Monteiro [2014] EWCA Crim 747; [2014] 2 Cr. App. R. (S.) 62 93
R. v Haining [2016] EWCA Crim 854. 100–1
R. v Hardy [2020] EWCA Crim 398; [2020] 2 Cr. App. R. (S.) 37 267–68
R. v Hatfield [2009] EWCA Crim 1589 210–11
R. v Henning [2015] EWCA Crim 879; [2015] 2 Cr. App. R. (S.) 37 26–27
R. v Inglis [2010] EWCA Crim 2637; [2011] 1 W.L.R. 1110. 187
R. v James [2011] EWCA Crim 2630 267–68
R. v Jones [2018] EWCA Crim 1499 210–11
R. v Jurisic [1998] NSWSC 423 103
R. v Kelly [2011] EWCA Crim 1462; [2012] 1 W.L.R. 5 . . . . 220, 221
R. v Khan (Mohammed Gulnawaz) [2016] EWCA Crim 125 207–8
R. v King [2013] EWCA Crim 1599; [2014] 1 Cr. App. R. (S.) 73 99
R. v Laverick [2015] EWCA Crim 1059; [2015] 2 Cr. App. R. (S.) 62 269–70
R. v Lawrence (1989) 11 Cr App R (S) 580 261
R. v Leader [2014] EWCA Crim 300. 207–8
R. v Lewis [2012] EWCA Crim 1071 269–70
R. v Maka [2005] EWCA Crim 3365; [2006] 2 Cr. App. R. (S.) 14 210–11
R. v Markham and Edwards [2017] EWCA Crim 739;
  [2017] 2 Cr. App. R. (S.) 30 262–63
R. v McC [2014] EWCA Crim 909 . . . . 13–14, 16–17
R. v McKay [2017] EWCA Crim 2299; [2018] 1 Cr. App. R. (S.) 36 203–5
R. v Moriarty [2018] EWCA Crim 1590. 212
R. v Murphy [2019] EWCA Crim 438. 269–70
R. v Nancarrow [2019] EWCA Crim 470; [2019] 2 Cr. App. R.(S.) 4 224
R. v Noel [2017] EWCA Crim 782; [2018] 1 Cr. App. R. (S.) 5. 254
R. v Nur [2015] 1 R.C.S. 773. 182

R. v *Oosthuizen* [2005] EWCA Crim 1978; [2006] 1 Cr. App. R. (S.) 73........ 202–3
R. v *P*; R. v *Blackburn* [2007] EWCA Crim 2290; [2008] 2 All E.R. 684.......... 175
R. v *Peters* [2005] EWCA Crim 605; [2005] 2 Cr. App. R. (S.) 101 .... 103, 286
R. v *Pinto* [2006] EWCA Crim 749; [2006] 2 Cr. App. R. (S.) 87............. 160–61
R. v *Plaku* [2021] EWCA Crim 568; [2021] 4 W.L.R. 82.................... 267–68
R. v *Planken* [2017] EWCA Crim 1807; [2018] 1 Cr. App. R. (S.) 24 207–8
R. v *Poulton and Celaire* [2002] EWCA Crim 2487.......................... 261
R. v *Price* [2016] EWCA Crim 1919................................... 100–1
R. v *Price* [2018] EWCA Crim 1528................................... 210–11
R. v *Quick* [2017] EWCA Crim 66; [2017] 1 Cr. App. R. (S.) 54 .... 209, 211–12
R. v *Racman* [2014] EWCA Crim 2133; [2015] 1 Cr. App. R. (S.) 18 202–3
R. v *RB* [2020] EWCA Crim 643; [2021] 1 Cr. App. R. (S.) 1................... 245
R. v *Rees* [1978] Crim. L.R. 298... 194
R. v *Rehman* [2005] EWCA Crim 2056; [2006]
   1 Cr. App. R. (S.) 77 .... 91–92, 93–95, 223
R. v *Robinson* [2015] EWCA Crim 1839; [2016] 1 Cr. App. R. (S.) 35 290
R. v *Rugg* [1997] 2 Cr App R (S) 350, CA (Crim Div)......................... 36
R. v *Saw* [2009] EWCA Crim 1; [2009] 2 Cr. App. R. (S.) 54 289–90
R. v *Simmons* (1995) 16 Cr. App. R. (S.) 801 210–11
R. v *Smith (Christopher)* [2015] EWCA Crim 1482; [2016]
   1 Cr. App. R. (S.) 8... 217, 222–23, 248
R. v *Smith* [2017] EWCA Crim 1174; [2017] 2 Cr. App. R. (S.) 42 213–14
R. v *Smith* [2018] EWCA Crim 1621 210–11
R. v *St Albans Crown Court ex parte Cinnamon* [1981] Q.B. 480; [1981]
   2 W.L.R. 681 189
R. v *Stockdale* [2005] EWCA Crim 1582 202–3
R. v *Tatomir* [2015] EWCA Crim 2167; [2016] Crim. L.R. 503............... 202–3
R. v *Taylor* [2012] EWCA Crim 630; [2012] 2 Cr. App. R. (S.) 98 ....27–29, 32, 78–79
R. v *Teklu* [2017] EWCA Crim 1477; [2018] 1 Cr. App. R. (S.) 12............... 249
R. v *Thelwall* [2016] EWCA Crim 1755; [2017] Crim. L.R. 240 .... 99, 289–90
R. v *Thompson* [2015] EWCA Crim 1575; [2016] 1 Cr. App. R. (S.) 26........... 217
R. v *Thompson* [2018] EWCA Crim 639; [2018] 2 Cr. App. R. (S.) 19......... 211–12
R. v *Tuka* [2017] EWCA Crim 2210 224
R. v *Tunney* [2006] EWCA Crim 2066; [2007] 1 Cr. App. R. (S.) 91 205
R. v *Turner* (1975) 61 Cr. App. R. 67..................................... 30–31
R. v *Waters and Others* [2021] EWCA Crim 1356........................ 255–56
R. v *Webbe* [2001] EWCA Crim 1217; [2002] 1 Cr. App. R. (S.) 22........... 289–90
R. v *Williscroft* [1975] VR 292... 156–57
R. v *Woods* [2020] EWCA Crim 84.................................... 267–68
R. v *Woolin* [1999] 1 A.C. 82; [1998] 3 W.L.R. 382 187
R. v *Wright and Bing* [2017] EWCA Crim 1195 212
R. v *Zehkov* [2013] EWCA Crim 1656; [2014] 1 Cr. App. R. (S.) 69 224
R. v *Kovali* [2013] EWCA Crim 1056; [2014] 1 Cr. App. R.(S.) 33............ 267–68
Re *Loughlin* [2017] UKSC 63; [2017] 1 W.L.R. 3963...................... 175–76
State v Evans 311 N.W.2d 481 (Minn. 1981) 103
US v Pitera 795 F.Supp. 546 (1992)................................. 78–79, 85
Wong v The Queen [2001] H.C.A. 64 230–31
Young v Bristol Aeroplane Company, Limited [1944] K.B. 718............... 196–97

Table of Statutes

Armed Forces Act 2016 151–52
Assaults on Emergency Workers
   (Offences) Act 2018 151–52
Coroners and Justice
   Act 2009 151–52
   s.118-124, 127 144–45
   s.120(11)(b) 13–14, 16–17, 27
   s.120(3) 288–89
Counter-Terrorism and Border
   Security Act 2019 151–52
Counter-Terrorism and Sentencing
   Act 2021 151–52
Crime (Sentences) Act 1997 151–52
Crime and Disorder Act 1998
   s.80 .... 144–45, 195,
                            230–31, 288–89
   s.81 .... 144–45, 195, 288–89
Crimes (Sentencing) Act 2005
   s.133C (A.C.T.) 78–79
Criminal Appeal Act 1907 190
   s.1 144–45
   s.4(3) 192
Criminal Appeal Act 1966 193
   s.1 144–45
   s.4(2) 192–93
Criminal Appeal Act 1968
   s.11(3) 192–93, 206–8, 211–12
   s.29 206–7
   s.50 163–64
Criminal Appeal Act 1995 151–52
Criminal Justice Act 1925
   s.40(2) 149–50
Criminal Justice Act 1948
   s.17 149–50
Criminal Justice Act 1982
   s.37 .... 159, 168
Criminal Justice Act 1988 Part IV... 208
Criminal Justice Act 1988
   s.36 208
   ss.35 and 36 149–50

Criminal Justice Act 1991 ..5–6, 151–52
   s.1(2)(a) 6
   s.1(2)(b) 6
Criminal Justice Act 1993 151–52
Criminal Justice Act 2003 ....6–7, 5–6,
                  7–8, 119, 151–52, 228
   s.142 .... 6–7, 26–27
   s.145 171–72
   s.152 26–27
   s.153 26–27
   s.167 144–45
   s.172 202–3
   s.189 211–12
   Sch.21 .... 103, 183–84, 219–20
Criminal Justice and Courts
   Act 2015 151–52
Criminal Justice and
   Immigration Act 2008 151–52
Criminal Law Act 1977 s.3 159
Crown Cases Act 1848 190–91
Drug Trafficking Act 1994 151–52
Fraud Act 2006 s.1 269–70
French Criminal Code
   art 132-1 13–14
French Penal Code 79
Habitual Criminals Act 1869 146–47
Judicature Act 1873 193
Legal Aid, Sentencing and
   Punishment of Offenders
   Act 2012 151–52
Magistrates' Courts
   Act 1980 s.32 163–64
Misuse of Drugs Act 1971
   s.27 163–64
   s.4(3) 106–7
   s.5(3) 106–7
Motor Car Act 1903 149–50
Murder (Abolition of Death
   Penalty) Act 1965 s.1 31–32,
                               159, 183–84

xx   TABLE OF STATUTES

Offences against the Person Act 1861
    s.5 159
    s.18 269–70
    s.61 145–46
Offender Rehabilitation
    Act 2014. 151–52
Offensive Weapons Act 2019. . . . 151–52
Penal Servitude Act 1891 s.1 145–46
Police, Crime, Sentencing and
    Courts Act 2022 . . . . . 151–52, 181
Powers of Criminal Courts
    (Sentencing) Act 2000 151–52
    s.109 184–85
Proceeds of Crime Act 2002 151–52
    Sch.2 para.1 182
Psychoactive Substances
    Act 2016. 151–52
Senior Courts Act 1981
    s.2 144–45
    s.45 158
Sentencing Act 2020. . . . . 7–8, 119,
              145 , 151–52, 166, 199,
              219–20, 227, 228, 246–47,
    s.52 . . . . 227, 228
    s.57 . . . . 7, 26–27, 74–76,
              81, 82, 106, 129–30,
              148–49, 154–55, 173,
              176–77, 182, 209,
              283–84,
    s.59 . . . . 246–47, 268,
              270–71, 273, 274
    s.60 268
    s.63 . . . . 26–27, 46, 68–69,
              138–39, 153–55 ,
              155–56, 162, 246–47
    s.64 170–71
    s.65 170–71
    s.66 170–71
    s.68 170–71
    s.69 170–71
    s.71 170–71
    s.72 170–71
    s.73 . . . . 176, 177, 181, 263
    s.74 . . . . 175–76, 263
    s.77 . . . . 172, 178, 200–1
    s.80 165–66
    s.83 184
    s.89 138
    s.109 156–57
    s.120 168
    s.174 and Sch.6 88–89
    s.204 153–54
    s.208 156–57
    s.223 159
    s.230 . . . . 26–27, 153–55
    s.231 . . . . 7–8, 26–27, 153–55
    s.277 166
    s.286 . . . . 167, 211–12
    s.311 . . . . 93–95, 180, 187, 220, 223
    s.312 . . . . 180, 181
    s.313 . . . . 138, 180, 182
    s.314 180
    s.315 . . . . 31–32, 180
    s.325 264–65
    s.346 166
    s.399 182
    ss.42-43 163–64
    ss.64 to 72. 263
    ss.133-146 163–64
    ss.152-161 164–65
    ss.200-220 163–64
    ss.233-248 185
    ss.252A, 265, 278. 184
    ss.258, 274, 285 184
    ss.259, 275 and 321,
        and Sch.21 183–84
    ss.268A and 282A 184
    ss.273 and 283 184–85
    ss.279 and 285 166
    ss.311-315 . . . . 31–32, 180
    ss.330-342 163–64
    ss.343-358 163–64
    ss.359-364 164–65
    ss.387-392 175–76
    Schs.18 and 19 . . . . . . 164–65, 169–70
    Sch.19 166
    Sch.21 . . . . 103, 184, 219–20, 286
    Sch.21 para.4 . . . . 220, 221
Serious Crime Act 2015 151–52
Serious Organised Crime
    and Police Act 2005 151–52,
                                  175–76
Sexual Offences Act 2003
    Schs.3 or 5 164–65
Terrorism (Restriction of Early
    Release) Act 2020 151–52
Terrorism Act 2006. 151–52
    s.5 214

The Criminal Justice Act 2003
(Commencement No.8 and
Transitional and Saving
Provisions) Order 2005 (SI
2005/950). 7–8

Theft Act 1968
  s.17 269–70
  s.7 135–36
  s.8 253–54
  s.9 137

Other Authorities

Criminal Practice Directions
   [2015] EWCA Crim 1567
   para.M.3 29

HC Deb 29 July 1907 vol
   179 cc663 192

List of Abbreviations

BAME	black and minority ethnic
CACD	Court of Appeal (Criminal Division)
CCSS	Crown Court Sentencing Survey
DTO	Detention and Training Order
IPP	Imprisonment for Public Protection
s	section
SOCPA	Serious Organised Crime and Police Act 2005

Introduction

'Would you tell me, please, which way I ought to go from here?'
'That depends a good deal on where you want to get to,' said the Cat.
'I don't much care where–' said Alice.
'Then it doesn't matter which way you go,' said the Cat.
'–so long as I get SOMEWHERE,' Alice added as an explanation.
'Oh, you're sure to do that,' said the Cat, 'if you only walk long enough.'[1]

This work focuses upon efforts to structure judicial discretion at sentencing in the name of achieving consistency, this being generally seen as a requirement of fairness and natural justice. If the same offence sentenced in Brighton and Birmingham by comparable offenders in comparable circumstances receives wildly different sentences, normative standards of justice almost inevitably lead to the conclusion that something has gone wrong with the administration of justice.

But a test of 'would a right-thinking member of the public think something has gone wrong with the administration of justice' is not sufficiently clear to correct the perceived error. So, unlike Alice in the epigraph above, in the pursuit of consistency, we must care about where we are going—*somewhere* will not do. And so, this work seeks to examine the concept of consistency to ascertain what it actually is. That, in turn, will enable an examination of (i) the current understanding of consistency; (ii) current methods used in an attempt to achieve consistency; and (iii) what is needed to achieve (or better achieve) consistency.

---

[1] Lewis Carroll, *Alice in Wonderland* (Macmillan and Co. 1866).

Achieving Consistency in Sentencing. Lyndon Harris, Oxford University Press. © Lyndon Harris 2022.
DOI: 10.1093/oso/9780192859266.003.0001

As a means of examining current methods of achieving consistency, this work uses England and Wales as a case study throughout. The jurisdiction of England and Wales has a long history of discretion at sentencing, and has, through various methods, developed a complex system of guidance at sentencing as a means of promoting consistency. It is a jurisdiction which (i) values flexibility and individualization; (ii) has in place a mature system of sentencing guidance, and in particular, a sentencing guidelines system that is twenty years old; and (iii) has as its dominant principle retributive proportionality (a feature of most Western systems). In short, the jurisdiction of England and Wales provides a very good case study for the examination of measures designed to achieve consistency in sentencing.

While therefore this work has a focus upon England and Wales and the particular provisions and practices that operate in this jurisdiction, it is hoped that this work will be of wider interest to those in other jurisdictions which place a value of consistency. There are many lessons (good and bad) to be learned from the English and Welsh experience which could be utilized in other systems worldwide as a means of promoting consistency in sentencing. Thus, this work flits between theoretical discussion, blind as to jurisdiction, and detailed discussion of the particular system in force in England and Wales in 2022. Those sections which consider the English and Welsh system seek to draw conclusions that are practically useful both to England and Wales and any other jurisdiction which has an interest in consistency.

So, rather than, as Alice and the Cheshire Cat would have us do and meander *somewhere* without a care for where we are headed, this work begins with some background on the system in place in England and Wales so as to provide some context to the later discussion. It then moves swiftly to a theoretical and empirical exploration of consistency, individualized justice, and discretion, before considering in detail measures utilized in England and Wales to promote consistency. This work concludes with an analysis of both the effectiveness of the measures in place in England and Wales and identifying lessons for other jurisdictions seeking greater consistency in their sentencing system.

And so with that said, let's begin at the beginning and go on until we come to the end.

1
Sentencing in England and Wales

The severity of the sentence imposed should reflect the seriousness of the offence committed.[1]

Introduction

England and Wales operate a principally retributive scheme with the nature and severity of the sentence determined, principally, by the seriousness of the offence for which an offender falls to be sentenced. There are, however, further (arguably competing) considerations which impact upon the decision to impose a sentence of a particular type and severity.

This chapter contains a summary of the sentencing scheme in England and Wales which serves to provide context to the later enquiry into consistency in sentencing. While consistency could be achieved—and measured—in numerous ways, the extent to which a system can be said to be consistent depends upon the principle(s) to which it seeks to conform. For instance, a regime which required sentences of ten years' imprisonment to be imposed for all violent offences would, on some measure, be consistent. However, in a regime which sought to reflect the harm caused by an offence, it would be inconsistent as it would result in the same sentence being imposed for offences which involved disparate levels of harm. Similarly, a regime which sought to sentence by reference to risk of future offences could be considered to be consistent if it sentenced on the basis of the offender's culpability, but it could not be said to be consistent with its consequentialist aims. In the search for consistency, therefore, the key question is 'consistent with what'?

---

[1] Home Office, *Making Sentencing Clearer: A Consultation and Report of a Review by the Home Secretary, Lord Chancellor and Attorney General* (Home Office 2006) 3.

Achieving Consistency in Sentencing. Lyndon Harris, Oxford University Press. © Lyndon Harris 2022.
DOI: 10.1093/oso/9780192859266.003.0002

This work will seek to argue that the concept of consistency is agnostic to the principle(s) which are sought to be realized and that consistency can be present in a regime which pursues any principle(s), whether they might be regarded as flawed, unjust, or even barbaric. A regime which mandated that amputation of the hands of thieves, for instance, might properly be considered to be barbarous, yet it certainly could be said that the punishment was—on one definition of the concept—consistent. The same is true for regimes which include in the sentencer's arsenal the death penalty. Moreover, it could be ordinally (though perhaps not cardinally) proportionate. That is not to legitimize such means of punishment of course but merely to recognize that as a critical tool, consistency remains silent as to the merits or otherwise of a particular scheme. By way of analogy, a speed camera is a tool used to measure the velocity at which vehicles travel, intended to detect those which exceed the prescribed limit for the purposes of punishment. The speed camera makes no comment as to the propriety of the 70 miles per hour limit applicable to a motorway in England and Wales. It would perform its same function if the speed limit were 70, 140, or 210 miles per hour. Although the speed camera has other aims—such as facilitating the punishment of those who have transgressed—it serves a tool to analyse the extent to which a speed limit is observed. Consistency, as a critical tool, may therefore be deployed to evaluate the extent to which a regime is consistent with its aims, but being agnostic as to the merits of those aims.[2]

This work explores the concept of consistency through the lens of the sentencing scheme in England and Wales. England and Wales has a very developed sentencing scheme, with a clear and longstanding tripartite relationship between the legislature, judiciary, and a guidelines body, the Sentencing Council. As such, the scheme in place in England and Wales—with its principally retributive scheme and well-established system of guidelines—provides an excellent example of the wide range of measures that can be employed as a means of promoting consistency in

---

[2] This conception of principles is recognized in Gardner's chapter in Ashworth's festschrift, where Gardner draws a distinction between principles which are 'reason-giving' only if they are 'good' principles and those which are treated as 'good' principles merely because they are adhered to. See John Gardner, 'Ashworth on Principles' in Lucia Zedner and Julian V. Roberts (eds), *Principles and Values in Criminal Law and Criminal Justice: Essays in Honour of Andrew Ashworth* (OUP 2012) 4–5.

sentencing. Accordingly, although the focus appears to be domestic, it is hoped that this exploration is of some utility to those with an interest in sentencing and consistency internationally, as many of the lessons to be learned apply to schemes far beyond England and Wales.

It is therefore necessary to set out the scheme prevailing in England and Wales so as to provide the context for the later enquiry into the means of structuring discretion to promote greater consistency in sentencing.

The overarching principle

Sentencers in England and Wales are given their powers and duties at sentencing in the context of a principally retributive scheme. Retributivism, most notably advocated by von Hirsch, mandates that a sentence addresses 'offenders as a moral agent, as having the capacity to assess and to respond to an official evaluation of their conduct'.[3] It is founded upon the 'intuitive' link between desert and punishment to censure transgressive behaviour, achieved by the imposition of a proportionate punishment designed to respect the rule of law values of certainty and predictability while operating as a deterrent.[4] While there are competing accounts of retributivism, the scheme in England and Wales is insufficiently precise to discern between the various accounts with confidence.

The sentencing scheme makes reference to the seriousness of the offence for which the offender falls to be sentenced which is, in turn, assessed by reference to the culpability of the offender and the harm present in the offence. Parliament legislated this approach in the Criminal Justice Act 1991, though the origins of this approach pre-date that enactment, the courts having sentenced by reference to the severity of the crime since at least the late 1800s.[5] Ashworth and Player criticized the 1991 Act's failure to declare clearly that proportionality was the principle by which

---

[3] Andrew Ashworth and Rory Kelly, *Sentencing and Criminal Justice* (7th edn, Bloomsbury 2021) 77.
[4] ibid 76.
[5] Julian V Roberts and Andrew Ashworth, 'The Evolution of Sentencing Policy and Practice in England and Wales, 2003–2015' (2016) 45(1) Crime and Justice 307, 308–358, 308.

sentencing should be conducted, though this was clear from the White Paper preceding the Act.[6]

Section 1(2)(a) of the 1991 Act made reference to the seriousness of the offence and placed limitations on the court's ability to impose custodial and community sentences by reference to offence seriousness. Section 1(2)(b) operated as an exception to this approach in circumstances where considerations of public protection required such a sentence. It is evident, therefore, that the 1991 Act brought about, more clearly than before, a form of limiting retributivism in sentencing in England and Wales. Sentences were therefore determined principally by the seriousness of the offence, but with other considerations capable of influencing the decision. The 'seriousness' of the offence was not defined but as Ashworth and Kelly noted, the principle of proportionality was clear from the White Paper preceding the Act.[7]

Proportionality may be subdivided into ordinal and cardinal proportionality. The former concerns the relative seriousness of one offence to another, for instance, an assault causing a bruise is less serious than an assault causing a fractured jaw. The latter 'relates the ordinal ranking to a scale of punishments'.[8] Notably, upon the enactment of the 1991 Act, the maximum sentences for criminal offences remained untouched. There was, therefore, no determined recalibration of ordinal or cardinal proportionality, though prison numbers almost doubled in the supervening years.[9] This speaks to the continuation (and formalization) of desert as the guiding principle at sentencing.

The Criminal Justice Act 2003 'reaffirmed a number of existing sentencing provisions and introduced a raft of changes'.[10] Proportionality remained the guiding principle, with other considerations at play. The scheme, however, now contained a legislative provision as to the objects of sentencing: section 142 of the 2003 Act listed for the first time the purposes of sentencing which comprised a mixture of retributive and consequentialist concerns.[11] This has since been repealed and re-enacted in a

---

[6] Andrew Ashworth and Elaine Player, 'Criminal Justice Act 2003: The Sentencing Provisions' (2005) 68(5) Modern Law Review 822–838, 822.
[7] Ashworth and Kelly (n 3) 98.
[8] Ashworth and Kelly (n 3) 77.
[9] Ministry of Justice, *Offender Management Statistics Quarterly: Prison Population: 30 September 2015* (Ministry of Justice 2015) cited in Roberts and Ashworth (n 5).
[10] Roberts and Ashworth (n 5).
[11] There is a fuller discussion of this provision in Chapter 6.

large consolidation exercise, now known as the Sentencing Act 2020 or 'Sentencing Code'.

Section 57 of the Sentencing Act 2020 provides that these purposes—in the case of those aged eighteen or over when convicted only—are:

(a) the punishment of offenders,
(b) the reduction of crime (including its reduction by deterrence),
(c) the reform and rehabilitation of offenders,
(d) the protection of the public, and
(e) the making of reparation by offenders to persons affected by their offences.[12]

Ashworth and Kelly criticized the lack of clarity stemming from a list of competing purposes of sentencing with no clear hierarchy or guidance as to how one should discern the correct approach in a given case and suggested that it is open to question as to whether there is in fact a primary rationale in the English and Welsh scheme.[13] Yet this is capable of justification and rationalization if one conceives of retributivism as an imprecise concept and of the task of a sentencer to be two distinct, sequential, steps: first, to determine the proportionate range by reference to desert; and second, to rely upon the statutory purposes of sentencing to determine where in the proportionate range a sentence ought to fall. This encapsulates the essence of Norval Morris' theory of limiting retributivism: a sentence must not be undeserved, but desert is imprecise, like cases should be treated alike unless there are utilitarian reasons to the contrary, perhaps most importantly for the present enquiry, unequal penalties can still be just.[14]

While the scheme in England and Wales may not expressly subscribe to the latter doctrine, the essence of Morris' limiting retributivism is captured by the requirement that the sentence to be imposed is to be driven by the seriousness of the offence but with other, non-retributive,

---

[12] Sentencing Act 2020 s 57 (1) and (2).
[13] Ashworth and Kelly (n 4) 66–67.
[14] Norval Morris, *Madness and the Criminal Law* (University of Chicago Press 1982) 192, 198, cited in Richard S Frase, 'Norval Morris's Contributions to Sentencing Structures, Theory, and Practice' (2009) 21(4) Federal Sentencing Reporter 254, 255–260, 255.

considerations capable of impacting upon the nature and severity of the sentence.[15]

By way of illustration, take an offence of dwelling burglary. Suppose the proportionate range is eighteen months to three years' imprisonment. Within that range of proportionate sentences, the purposes of sentencing may influence the sentence to be imposed. If a sentence prioritizing rehabilitation is considered to be appropriate, then something towards the lower end of that proportionate scale is perhaps to be expected; conversely, a sentence prioritizing punishment or deterrence may result in a sentence towards the top of that range. At no point is a disproportionate punishment permitted as the purposes cannot legitimize a sentence beyond the proportionate range. The purposes are a secondary consideration which cannot override the primary rationale, retributive proportionality.

While that might reconcile the approach adopted in England and Wales with an established and accepted theoretical framework, it does not deal with the obvious extension to Ashworth and Kelly's point; while unequal sentences may be just, based on the differing considerations between cases, could different sentences be justified in the same case? Put another way, continuing with the example in the previous paragraph, could a sentence of eighteen months and a sentence of three years be justified, if different judges took different views as to the appropriate disposal? The following chapters consider this point, but it suffices to say that at present, there is ambiguity in the England and Wales scheme. Evidently, whether that amounts to inconsistency rather depends on the definition of that concept that one adopts.

Additionally, the principle of parsimony is a clear feature of the statutory scheme; Parliament has legislated that sentences must be of a length that is the shortest period which is commensurate with the seriousness of the offence.[16] Again, this is subject to other, non-retributive

---

[15] The Criminal Justice Act 2003 (the sentencing provisions of which were largely brought into force on 4 April 2005, see The Criminal Justice Act 2003 (Commencement No 8 and Transitional and Saving Provisions) Order 2005 (SI 2005/950) effected widespread reforms as to the sentences which a court could impose upon an offender, providing courts with greater choice as to the way in which it could respond to crime. These reforms operated within the overarching scheme driven by retributivism, however. This regime has since been repealed and re-enacted in the Sentencing Act 2020 on 1 December 2020.
[16] Sentencing Act 2020 s 231 (2).

considerations. Given the lack of precision around the principle of desert, this provision perhaps has less impact than was intended. In practice it is something frequently said in mitigation, though its impact is difficult to discern.

And so, it is these principles to which sentencers are required to adhere. In so doing, consistency is—at least—a latent aim: the scheme seeks to impose sentences in accordance with these principles. Inconsistency as to this may result in the principles not being realized to the extent that the scheme desires.

The tension between principles and the 'real world'

While regard to principles is important—for it produces a more coherent and theoretically satisfying account—the relevance of the real-world practice cannot be ignored. While principles may be neutral to factors such as social class, gender, race, religion, or political persuasion, it is important to be cognizant of the practicalities of how these factors impact sentencing practice.

For instance, the principle of proportionality, encompassing considerations of culpability and harm, pays no regard to the gender of the offender. The legislation providing for this approach is drafted in gender neutral language, as are the sentencing guidelines; yet gender has a role to play in the consideration of the application of sentencing principles. It must be recognized that female offenders are more likely to be involved with crime through domestic abuse, coercion, and controlling behaviour, which is likely to have a deflationary effect in the consideration of their culpability.[17] Conversely, there is some evidence that female offenders receive comparatively harsher sentences than their male counterparts when sentenced for assault offences involving intoxication.[18]

---

[17] Ministry of Justice, Female Offenders Strategy, Cm 9642 (Ministry of Justice 2018) 11.
[18] Carly Lightowlers, 'Drunk and Doubly Deviant? The Role of Gender and Intoxication in Sentencing Assault Offences' (2019) 59(3) British Journal of Criminology 11, 19–25, 19. There is other empirical evidence that suggests for assault, drugs, and burglary offences, males receive significantly harsher sentences than female counterparts, when controlling for relevant case characteristics, however, see Jose Pina-Sanchez and Lyndon Harris, 'Sentencing Gender? Investigating the Presence of Gender Disparities in Crown Court Sentences' [2020] Criminal Law Review, 3. More work is clearly needed on the gender impact across different offence groups.

Similarly, it is accepted that on a retributive account, a guilty plea reduces the severity of the sentence and that this is a perfectly proper consideration which in the principle of proportionality is neutral to race (and other non-legally relevant factors). However, in practice several studies have demonstrated that black and minority ethnic (BAME) defendants are more likely to plead not guilty than white defendants.[19] This element of a reduction in sentence (and the application of the principle of proportionality) is therefore a less significant feature in the sentencing of BAME offenders than is the case for white offenders.

While a principle may be in theory neutral to legally irrelevant factors, it is clear that in practice the position may be very different. The consideration of consistency in sentencing—and methods of promoting more consistency in the determination of sentence—must therefore be cognizant of this disconnect between theory and practice of sentencing. Consideration of the methods utilized to promote greater consistency must evaluate their relative efficacy against the background of the empirically evidenced divergence between practice and theory.

Conclusion

The consideration of the concept of consistency in sentencing in this work concerns sentencing in England and Wales, yet the lessons to be learned are of universal application, not least because of the popularity of retributive sentencing schemes and sentencing guidelines bodies around the world.

England and Wales subscribes to a sentencing scheme prioritizing retributive proportionality, encapsulating an assessment of offender's culpability and the harm present in the offence. This produces a range of permissible sentences which may be legitimately imposed in accordance with the principle. The eventual sentence is informed by other factors, enabling the sentencer to choose a sentence within the permissible range. The consideration of consistency is therefore a consideration of the extent to which sentencing in England and Wales is consistent with these

---

[19] Ministry of Justice, 'Black, Asian and Minority Ethnic disproportionality in the Criminal Justice System in England and Wales' (Ministry of Justice 2016) 19.

principles, and the later examination concerns measures in place to promote sentencing practice which is consistent with these principles.

The theoretical work in the early stages of this text may be utilized as a critical tool to evaluate the measures in place (or devise measures to be put in place) in other jurisdictions subscribing to different principles. While that might be criticized as having a wanton disregard for principles (as it is agnostic to the particular principles adopted by a particular scheme), it is submitted that such an exercise is better viewed as acknowledging different and conflicting principled accounts of sentencing theory. It may be utilized as a deliberately neutral tool as a means of evaluating the efficacy of a particular scheme's pursuit of its underlying principles. As will be developed, while individual schemes may pursue different (perhaps subtly different) sentencing rationales, the pursuit of consistency, properly conceived, is universal.

2
Conceptualizing consistency in sentencing

Consistency in punishment—a reflection of the notion of equal justice—is a fundamental element in any rational and fair system of criminal justice....[1]

Introduction

The need for, and importance of, consistency in sentencing

Consistency is a fundamental property of a fair sentencing system. It is a familiar concept; put crudely, it is the notion that like cases should be treated alike. However, that overly simplistic description belies the reality of what is in fact a complex concept lacking clarity. While most Anglo-Saxon jurisdictions place emphasis on the need for consistency in sentencing,[2] continental European jurisdictions tend to favour individualized justice over the desire to be consistent.[3] Whereas a common law

---

[1] *Lowe v The Queen* [1984] HCA 46.
[2] See eg the Sentencing Commission for Scotland, *The Scope to Improve Consistency in Sentencing—Report 2006*, para 6.3; Coroners and Justice Act 2009 s 120(11)(b); *R. v Blackshaw* [2011] EWCA Crim 2312; [2012] 1 WLR 1126 at [14]; Lord Justice Leveson when stressing the importance of consistency in sentencing during his evidence to the House of Commons Justice Committee on the Annual Report of the Sentencing Council, 13 January 2012 (2010–2012) HC 1711 I; *R. v McC* [2014] EWCA Crim 909 at [23]; Jose Pina-Sanchez and Robin Linacre, 'Refining the Measurement of Consistency in Sentencing: A Methodological Review' (2016) 44 International Journal of Law, Crime and Justice 68.
[3] For example, article 132-1 of the French Criminal Code requires that any sentence must be individualized; section 80 of the Danish Penal Code requires a consideration of the offence but also of the offender's 'general personal and social characteristics, his situation before and after the crime as well as his motivations for the crime' (a translation from Rasmus H Wandall,

jurisdiction seeking consistency may opt for a guidelines body, legislation placing restrictions on judicial discretion or a consideration of comparable cases (or a combination of those measures), a jurisdiction primarily concerned with individualized sentencing would naturally grant a wider discretion to the individual sentencer, placing emphasis upon imposing the appropriate sentence on the individual, with little or no focus upon consistency as between different cases.[4]

In order to examine the concept of consistency in a theoretical and practical context, this work uses England and Wales as its case study. England and Wales is the ideal jurisdiction as it is one which has, for some considerable time, placed emphasis on the benefits of consistency and in order to promote that concept, has developed its sentencing scheme in a way that features three key institutions—Parliament, the Court of Appeal (Criminal Division) (CACD), and the Sentencing Council—each of which has formally expressed a commitment to promote consistency in sentencing. This chapter focuses upon the theoretical aspects of the concept of consistency and the following discussion, though general in nature, should be considered against the background of the sentencing scheme prevailing in England and Wales, as set out in Chapter 1. England and Wales is thus the vehicle by which a broader analysis of the concept of consistency and methods employed to pursue it can be explored.

In those jurisdictions explicitly placing an emphasis on consistency, the benefits are well-known; more consistent sentencing practice results in more accurate provision of legal advice, increased transparency and legitimacy, and greater efficiency.[5] The core theoretical justification for the need for consistency in sentencing concerns fairness and equality. This finds its origins in the rule of law, and the common law norm of equal

---

'Resisting Risk Assessment? Pre-sentence Reports and Individualized Sentencing in Denmark' (2010) 12(3) Punishment & Society 329.

[4] There is of course an argument to say that the individualized nature of sentencing merely adopts a proportionality-based approach employing a wider definition of 'offence seriousness'. In subsequent chapters it will be argued that an individualized approach to sentencing is not inconsistent with the concept of consistent in sentencing; on the contrary, it will be argued that it is vital to it.

[5] See eg the Sentencing Commission for Scotland (n 2) para 6.3 and *R. v Caley* [2012] EWCA Crim 2821; [2013] 2 Cr App R (S) 47 at [28] and [29].

justice.[6] With wide-ranging benefits and strong normative arguments for the reduction of inconsistency in sentencing[7] it is no surprise that consistency has attracted interest in many jurisdictions. This chapter seeks to bring some clarity to the concept of consistency through the pursuit of a more principled approach. A 'definition' lacking in clarity would be an ironic failing for this concept; as will be demonstrated, vague principles lead to imprecise application and thus, a lack of consistency.

The basic concept

When asked to explain the concept of consistency in sentencing, academics, judges, and practitioners will often resort to something resembling the following form of words: like cases should be treated alike.[8] This neatly encapsulates the basic idea that similarly situated offences and offenders should receive similar treatment. Ashworth suggests that this basic description—treating like cases alike—should be accompanied by the converse, namely treating different cases differently.[9] This general description however leaves many issues unresolved; the two most important of which are perhaps what constitutes 'like' treatment and how to determine a 'like' case. Without an answer to that question and questions like it, the concept has little use as a critical tool.[10] A counter to this view is that perhaps favoured by those in common law systems, namely to resist the temptation to define everything, for through definition comes restriction. But as will be seen, in this context at least, that is superficial at best.

---

[6] Mirko Bagaric and Athula Pathinayake, 'The Paradox of Parity in Sentencing in Australia: The Pursuit of Equal Justice that Highlights the Futility of Consistency in Sentencing' (2013) 77(5) Journal of Criminal Law 399, 400.
[7] Patricia L Brantingham, 'Sentencing Disparity: An Analysis of Judicial Consistency' (1985) 1(3) Journal of Quantitative Criminology 281, 282.
[8] See eg Michael Tonry, 'Punishment Policies and Patterns in Western Countries' in Michael Tonry and Richard S Frase (eds), *Sentencing and Sanctions in Western Countries* (OUP 2001) 6; Brantingham, 'Sentencing Disparity' (n 7) 282; Andrew Ashworth, 'Disentangling Disparity' in Donald C Pennington and Sally Lloyd-Bostock (eds), *The Psychology of Sentencing: Approaches to consistency and disparity* (Centre for Socio-Legal Studies 1987) 24.
[9] Andrew Ashworth, 'Structuring Sentencing Discretion' in Andrew von Hirsch, Andrew Ashworth, and Julian V Roberts (eds), *Principled Sentencing: Readings on Theory and Policy* (3rd edn, Hart 2009) 253.
[10] Ashworth (n 8) 24.

Most accounts concern differences in sentencing decisions and the extent to which they are objectionable or justifiable, with the focus predominantly upon the sentencing outcome. This is often performed by a comparison with previously determined cases. Some accounts focus solely on the approach to sentencing reflecting the strong value placed in the discretion traditionally afforded to sentencers.[11] Some consider that the concept has the status of a principle of sentencing, though many do not go so far.[12] There is, however, widespread agreement that some form of consistency in sentencing is necessary.[13] The principal disagreement with which this chapter is concerned comes in the form of what constitutes an inconsistency or disparity, and how it may be identified.

Notwithstanding the widespread agreement on its importance and value within the Anglosphere, there is disagreement as to what the term actually means, and it is widely accepted that the concept is stricken with complexity and confusion. Some attribute the confusion—at least in part—to the fact that 'the concept of disparity is far from clear ... the simple term 'equality' or 'disparity' hides a variety of complex conceptual problems'.[14] Whereas many guidelines bodies and legislatures around the world place great emphasis upon the importance of consistency—and moreover, many regard it as a critical feature of fair sentencing[15]—those

---

[11] Sir Brian Leveson, 'The Parmoor Lecture: Achieving Consistency in Sentencing', 24 October 2013 <https://www.judiciary.gov.uk/wp-content/uploads/JCO/Documents/Speeches/leveson-parmoor-lecture-20131031.pdf> accessed 31 December 2021.

[12] For example, Etienne takes the view that parity is a 'first principle' of sentencing, see Margareth Etienne, 'Parity, Disparity and Adversariality: First Principles of Sentencing' (2005–2006) 58 Stanford Law Review 309, 310. However, this work adopts the view that consistency is not a principle of sentencing, attaining the same status as proportionality or parsimony, but instead, considers consistency to be a concept concerned with the application of sentencing principle.

[13] Jose Pina-Sanchez and Robin Linacre, 'Sentencing Consistency in England and Wales: Evidence from the Crown Court Sentencing Survey' (2013) 53(6) British Journal of Criminology 1118 and Jose Pina-Sanchez and Robin Linacre, 'Enhancing Consistency in Sentencing: Exploring the Effects of Guidelines in England and Wales' (2014) 30(4) Journal of Quantitative Criminology 731.

[14] Petrus C Van Duyne, 'Backgrounds of Disparity in the Administration of Criminal Law' in European Committee on Crime Problems, *Disparities in Sentencing: Causes and Solutions* (Council of Europe 1989) 67.

[15] See eg, in relation to England and Wales, Coroners and Justice Act 2009 s 120(11)(b); Lord Justice Leveson when stressing the importance of consistency in sentencing during his evidence to the House of Commons Justice Committee on the Annual Report of the Sentencing Council, 13 January 2012 (2010–2012) HC 1711 I; *R. v Bond* [2013] EWCA Crim 2713; [2014] 2 Cr App R (S) 3 [14]; *R. v McC* [2014] EWCA Crim 909; Jose Pina-Sanchez and Robin Linacre, 'Refining the Measurement of Consistency in Sentencing: A Methodological Review' (2016) 44 International Journal of Law, Crime and Justice 68. In relation to Scotland, see the Sentencing Commission for Scotland (n 2) Foreword.

jurisdictions routinely fail to provide a definition for the concept. This is problematic; as Krasnostein and Freiberg asked in the title of their paper on consistency in an individualistic sentencing framework: 'If you know where you're going, how do you know when you've got there?'[16] The 'where are we going?' is a sentence that is imposed in accordance with the principle(s) subscribed to by the particular sentencing scheme in question; in this work, utilizing England and Wales as the vehicle for this enquiry, that is a retributively proportionate sentence (informed by other, consequentialist, considerations), as discussed in Chapter 1.

The structure of this chapter

This chapter will examine what is meant by the term 'consistency' in sentencing, exploring the role it plays in the sentencing system in England and Wales which places an emphasis upon the need for like cases to be treated alike. In doing so, the chapter will consider concepts which are integral to the notion of consistency, and critique different accounts of consistency, including one from a prominent English judge and then Chairman of the Sentencing Council of England and Wales.

The first part of the chapter explores to what extent the concept of consistency overlaps with that of disparity, critically examining the two in an attempt to reconcile any differences in the terms. Thereafter, the chapter explores in-depth the notion of treating like cases alike, unpacking different interpretations of the phrase. Next, I consider two key debates concerning consistency in sentencing; consistency of approach and consistency of outcome, and the closely related issue of whether consistency is best viewed as a substantive concept, a procedural device, or an amalgam of the two. The chapter will then conclude by drawing the threads together in an attempt to construct a credible account of consistency in sentencing which may be employed as a critical tool to assess the success of the pursuit of consistency in the any sentencing system.

---

[16] Sarah Krasnostein and Arie Freiberg, 'Pursuing Consistency in an Individualistic Sentencing Framework: If You Know Where You're Going, How Do You Know When You've Got There?' (2013) 76 Law and Contemporary Problems 265.

Having explored the complex issues concerning consistency in sentencing, this chapter will argue that it is possible to simplify matters, and suggest that:

(1) inconsistency and disparity refer to the same concept;
(2) in order to use consistency in sentencing as a critical tool to assess the propriety of sentencing decisions, the concept has to feature both procedural and substantive elements incorporating both consistency of approach and consistency of outcome;
(3) consistency should not be overtly pursued as an aim of a sentencing system; and
(4) instead, the pursuit of principled sentencing results in consistency as the proper application of principle would result in an appropriate sentence being imposed in every case.

While consistency is a beneficial element to a sentencing system, as an aim in itself it is unprincipled. It must be tied to a legitimate substantive principle (or principles) which underpin the sentencing scheme in question in order to be an effective device. Without a legitimate principle at its heart, it is agnostic to the substantive foundations of the sentencing scheme and becomes merely an empty tool by which any scheme—fair or otherwise—could be assessed.

The scope of the basic concept

Are consistency and disparity interchangeable terms?

There is—rather ironically—a degree of inconsistency in the way in which the concept of treating similar cases similarly is described. For example, Krasnostein and Freiberg consider that '[d]isparity [is] the converse of consistency'[17] and therefore use the terms 'disparity' and 'inconsistency' interchangeably, whereas others use the terms in conjunction and

---

[17] ibid 265.

therefore appear to regard them as (perhaps discretely) different concepts.[18] The predominant view however is that consistency and disparity are two sides of the same coin[19] representing a concept concerned with fairness and justice in the imposition of sentences following a criminal conviction.

'Disparity' is a term which appears to be broadly used in one of two ways: first, to describe a sentencing decision which is *unjustifiably* different to cases which are like it or unjustly similar to cases which are different to it; and second, to describe a sentencing decision which is different or similar to other sentencing decisions, *with no value judgment as to the propriety of that difference or similarity*. The term 'inconsistency' appears to be used to describe the former, carrying with it a value judgment as to the legitimacy of the perceived difference, thus involving an analysis of the sentencing decision at hand, not simply a bare comparison between the outcomes.

Accounts of disparity that require a bare comparison between sentencing decisions are in the minority, notwithstanding the fact that such an interpretation would be more in line with the dictionary definition of the term. Spohn states that '[d]isparity is a difference in treatment or outcome that does not necessarily result from intentional bias or prejudice' and '[s]entencing disparities reflect differences in the sentences imposed on similarly situated offenders by judges in different jurisdictions, by judges in the same jurisdiction, or by individual judges.'[20] Such accounts can be dismissed as incomplete. In the absence of a secondary stage analysing the difference (or similarity) identified, such accounts are of no utility as a critical tool; the application of the definition of disparity

---

[18] See eg Brantingham, 'Sentencing Disparity' (n 7) and Cyrus Tata and Neil Hutton, 'What "Rules" in Sentencing? Consistency and Disparity in the Absence of 'Rules' 1998 (26) International Journal of the Sociology of Law 339, 339

[19] However, it is correct to note that in numerous discussions where the terms are used together, it is not always clear whether that is to differentiate them or for the avoidance of doubt as to what is being discussed. For example, in discussing the discretionary decision-making process, Tata appears to use the two terms as synonyms, see Cyrus Tata, 'Sentencing as Craftwork and the Binary Epistemologies of the Discretionary Decision Process' (2007) 16(2) Social and Legal Studies 425, 438, whereas Spiegelman uses the terms in conjunction with one another, thereby implying they are different concepts, see James Spigelman, 'Consistency and Sentencing' (2008) 82 Australian Law Journal 450.

[20] Cassia Spohn, *How Do Judges Decide? The Search for Fairness and Justice in Punishment* (Sage 2009) 129, 166. It is worth noting that Spohn's definition appears to be rather narrow, focusing upon treating like cases alike but not on treating different cases differently.

would not yield any information as to the propriety of the sentencing decision under scrutiny. The term disparity is therefore often accompanied by a qualification such as 'unwarranted' or 'unjustified'. This however serves only to bring the definition into line with the dominant account of the concept and accordingly it can be dismissed. It can therefore be concluded that disparity (and consistency) must import a value judgment as to the propriety of the decision under scrutiny if it is to have any utility as a critical tool, either in the search for consistent sentencing practices or in evaluating the propriety of a sentence imposed in an individual case.

Other accounts are in broad agreement as to the meaning of the concept and merely differ on the label: disparity versus inconsistency. The majority view is perhaps best characterized by Ashworth's account, and requires both a simple comparison between the result of the sentencing decision and an assessment of the underlying reasoning for it. Ashworth suggests that disparity 'is a word which calls attention to a form of injustice, to decisions which have resulted in an unfair distribution of burdens and benefits',[21] therefore linking disparity with unfairness, although the concept of fairness is not explored in this context. Developing the idea, Ashworth calls upon the 'principle' which 'seems to express the core of parity against which various practices and decisions are measured ... the widely held precept of formal justice: treat like cases alike'.[22] This was echoed in his later writing on the topic, where he stated that '[d]isparity in sentencing occurs when similar cases are dealt with differently, and where different cases are treated without reference to those differences'.[23] This therefore calls attention to the imposition of the appropriate sentence in a particular case (or perhaps to be more accurate, the imposition of a not incorrect sentence);[24] cases which do not conform to this ideal risk being treated differently to similar cases or similarly to different cases. One interpretation of this account is that the sentencing decision in question is compared with an actual case or cases said to be 'like' it in order to establish whether or not disparity exists. The precise

---

[21] Ashworth (n 8) 24. This focus upon injustice is repeated in later work, eg Ashworth (n9) 253.
[22] Ashworth (n 8) 24.
[23] Ashworth (n 9) 253.
[24] See 'Permissible range of sentences and the pursuit of principled sentencing' later in this chapter.

methodology remains somewhat unclear. As will be seen, in England and Wales, in practice, this is an approach which has been criticized.

Having eliminated the definition requiring only a bare comparison between sentencing outcome, henceforth, parity and disparity will be used synonymously with consistency and inconsistency. Consistency will be taken to express the concept that like cases are treated alike and different cases are treated differently, where for that purpose, a difference (or similarity) in sentence is identified and then analysed to establish whether or not it is justified; an unjustified difference (or similarity) will indicate an inconsistency.

Permissible range of sentences and the pursuit of principled sentencing

Having established that analysing consistency in sentencing involves a comparative exercise forming the basis of the evaluation of the propriety of the decision in question, it is necessary to establish the subject of the comparison. This is the point of departure with many established accounts of consistency. Whereas those accounts involve a comparison with other cases (and so consider whether cases are consistent with one another), the account of consistency I advocate relies upon a consideration of the appropriate sentence by reference to established sentencing principle(s). The question is therefore not whether a particular decision is sufficiently 'like' others which are deemed to be sufficiently 'like' it, but whether a particular decision can be considered to be an appropriate application of the principle(s), thereby producing an appropriate sentence. As will be explored, if the subject of the comparison is a moving target, there is manifest difficulty in performing an accurate comparison.

It is therefore necessary to establish what would be an 'appropriate' sentence for a particular offence, or, put another way, it is necessary to establish what constitutes the proper application of sentencing principles in a given case. As discussed in Chapter 1, and using England and Wales as an example, the appropriate sentence in that jurisdiction is determined by a principally retributive set of principles; proportionality determines an acceptable range of sentences within which other, consequentialist, considerations determine the sentence.

As is trite, in desert theory, it is generally accepted that there is no single *correct* sentence for any given criminal offence. By the application of established sentencing principles, it is possible to establish a range of 'not wrong' sentences. This echoes Morris' 'not undeserved' range of sentences in which he conceived of the concept of desert as a limiting, rather than a defining, principle. He argued that retributivism set the upper (and sometimes lower) limits for punishment and within that range of 'not undeserved' sentences, consequentialist considerations could legitimately determine the sentence to be visited upon the offender.[25] Where a sentence falls within this range, the sentence can be said to be consistent (with sentencing principles) and therefore appropriate. This is notwithstanding the fact that sentences could be disparate within that range.[26]

This concept will be explored more fully in Chapter 4 where the role that consistency has to play in sentencing systems placing emphasis on individualization is examined. For the purposes of this chapter however, it suffices to describe the concept of a range of 'permissible sentences' within which a sentencing decision can be said to be consistent. Accordingly, the question of whether a sentence is consistent in England and Wales requires a consideration of the extent to which the sentence falls within the permissible range of sentences, or, put another way, is consistent with the sentencing principles underpinning the sentence scheme.

Treating like cases alike

The interpretation of the term 'treating' represents one of the major divergences of opinion as to the role and extent of consistency in sentencing. It is an issue which is at the heart of consistency as it impacts upon the very nature of the concept.

Perhaps the most obvious interpretation is that the treatment referred to is the sentencing outcome, that is the nature and/or length of the sentence imposed. For example, where two cases receive sentences of one and ten years respectively, the sentences are different and therefore the

---

[25] For a discussion see Richard S Frase, 'Limiting Retributivism' in von Hirsch, Ashworth, and Roberts *Principled Sentencing* (n 9) 135.
[26] Ibid 137.

cases have not been treated alike. This appears to be the way in which the basic concept is interpreted by the majority,[27] constructing a concept concerned with the variability that remains having accounted for legally relevant factors.[28] As will be seen however, a version of consistency only concerned with sentencing outcome is theoretically flawed.

An alternative interpretation is that 'treating like cases alike' refers to the way in which the sentencing decision is arrived at, though this is perhaps a little deviation from the natural meaning of the words. This concerns the procedural mechanisms applied in order to determine the sentence. Where two cases of common assault are sentenced, one by reference to a guideline applicable to assault offences, and the other by reference only to the sentencer's intuition, the two cases have been decided by different procedures and therefore have not been treated alike.[29] This interpretation has limitations however as it naturally lends itself to a definition of consistency restricted to consistency of approach, rather than considering the outcome which, in the above example, could be identical.

A third interpretation is that the treatment referred to is the impact of the outcome of the sentence on the individual defendant, sometimes referred to as 'equity'. It requires a comparison between sentence outcomes, as in the first interpretation, but also an assessment of the severity of the sentence in relation to the individual. This proceeds on the basis that it is incorrect to assume that each unit of punishment (eg one month of imprisonment or each £10 of a fine) has an objectively quantified punitive impact.[30] For example, it is generally accepted that imprisonment impacts more greatly on a person in their old age, than a person in their youth, or on a person of ill health as compared to a person of good health, and as such an adjustment in the sentence imposed will likely follow. A clearer example is a £1,000 fine imposed on a professional footballer earning

---

[27] See for example Lisa Stolzenberg and Stewart J D'Alessio, 'Sentencing and Unwarranted Disparity: An Empirical Assessment of the Long-Term Impact Sentencing Guidelines in Minnesota' (1994) 32(2) Criminology 301; Tonry, 'Punishment Policies and Patterns in Western Countries' (n 8); Frase (n 25); and Richard S Frase, 'Theories of Proportionality and Desert' in Joan Petersilia and Kevin R Reitz (eds), *The Oxford Handbook of Sentencing and Corrections* (OUP 2012).
[28] Stolzenberg and D'Alessio, 'Sentencing and Unwarranted Disparity' (n 27) 301.
[29] See eg Leveson (n 11).
[30] Andrew Ashworth and Elaine Player, 'Sentencing, Equal Treatment and the Impact of Sanctions' in Andrew Ashworth and Martin Wasik (eds), *Fundamentals of Sentencing Theory* (OUP 1998) 255.

£250,000 per week, and the same fine imposed upon a person who is unemployed and without independent wealth. While many regard equity to be a separate consideration, falling outside of the definition of consistency,[31] others would consider that a comparison of sentencing outcomes for the purpose of a determination of consistency in sentencing must account for individual differences pertaining to the offender which affect the impact of a sentence on the individual (see for example the decision of the High Court of Australia in *Lowe v The Queen*).[32] Such a construction has difficulties in a retributive framework, however. Easton describes such an approach as 'sailing in dangerous waters' and questions whether it can be properly defended in on retributive grounds.[33] Piper considers 'that there is no clearly-articulated penal justification for allowing [impact] mitigation to have effect' but suggests that impact is capable of justification by retributive reasoning.[34] Ashworth and Player justify such an approach on grounds of fairness, but recognize practical difficulties in doing so within a proportionality-based sentencing system.[35] Interpreting 'treatment' in this way is more comfortable within a system which places emphasis upon individualized sentencing. As briefly mentioned at the outset of this chapter, I will argue that individualized justice and consistency are not (necessarily) at odds. However, permitting a reduction in sentence to account for the relative impact of a sentence on a particular offender arguably undermines the principle in whose name it is justified. By requiring such a reduction, although one might argue that such a sentence is in fact consistent (by reference to the relative punitive 'bite') the message communicated to the victim and society[36] is likely to be one of inconsistency.

---

[31] See eg John W Raine and Eileen Dunstan, 'How Well do Sentencing Guidelines Work?: Equity, Proportionality and Consistency in the Determination of Fine Levels in the Magistrates' Courts of England and Wales' (2009) 48(1) The Howard Journal 13.

[32] [1984] HCA 46.

[33] Susan Easton, 'Dangerous Waters: Taking Account of Impact in Sentencing' [2008] Criminal Law Review 105.

[34] Christine Piper, 'Should Impact Constitute Mitigation?: Structured Discretion versus Mercy' [2007] Criminal Law Review 141.

[35] Ashworth and Player, 'Sentencing, Equal Treatment and the Impact of Sanctions' (n 30).

[36] Ashworth and Player would justify excluding the offender from this point on the basis that sentencing theories of censure and communication assume that offenders with sufficient autonomy to understand why a punishment has been imposed upon them and respond accordingly are similarly capable of understanding why a co-defendant with a similar criminal history receives a discounted sentence on the basis that he suffers from a life-threatening illness. See Ashworth and Player (n 30) 271.

Proponents of equity would regard equality of treatment as an overly simplistic approach guaranteed to ensure inconsistency on the basis that equality of treatment fails to account for inherent differences capable of affecting the relative severity of the sentence. As noted earlier, a flat £1,000 fine for speeding would constitute equal treatment but not equitable treatment as it would impact upon a rich person less than a poor person. This unfairness is derived by the reference to a narrow class of factors (eg offence only) as opposed to a wider class, producing a more nuanced, individualized, outcome. The criticism that promoting equality over equity ensures inconsistency (and is therefore unfair) is therefore well founded.

As will be seen, this work argues that the appropriate interpretation is a combination of the first and second, namely that treatment refers to both outcome and approach. So, what of equity? Further, it is suggested that consistency is concerned with principled sentencing, and therefore considerations of equity could be encompassed within the determination of sentence, not the consideration of consistency of sentencing. Depending on the view one takes as to the way in which sentences should be determined, equity could be considered to be encompassed within a definition of proportionality, or as a separate consideration.[37]

The nature of consistency in sentencing

A consistent approach or a consistent outcome?

A closely related issue about which there is disagreement is whether or not consistency should be seeking to achieve a consistent approach to sentencing, or consistent sentencing outcomes. As established, consistency requires that similar cases are treated similarly (and different cases are treated differently). Consistency of approach interprets 'treatment'

---

[37] For example, where offence seriousness is regarded as encompassing a consideration of both offence and offender, equity could be considered to fall within the definition of proportionality. Alternatively, where offence seriousness is viewed as restricted to the offence itself, matters of personal mitigation would be considered separate to the application of the principle of proportionality. The position adopted in this work is therefore that there is a role for impact to play, but that it does not weigh in on considerations of consistency.

to refer to the mechanism by which a sentencing outcome is arrived at, whereas consistency of outcome interprets 'treatment' to refer to the substantive effect of the sentencing decision. These two versions of consistency are sometimes posited as being in conflict, however as will be seen, such a view is not sustainable on analysis.

That consistency of approach is a prerequisite for a sentencing system placing some value—even on theoretical grounds alone—in consistent sentencing practice would appear to be uncontroversial. Ashworth and Kelly have described the current situation in England and Wales in relation to the purposes of sentencing, where no single purpose is given primacy, as 'the worst of pick-and-mix sentencing', commenting that the fact that individual sentencers are permitted (or even required) to follow their own penal philosophies seemed to invite inconsistency.[38] Quoting a (now dated) study by Hogarth, Ashworth noted that it was 'fairly well established' that different penal philosophies of judges was a major cause of disparity.[39] As will be seen, this not only impacts upon sentencing procedure but also sentencing outcomes.

Consistency of approach requires a common process to the determination of sentence but can take numerous different forms. For example, in England and Wales, Parliament has required courts to impose sentences that are proportionate to offence seriousness,[40] parsimonious,[41] and by reference to prescribed aims of sentencing.[42] Other procedural mechanisms, such as sentencing guidelines or guidance issued by appellate courts, take different forms with different levels of prescription. These differing mechanisms would likely have to operate in a less prescriptive manner given both their status and their importance to the scheme: compare, for example, the statutory requirement to determine sentence by reference to offence seriousness[43] (a central pillar in the principally retributive scheme) and the approach required by sentencing guidelines

---

[38] Andrew Ashworth and Rory Kelly, *Sentencing and Criminal Justice*, 7th edn (Bloomsbury 2021), 67.
[39] ibid 66.
[40] Sentencing Act 2020 s 63 (formerly Criminal Justice Act 2003 s 152).
[41] Sentencing Act 2020 s 231 (formerly Criminal Justice Act 2003 s 153).
[42] Sentencing Act 2020 s 57 (formerly Criminal Justice Act 2003 s 142).
[43] Sentencing Act 2020 ss 63 and 230 requires a sentence to be commensurate with the seriousness of the offence and that offence seriousness is assessed by reference to the offender's culpability and harm caused, intended or which might have been foreseen.

issued by the Sentencing Council in England and Wales (which, as will be seen, structure the sentencing decision in accordance with the principle of retributive proportionality).[44] In England and Wales these mechanisms coexist and largely work in harmony.[45] The combined effect of these mechanisms is considered in detail in Chapter 9, following a consideration of each in isolation. At this juncture, it suffices to note that consistency of approach is frequently multi-layered, with principles of sentencing operating alongside purer mechanisms of ensuring consistency such as sentencing guidelines.

Some consider that consistency refers only to consistency of approach. The Sentencing Council has a statutory duty to have regard to the need to promote consistency in sentencing, yet the statute provided no definition for that purpose.[46] Accordingly it fell to the Council to define it and at its first meeting in April 2010, the Council members agreed a statement of purpose, which included the following statement:

> The Sentencing Council for England and Wales will ... promote a clear, fair and consistent approach to sentencing ....[47]

Sir Brian Leveson, a Lord Justice of Appeal and then Chairman of the Sentencing Council, said in a speech regarding the function and operation of the Council: 'I frequently put it that the guidelines define a common approach to sentencing, leaving the eventual outcome to the discretion of the judge based on the facts and circumstances of the case before him/her.'[48] This has been adopted by subsequent Chairmen of the Council, most recently by Sir Tim Holroyde, current Chairman of the Sentencing

---

[44] The offence-specific sentencing guidelines issued by the Sentencing Council adopt the same multi-step structure: at Step One they require a court to consider an exhaustive list of factors in order to determine the harm and culpability present in the offence for the purposes of arriving at a starting point.

[45] For example, the Court of Appeal (Criminal Division) have interpreted guidelines (eg *R. v Henning* [2015] EWCA Crim 879; [2015] 2 Cr App R (S) 37) and statutory provisions (eg *Attorney General's Reference (No 27 of 2013) (R. v Burinskas)* [2014] EWCA Crim 334)); [2014] 2 Cr App R (S) 45, and guidelines have interpreted and amplified statutory provisions, such as the assessment of offence seriousness (eg Sentencing Council, *Assault Offences Definitive Guideline* (Office of the Sentencing Council 2011)).

[46] Coroners and Justice Act 2009 s 120(11)(b).

[47] Minutes of Meeting: April 2010, Sentencing Council of England and Wales <https://www.sentencingcouncil.org.uk/publications/item/minutes-of-meeting-april-2010/> accessed 9 September 2016, 7.

[48] Leveson (n 11) 5.

Council when giving evidence to the Justice Select Committee of the House of Commons: 'The aim of the guidelines is to increase consistency in sentencing; that is to say, taking a consistent approach to sentencing cases, not necessarily leading to the same outcome because the circumstances of offences always vary.'[49] It is this (narrow) definition of consistency which has been used by the Council when it has conducted its empirical research into consistency.[50] A stark example of this in practice would be in applying a Sentencing Council guideline, it would be permissible for two judges to place the same offence/offender scenario into two different categories (producing different starting points and likely different eventual sentences) while remaining faithful to the notion of consistency subscribed to by the Council. Such flexibility risks (or perhaps invites) inconsistency as the application of the procedural device is left to the individual sentencer, with different results almost inevitably produced.[51] In such a circumstance, the procedural mechanism is unable to assist the sentencer in any substantive way in arriving at the appropriate conclusion. Of course, a more rigid mechanism of ensuring consistency of approach would reduce the flexibility and therefore limit the risk of such inconsistency; such a measure would however fetter judicial discretion which would be a retrograde step for a sentencing system employing a wide definition of the principle of proportionality encompassing many non-retributive factors.[52] The wider the definition of proportionality the greater the discretion afforded to sentencers must be if they are to be able

---

[49] House of Commons, Justice Select Committee, 'The Work of the Sentencing Council', HC 1184, Oral Evidence, 2 February 2021, Q2.

[50] Sentencing Council, 'The Impact of Three Guidelines on Consistency in Sentencing' (Office of the Sentencing Council, 2021) 4 and Sentencing Council, 'A Review of Consistency in Sentencing' (Office of the Sentencing Council, 2021),

[51] See John Hogarth, *Sentencing as a Human Process* (University of Toronto Press 1971) 91 as to the differences in penal philosophies, effectiveness of different kinds of sentence, and the importance of each of the purposes of sentencing among judges, evidenced by his study of Canadian magistrates. The variation evident in his study when viewed in an English and Welsh context of a range of purposes of sentences, none of which have been given priority by Parliament and an absence of data from the Sentencing Council as to the relative effectiveness of different types of sentence despite the fact that the mandate to do so results in the inevitable conclusion that such variation in sentencing decisions in England and Wales is a product of a system affording sentencers with a wide discretion. von Hirsch, referencing Marvin Frankel, described how 'wide-open discretion' permits disparity, see Andrew von Hirsch, *Doing Justice* (Hill and Wang 1976) 29.

[52] Julian V Roberts and Lyndon Harris, 'Reconceptualising the Custody Threshold in England and Wales' (2017) 28(3) Criminal Law Forum 477.

to 'do justice in an individual case'[53] and accordingly any reduction in discretion would impinge upon the principle of individualization.[54] As will be revisited, there appears to be a tension between individualization and the search for consistency.

Proponents of a version of consistency limited to consistency of approach rely upon the need to do justice in a particular case[55] and trumpet the flexibility inherent in such an account of consistent sentencing. Consistency of approach, it is said, still delivers the benefits associated with consistency such as greater legitimacy through increased public understanding and confidence in the system as well as the rule of law values of clarity and certainty, without unduly constraining judicial discretion.[56]

A related criticism is that consistency of approach places itself at the mercy of the substantive law to which it applies. As a procedural device it is (largely) an empty vehicle, requiring compliance with any mechanism, principled or otherwise, in order to achieve the desired goal of treating offenders in the same way by a common process of determining sentence.[57] As such, its utility in producing appropriate sentences, or more principled sentencing, hinges almost entirely upon the procedure (and thus the substantive principle beneath it) to which it applies. For example, a procedure requiring the determination of sentence to be based on an assessment of the harm caused, to the exclusion of an assessment of culpability, would serve the aim of consistency of approach but would result in disproportionate sentences in, for example, cases of mercy killing. An extreme example would be a procedure that applied to offenders who had brown hair, and another procedure for offenders without brown hair.

---

[53] See eg *R. v Taylor* [2012] EWCA Crim 630; [2012] 2 Cr App R (S.) 98 at [13].
[54] This will be explored in further detail in Chapter 3.
[55] This is a function that the Lord Chief Justice and the Court of Appeal (Criminal Division) has repeatedly placed emphasis on: see Criminal Practice Directions [2015] EWCA Crim 1567 (as amended) para M.3; *R. v Blackshaw* [2011] EWCA Crim 2312; [2012] 1 Cr App R (S) 114 at [14] and *R. v Erskine* [2009] EWCA Crim 1425; [2009] 2 Cr App R 29 at [3] as examples. This also extends to the Sentencing Council, see Sentencing Council, 'A Review of Consistency in Sentencing' (Office of the Sentencing Council, 2021).
[56] Sarah Krasnostein, 'Pursuing Consistency: The Effect of Different Reforms on Unjustified Disparity in Individualized Sentencing Frameworks' (PhD thesis, Monash University 2015) 77.
[57] It is perhaps right to note that procedural mechanisms are capable of having substantive effect, such as the procedure for a trial (prosecution presents its case before the defence) or the procedure for disclosure of unused material enforce a substantive right enshrined in article 6 of the European Convention of Human Rights, but these are means of effecting the substantive right and exist independently to the right itself.

While the aim of consistency would be in one respect achieved, the procedural device delivers sentencing decisions which are unjust and made in reference to legally irrelevant factors.

Consistency of approach inevitably has *an* impact upon sentencing outcomes, achieving greater consistency of outcome—and this is something that in adopting its narrow definition of consistency, the Sentencing Council acknowledges:

> Consistency of approach in the use of Sentencing Council guidelines means that sentencers all work through the same step by step approach as set out in the guidelines. This supports sentencers in coming to a similar starting point and sentencing category range in similar cases.[58]

The degree of that impact will depend on the prescription of the method employed and the extent to which the approach is related to the outcome. For example, where all persons are sentenced on the basis of the principle of proportionality, *a priori*, there will be greater consistency of outcome than if there was no common approach to sentencing: a common approach narrows the scope for unwanted or unjustified variability in, for example, the assessment of offence seriousness, with the inevitable result that sentencing outcomes in similar cases are more closely aligned. Conversely, an approach which required all convicted offenders to be sentenced by a judge of a particular seniority, or by a judge wearing a particular judicial dress, would be likely to have a negligible impact due to its weak nexus to the desired outcome. Thus, the extent to which the common approach is successful obviously depends upon its nature.

Turning to consider consistency of outcome, there is more than one way in which it can be achieved, providing a range of results dependent upon the extent to which the system wishes to be prescriptive. Perhaps the most commonly recognized mechanism for achieving consistency of outcome—at least in England and Wales—is a statutory requirement to impose a particular sentence (type or length) on a particular class of offender, often referred to as a mandatory or minimum sentence.[59] Other

---

[58] Sentencing Council, 'A Review of Consistency in Sentencing' (Office of the Sentencing Council 2021) 10.

[59] England and Wales have various minimum sentences which must be imposed where the conditions are met, subject to an 'escape clause' to avoid grossly disproportionate sentences.

methods of achieving a consistent outcome may come in the form of guidance from appellate courts, for example indicating the appropriate range for a certain type of offence,[60] or from sentencing guidelines issued by a sentencing guidelines body.[61]

Some consider that consistency of outcome is concerned with uniformity of outcome.[62] This has the potential to mislead, however; consistency of outcome operates on a scale, from uniformity (ie identical sentencing outcomes) to broad similarity (ie differences between sentences are within an acceptable margin). A sentencing guideline adopting a narrative approach may afford the sentencer sufficient discretion to reflect the individual features of a case, thereby seeking to achieve greater consistency of outcome but without pursuing uniformity of outcome. Conversely, a statutory requirement to impose a particular sentence upon the conviction of a particular offence may achieve uniformity of outcome at the expense of individualization.

A strong criticism of mechanisms of ensuring consistency of outcome is that they risk treating different cases as though they are similar.[63] Consider the following situation. A minimum sentence of three years exists for burglary in a sentencing system based on the principle of retributive proportionality. The first offender's offence is 'worth' two years by reference to the principle of proportionality whereas the second is worth three years. The minimum sentence requires a disproportionate sentence to be imposed in the first case but (by chance) the appropriate sentence in the second case. As a tool for ensuring consistency of outcome, it succeeds, as both offences of burglary receive sentences of three years. That result is however that a disproportionate sentence is imposed in one case, and therefore the minimum sentence requires different cases to be treated as though they are alike. This is often the result of minimum or mandatory sentencing regimes which operate by reference to a small

---

[60] For an example see *R. v Turner* (1975) 61 Cr App R 67, CA (Crim Div).
[61] The most obvious example is perhaps the Minnesota Grid, which is based on a two-dimensional matrix and assesses offence severity and criminal history score to arrive at a presumptive sentence. This creates a rather prescriptive approach which is likely to achieve consistency of outcome due to its rigid procedure and simple matrices. The approach taken in England and Wales adopts a narrative, more nuanced and flexible approach which is less likely to produce a high level of consistency of outcome. This will be explored in detail later in this work.
[62] Krasnostein, 'Pursuing Consistency, citing the Australian Law Reform Commission (n 56) 79.
[63] Tonry (n 8) 20.

number of relevant factors such as offence type, or a combination of offence type and number of previous convictions.[64] The preference given to these few 'headline' factors runs contrary to the (generally) accepted notion that legally relevant factors to sentence extend beyond simply offence type and criminal history.[65]

This criticism however depends entirely on the mechanism used to achieve consistency of outcome. For example, a system where an appellate court provides judgments with guidance on the appropriate sentencing ranges for a type of offence, broken down by category with case examples, may allow sufficient discretion to enable the sentencer to 'do justice in an individual case'[66] and appropriately reflect the individualities of an offence. Incidentally, a criticism of such an approach is that the extent to which outcomes are consistent is reduced by the wide (or at least wider) discretion afforded to the sentencer. Accordingly, consistency of outcome is best viewed as a sliding scale, from absolute uniformity of sentence to broadly similar sentences. It is capable of dealing quite adequately with the criticism that consistency of approach requires different cases to be treated similarly, however the extent to which that is the case depends entirely upon the mechanism employed.

Is consistency a procedural or substantive concept?

With the foregoing in mind, a key question is whether consistency is to be viewed as a substantive concept or merely a procedural device and whether they are mutually exclusive.

The competing views are thus: on the one hand, consistency is a procedural mechanism requiring that sentences are determined in the same manner. Consistency therefore merely operates as the vehicle by which one arrives at the desired destination. On this view, consistency is not concerned with substance, only that all persons in a relevant class are treated consistently. For example, consider that the mechanism for ensuring consistency is the application of the proportionality principle. In

---

[64] For examples in England and Wales, see the Sentencing Act 2020 ss 311–315 and the Murder (Abolition of Death Penalty) Act 1965 s 1.

[65] Tonry (n 8) 20.

[66] See eg *R. v Taylor* [2012] EWCA Crim 630; [2012] 2 Cr App R (S) 98 at [13].

two identical cases sentenced by two judges, where both apply the principle of proportionality, a difference in sentence, for example three years for the first offender and four years for the second, will not be regarded as inconsistent. The result is immaterial as consistency as a procedural mechanism (in this case, the principle of proportionality) is concerned only with formal equality; where the sentencing decision is taken in accordance with the predetermined mechanism, there is consistency in sentencing. Accordingly, consistency as a procedural mechanism is concerned with consistency of approach. That said, consistency of outcome will be (to some extent) a by-product, as considered in the previous section of this chapter. Consistency as a procedural mechanism merely applies the substantive sentencing law, whether that be the duty to apply the principle of proportionality contained in primary legislation, sentencing guidelines, or a statutory provision requiring a mandatory sentence.

The alternate view is that consistency is a substantive concept: an end in itself. This relies upon the existence of an individual's 'right' to have a similar sentence imposed upon them to that imposed in similar cases. Yet this must exist without recourse to sentencing principles such as equity or proportionality, otherwise the concept is a procedural device ensuring the application of such principle. It is difficult to conceive of many situations in which a complaint of inconsistency could exist without the complaint being that there was a procedural deficiency (eg a guideline was not applied or wrongly applied) or misapplication of a principle of sentence (eg the principle of proportionality was not or wrongly applied). Accordingly, the existence of consistency as a substantive concept is limited, occurring only where there is no procedural impropriety but where a 'right' to a particular sentence exists. Such would arise only in a multiple defendant scenario in which, *ceteris paribus*, two defendants receive different sentences in circumstances where each sentence is within the permissible range for that offence having been imposed in accordance with the requisite procedure. As it is not possible to justify the difference in sentences by reference to legally relevant factors, there exists an inconsistency thereby giving rise to an entitlement to an adjustment on grounds of fairness and justice.[67]

---

[67] This could of course conceivably operate where there was a sense of grievance at the unjustified similarity of treatment where, for example, a defendant had a worse criminal history.

Consistency is predominantly a procedural mechanism for ensuring that sentences are imposed in accordance with the principles underpinning the regime. This necessarily imports a degree of substance to the concept; without consideration of the underlying principles, the concept would merely be an empty device which was blind to substance and facilitated unprincipled sentences. There is also scope for consistency as a substantive concept to coexist in limited circumstances where a sentence has been imposed in accordance with the appropriate procedure, yet there is still a complaint of inconsistency on grounds of unfairness.[68]

In summary, therefore, consistency exists as a procedural device concerning both consistency of approach (in requiring adherence to a common procedure) and consistency of outcome (in that a more consistent procedure will result in more consistent outcomes). Consistency as a substantive concept however operates solely in relation to consistency of outcome as it concerns a right to a particular outcome arising out of a completely separate consideration to whether or not the sentence was imposed in accordance with a common process.

Conclusion

A credible account of consistency

Based on the foregoing discussion, consistency is best viewed as an amalgam of the various accounts of consistency currently theorized; it consists of both a procedural element and a substantive element, with a focus upon consistency of approach but incorporating a degree of consistency of outcome. Further, consistency represents the concept of treating like cases alike and different cases differently, where 'treating' refers both to the process by which the sentencing decision is taken, and the outcome of that decision. It falls then to construct a credible, theoretically sound definition of consistency.

---

[68] There is some support for this view, see eg Etienne 'Parity, Disparity and Adversariality' (n 12).

CONCEPTUALIZING CONSISTENCY IN SENTENCING   35

This version of consistency produces two routes to establishing whether or not a particular sentence can be said to be consistent:[69] (i) the procedural route and (ii) the substantive route. In both cases, there must be an improper sentencing outcome; a procedural impropriety absent an improper sentencing outcome will establish an inconsistency but will be insufficient to warrant an alteration to the sentence.[70] An improper sentencing outcome is one which falls outside of the permissible range of sentences for the offence in question.

The procedural route will arise most commonly. The complaint that there has been a procedural deficiency resulting in an improper result will arise most commonly. Consider a scenario where defendant X receives a sentence of four years for a robbery. In circumstances where it can be established (by reference to sentencing principles, sentencing guidelines, or comparable cases) that four years is outside of the permissible range, the complaint will be that due to a procedural impropriety (eg non- or improper application of a guideline or sentencing principle), the resultant sentence is improper on the basis that it is not capable of justification by reference to legally relevant factors; in essence, the sentencer has miscalculated the sentence, giving too little or too much weight to a relevant factor, not considered a relevant factor, or considered an irrelevant factor. The deficiency in procedure has resulted in an improper sentencing outcome. There is of course a substantive element here: the procedure requires the proper application of the substantive principle and in that way, the concept is a hybrid of the two. It is not possible to divorce the procedural element from the substantive principle, as the former is the method by which the latter is realized. Notwithstanding this, this can be properly described as the 'procedural route'.

The substantive route will arise far less frequently. The complaint that the result is improper arises only in a multiple defendant scenario and

---

[69] Based on the foregoing discussion, 'consistent' means consistent with sentencing principles and having been imposed by an application of appropriate procedure.
[70] Certainly, in current practice, the CACD is concerned with the sentencing outcome, and less concerned with procedural impropriety. However, it is acknowledged that a procedural deficiency, eg a failure to apply a guideline, will create a technical inconsistency of approach, even though no inconsistency of outcome exists just by virtue of the failure to apply the guideline. In such a scenario, there is no requirement to make an adjustment to the sentence as despite the procedural impropriety, the resultant sentence can still be said to be 'appropriate' as it falls within the permissible range of sentences.

exists where there is nothing objectionable about the sentence in isolation, that is there is no procedural impropriety and the sentence is within the permissible range. Consider the scenario where defendant X receives a sentence of four years for a robbery, and his co-defendant, Y, receives a sentence of three years in circumstances where all legally relevant factors are identical. Where both X and Y's sentences are within the permissible range, the claim is therefore not that X has a 'right' to a three-year sentence because it is the same as Y, but that three years is also an appropriate sentence for X's offence and there is no justification for the difference in treatment (ie three years for Y and four years for X). A reduction is justified because of a legitimate sense of grievance based on substantive unfairness: there is no legally relevant reason to justify the differential treatment.

Where, however, X's sentence is within the permissible range but Y's sentence is outside of the permissible range, this would (first) be objectionable under the procedural route described above in relation to Y's sentence. But to reduce X's sentence simply because Y received a lesser sentence would be to require the substitution of a correct sentence (four years) with an incorrect sentence (three years); as a matter of principle, that cannot be. Yet, there is injustice between X and Y. Under the substantive and procedural route, there can be no legitimate sense of grievance held by X. The difference in treatment is capable of explanation on the basis that X's sentence is appropriate and there is no legitimate sense of grievance created by an incorrect application of the principle(s) in Y's case. This notion is supported by case law from the Court of Appeal.[71]

While this focus upon outcome under the substantive route at first blush appears to be contrary to the emphasis this chapter has placed on approach, it is in fact entirely explicable. In constructing an account of consistency that is principally procedural with a subsidiary substantive element, the focus is predominantly upon achieving consistent sentencing outcomes through a consistent approach by the proper application of sentencing principle(s). However, whereas a procedural impropriety will result in a technical inconsistency (ie the sentence has not been determined in accordance with established sentencing principles or

---

[71] See eg *R. v Butcher* (1989) 11 Cr App R (S) 104, CA (Crim Div), *R. v Rugg* [1997] 2 Cr App R (S) 350, CA (Crim Div), and *R. v Bailey* [2011] EWCA Crim 1585.

procedure), absent an improper result, the practical effect is nil. The presence of an improper sentencing outcome demonstrates an impropriety which (in practice) needs to be addressed. Therefore, the focus upon an 'improper result' is the best indicator that there has been an inconsistency resulting in an unfairness.[72]

On this account of consistency, the concept is predominantly a procedural mechanism, operating as a vehicle to deliver the ultimate aim: principled sentencing. Developed sentencing systems subscribe to one or more principles. In England and Wales, the principle of retributive proportionality governs the general approach to sentencing; sentencing guidelines narrow the variability in the application of that principle, as does guidance from the appellate courts and consideration of comparable cases. Adherence to the procedure should produce an appropriate result; if it does not, the procedure has not been correctly followed. Additionally, in a multiple defendant case, consistency as a substantive concept has a role to play in isolation, where there exists a legitimate grievance in the difference in sentencing outcomes imposed.

As such, consistency—save for the rare multiple defendant scenario described in the previous paragraph—is properly conceived of as being concerned with the pursuit of principled sentencing as opposed to the predominant focus being on a consistent outcome. This places consistency on a more solid theoretical footing but raises the question as to whether or not the pursuit of consistency is a red herring. Should we seek to impose consistent sentences, or should we seek to impose principled sentences? If every case is sentenced in accordance with established principle, adhering to any required procedure, there would be absolute consistency as there would be no sentence imposed which fell outside of the permissible range of sentences for a given offence. Taking the robbery case used above as an example in a principally retributive scheme, defendant X ought to receive four years' custody not because other offences committed by similarly situated offenders received four years but because four years is a correct sentence (within the permissible range) in the individual case; to sentence otherwise would be unprincipled.

---

[72] This works for both 'routes' as described earlier but is most likely to occur in relation to the 'procedural route'.

Accordingly, consistency is therefore to sentence in accordance with established sentencing principles and in adherence to established sentencing procedure. It should not be actively pursued but should rather be the by-product of a consistently correct application of sentencing principles. A sentence that is inconsistent with other sentences imposed upon similarly situated offenders for similar offences is not objectionable because it is out of line with comparable cases, but may be objectionable because something has gone awry in the determination of sentence and the resultant sentence is unprincipled. In the multiple defendant scenario described above, an adjustment in sentence is required on grounds of fairness and to avoid an arbitrary difference in sentences.

A revised definition

The beginning of this chapter began with a working definition of consistency: like cases should be treated alike and different cases should be treated differently. It was established that consistency and disparity refer to the same concept, discounting definitions which did not require an analysis of the sentencing decision (operating on a bare comparison between sentencing outcomes). It was then argued that 'treatment' predominantly referred to the manner in which the sentencing decision was made, encompassing an element of substantive consistency limited to the underlying principles of the sentencing scheme. Additionally, it was suggested that in a multiple defendant scenario, 'treatment' also referred to the sentencing outcome as an aim in isolation. This was on the basis that consistency ought to be primarily concerned with the application of sentencing principle or procedure (ie consistency as a procedural mechanism) which results in more consistent outcomes, and only when a multiple defendant scenario arises, should it actively concern itself with consistency of outcome (ie consistency as a substantive concept). It is now possible to revise the definition discussed at the outset of the chapter.

> Achieving consistency in sentencing requires sentences to be determined only by the application of established principles, having regard

only to legally relevant factors, in a manner which follows an established fair procedure.

In a principally retributive framework, this entails the production of a range of sentences proportionate to the seriousness of the offence. A particular sentence within the range can then be chosen with reference to other established principles, secondary to proportionality, and imposed following an established fair procedure.

In a multiple defendant scenario in which the sentences are within the permissible range, any residual variation in sentence not capable of justification by reference to legally relevant factors will constitute an inconsistency and will merit an adjustment in sentence.

That definition can be summarized in the following steps:

(1) Identify the procedural mechanism(s)[73] used to ensure consistency of approach and consistency of outcome;
(2) Determine whether or not there has been a deficiency in the application of the mechanism or mechanisms;
  (a) Determine whether or not the outcome falls outside of the permissible range of sentences;
  If it does not, and there is no co-defendant, the outcome is justified and is not inconsistent;
  If it does, go to step (3);
(3) Determine the correct sentencing outcome by virtue of the appropriate application of the mechanism(s) in question; the resultant sentence is a consistent sentence in line with like cases;
  If there is a co-defendant go to step (4);
  If there is no co-defendant, there are no further steps.
(4) Where there is a difference or similarity between the sentences imposed on co-defendants where the defendant's and the co-defendant's sentences are within the permissible range, assess whether or not that difference or similarity is justified by reference to legally relevant factors;

---

[73] This work uses the term 'procedural mechanism' in the broad sense, ie to encapsulate sentencing principles, guidelines, and statutory provisions.

If it is justified, the defendant's sentence is not inconsistent;
If it is not justified, the defendant's sentence is unjustified and therefore inconsistent; the judge should then adjust the defendant's sentence accordingly.

This chapter has attempted to bring clarity to the concept of consistency, reconciling differences among the competing accounts and deriving from the discussion a step-by-step process that can be used in both theory and in practice. It has been argued that this presents a more theoretically sound account of consistency in which the emphasis is placed upon principled sentencing as opposed to consistent sentencing for the sake of being consistent. The revised definition comprises a predominantly procedural approach but recognizes the need for recourse to consistency as a substantive concept to (i) ensure outcomes are principled and (ii) to alleviate any residual variation which is unjustifiable. This represents an amalgam of procedural and substantive law, incorporating both consistency of approach and consistency of outcome to enable the concept of consistency in sentencing to act as a critical tool in assessing whether or not a particular sentence is justified in the particular scheme at hand. This conception of consistency may be utilized as a critical tool in any sentencing scheme. Later, as an illustration of its utility, it will be utilized to assess the extent to which the sentencing scheme in England and Wales achieves consistency.

The account proffered here, with its focus upon principles, will produce a normatively sound and conceptually clear approach to the assessment of consistency in sentencing. However, the realities of sentencing practice cannot be overlooked. For instance, while retributive proportionality is neutral to factors such as age, social class, race, gender, and religion, empirical evidence demonstrating that in practice, the principle is undermined by an inconsistent application according to legally irrelevant factors must be confronted. It would be easy (but remiss) to simply say that this is a theoretical consideration and that as the principles are neutral to factors such as race and gender, it is unnecessary to consider the extent to which legally irrelevant factors impact the application of the principles, simply because they *ought* not to.

This work undertakes an assessment of the extent to which current measures for promoting consistency achieve their stated aim;

such an assessment that was wilfully blind to the realities of practice—notwithstanding the theory—would be incomplete and of limited utility. Accordingly, the following chapter considers the international empirical evidence of inconsistency in sentencing both in relation to the inability of sentencers to apply the relevant principles accurately in determining sentence and also in relation to the effect of legally irrelevant factors which may or may not affect the determination of sentence. This will inform the later discussion as to the relative effectiveness of measures employed to achieve consistency. By considering the approach in England and Wales with this empirical literature in mind, the efficacy of measures designed to promote consistency can, at a high level, be assessed such that lessons can be learned both in this jurisdiction and abroad.

3
Dangers of discretion: Empirical evidence of inconsistency

Discretion allows decision makers more easily to consult illegitimate considerations and does nothing to stop them making mistakes...[1]

Introduction

In 1977, Frankel considered the 'lawlessness' present in sentencing, noting a lack of guidance as to factors which should be weighed in moving a sentence towards one or other end of the range permitted by legislation gave sentencers extremely wide discretion but risked inconsistency.[2] He stated:

> It might be supposed by some stranger arrived in our midst that the criteria for measuring a particular sentence would be discoverable outside the narrow limits of the statutes and would be known to the judicial experts rendering the judgments. But the supposition would lack substantial foundation.[3]

Is this borne out by the empirical literature? Have matters improved since Frankel's work? This chapter endeavours to answer those questions.

---

[1] Carl E Schneider, 'Discretion and Rules' in Keith Hawkins (ed), *The Uses of Discretion* (Clarendon 1992) 68.
[2] Marvin E Frankel, 'Lawlessness in Sentencing' (1972) 41 University of Cincinnati Law Review 4.
[3] ibid.

Discretion at sentencing can polarize opinion. One view is that discretion is vital to the fair disposal of a criminal case, allowing the judge to do justice to the individualities of the offence *and the offender* before the court; the other is that discretion is equivalent to lawlessness and chaos[4] and ought to be tightly constrained. Perhaps there is truth in both propositions. This chapter examines the empirical literature in relation to inconsistencies in sentencing. Many of the studies occur in jurisdictions where discretion at sentencing is subject to limited structure and constraint; it is thought that the much of the inconsistency flows from the existence and exercise of discretion in the absence of effective structure. It is this absence of robust structure to which Schneider was referring in the quotation at the head of this chapter. It is submitted that as a general proposition, the statement is true. Unregulated discretion carries real—not merely theoretical—dangers which can result in inconsistent sentences.

With that firmly in mind, this chapter seeks to establish two main propositions. First, that there is inconsistency[5] in sentencing, and secondly that such inconsistency cannot be explained by legitimate factors such as crime rate or offence seriousness. This chapter considers what the empirical literature demonstrates in relation to consistency in sentencing. It then applies the literature to the definition of consistency proposed in Chapter 2 and asks whether, in that respect, methods of promoting consistency employed are fit for purpose. Again, the scheme in England and Wales will be used as tool to evaluate these methods against the literature, from which wider lessons can be learned.

The critical framework

This chapter uses the definition of consistency arrived at in Chapter 2 as a critical tool to analyse the empirical literature on

---

[4] ibid.
[5] In this chapter, the term 'consistency' refers to the definition proposed in Chapter 2 and the term 'inconsistency' should be read accordingly.

consistency in sentencing. It is convenient then, briefly to revisit the definition. It will be recalled that while the definition is not jurisdiction-specific it does focus upon the principally retributive scheme used in this jurisdiction. Its focus on principles is therefore a focus on proportionality in the retributive sense, though as described in Chapter 2, other factors may be relevant.

The definition used is therefore as follows:

Achieving consistency in sentencing requires sentences to be determined only by the application of established principles, having regard only to legally relevant factors, in a manner which follows an established fair procedure.

In a principally retributive framework, this entails the production of a range of sentences proportionate to the seriousness of the offence. A particular sentence within the range can then be chosen with reference to other *established* principles, secondary to proportionality, and imposed following an established fair procedure.

The chapter adopts two premises. First, the accepted normative position that a degree of consistency in sentencing is desirable. Secondly, that consistency should not seek comparisons between two (or more) 'similar' cases and rather focus upon an application of sentencing principles relevant to the determination of sentence.[6]

This chapter therefore analyses the empirical literature regarding structured discretion and consistency from jurisdictions operating a form of retributivism. This will identify the extent to which these systems achieve consistency and therefore provide a basis from which the success of measures employed for this purpose can be assessed. This chapter seeks to demonstrate that there exists unexplained and objectionable disparity in sentencing within retributive schemes and to lay the groundwork for the claim, made later in this work, that to promote consistency in sentencing, judicial discretion must be robustly structured.

---

[6] This second proposition is disputed in some of the disparity literature which, as discussed in Chapter 2, proceeds on the basis of 'like with like' comparisons.

Empirical literature on consistency in sentencing

Introduction

This exploration of the search for consistency in sentencing is concerned with principally retributive sentencing schemes and, as discussed in Chapter 1, the scheme in force in England and Wales is a paradigm example from which a close study can yield valuable lessons. Sentence in England and Wales is therefore predominantly driven by the sentencer's assessment of the harm and culpability present in the offence.[7] In a scheme that involves a case-by-case judgment as to the seriousness of retributively significant case characteristics, there is bound to be a degree of variability. Judge 1 might consider case A to score 7/10 on a scale of seriousness or be 'worth' a sentence of six years' imprisonment, whereas judge 2 might consider it to score 8/10 or six years and six months.[8] It is suggested that such 'inconsistency'—in the literal sense of the term—is normatively acceptable.[9] Indeed, we know that retributivism is an imprecise concept and therefore a degree of variance must be accepted. A strict mathematical approach to sentencing is to be resisted, not least because it is difficult to adopt such a precise approach to a concept which is recognized to be imprecise. Having said that, there clearly comes a point beyond which the variability in sentence would be normatively impermissible.[10] If it did not, then there would be no consistency or inconsistency, just a free for all which would run contrary to rule of law principles of certainty and clarity and the principle of natural justice.

As discussed in Chapter 2, the application of the principle of proportionality produces a range within which a sentence will not be inconsistent. This requires the identification of where the range ends, a sentence beyond which a sentence will be said to be inconsistent. But a

---

[7] Sentencing Act 2020 s 63.
[8] The issue is further complicated because not only might the judges disagree as to the seriousness of the offence, ie its 'score' on a scale of 1 to 10, but they may also disagree on how to translate that into a sentence, ie one might consider a 6/10 is six years whereas the other might consider it is eight years.
[9] As will be discussed, this does not mean that the sentence is absent of any inconsistency; if the reason for the slight (but acceptable) variation was due to race, this would be inconsistent.
[10] Andreas von Hirsch, *Deserved Criminal Sentences* (Hart 2017) 22, 58 and in particular, 104.

strict mathematical approach to determining the range is clearly inappropriate as an attempt to ascribe a numerical figure—say 20 per cent or 30 per cent—either side of the appropriate sentence is arbitrary, assuming that the range is limited to a particular percentage of the 'appropriate sentence' and it assumes that the 'appropriate sentence' is the middle of that range.

That said, it is possible to say, in certain circumstances, that a sentence is inconsistent with the principle. For instance, a variability of say, 100 per cent, for example an offence which, if sentenced by judge 1 received a sentence of four years, but if sentenced by judge 2 received a sentence of eight years, both sentences would clearly not be retributively proportionate (and thus at least one would be normatively inconsistent with the other): proportionality may be imprecise but it is not that imprecise. But that is an obvious case. This work does not suggest a figure beyond which a sentence would be regarded as inconsistent. Such an exercise would require extensive empirical research such as a study of appellate sentencing decisions or qualitative research with judges, lawyers, or the public, for instance. In any event, such an exercise adopts a mathematical approach to sentencing which is antithetical to the qualitative approach to principles such as proportionality.

Instead, it suffices to note three points for the purposes of this chapter. First, that some studies may identify such a wide range of sentences that it is possible to say with some confidence that *unjustified inconsistency* exists; naturally the limits of that range will be subject to debate.[11] Conversely, some studies will identify variability which may fall within the proportionate range which will not, *prima facie*, evidence inconsistency. Secondly, that sentences within the proportionate range may contain unjustified inconsistency. If there is no legally relevant reason for distinguishing between two offenders, then such inconsistency may be unjustified. This will of course depend on the extent to which the study is able to control for case characteristics in order to isolate the factor of interest to the study. Thirdly, that all sentences within the proportionate range will be presumed to be justifiable unless there are data which accurately evidences

---

[11] It is interesting to note that von Hirsch suggests 10–15 per cent would be permissible but 20–30 per cent would not, see ibid 104.

that any differential treatment is legitimate[12] (*justified inconsistency*) or illegitimate[13] (*unjustified inconsistency*).

It is notable that much of the literature considered in this chapter either does not engage with the discussion as to a 'correct' definition of consistency, nor does it suggest an appropriate (even approximate) figure of tolerable disparity; it merely considers the extent to which sentences differ and seeks to draw conclusions as to whether such differences are justifiable. This divergence of opinion as to the definition of consistency (and potential to 'over-interpret' data) does not undercut the principal aim of this chapter, however, namely to demonstrate that there is unexplained and objectionable disparity in sentencing.

Methodological challenges

For useful analysis on consistency within a retributively proportionate scheme, detailed case data are essential. It will be, of course, necessary to isolate factors which are relevant to the assessment of seriousness in order to obtain meaningful data as to the extent to which sentencers are consistent. A bare comparison between groups, say by reference to gender, geographical location, or age will no doubt provide data that suggest inconsistency, either by virtue of a wide range (indicative that the principle of proportionality is being misapplied) or by virtue of a higher or lower average sentence for a particular group. Such 'gross' results—those without taking appropriate account of case characteristics—provide little assistance. Instead, it is the 'net' results—those which have (so far as is possible) controlled for the various characteristics affecting the assessment of seriousness—which are most informative. For example, if considering gender, it is necessary to control for the fact that male defendants are typically sentenced for more serious offences than female defendants. This presents methodological challenges which are not new; it is accepted that multivariate analyses are superior when seeking to conduct this type of research as such an approach enables researchers to control for case

---

[12] This may be where one sentencer relies upon a particular principle, say deterrence, to determine the sentence within the permissible range, but it would have been justifiable to choose another principle, resulting in a different sentence with the range.

[13] For instance, this may be where the choice of principle, say deterrence, is not justifiable owing to the particular circumstances, where too much or little weight is placed on a particular factor, or where reference is made to non-legal factors.

characteristics affecting offence seriousness.[14] Once such controls are conducted, it is far easier to confidently assess the state of play viz. inconsistency and potential discrimination.

Methods are continually advancing and so one must be cautious when considering the extent to which controls for offence seriousness were conducted in older studies. For instance, a 1980s Canadian study analysed cases from two municipalities, one urban and one suburban, finding intra-judge consistency but inter-judge disparity.[15] Variations in sentence lengths were analysed after consideration of differences in case facts, offender characteristics, system factors, and judge characteristics. The analysis demonstrated that 65 per cent of variation regarding sentence type and 67 per cent of the variation in sentence length could be explained.[16] The residual 30–35 per cent variation is, on any view, significant. However, caution must be exercised as the method of control employed was somewhat approximate; for instance the study gave a '+1' score to each aggravating factor (and the converse to each mitigating factor). This is of course blind to the readily accepted notion that factors are not of equal weight and therefore the control can limit, not eradicate, the effect of case seriousness on the results.[17] For example, the absence of previous convictions will vary depending upon the context, including the conviction offence and the age of the offender. That is not to say such data are useless, but rather, reliance on such data must be appropriately weighted.

There is much to be said for using both 'real' cases, that is analysing real sentencing decisions in court or those handed down on paper, and hypothetical cases, in other words simulated scenarios. In the case of the former, another Canadian study critiqued the methodological limitations in studies seeking to analyse past sentencing decisions as, it was posited, such studies required an assumption that each variable was identical save for the variable of interest.[18] In the case of the latter, one judge

---

[14] Jose Pina-Sanchez, Julian Roberts, and Dimitrios Sferopoulos, 'Does the Crown Court Discriminate Against Muslim-Named Offenders? A Novel Investigation Based on Text Mining Techniques' (2019) 59(3) British Journal of Criminology 718–736, 720.
[15] Patricia Brantingham, 'Sentencing Disparity: An Analysis of Judicial Consistency' (1985) 1(3) Journal of Quantitative Criminology 281.
[16] ibid 303.
[17] See eg Julian V Roberts 'Punishing, More or Less: Exploring Aggravation and Mitigation at Sentencing' in Julian V Roberts (ed), *Mitigation and Aggravation at Sentencing* (CUP 2011) 13.
[18] Ted S Palys and Stan Divorski, Explaining Sentence Disparity (1986) 28 Canadian Journal of Criminology 347, 348.

participating in a hypothetical case study commented: 'The trouble with these sentencing exercises is that you tend to be paper tigers. You sentence hard. It's a different thing when you're actually doing it yourself.'[19] This underlines the value of sentencing disparity studies encompassing both 'real cases' (to avoid the results being affected by the hypothetical nature of the exercise) and hypothetical cases (to avoid the assumptions referred to which would affect the overall analysis).

Additional methodological challenges are presented in obtaining data already collected. First, large state-collected datasets such as the Crown Court Sentencing Survey in England and Wales did not record data on the ethnicity of the defendant. Further, traditionally, Ministry of Justice data were aggregated, which precluded regression techniques.[20] Some datasets do not contain data on case characteristics or aggravating and mitigating features. In some cases, current data are not available; the decision to cease the Crown Court Sentencing Survey in 2015 provides one such example. In its recent paper on consistency, the Sentencing Council reviewed different approaches to measuring consistency.[21] It noted that the 'main threat' to the validity of studies was the ability to control for relevant case characteristics to ensure like was being compared with like and that various approaches have been utilized over time, including randomization, fictional studies and controlled statistical modelling. This chapter considers the use of each of these methods.

Finally, there are challenges in the way in which multiple offence cases are recorded and analysed. This is because, despite there being general principles in relation to the way in which such cases ought to be dealt with (in England and Wales at least)[22] sentencers may take different approaches. For instance, in England and Wales, despite a statutory duty to apply guidance on the topic, a sentencer sentencing

---

[19] Malcolm Davies and Jane Tyrer, '"Filling in the Gaps"—A Study of Judicial Culture: Views of Judges in England and Wales on Sentencing Domestic Burglars Contrasted with the Recommendations of the Sentencing Advisory Panel and the Court of Appeal Guidelines' [2003] Criminal Law Review 243.
[20] Pina-Sanchez (n) 720.
[21] Sentencing Council, A Review of Consistency in Sentencing (Office of the Sentencing Council 2021).
[22] Sentencing Council of England and Wales, *Offences Taken into Consideration and Totality Guideline* (Office of the Sentencing Council 2012).

a single offender for three offences may (i) impose a sentence for the most serious count, increasing the sentence beyond that which is proportionate to reflect the other offences, and impose sentences on those to run concurrently (or impose no separate penalty); (ii) impose consecutive sentences on each count, reducing one or more to account for the principle of totality; or (iii) impose a proportionate sentence on the most serious count, and a mixture of consecutive and concurrent sentences on the other counts to achieve a total sentence which accords with the principle of totality. This causes problems for the assessment of consistency as comparisons often proceed on the assumption that the sentences imposed are proportionate and not (necessarily artificially) increased or reduced to account for the existence of other offences. Similarly, offences taken into consideration[23] cause potential problems as the sentence for the conviction offence will be increased to take account of other offences which have not been charged and for which there is no conviction. For instance, there could be a conviction for one burglary for which sentence is imposed for ten burglaries. This causes obvious problems for any assessment of consistency and at present, it appears that it is not possible to control for such problems when using large datasets such as the Crown Court Sentencing Survey or Ministry of Justice data.

With those cautionary words firmly in mind, the chapter proceeds to consider the literature and establish the extent to which it can be said that sentencing in retributively proportionate schemes satisfies the definition of consistency proposed in Chapter 2.

Geographical differences and 'local justice'

Inconsistencies attributable to geographical differences exist and may be justifiable. Geographical inconsistency is not limited to sentencing, however; it has been demonstrated that there is a statistically

---

[23] The process in England and Wales whereby an offender can admit other offences and be sentenced for all the offences, but the sentence will be limited by the maximum sentence for the conviction offence. This procedure provides a convenient way for an offender to guarantee being released from prison with a 'clean slate' (in the sense that he/she does not need to fear prosecution for offences committed prior to the imposition of their sentence).

significant variance in inter-court practices extending to court procedure, the decision regarding bail, and the determination of venue for trial.[24] An obvious justification for such inconsistency in sentencing would be disparate case loads. For instance, more serious crime (or more crime of a particular type) may be committed in Greater London than in Cornwall. The inconsistency may therefore be justified on the basis that by the application of the principle of retributive proportionality, the areas in which more serious cases are dealt with quite properly have a greater custody rate or longer average custodial sentence length.

It is not the case that geographical inconsistencies can always be justified, however and there is a range of empirical evidence that certain 'local practices' exist (or have existed) in sentencing. A particularly stark example comes from anecdotal evidence that until comparatively recently, the City of Westminster Magistrates' Court in effect operated its own sentencing guideline (separate to the guideline issued by the Sentencing Guidelines Council which applied nationwide) in relation to offences of 'pick-pocket' theft, on grounds of prevalence.[25] This was of doubtful legality. Not all geographic variation stems from such orchestrated local practices, however. The following paragraphs consider international studies evidencing 'local justice' and geographical inconsistency.

The Halliday Report—a review of the sentencing framework in England and Wales published in 2001—considered the 'case for change' in sentencing in this jurisdiction. The report referred to significant disparity in the percentage of defendants sentenced to immediate custody in magistrates' courts in 1998 and 1999. Taking the offence of dwelling burglary as an example, the lowest recorded value was 5.9 per cent in 1998 and 12.8 per cent in 1999 as compared with the highest recorded value of 69.6 per cent in 1998 and 50.0 per cent in 1999.[26] Even allowing for local variance on the basis of differing rates of crime, crime seriousness and a

---

[24] Andrew Herbert, 'Mode of Trial and the Influence of Local Justice' (2004) 43(1) The Howard Journal 65.
[25] Sentences, The Defence Brief, 6 February 2013 <http://defencebrief.blogspot.com/2013/02/sentences.html> accessed 21 November 2021; Andrew Ashworth, 'What if Imprisonment Were Abolished for Property Offences?' The Howard League for Penal Reform, 5 < https://howardleague.org/wp-content/uploads/2016/03/What-if-imprisonment-were-abolished-web.pdf> accessed 21 November 2021.
[26] John Halliday, 'Making Punishments Work: Report of a Review of the Sentencing Framework for England and Wales' (London: Home Office, 2001) Appendix 2, Table 6.

different 'type' of offender,[27] this disparity appears to be so significant that justification on the basis of geographical differences (and other, legally relevant, factors) seems highly unlikely. A custody rate of 6–70 per cent in 1998 can be taken as *prima facie* evidence that unjustified inconsistency exists, though its precise extent may be unclear from the data. The report concluded that there was widespread inconsistency by reference to geographical area which was 'difficult to explain or justify', notwithstanding the lack of precision with which such assessments of seriousness suffer. Reference to 'local prevalence' was made, citing this as a significant factor in geographical differences—in essence, an example of the local practices referred to earlier. As will be considered in Chapter 6, the Court of Appeal (Criminal Division) has sought to provide guidance on this issue to avoid unjustified inconsistency. The evidence remains, however, that there is geographical variation which is not explained and not justified, tending towards a conclusion that some sentencing principles, in particular the principle of proportionality, are being mis- or dis-applied.

A 2003 report found significant inconsistencies in the custody rate which were attributable to geographic location: in magistrates' courts in Merseyside, the custody rate for burglary was 25 per cent, whereas in Staffordshire it was 45 per cent, despite the incidence of burglaries being the same.[28] The report noted that although the discrepancy could reflect 'other differences', the analysis of the data suggested that that was not the case and that the inconsistency was not wholly attributable to legitimate—legally relevant—factors. From this gross inconsistency evidenced by this study we can infer unjustified inconsistency, on the basis that the extent of the inconsistency is such that it would fall outside of the permissible range of sentences, on a normative basis.[29] It therefore provides evidence that the principle of proportionality is not being correctly applied.

Roger Tarling conducted an analysis of sentencing practices in the magistrates' courts in relation to males aged twenty-one or over, sentenced for indictable offences with data collected from 1975. The study used qualitative and quantitative methods, finding unexplained disparity

---

[27] For instance, a higher percentage of first-time offenders in a particular area.
[28] Patrick Carter, *Managing Offenders, Reducing Crime: A New Approach* (Home Office 2003) 20.
[29] As to this, see Andreas von Hirsch, *Deserved Criminal Sentences* (Hart 2017) 104.

among the thirty magistrates' courts which were studied.[30] Some twenty-five years later, Tarling revisited the study and repeated the analysis on data collected from 2000. The study found that there had been a significant increase in the rate of imprisonment (6.8 per cent in 1975, 15.5 per cent in 2000),[31] a range of 16 per cent in 1975 and 19.1 per cent in 2000 when the use of immediate imprisonment was examined, but no material change in the use of fines.[32] The 2000 study found factors such as case and offender characteristics could not explain the entirety of the variation found. As a study which controlled for offence seriousness and other factors which might legitimately have impacted upon the sentencing decision, this study provides particularly strong evidence of unjustified inconsistency within the permissible range.

A 2007 Ministry of Justice study divided England and Wales into forty-two criminal justice areas and assessed both magistrates' courts and the Crown Court. The study analysed data concerning the custody rate, custody length, and (in the Crown Court only) the rate of imprisonment for public protection (IPP) and life sentences.[33] The study found:

(1) Custody rates ranged from 6 to 16 per cent in the magistrates' courts and 45–68 per cent in the Crown Court;
(2) the average custodial sentence in months in the magistrates' courts ranged from 2.4 to 3.6 months, and in the Crown Court from 19.5 to 25.3 months; and
(3) the rate of IPP and life sentences ranged from 1.3 to 4.3 per cent.[34]

---

[30] Roger Tarling, *Sentencing Practice in Magistrates' Courts: A Home Office Research Unit Report* (Home Office 1979).
[31] Roger Tarling, 'Sentencing Practice in Magistrates' Courts Revisited' (2006) 45(1) The Howard Journal 29.
[32] The range was 30.1 per cent and 29.6 per cent in 1975 and 2000 respectively.
[33] Both the IPP and the life sentence are indeterminate sentences whereby a court imposes a minimum term which the offender must serve before release may be considered by the Parole Board. The minimum term is imposed by reference to the seriousness of the offence, whereas the continued detention (or release) is determined by considerations of public safety.
[34] Thomas Mason, Nisha de Silva, Nalini Sharma, et al, *Local Variation in Sentencing in England and Wales* (Ministry of Justice 2007), 7. Note that the IPP sentence was a form of indeterminate sentence available to Crown Courts in England and Wales between 2005 and 2012; between 2005 and 2008, courts were required make certain assumptions about offenders leading to the mandatory imposition of the IPP sentence in certain cases. It is widely considered to be akin to a life sentence (and widely considered to have been a legislative error to enact the sentence in the way chosen).

The data were assessed and a number of hypotheses were tested, including that sentencing practice and local crime rates are related, and that severity of sentencing within a criminal justice area is related to the seriousness of offences being sentenced by the courts. Among the various findings, the study revealed that geographical variance in sentencing practice was 'not well explained' by the data on crime and seriousness of offences sentenced,[35] and that in fact the seriousness of the offences provided only a partial explanation for the variation.[36] The absence of a significant relationship between differing geographical factors and the eventuating disparity in sentencing practice found by the Ministry of Justice study is supported by earlier research by Tarling and Herbert.[37] Again, the strong conclusion must be that the absence of an explanation for such variance supports the hypothesis that the principle of proportionality is not correctly applied and that sentencers are unable—at least with a sufficient degree of precision and consistency—to assess the seriousness of an offence and more importantly the appropriate and proportionate sanction. It is right to note, of course, that this was at a time when there were few sentencing guidelines in force in England and Wales; the general point remains, however, that sentencers struggle to accurately and consistently apply the principle of proportionality in the absence of sufficiently structured discretion.[38] Most recently, in 2020, an analysis of sentences in assault cases was conducted, with the result that there was 'sentence variation', that is, inconsistency, both inter- and intra-court centres, but that

---

[35] ibid 13.
[36] The methodology involved placing each of the offences to be sentenced into one of ten categories according to its seriousness. This seriousness ranking was derived from previous practice. Although the report provides insufficient detail regarding this exercise, the reliance upon past practice tends towards the conclusion that the seriousness score concerns the offence for which the offender is convicted in the abstract, rather than a closer evaluation of the individual circumstances of an offence. For example, a manslaughter could be more or less serious than a robbery. The seriousness scale therefore presents potential problems concerning the accurate assessment of seriousness according to the proportionality and attendant inaccuracy in the results of this study.
[37] Thomas Mason, Nisha de Silva, Nalini Sharma, et al, *Local Variation in Sentencing in England and Wales* (n 34) 22 et seq.
[38] Later in this work the effect of various methods of structuring discretion will be considered. Kaplow has considered the differences between 'balancing' as a form of decision-making (the example given is the negligence test in tort) and structured discretion procedures (the example given is proportionality in constitutional law) and prefers balancing. Although sentencing is not considered, the discussion is of interest as to the utility of structured discretion as a method.

much of the variation was attributable to legally relevant factors, in other words it was warranted, rather than unwarranted.[39]

Disparity studies from other jurisdictions with a principally retributive scheme can also be instructive. A four-year study of four magistrates' courts locations in Victoria, Australia found variations in the custody rate for theft offences, with the range extending from 12.0 per cent to 40.3 per cent. It found that in one of the courts, a fine was the most common penalty for theft offences, whereas it was imprisonment in the other three locations, and that there was an 18 per cent difference in the average length of sentence imposed between the two courts with the highest and lowest average custodial sentence length.[40] The study concluded that the results suggested that sentencing in Victoria was affected by a considerable degree of variation in sentencing outcomes.[41] That said, this study provides a paradigm example of the need for caution when interpreting disparity studies. It is essential to understand the impact of two features, first that the study did not control for offence seriousness and secondly that the data provided are median and mean averages presenting an impression of the disparity between the courts as between rural, semi-rural, and suburban court centres. It is possible that from such gross inconsistency one can infer unjustifiable inconsistency on the basis that a degree of the variation falls outside of the proportionate range (suggesting the consensually arrived at principles of sentencing are not being properly interpreted or applied); certainly, the custody rate of 12–40 per cent would tend toward that conclusion on a normative definition of consistency (bearing in mind von Hirsch's view referred to earlier that 10–15 per cent may be acceptable but 20–30 per cent would not). As a result of its methodological limitations, there is a danger of placing too much weight on this study.[42]

---

[39] Ian Brunton-Smith, Jose Pina-Sanchez, and Guanguan Li, 'Re-assessing the Consistency Of Sentencing Decisions in Cases of Assault: Allowing for Within Court Inconsistencies' (2020) 60(6) British Journal of Criminology 1438.

[40] Clare Farmer, Ian Parsons, and Mirko Bagaric, 'Inconsistencies in Sentencing of Theft Offenders in Victoria: Implications for the "Instinctive Synthesis"' (2017) 44 Australian Bar Review 318.

[41] ibid 336. The inconsistency is attributed to the 'instinctive synthesis' approach to sentencing adopted in Australia; the article concludes with a call for measures to bring greater consistency to sentencing in Australia.

[42] Further work would be needed to isolate the cause of the disparity and the extent to which it can be said to be objectionable. It would then be possible with a far higher degree of certainty to comment on the existence and extent of the unjustified inconsistency evidenced by this study.

It is evident that the literature demonstrates inconsistency between different geographical areas exists.[43] There is good evidence of gross disparity, with good controls for case characteristics, providing strong evidence of unjustified disparity between different geographical areas. Other studies provide, by inference, evidence of unjustified inconsistency arising from unexplained inconsistencies within the proportionate range. From this we may strongly infer sentencers' inability or unwillingness to apply the principles underpinning the sentencing scheme with a sufficient degree of precision.[44]

Drawing upon other research, Herbert attributed a significant proportion of sentencing inconsistency to the existence and perpetration of local practices rather than differences between sentencers and their interpretation of the facts.[45] Yet, as will be seen, there is strong evidence that the subjective interpretation of the facts and the application of the law to them is a source of unjustified inconsistency. It falls then, to consider the empirical evidence as to the impact of the 'human' element of the sentencing process.

The 'human' element

To what extent is unjustified inconsistency a product of an inability to be consistent, despite best efforts? Or, put another way, to what extent does the 'human' element in sentencing result in unjustified inconsistency? The claim is that as the sentencing process relies heavily upon a subjective interpretation of the facts of the case and the law applicable to it, irrespective of a desire to be consistent, there are likely to be elements of inconsistency stemming from the fact that decision-makers are

---

[43] Such conclusions are also supported by wider reviews of disparity literature, such as the Canadian Sentencing Commission which considered research into geographical variation, see Canadian Sentencing Commission, *Sentencing Reform: A Canadian Approach* (Minister of Supply and Services Canada 1986). It found that differences in sentence lengths across jurisdictions in Canada provided strong evidence of '*considerable*' inconsistency. The Sentencing Commission for Scotland considered similar research in its jurisdiction, noting similar inconsistencies but it was more circumspect about whether it could confidently be said to be unjustified.
[44] In absence of evidence of a practice of wilfully disapplying the principles, it must be assumed that the inconsistency arises from imprecision.
[45] Herbert, 'Mode of Trial and the Influence of Local Justice' (n 24) 66.

individuals. In addition to this, the subjective interpretation of facts (and to a lesser extent, the law) and its conversion into a sentence may be influenced by sentencers' own penal philosophies. This can manifest itself in different ways; for instance, a sentencer might consider that general sentencing policy is unduly or insufficiently punitive, or that a particular genus of crime should be dealt with more severely or more leniently than accords with current practice. Such views, if permitted to influence the sentence imposed, may result in a degree of inconsistency. Although much of the literature concerning this issue considers the effect of the sentencers' individual views, it does not address the idea that within reason, such disparity may be acceptable. There is empirical evidence, of differing strengths, to evidence the human element in sentencing and its role in the existence of unjustified inconsistency. From early, less sophisticated studies to current more robust research, there is a clear narrative of unjustified inconsistency in sentencing stemming from the involvement of individual assessments of case characteristics and differing penal philosophies.

The Halliday report, referred to earlier in this chapter, concluded that in a scheme which retained a high degree of discretion, inconsistency of approach was inevitable and that while individuals were likely to agree as to the relative severity of an offence, they were less likely to agree as to the corresponding severity of sentence which ought to be imposed in response.[46] The report acknowledged that precision was 'elusive' but observed that the variation identified by the research was 'difficult to justify', providing further evidence of problems arising from the application of sentencing principles in the determination of sentence.

A more recent study in England and Wales involving five sample scenarios presented to fifty-seven judges sitting at eleven court centres asked the judges to sentence the five fictional domestic burglary cases. By way of example, in one case, the mean sentence across the eleven court centres was 44.39 months with a range of a mean of thirty-three months in one court centre to sixty-nine months in another.[47] Another of the cases revealed perhaps an equally fundamental disagreement as to the seriousness of the offence, where all but two judges opted for a

---

[46] Halliday, 'Making Punishments Work' (n 26) 3 and 6.
[47] Davies and Tyrer, '"Filling in the Gaps"—A Study of Judicial Culture' (n 19) 255.

non-custodial sentence. The range of non-immediate custodial disposals extended from a conditional discharge to a suspended sentence with the most severe sentence being one of nine months' imprisonment (immediate).[48] As a hypothetical case study, this has the benefit of an absolute control for case seriousness, isolating with a high degree of precision the 'human element'. As Morris and von Hirsch have argued, a degree of justifiable disparity is expected as a result of the lack of precision with which a deserved sentence can be identified, yet there are of course limits to this imprecision. A sentencing range in one sample case in which the upper limit of the range was more than twice the lower limit demonstrates quite pronounced inconsistency. As argued earlier in this chapter, this would fall outside the range of permissible sentences on a normative conception of consistency, thereby evidencing unjustified inconsistency.

Such findings are numerous and manifest across the literature from many principally retributive sentencing systems around the world. An early US study of real cases found that although judges maintained their relative positions on the scale of severity (some being consistently more severe than others), the judges often displayed idiosyncrasies with respect to certain offence types.[49] Despite this study's methodological limitations, with weak controls for case seriousness, the conclusion has been consistently supported by later studies.

Perhaps of greatest importance is John Hogarth's major work on sentencing for which he interviewed magistrates in Ontario, Canada, to discern the differing perspectives which informed their sentencing decisions. He concluded that one can explain more about sentencing by knowing a few things about the judge than by knowing a great deal about the case.[50] While this may be somewhat hyperbolic, the essence of his conclusion is that the human element of the sentencing process is undeniably influential on the sentence imposed. This is supported by numerous studies since Hogarth's seminal work. His study demonstrated that disparity existed by virtue of the difference between sentencers' beliefs and the inability to homogenously assimilate case information and the principles of sentencing, translating one into the other. Remaining with Canada, a later study

---

[48] ibid 261.
[49] Frederick Joseph Gaudet, *Individual Differences in the Sentencing Tendencies of Judges* (Archives of Psychology 1938) 55.
[50] John Hogarth, *Sentencing as a Human Process* (Toronto University Press 1971) 22.

conducted by Palys and Divorski underlined the need for any assessment of sentencing disparity to encompass studies of both real cases (to avoid the results being affected by the hypothetical nature of the exercise) and hypothetical cases (to avoid the necessary assumptions identified by Palys and Divorski affecting the overall analysis).[51] The study, involving five hypothetical cases sentenced by 206 judges, demonstrated significant disparity attributable to the judge imposing the sentence; one such case involving an armed robbery saw a range of a suspended sentence to immediate custody of thirteen years.[52] Such would, self-evidently, fall outside the proportionate range of sentences and therefore provides *prima facie* evidence of unjustified inconsistency.

Research in Scotland conducted in relation to real cases found similar results. Hutton and Tata studied 1,281 cases previously sentenced by ten sheriffs and found that some sheriffs consistently imposed sentences longer or shorter than the overall mean. The mean length of sentence passed by individual sheriffs ranged from thirteen months to 24.69 months, a range approaching 100 per cent. Additionally, there was both consistency and disparity present in the lengths of sentences imposed in similar cases.[53] This real case study supports conclusions from the earlier literature that individual judges' views may directly affect the sentences they impose. The simultaneous finding of consistency and disparity appeals to logic—that some sentencers will be consistently tougher than others—but remains a concern, particularly when the mean length of sentence imposed among a small sample of sentencers varied to a significant extent. The finding that some were consistently more punitive than others would tend towards the conclusion that sentencers' personal penal philosophies impacted the determination of sentence. Different sentencers may have different cardinal bases attributable to their personal penal philosophy, or alternatively, an inaccurate conception of the principle of proportionality. Similarly, sentencers may have different conceptions of ordinal proportionality, again, attributable to personal penal philosophies. This study would appear to also support the hypothesis that sentencers struggle to apply the principle of proportionality accurately;

---

[51] Palys and Divorski, Explaining Sentence Disparity (n 18) 347, 348.
[52] ibid 354.
[53] Neil Hutton and Cyrus Tata, *Patterns of Custodial Sentencing in the Sheriff Court* (The Scottish Office Central Research Unit 1995).

notwithstanding that it is possible to be more consistently punitive or lenient, the study illustrates a residual degree of inconsistency. This raises two distinct issues: first that the inaccuracy of the principles may require greater guidance, and secondly greater restriction upon sentencers' discretion may limit the effect of sentencers' personal philosophies. Both issues will be considered later in this work.

Returning to the United States, a study of real cases found that where a number of judges were tasked with imposing sentence in the same cases, although the majority of sentences imposed averaged in comparable severity, there was a tendency to very different opinions about which particular cases deserved more severe or more lenient punishment.[54] That is to say that the judges had different conceptions of ordinal proportionality.

This snapshot of the literature is supported by meta-reviews conducted by national sentencing bodies. The Canadian Sentencing Commission conducted a meta-review of the literature concluding that, *inter alia*, the identity of the sentencing judge and their particular sentencing philosophy is closely associated with the sentencing outcome.[55] Notably, the Commission's report linked this inconsistency with an absence of sufficient guidance on the approach to sentencing. In particular, they found that the absence of an agreed approach to sentencing was only one part of the problem; the Commission concluded that additional guidance was necessary as the concepts used to articulate a common theory of sentencing would result in different interpretations as to the principles.[56] The Sentencing Commission for Scotland conducted a similar review and found support for the view that the subjective element of the process resulted in inconsistency.[57]

The consensus is therefore that unjustified inconsistency exists in part as a result of the human element in the sentencing process. The literature, over decades, through real and hypothetical case studies demonstrates that the subjective element to sentencing, that is, the individual assessment of case characteristics and offence seriousness (and their

---

[54] Paul J Hofer, Kevin R Blackwell, and R Barry Ruback, 'Effect of the Federal Sentencing Guidelines on Inter-judge Sentencing Disparity' (1999) 90(1) Journal of Criminal Law and Criminology 239.
[55] The Canadian Sentencing Commission, *Sentencing Reform* (n 43) 77.
[56] ibid 107.
[57] 'The Scope to Improving Consistency in Sentencing', The Sentencing Commission for Scotland (Scottish Executive 2006) 19–21 and Annex B.

application to sentencing principles) in addition to different penal philosophies impacts upon sentence determination and leads to inconsistencies, some of which are unjustified.

Sex/Gender

It is widely accepted that offenders should not receive different treatment solely as a result of their sex/gender.[58] The simplicity of that agreed position belies the true complexity of the issue, however. There are legal factors which may correlate with a particular gender, such as primary caring responsibilities, lower (perceived) risk[59] and the commission of lower-seriousness offences. These factors may feed into the assessment of the seriousness of an offence or alter the resultant sentence on the grounds of what is described as 'personal' mitigation. Accordingly, evidence of gross inconsistency offers little to the consideration of the existence of *unjustified* inconsistency in this context as it may well be that such inconsistency is justified by the correlation with other, relevant factors. It is therefore necessary to consider the extent to which disparities are attributable solely to gender.

The existence and nature of sex/gender disparities at sentencing have typically polarized opinions. Despite this, some of the literature speaks of one or other position being 'generally accepted'.[60] It is possible, however, to identify (broadly) three theses. One view is that female offenders receive disproportionately *lenient* sentences in comparison to their male

---

[58] The literature refers to sex and gender and as such, this work adopts the term used in the particular literature being discussed. With regard to the treatment of offenders, see eg Andrew Ashworth and Rory Kelly, *Sentencing and Criminal Justice* (7th edn, Bloomsbury 2021) 88, Baroness Jean Corston, *A Report by Baroness Jean Corston of A Review of Women with Particular Vulnerabilities in the Criminal Justice System* (Home Office 2007) 23.

[59] There is an extensive body of literature concerning risk assessment tools and the legitimacy or otherwise of taking account of certain factors when seeking a predictive assessment of how likely an offender is to recidivate. Space prevents further enquiry into this aspect of sentencing and consistency, however. For more information, see for example, Kelly Hannah-Moffat, 'Algorithmic Risk Governance: Big Data Analytics, Race and Information Activism in Criminal Justice Debates' (2018) 23(4) Theoretical Criminology 1; Lori D Moore and Irene Padavic, 'Risk Assessment Tools and Racial/Ethnic Disparities in the Juvenile Justice System' (2011) 5(10) Sociology Compass 850.

[60] For example, Frances Heidensohn and Marisa Silvestri, 'Gender and Crime' in Mike Maguire, Rod Morgan, and Rob Reiner (eds), *The Oxford Handbook of Criminology* (5th edn, OUP 2012) 352.

counterparts. This is grounded in presumed leniency towards female offenders, often described as male or judicial chivalry. The other is that female offenders receive disproportionately *severe* sentences in comparison to their male counterparts. This is grounded in the view that a female offender is 'doubly deviant', with female offenders receiving harsher sentences as punishment for not conforming with societal expectations of femininity.[61] The third view, seemingly in the minority, combines the two; while gender results in disproportionate sentences, it is the offence (and context) which determine whether or not that manifests in an unduly severe or lenient sentence, and not gender *per se*.[62] While the weight of the literature supports the hypothesis that women are treated more leniently than men, there is a minority view that female offenders are more likely to be sentenced to short custodial sentences and to be remanded in custody than male offenders.[63]

The chivalry theory has a solid evidence-base, at least in so far as female offenders benefiting from more lenient sentences. In the 1990s, Steffensmeir, Kramer, and Streifel reviewed the empirical literature, concluding that 'a fairly persistent finding has been that adult female defendants are treated more leniently than adult male defendants'.[64] They identified various methodological limitations of past studies including weak controls for offence seriousness and previous criminal history, two legal factors which are known to impact upon sentence determination in a significant way.[65] They concluded that the research demonstrated fairly consistently that female offenders were treated more leniently than male offenders. The study following the literature review was, at the time, one of the most comprehensive and methodologically sound study of its type.[66] Controlling for 'all other variables'[67] the study found that male offenders were 1.77 times more likely to be incarcerated than female offenders. It

---

[61] Carly Lightowlers, 'Drunk and Doubly Deviant? The Role of Gender and Intoxication in Sentencing Assault Offences' (2018) 59(3) British Journal of Criminology, 693
[62] Lightowlers notes that this manifests in the form of more lenient sentences for female offenders for property offences but more severe sentences for more serious and personal offences owing to the latter being seen as un-woman-like behaviour. See ibid.
[63] Carol Hedderman, 'Government Policy on Women Offenders: Labour's Legacy and the Coalition's Challenge' (2010) 12(4) Punishment and Society 485.
[64] Darrell Steffensmeir, John Kramer, and Cathy Streifel, 'Gender and Imprisonment Decisions' (1993) 31(3) Criminology 411.
[65] ibid 412.
[66] ibid 419.
[67] ibid 423.

was observed, perhaps unsurprisingly, that the effects of gender on the sentencing decision were weak when compared with criminal history or offence severity; that is perhaps expected, given gender is a non-legal factor and the two former factors are legitimate (indeed central) sentencing considerations. In relation to sentence length, gender contributed 'very little' to the variation in sentence and failed to reach the standard of statistical significance in sixteen of the twenty offence categories studied. When testing for interactive effects, proportionate increases in offence severity tended to increase the length of a sentence more for males than females. The findings therefore may seem somewhat underwhelming; there is inconsistency (particularly in the 'in/out' decision) but it is moderate or, when it comes to sentence length, non-existent. In relation to the decision whether or not to imprison, a variance of 12 per cent was found.[68] While this may provide evidence of inconsistency, this study is inconclusive as to whether that inconsistency is justified.

A recent US review of the literature found that overall, female offenders received less severe sentences than male counterparts, but that more recent research suggested that there was greater parity than had been found previously.[69] It was noted that literature disagreed as to the basis for the chivalrous view that females are seen as less threatening and less culpable; some scholars have dismissed this as 'simplistic' and limited only to those offenders or scenarios which fit a specific construction of femininity.[70] Drawing on other studies, Bontrager, Barrick, and Stupi note that this judicial chivalry relies upon additional factors as child caring responsibilities, increased cost of imprisoning women, and the greater likelihood of rehabilitation. They describe these as extra-legal factors, tending towards the conclusion that if influential, there may be objectionable disparity. While there may be a justifiable objection to such stereotypes, it is right to recognize that such factors can legitimately influence the determination of sentence. Within a limiting retributivist scheme, these considerations could (within reason) justify a different sentence imposed on a male and female offender for otherwise identical offences as they are capable of

---

[68] ibid 432.

[69] Stephanie Bontrager, Kelle Barrick, and Elizabeth Stupi, 'Gender and Sentencing: A Meta-analysis of Contemporary Research' (2013) 16(2) The Journal of Gender, Race, and Justice 349.

[70] Christy A Visher, 'Gender, Police Arrest Decisions, and Notions of Chivalry' (1983) 21(1) Criminology 5.

being factors relevant to consequentialist aims of sentencing. The gender disparity therefore *may* be objectionable, but the existence of such difference is by no means conclusive. Examination of data from the US Sentencing Commission found that female offenders were less likely to receive custodial sentences and typically received more lenient sentences than their male counterparts but that legal factors accounted for a considerable portion of the gender gap in sentencing.[71] In England and Wales, there is recent evidence to support the claim that if disparity exists, it is not as pronounced as many would claim; female offenders typically have fewer previous convictions,[72] commit less serious crime,[73] and are more likely to be dealt with by the magistrates' courts[74] (which have limited sentencing powers compared with the Crown Court for comparable offences).

By contrast, the 'evil women' theory considers that female offenders who deviate from social norms of femininity by committing, for example, violent crime are disproportionately punished, in part due to the perception of heightened risk or danger. Again, while this may be objectionable, it is capable of justification as the factors referred to—need for public protection, amenability to rehabilitation, culpability, and so on—are legal factors which may legitimately influence sentence. An important finding of Bontrager, Barrick, and Stupi's study and meta-review of the literature was that the inclusion of important control variables undermines the level of support for the chivalry theory. The report concluded that over a significant period of time, the literature demonstrated support for the chivalry theory, but that it declined over time. They further concluded that the research supported theories of greater leniency towards female offenders and that the studies 'clearly demonstrate that women have a sentencing advantage over males charged with similar crimes and with comparable offense histories'.[75] However, more recent data, from 2000to

---

[71] Jill K Doerner and Stephen Demuth, 'Gender and Sentencing in the Federal Courts: Are Women Treated More Leniently?' (2014) Criminal Justice Policy Review 242–269, 245–246.
[72] In 2017, 11 per cent of female offenders had 156 or more previous convictions whereas 89 per cent of male offenders had fifteen or more previous convictions, and of the 82 per cent who had a 'criminal history', 87 per cent were male whereas 13 per cent were female, *Statistics on Women and the Criminal Justice System 2017: A Ministry of Justice publication under Section 95 of the Criminal Justice Act 1991* (Ministry of Justice 2018), 36 and 101.
[73] ibid 102 and 119.
[74] ibid 40.
[75] Bontrager, Barrick, and Stupi, 'Gender and Sentencing' (n 69) 365.

2006, demonstrated that the extent to which female offenders enjoyed preferential sentencing outcomes over male counterparts had dwindled such that it could no longer be said that female offenders received 'significantly shorter' sentences or lower odds of incarceration. This meta-review of the empirical research strongly suggests that the extent of the objectionable disparity is less extensive than much of the literature had hitherto stated.

In relation to the mixed theory, Doerner and Demuth found that legally relevant factors had disparate effects for male and female offenders.[76] For example, previous convictions were more influential in the sentencing decision for female offenders. Their study also established that non-legal factors had disparate effects in correlation with gender, for example the presence of a high school education increased the severity of sentence for female but not male offenders. This provides support for the proposition that conceiving of gender and sentencing as one dimensional is overly simplistic and that the 'hybrid' theory is more credible. This is also supported by recent work by Lightowlers. Her study demonstrates that although male offenders receive more severe sentences than female counterparts, the legally relevant factor of intoxication adversely affects female offenders, resulting in *reduced* leniency.[77] This paints a rather more complex picture than the more simplistic chivalry versus 'evil women' debate. It suggests that there are elements of both theories at play, say where women who are intoxicated are disproportionately punished for being 'doubly deviant', as Lightowlers suggests, but within an overarching chivalrous approach to sentencing female offenders.

Most recently, the Sentencing Council of England and Wales conducted a review of sentencing data to explore the relationship between a defendant's sex (and ethnicity) and the sentence imposed upon them for drug offences in England and Wales.[78] Having explored the likelihood of receiving immediate custody and the length of any custodial sentence imposed, the research concluded that 'after controlling for many (but

---

[76] Doerner and Demuth, 'Gender and Sentencing in the Federal Courts' (n 71) 261.
[77] Lightowlers (n 61).
[78] Sentencing Council, *Investigating the Association between an Offender's Sex and Ethnicity and the Sentence Imposed at the Crown Court for Drug Offences* (Office of the Sentencing Council 2020) <https://www.sentencingcouncil.org.uk/wp-content/uploads/Sex-and-ethnicity-analysis-final-1.pdf> accessed 31 December 2021.

not all) of the main factors that sentencers are required to take into account ... an offender's sex [is] associated with different sentencing outcomes'. Crucially, the research used the Crown Court Sentencing Survey (CCSS) data which allowed for factors concerning culpability to be controlled, producing a clear and reliable conclusions. In relation to drugs offences, the research concluded that the odds of a male offender receiving an immediate custodial sentence were 2.4 times the size of the odds for a female offender and that males received custodial sentences of five months (or 14 per cent) longer than female offenders.[79] This analysis was able to control for a greater number of factors than the 2016 Ministry of Justice study, which found a greater degree of inconsistency attributable to sex/gender.[80]

In sum, the literature is generally consistent;[81] a degree of inconsistency attributable to sex/gender exists but taken as a whole, later work demonstrates that the issue is not as straightforward as the chivalry versus 'evil woman' literature suggests. Sex/gender are complex sentencing factors which manifests in different ways. Further work as to the interaction between sex/gender and other legal factors is plainly necessary in order to identify more accurately the extent to which inconsistency linked to gender is unjustified. It is beyond the scope of this work to delve deeper into the issue; it suffices to note that it is empirically proven that sex/gender disparities exist in sentencing, with the empirical evidence largely supporting the chivalry theory rather than the evil women theory. Even applying a flexible limiting retributivist scheme providing a sentencer with discretion to prioritize certain considerations thereby justifying differential treatment, there is legitimate concern as to the existence of unexplained disparity in sentencing attributable to gender. As a factor which is not considered to be legally relevant to the determination of sentence, the literature provides strong support for the view that gender inappropriately impacts upon the application of sentencing principles.

---

[79] ibid 2-3.
[80] ibid 14.
[81] Farrell, Ward, and Rousseau observe that '[d]ecades of research confirm that women receive less-severe sanctions than men across all phases of the criminal justice system'. Amy Farrell, Geoff Ward, and Danielle Rousseau, 'Intersections of Gender and Race in Federal Sentencing: Examining Court Contexts and the Effects of Representative Court Authorities' (2010) 14 Journal of Gender, Race & Justice 85.

Race/Ethnicity

Race[82] presents an obvious challenge to the application of equality.[83] A large body of research has explored the question of whether racial and ethnic minority offenders have been sentenced differently from white offenders convicted of comparable offences. The overarching question is whether there is inconsistency present in sentencing which can be attributed to the race of the offender. This could take the form of general evidence of inconsistency: say, members of a particular racial group receiving different treatment attributable to their race; for example, that black offenders receive higher sentences than white offenders for offences of comparable severity. Additionally (or alternatively), it might be the case that certain legal factors interact with race as a characteristic and produce different treatment for a particular racial group. For example, black offenders may be less likely to plead guilty to offences than white offenders and therefore receive higher sentences. Similarly, there may be non-legal factors which interact with race; for instance, if Asian offenders are more likely to have a university education than black offenders, a disparity may result from the latter factor which is correlative with race.

It should be noted from the outset that there appears to be little dispute that gross inconsistencies in relation to race exist, both within the criminal justice system more generally but also within sentencing.[84] In such circumstances, we must ask whether such inconsistency is justified (within a scheme which depends on flexibility and discretion) or not.[85] While, continuing with the earlier example, it may not be satisfactory if black offenders are less likely to plead guilty to criminal offences as this is likely to result in gross inconsistency to level criticism at sentencing judges or the sentencing process for this deficiency seems premature. That

---

[82] The literature refers to race and ethnicity and as such this work adopts the term used in the particular piece of literature being discussed.

[83] Ashworth and Kelly (n 58) 186 et seq.

[84] David Lammy MP, *The Lammy Review: An Independent Review into the Treatment of, and Outcomes for, Black, Asian and Minority Ethnic Individuals in the Criminal Justice System* (Ministry of Justice 2017) 5.

[85] It is of course necessary to note that simply because disparity could be justified, by reference to the various purposes of sentencing contained in s 63 of the Sentencing Act 2020, that does not mean that such disparity is in fact justified. It is submitted that only a case-by-case analysis of sentencing decisions could truly ascertain, on such a granular level, whether disparity is justifiable or not.

is of course not to say that such a situation is immune from criticism—it is not. But to level criticism at sentencing judges or the sentencing process legitimately, it must be established that there is some unjustified inconsistency in *the sentencing determination* when deciding the appropriate reduction in sentence for pleading guilty:[86] using the aforementioned critical framework, this requires consideration of whether the data suggest the principle of proportionality is being properly applied.

Hudson found disparities in sentencing in relation to black offenders, only a proportion of which was capable of justification by reference to legally relevant factors.[87] While the initial analysis revealed a pronounced disparity, consideration of the offence type (robbery and drugs offences being disproportionately committed by black offenders, for instance) reduced the extent of the disparity. Irrespective of the presence and extent of discrimination elsewhere in the system, efforts to control for various legally relevant factors produced results which affirmed previous findings that black offenders progressed more quickly through non-custodial disposals than white offenders.[88] In particular, Hudson found that in cases of offences against the person, there was 'a direct race effect on sentencing which produces custodial sentences in circumstances where white defendants would receive non-custodial disposals'.[89] This provides strong evidence of mis- or dis-application of sentencing principles resulting in unjustified inconsistency.

Hood's seminal study of Crown Court sentencing practices found a 'residual race difference' of a greater likelihood of a custodial sentence in the region of 5 per cent for black offenders.[90] The data required a degree of estimation, with Hood seeking to control for factors such as the composition of the cases coming before the courts, including the proportion of black offenders and the fact that they were generally being sentenced for more serious offences. Interestingly, the study found that 13 per cent of the disparity—the lengthier sentences imposed on black

---

[86] In England and Wales, since 2007 there has been a sentencing guideline which regulates the reductions made for pleading guilty. The details and effect of this guideline will be explored later in this work.
[87] Barbara Hudson, 'Discrimination and Disparity: The Influence of Race on Sentencing' (1989) 16(1) Journal of Ethnic and Migration Studies 23–34, 27.
[88] ibid 29.
[89] ibid 30.
[90] Roger Hood, *Race and Sentencing* (OUP 1992) 78.

defendants—was attributable 'almost entirely to the greater propensity of black defendants to plead not guilty'.[91] Ashworth and Kelly note that although Hood's study is more than thirty years old, it is more nuanced and wide-ranging than other studies and thus continues to make a powerful case for vigilance rather than complacency regarding racial discrimination in sentencing.[92] More recently, in England and Wales, the Sentencing Council reviewed CCSS data for sentencing in drugs cases, considering ethnicity and sex.[93] The research found that the odds for Asian and Other[94] ethnicity offenders were each 1.5 times the size of the odds for white offenders, and that the odds of a black offender receiving an immediate custodial sentence were 1.4 times the size of the odds for a white offender.[95] Additionally, it was found that Asian offenders received custodial sentences that were on average around one month (or 4 per cent) longer than the sentences imposed for white offenders, but no differences were found when comparing the custodial sentence lengths of white offenders with black and Other ethnicity offenders. Importantly, this study controlled for multiple case factors including harm and culpability factors, aggravating and mitigating factors, guilty plea, and age. This analysis was able to control for a greater number of factors than the 2016 Ministry of Justice study, which found a greater degree of inconsistency attributable to sex/gender.[96]

In the United States, Rehavi and Starr found that although legally relevant factors could explain much of the disparity present in case data, significant gaps remained. They concluded that there was 'robust evidence that black male federal arrestees ultimately face longer prison terms than whites arrested for the same offenses with the same prior records'.[97] Spohn observed that studies conducted between 1930 and 1970

---

[91] ibid. Others have also made this claim, see eg Lammy, 'The Lammy Review' (n 84) and Michael Tonry, *Punishment and Politics: Evidence and Emulation in the Making of English Crime Control Policy* (Willan 2004) 78.

[92] Ashworth and Kelly (n 58) 189 et seq.

[93] Sentencing Council, *Investigating the Association between an Offender's Sex and Ethnicity ...* (n 78).

[94] The 'Other' ethnicity group includes Chinese, Japanese, or South-East Asian offenders, Middle Eastern offenders and any other ethnic group not counted within white, black, or Asian. Footnote in original source material.

[95] Sentencing Council (n 78) 3.

[96] Sentencing Council (n 78) 14.

[97] M Marit Rehavi and Sonja B Starr, 'Racial Disparity in Federal Criminal Sentences' (2014) 122(6) Journal of Political Economy 1320.

concluded that racial disparities in sentencing reflected 'overt racial discrimination'.[98] Reviewing recent studies in non-capital cases, Spohn asserted that the suspicion that race and/or ethnicity is a factor in sentencing (though not the primary determinant) had been confirmed. Further US studies have found a 'direct race effect',[99] although the extent of the inconsistency varies. Testing for interactive effects of race and gender has found that black female offenders on average received longer sentences (about three months) than white female offenders.[100] Though providing some evidence of net inconsistency, the weight which may be placed on this rests heavily on the extent to which the controls are rigorous as the evidence of disparity is minimal.

A recent multivariate study commissioned by the Ministry of Justice found that those self-reporting as belonging to an ethnic minority were more likely to be sentenced to custody than those self-reporting as white; the data revealed statistically significant increases for those self-reporting as black, Asian, or Chinese.[101] This robust study produced evidence of both gross and net disparities, the latter being the product of controls for certain case characteristics. Having controlled for variables such as previous convictions, previous cautions, age, and offence group, the data revealed a 50–55 per cent increase in the likelihood of being sentenced to imprisonment for those self-reporting at Asian or black, and an 80 per cent increase in the likelihood of being sentenced to imprisonment for those self-reporting at Chinese, as compared with being white. There was no increase in odds for those self-reporting as mixed. The study also sought to evaluate the interactive effects of race and certain characteristics. Focusing upon the plea, it was noted that white offenders are more likely to plead guilty than black, Asian, or Chinese offenders.[102] The study concluded that while plea could partially explain the association between race and sentencing, there remained a direct association between racial

---

[98] Cassia Spohn, 'Racial Disparities in Prosecution, Sentencing, and Punishment' in Sandra Bucerius and Michael Tonry (eds), *The Oxford Handbook of Ethnicity, Crime, and Immigration* (OUP 2014) 180.
[99] Cassia Spohn, 'Thirty Years of Sentencing Reform: The Quest for a Racially Neutral Sentencing Process' (US Department of Justice 2000).
[100] Steffensmeir, Kramer, and Streifel, 'Gender and Imprisonment Decisions' (n 64) 430.
[101] Kathryn Hopkins, Noah Uhrig, and Matthew Colahan, 'Associations between Ethnic Background and Being Sentenced to Prison in the Crown Court in England and Wales in 2015' Ministry of Justice Analytical Services (Ministry of Justice 2016) 1.
[102] This has been stated elsewhere, see eg Tonry, *Punishment and Politics* (n 91) 78.

group and the likelihood of receiving a custodial sentence.[103] This evidence of a residual and unexplained inconsistency suggests problems with the application of the principle of proportionality and also perhaps with the determination of sentence within the proportionate range attributable to race.

The UK data are strong and consistent, particularly as it presents similar results some twenty-five years apart, from Hudson and Hood in 1989 and 1992 to Ministry of Justice data in 2016; there is evidence of unjustified inconsistency which is attributable to the race of the offender. While studies from other jurisdictions are of more limited value, the view given by the US studies supports that provided by the UK data. This does not, however, paint a precise picture of the extent of unjustified inconsistency on grounds of race but merely shows that there is a consistent body of literature demonstrating that studies in various jurisdictions, from various times, employing differing methods have produced evidence that non-white offenders are more likely to be sentenced to custody than white offenders and more likely to receive a lengthier custodial sentence than white offenders, when attempting to control for other variables. That such disparity ought to be addressed is entirely uncontroversial, though there may be disagreement as to the way in which remedial steps ought to be taken.[104] It might be said that this is a 'sentencing problem' and therefore it ought to be addressed with sentencers and the structures placed around the sentencing process. On the other hand, there may be factors which are better addressed earlier on in the process, such as the disparity in guilty pleas between white and black defendants.[105] This clearly—and rightly—leads to inconsistency in sentences imposed, but not one which is objectionable on sentencing principles. That is not to say that it is not objectionable *per se*.

---

[103] Hopkins, Uhrig, and Colahan, 'Associations between Ethnic Background and Being Sentenced to Prison...' (n 101) 8.

[104] Michael Tonry noted the many grounds on which policies leading to such results ought to be repealed and recommended an 'audit' of racial disparities in the criminal justice system. See Tonry (n 91) 87.

[105] For a discussion as to whether the sentencing stage is too late to promote equality, see Rory Kelly and Andrew Ashworth, 'State Responses to Criminal Offences in England and Wales' in Matthew Dyson and Benjamin Vogel (eds), *The Limits of Criminal Law: Anglo-German Concepts and Principles* (Intersentia 2018) 345–61.

The literature is inconclusive as to whether the unjustified inconsistency is a product of the misapplication of the principle or proportionality (producing sentences outside the proportionate range), or a disapplication of sentencing principles attributable to conscious or unconscious biases towards non-white defendants (producing differential treatment within the proportionate sentencing range). What is clear, however, is that unjustified inconsistency attributable to race exists and that remedial action is necessary to address the injustice.

Intersectionality

Although this chapter has considered the two primary illegitimate factors which impact upon sentencing consistency in near isolation, it is important to note the interaction between them (and other factors) and the combined effect upon the present inquiry. Race and gender have been recognized as the dominant non-legal factors in the sentencing disparity literature for some time. By contrast, the extent to which these (and other such factors) interact, correlate, or coalesce—that is, intersectional factors—is a comparatively recent area of study.[106] Intersectionality literature argues that definitions of race and ethnicity are impacted by gender and vice versa.[107] The argument is therefore that such single-factor studies are incomplete, not providing a full and informed account. For instance, considering the gender disparity in the Lightowlers' study would give the impression of a chivalrous approach, yet when the interaction with intoxication is considered, the effect of gender is transformed, as we know that intoxication has a differential impact for the male and female genders.

Hitherto in the sentencing disparity debate, intersectionality research is barely mentioned. This is despite an increasing number of intersectional research studies into crime and criminology.[108] A 2010 study in the

---

[106] For the purposes of this chapter, the definition of intersectionality and intersectional adopted is as follows: 'the concept or conceptualisation that each person has an assortment of coalesced socially constructed identities that are ordered into an inequitable social stratum', from Hillary Potter, *Intersectionality and Criminology: Disrupting and Revolutionizing Studies of Crime* (Routledge 2015) 3.
[107] ibid 8.
[108] ibid 145.

74   ACHIEVING CONSISTENCY IN SENTENCING

United States considered the extent to which race and gender intersected at sentencing based on the composition of the courtroom staff, finding that courtrooms with greater female and ethnic staff were more inclined to leniency and increased representation of black prosecutors saw greater leniency for black female offenders.[109] More research is clearly needed.

It seems as though sentencing disparity scholars are slowly moving away from the traditional offence-based approach, exemplified by studies such as Palys and Divorski. More modern studies—even those concerned with single factors—avoid the sole focus upon offence characteristics and consider offender characteristics too. That is not to say that the older studies ignored offender characteristics, but merely that they adopted a more traditional view, considering retributively significant factors such as previous convictions and factors such as employment (which might be said to be consequentialist and therefore of secondary relevance in a limiting retributivist scheme).

The relevance of, for instance, socioeconomic status and its interactions with race and gender are important in this regard as a greater proportion of women and persons of colour are situated in lower socioeconomic statuses than white men.[110] For instance, US data suggest that black women tend to be in less advantageous financial positions as they are less likely to have a partner and therefore are less likely to benefit from a second income, but if they do have a partner, their partner is more likely to have a lower income than the partners of white women.[111] When this is set against the data referred to in the Halliday report, for instance that sentencing outcome is influenced by employment status (and therefore financial position), it is easy to see how the focus on one factor can mask the true picture of inconsistency. This has as least two important consequences: first, that we are unaware of the extent to which the principle of proportionality (and in England and Wales, the purposes of sentencing listed in section 57 of the Sentencing Act 2020) are being mis- or disapplied, and secondly that true extent of inconsistency (and the extent to which it is unjustified) is masked. In relation to the second point, where a sentence is within the proportionate range, a focus upon one factor, such

---

[109] Farrell et al. (n 81) 122.
[110] Potter, *Intersectionality and Criminology* (n 106) 31.
[111] Potter (n 106) 31.

as gender, may create an impression that any residual variation may be unexplained but not unjustified as there is a degree of discretion and imprecision built into the sentencing scheme. A focus upon a fuller range of factors is likely to provide more accurate data enabling a higher quality analysis. Such a focus accords better with the recent increased interest in offender characteristics; Sentencing Council guidelines relating to the custody threshold, children and young persons and domestic abuse focus far more on factors which pertain predominantly to the offender rather than the offence, and in some cases, have nothing to do with the offence whatsoever.

The conclusion is obvious. Better data and analysis enable any remedial steps considered to be necessary to be more targeted and more effective. While there is a dearth of evidence as to inconsistency in sentencing having regard to intersectionality, the awareness of this knowledge gap will feed into the later analysis of the effectiveness of the current sentencing system in England and Wales in achieving the conception of consistency proposed in Chapter 2. This will ensure that the conclusions drawn later in this work will be more relevant to the current debate regarding race, gender, and similar factors. It is hoped that it will be in turn produce more accurate and better-quality analysis of the methods currently in place to structure the discretionary sentencing decision in principally retributive schemes.

Conclusion

This chapter has evaluated the literature on sentencing disparity. It is evident that there is strong, consistent evidence of inconsistency in sentencing. There appear to be various 'sources' including factors such as geographical variation and subjective assessments of particular cases, but also factors such as race and gender. It was argued that the existence of inconsistency in relation to these factors may not be unjustified as it is possible that they may feed into the assessment of the seriousness of the offence (or in England and Wales may be relevant to one of the five statutory purposes of sentencing contained in section 57 of the Sentencing Act 2020). That said, even if this unexplained inconsistency can be regarded legitimate on that basis—a difficult argument to sustain given the scale—there remains great cause for concern. The literature provides evidence of unjustified inconsistency in the form of sentences falling outside of the proportionate range and differential treatment between offenders by the imposition of sentences inside the proportionate range (where studies have isolated one factor, such as gender, and been able to attribute the residual variation to that factor). It is therefore evident that the application of the principles of sentencing, predominantly retributive proportionality, is currently imprecise resulting in a state of affairs which cannot be conceived of as conforming with a normatively sound definition of consistency.

4
Are individualized justice and consistency incompatible?

Individualized justice is prima facie at war with ... consistency.[1]

Introduction

The view expressed in the quotation by Frankel at the head of this chapter is shared by Krasnostein and Freiberg. In fact they appear to have gone further than the above epigraph, describing consistency and individualized justice as being in 'perennial conflict'.[2] Is that correct, and if so, how might such conflict be resolved?

This chapter explores the role that the concept of consistency has to play in a discretionary sentencing system. As established in Chapter 2, across the common law world, consistency is widely regarded as a necessary component of a fair sentencing system. However, in systems affording individual sentencers with varying degrees of discretion in the sentencing process, so too is the concept of individualized justice. Beginning with an exposition of individualized justice, this chapter examines in depth the concept of a permissible range of sentences as relied upon in Chapter 2. Having established the way in which individualized justice operates within a discretionary sentencing system, the chapter considers the way in which the concept of consistency interacts with it. The purpose of this chapter is to attempt to reconcile these apparently conflicting concepts.

---

[1] Marvin E Frankel, *Criminal Sentences: Law Without Order* (Hill and Wang 1973) 10.
[2] Sarah Krasnostein and Arie Freiberg, 'Pursuing Consistency in an Individualistic Sentencing Framework: If You Know Where You're Going, How Do You Know When You've Got There?' (2013) 76 Law and Contemporary Problems 265, 265.

Individualized justice requires that the determination of sentence ought to consider both the features of the offence and the offender but place a particular emphasis upon the characteristics of the individual. It is present in most, if not all, Western sentencing systems and is inextricably related to principles of sentencing and theories of punishment. It is therefore suggested that reference to tension between the two concepts is misguided and that the argument that individualized justice results in a loss of (or reduction in) consistency is not borne out by principled analysis. This chapter argues that principled sentencing permits (in fact, *requires*) individualization, it does not hamper it.

Individualized justice

The basic concept and its importance

The importance of individualized justice is generally accepted in the common law world, however the extent to which the concept is deployed varies. In the Australian Capital Territory, there is a statutory duty to 'have particular regard to the common law principle of individualised justice' when sentencing a young offender.[3] Justices of the Supreme Court of New South Wales have previously commented that 'if justice is not individual, it is nothing'.[4] In the context of sentencing Aboriginal and Torres Strait islander people in Australia, taking account of the disadvantaged treatment suffered by Aborigines and Torres Strait islanders has been held to be an application of equal justice, rather than a denial of it.[5] The Court of Appeal (Criminal Division) in England and Wales has similarly stressed the need to 'do justice in an individual case'.[6] Further, the US District Court has commented that 'individualised sentencing is so important to the constitutional scheme that any legislative attempt to

---

[3] Crimes (Sentencing) Act 2005 s 133C (ACT).
[4] *Kable v DPP (NSW)* (1995) 36 NSWLR 374.
[5] Justice Stephen Rothman, 'The Impact of Bugmy & Munda on Sentencing Aboriginal and Other Offenders', Ngara Yura Committee Twilight Seminar, 25 February 2014, available at <http://www.austlii.edu.au/au/journals/NSWJSchool/2014/6.pdf>, cited in Thalia Anthony, Lorana Bartels, and Anthony Hopkins, 'Lessons Lost in Sentencing: Welding Individualised Justice to Indigenous Justice' (2015) 39(47) Melbourne University Law Review 47.
[6] *R. v Taylor* [2012] EWCA Crim 630; [2012] 2 Cr App R (S) 98 at [13] per Gross LJ.

limit a defendant's ability to advocate mitigating circumstances to a jury is unconstitutional.[7] A pilot study conducted by Ashworth in the 1980s found that whereas judges considered consistency in sentencing to be an important feature, they were of the opinion that flexibility was needed in order to allow the court to do justice in an individual case.[8] The recognition of a need for consistency but also for individualized justice suggests that there is a 'balancing act' to be performed when sentencing in order to achieve these two ideals. If that is correct, this too envisages consistency and individualized justice as being in conflict to some degree.

Individualized justice is generally understood to refer to the notion that a sentence should be bespoke to the particular features of the case[9] and requires that the sentence is tailored to the particular offence and offender.[10] This is in contrast to systems which limit the determination of sentence, perhaps by the use of minimum and maximum sentences, or permitting sentence determination by reference to 'key' factors only, such as prior record and offence seriousness; individualized justice therefore encompasses a broader consideration of the case in order to balance often competing aims of punishment such as crime control measures legitimizing the pursuit of rehabilitation verses the need to punish.[11] There is a tendency to view individualized justice as necessarily rehabilitative, however it appears that at its core, individualized justice is agnostic as to whether the underlying theory is retributive, consequentialist, or mixed. Further, while individualization typically results in mitigation of sentence, both common law jurisdictions and continental systems endorse the aggravation of sentence in pursuit of the individualization of sentence.[12]

A system which does not adopt an individualized approach will tend to operate with a greater restraint on judicial discretion, limiting the extent to which a sentencer is able to reflect the nuances of the particular

---

[7] *US v Pitera* 795 F.Supp. 546 (1992) at p 564.
[8] Andrew Ashworth, *Sentencing in the Crown Court: Report of an Exploratory Study*, Occasional Paper No.10 (Centre for Criminological Research 1984) 20.
[9] Andrew von Hirsch, *Doing Justice* (Hill and Wang 1976) 27.
[10] Anthony, Bartels, and Hopkins, 'Lessons Lost in Sentencing' (n 5) 51.
[11] ibid 52.
[12] As an example, the French Penal Code devotes an entire section to the individualization of sentences and the aggravation of sentence is permitted both at the judgment stage and the sentence execution stage.

case in the sentences they impose.[13] When reviewing Victorian attempts to resolve the perceived tension between proportionality and individualized justice. In England and Wales, the concept has long-standing roots; Radzinowicz and Hood described the Victorian Criminal Law Commissioners' desire to preserve judicial discretion as stemming from the English common law tradition of leaving room to 'accommodate the peculiarities of individual cases'.[14] The result may be a sentence which differs from the normal or expected sentence in a given scenario and is justified by conceptions of fairness and justice to the individual offender.[15] Yet this definition of individualized justice, focusing upon the 'particular features of the case' is vague; unless a sentence is imposed arbitrarily, then all sentences are to some extent 'bespoke' and tailored to the individual. A tighter definition is needed.

The offence, the offender, or both?

While there is a general consensus as to the importance of individualized justice, there is disagreement regarding its scope. Does it permit an 'anything goes' approach to sentencing, providing that there is some rationale underpinning the 'alternative' sentencing disposal imposed by the court, or is it more structured and more principled? Are considerations limited to the offender, or are they broader than that?

While Doob and Brodeur note that individualization is often used to mask anarchy in sentencing as order and to market chaos as deliberation, they are clear in their view that the stronger justification for individualization is that the sentence should fit the individual offender.[16] Interestingly, they note that in the history of sentencing theory, it is

---

[13] See eg the description of the approach taken in England and Wales as compared with the US Sentencing Commission, as described by Hutton: Neil Hutton, 'Sentencing as a Social Practice' in Sarah Armstrong and Lesley McAra (eds), *Perspectives of Punishment: The Contours of Control* (OUP 2006) 159.

[14] Sir Leon Radzinowicz and Roger Hood, 'Judicial Discretion and Sentencing Standards: Victorian Attempts to Solve a Perennial Problem' (1979) 127(5) University of Pennsylvania Law Review 1294.

[15] For example, see *R. v Glover* [2010] EWCA Crim 1714 at [7] and *R. v Gibson* [2004] EWCA Crim 593; [2004] 2 Cr App R (S) 84 at [3].

[16] Anthony N Doob and Jean-Paul Brodeur, 'Achieving Accountability in Sentencing' in Phillip C Stenning (ed), *Accountability for Criminal Justice: Selected Essays* (University of Toronto Press 1995) 387.

evident that individualized justice began not as a mechanism of distinguishing between individuals but to enable the courts to distinguish between 'common criminals' and politically motivated offenders.[17] While this may encompass some consequentialist considerations, at its origin, individualized justice appears to have permitted an enquiry into circumstances of the offence as well as the offender, with a focus principally on the offence (and the offender's motivations for its commission). However, as Doob and Brodeur note, the emphasis now appears to be on the individual in a wider sense. This is presumably at least part due to the fact that in most systems, offence-based factors will be considered in any event.

Doob and Brodeur go on to set out their view of individualized sentencing 'at its best' describing a system which required the judge to assess the factors which spoke to that purpose.[18] Yet they accept that this is not the concept to which the term refers. They suggest two possible definitions, the first being so broad that it can be described as an 'anything goes' approach, so long as it is possible to form a *post hoc* justification. The second, 'less anarchistic' definition is that individualized justice requires the court to decide what the major goal of the sentence should be, and then to impose a sentence which best meets that goal.[19] It is worth noting that in England and Wales, that is similar to the current approach permitted by section 57 of the Sentencing Act 2020.

The former definition suffers from theoretical difficulties; the broader definition, permitting an 'anything goes' approach focuses upon the discretion of the judge, however this, as is implied by Doob and Brodeur's description of 'anarchy', pays no regard to rule of law principles such as clarity and certainty, in addition to the need for consistency. It would, however, accord with Hutton's view that much of the literature regards individualized justice as being without rules.[20] This first definition, requiring a *post hoc* justification for whatever disposal is identified is understandably rejected by Doob and Brodeur; it would be practically

---

[17] ibid.
[18] ibid 387.
[19] ibid 388.
[20] Neil Hutton, 'Visible and Invisible Sentencing' in Annie Hondeghem, Xavier Rousseaux, and Frédéric Schoenaers (eds), *Modernization of the Criminal Justice Chain and the Judicial System* (Springer 2016) 2.

problematic and antithetical to the general direction of travel as regards sentencing being increasingly principled and rule-driven.[21]

The latter definition better describes the way in which the concept is applied in practice in England and Wales: with a list of sentencing principles, none of which take precedence,[22] the court is permitted to sentence according to its own penal philosophy (within the bounds set by the purposes of sentencing). Yet this second definition subtly moves away from the offender-based focus which emanates from much of the literature and the case law. This definition is wider than many of the others discussed earlier in that it appears to be agnostic as to whether the focus ought to be on the offence or the offender. Such an approach, however, does encompass a principled approach to sentence determination as it is wedded to the purpose(s) of sentencing to which the particular system subscribes.

Hutton suggests that the 'discourse of "*individualised sentencing*" argues that each case is unique and that a just sentence can only be reached by the consideration of the detailed facts and circumstances of each individual case. Judges craft a bespoke sentence which fits the distinctive combination of facts and circumstances which make up the case and this in turn generates a sanction which achieves a "*just*" sentence.'[23] In doing so, Hutton identifies a wider definition of the concept to seemingly include offence-based in addition to offender-based factors. This, again, appears to move away from the more traditional view of the concept as being almost exclusively offender-based, but appears to enable its operation within the confines of sentencing principle. While each case may be unique—in the sense that no two cases are factually *identical*—the reliance upon judicial discretion and the concomitant experience of a sentencing judge appears to undermine the argument that cases are unique and therefore individualization commands a wide discretion to enable the court to 'do justice'. As Hood, and later Ashworth, noted, if experience

---

[21] See eg Norval Morris 'Towards Principled Sentencing' (1977) 37 Maryland Law Review 267; Sentencing Guidelines Council, *Overarching Principles: Seriousness Definitive Guideline* (Sentencing Guidelines Council 2004); Julian V Roberts and Jan W de Keiser, 'Democratising Punishment: Sentencing, Community Views and Values' (2014) 16(4) Punishment and Society 474; Northern Ireland Assembly, 'Sentencing guidelines mechanisms in other jurisdictions: Research Paper' (79/16) (Northern Ireland Assembly Research and Information Service 2016) 10.

[22] See s 57 of the Sentencing Act 2020 and Andrew Ashworth and Rory Kelly, *Sentencing and Criminal Justice* (7th edn, Bloomsbury 2021) 67.

[23] Hutton (n 20) 2.

is of value, then all cases cannot be unique and must be to some degree comparable.[24] The Hood/Ashworth rebuttal however runs contrary to the account of consistency proffered in Chapter 2 as it favours sentencing by comparison as opposed to by reference to principle. Is it impossible to view all cases as being unique but simultaneously rely upon the experience of sentencers in the determination of sentence? It appears that it is possible where the application of the experience concerns sentencing principles as opposed to other, comparable, cases (or the 'going rate'). Perhaps a better interpretation of Hutton's view is that cases are unique and therefore require a consideration of all of the circumstances in order to arrive at a just sentence. That is not to take away from Hutton's wider definition of individualized justice, however. It is capable of operating within a scheme grounded in sentencing principle, as noted earlier, but the individualization is likely to have a more muted impact than narrower definitions of the concept owing to the focus placed upon the offence as well as the offender. Such a definition therefore appears to fit more comfortably within a retributive scheme.

While there is evidently disagreement, the general view appears to be that the concept focusses upon the individual rather than other particulars of the offence. In *R. v Gladue*[25] the Canadian Supreme Court considered the issue, stating that '[s]entencing is an individual process and in each case the consideration must continue to be what is a fit sentence for this accused for this offence in this community'.[26] While seemingly adopting a slightly broader view than is traditional, encompassing offence-based factors into the equation, the general thrust of the judgment was to focus upon the individual's characteristics and how that might justify adopting a different course. Similarly, in *Bugmy v The Queen*,[27] the High Court of Australia described a submission that account should be taken of the systemic background of deprivation of the Aboriginal people as 'antithetical to individualised justice' which said 'nothing about a particular Aboriginal offender'.[28] In so doing, it seemingly adopted the approach

---

[24] Roger Hood, *Sentencing in Magistrates' Courts: A Study of Variations of Policy* (Stevens and Sons 1962) 16; Andrew Ashworth, 'Disentangling Disparity' in Donald C Pennington and Sally M Lloyd-Bostock (eds), *The Psychology of Sentencing* (Oxford Centre for Social-Legal Studies 1987) 24, 25–26.
[25] [1999] 1 SCR 688.
[26] At [93](5).
[27] [2013] HCA 37.
[28] At [41].

taken in *Gladue*, setting out its view that the concept of individualized justice predominantly concerned the individual offender (as opposed to the offence).

There is further support for this approach in practice; guidance issued jointly by the Home Office and Ministry of Justice on integrated offender management emphasizes the need to provide individual offenders with paths out of crime.[29] This recognition of individualized justice was also seen in the major Ministry of Justice consultation on sentencing and managing offenders in 2010, *Breaking the Cycle*.[30] The paper noted the scope to increase the use of community orders with rehabilitative requirements, thereby placing an emphasis on the need—at least in certain cases—for individualization. The paper also noted the use of community disposals in the case of young offenders, identifying the 'sustained focus on tackling the factors that contribute to the young person's offending behaviour'.[31] In the response to consultation, the Government noted the need to ensure certain offenders received more individualized treatment by the courts and throughout their sentences and to increase judicial discretion to enable a greater number of non-immediate custodial sentences to be imposed.[32]

Therefore, while there is a degree of disagreement as to the precise nature of individualized justice, it is clear that the emphasis—at the very least—is on the individual and their characteristics rather than the offence. 'Individualized justice' will henceforth in this work refer to the concept that requires the sentencing court to consider the features of the offence and the offender, placing particular emphasis upon the individual's characteristics, unless otherwise indicated.

---

[29] Integrated Offender Management: Key Principles: February 2015 (Home Office and Ministry of Justice, 2015) <https://www.gov.uk/government/uploads/system/uploads/attachment_data/file/406865/HO_IOM_Key_Principles_document_Final.pdf> accessed 1 January 2022. It is worth noting that this can be distinguished from sentencing on the basis that the guidance is concerned with the administration of sentence rather than its imposition, however it is suggested that it demonstrates a system-wide endorsement of individualized justice at a more general level.
[30] Ministry of Justice, *Breaking the Cycle: Effective Punishment, Rehabilitation and Sentencing of Offenders: Evidence Report* (Ministry of Justice 2010).
[31] ibid para 3.32.
[32] ibid paras 21 and 30.

Individualized justice: Structured discretion or carte blanche?

How much discretion is it appropriate for a court to have? Hutton regards the literature as consistent in the view that individualized justice carries with it an absence of rules. He asks the question 'How can the exercise of discretion by individual judges produce broad patterns of consistency in sentencing?'[33] This therefore appears to accord with the 'anything goes' view of individualized justice proffered by Doob and Brodeur.[34] Can individualized justice be reconciled with a theoretically sound sentencing system, or does it simply give a court *carte blanche* to do as it pleases?

Some judicial definitions of individualized justice are looser than that suggested by their academic counterparts. These general definitions include that individualized justice 'necessitates a broader inquiry into all aspects of the defendant's life and the crime committed'[35] and 'depends on the elementary proposition that the wide variation of circumstances of both the offence and of the offender must always be taken into account, so that the sentence is appropriate to the individual case'.[36] Whether one adopts the loose, judicial definition or a somewhat tighter, academic definition placing a greater emphasis on the individual, it is clear that individualized justice can incorporate retributive concerns as notwithstanding the focus to be placed upon the individual's characteristics, 'the severity of punishment should be a function of the seriousness of the offence'.[37]

The broader inquiry into the considerations of the offender's personal circumstances unrelated to the offence incorporates utilitarian values.[38] For this reason, conceptions of individualized justice are naturally drawn towards mixed theories, with limiting retributivism perhaps the most

---

[33] Hutton (n 20) 2.
[34] Doob and Brodeur, 'Achieving Accountability in Sentencing' (n 16) 387.
[35] *US v Pitera* 795 F.Supp. 546 (1992).
[36] James Spigelman, Chief Justice of NSW (2008), 'Consistency and Sentencing, Keynote speech to the National Judicial College of Australia', Canberra, 8 February 2008.
[37] Douglas N Husak, 'The Seriousness of Drug Offences' in Andrew Ashworth and Martin Wasik (eds) *Fundamentals of Sentencing Theory* (OUP 1998) 189.
[38] Richard F Frase, 'Limiting Retributivism' in Andrew von Hirsch, Andrew Ashworth, and Julian Roberts (eds), *Principled Sentencing: Readings on Theory and Policy* (3rd edn, Hart 2009) 137–39.

obvious. The focus on the offender—rather than the offence—however remains clear in much of the literature.

If one adopts Morris' limiting retributivism model—an approach using an 'exchange rate' between sanctions to allow for individualization within the bounds of proportionality[39]—individualized justice in fact appears to be a central feature. As noted by Frase:

> Sentencing severity can be precisely scaled to desert by means of sanction equivalency scales and interchangeable sanction. This would allow equally culpable offenders to receive very different forms of punishment that are deemed to have equivalent punitive bite but which can be tailored to the particular crime control, restorative justice or other needs of the particular case....[40]

This permits two outcomes: first, that sentences of differing severity (within the bounds set by proportionality) are imposed on equally culpable offenders who have committed an identical offence; or second, that the individualization merely allows a sentence of the same severity but of a different nature to be imposed on equally culpable offenders who have committed an identical offence. For the limiting retributivist, either approach would appear to be permissible and in accordance with principle.

But what of those who do not subscribe to retributivism as a limiting principle?[41] The approach permitted under Morris' model above would attract criticism regarding the 'morally problematic' situation of visiting differing degrees of punishment on equally culpable offenders, where punishment embodies blame.[42] Morris accepted that such a scenario could occur, but viewed equality as a guiding principle which applied only unless there were good reasons to impose different sentences.[43] Therefore, where other considerations, say, deterrence, applied, different

---

[39] Frase, 'Limiting Retributivism' (n 38) 138.
[40] ibid 139–40.
[41] See eg Andrew von Hirsch, 'Proportionality in the Philosophy of Punishment' (1992) 16 Crime and Justice 75.
[42] Andrew von Hirsch, 'Proportionate Sentences' in Andrew von Hirsch, Andrew Ashworth, and Julian Roberts (eds), *Principled Sentencing: Readings on Theory and Policy* (3rd edn, Hart 2009) 119.
[43] Richard S Frase, *Just Sentencing: Principles and Procedures for a Workable System* (OUP 2012) 83.

amounts of punishment would be permissible. Such a response does not appear to assuage the concerns of the defining retributivist; von Hirsch purports to offer a solution by recognizing 'the crucial difference between the comparative ranking of punishments on the one hand, and the overall magnitude and anchoring of the penalty scale on the other',[44] criticizing Morris for neglecting this distinction. Yet this 'solution'—a recourse to his ordinal and cardinal proportionality theory—is, with respect, nothing of the sort. Instead, it is merely a rejection of Morris' limiting retributivism in favour of von Hirsch's pure proportionality. By relying upon cardinal proportionality to anchor the penalty scale, and ordinal proportionality to guide the imposition of the appropriate sentence within that scale, von Hirsch simply reaffirms his stance and in so doing dismisses limiting retributivism.[45] It does not appear to advance the debate as to the conflict between pure and limiting retributivism. However, von Hirsch (with Martin Wasik) has advocated a limiting retributivist model in an article considering a more integrated system of non-custodial penalties which are not simply rehabilitative sentences as alternatives to punishment. Their proposal assumes 'full adherence' to desert principles but recognizes that utilitarian aims may be considered where they do not infringe proportionality requirements.[46]

Returning to the issue of the role individualized justice plays in such schemes, for the limiting retributivist, the role is clear. But does this reasoning not also assuage the concerns of the defining retributivist? The key here is surely the different sanctions of equal punitive bite, another form of individualization of sentence.[47] Individualized justice would permit considerations broader than purely offence seriousness to determine which of the equally severe sentences should be imposed. The von Hirsch criticism therefore appears to fall away. However, for the retributivist who considers there is only one appropriate disposal (as opposed to multiple disposals of the same severity), does individualized

---

[44] von Hirsch, 'Proportionate Sentences' (n 42) 120.
[45] ibid 119.
[46] Martin Wasik and Andrew von Hirsch, 'Non-custodial Penalties and the Principles of Desert' [1988] Criminal Law Review 555.
[47] This enables a court to individualize a sentence based on the impact of sentences on the individual before the court. This might manifest as a reduction in sentence by virtue of custody being more onerous for a person of advanced age or ill health, or a recognition that a community sentence may be more onerous than a short custodial sentence.

justice have a role? The key here is culpability, a core requirement of a retributive justification for sentencing. In the assessment of culpability, there is room for a broader consideration of the individual's characteristics to influence the sentence. For example, culpability does not simply have to operate as a proxy for *mens rea* but can involve a wider consideration of an individual's purpose and motivations. For an offender who committed a robbery, the purpose of the robbery—to obtain money to buy food for their starving family—can be a relevant consideration in the assessment of culpability. It is suggested therefore that individualized justice can have a role to play, even in a defining retributive scheme. However, as Tonry notes, only the most rigid retributivist would hold that there is only one appropriate sanction for a given offence.[48] Yet even for the strictest retributivist, individualization of sentencing is not precluded; a wider consideration of the offence and offender such as that required by individualized justice can be incorporated within such a theory.[49]

In relation to consequentialist approaches to punishment, a form of individualized justice is capable of justification by a different route. Consequentialist theory justifies punishment by reference to its effects, namely that the imposition of punishment can reduce criminal actions and is therefore morally acceptable and rational. The theory principally revolves around three key mechanisms: deterrence, incapacitation, and rehabilitation.[50] At a rather general level, it is immediately apparent how individualized justice interacts with two of these three strands of consequentialist sentencing theory. Incapacitation and rehabilitation necessarily involve consideration of the offender's personal circumstances in order to assess the likelihood of any punitive measure achieving its crime control goal. As for deterrence, closer inspection is required.

Rehabilitation is the most compatible with individualized justice. Sentencing disposals justified by a rehabilitative rationale include treatment,[51] for example, to tackle substance dependency, a predilection for indecent images of children or difficulties in controlling one's temper. In

---

[48] See eg Michael Tonry, 'Individualizing Punishments' in von Hirsch, Ashworth, and Roberts (eds), Principled Sentencing (n 42) 356.
[49] This of course depends on how one views the definition of '*offence*' in relation to the object to which the punishment must be proportionate.
[50] See eg Ashworth and Kelly (n 22) 68–76.
[51] ibid 73–74.

England and Wales, explicitly rehabilitative disposals exist as requirements as part of a sentence to be served in the community.[52] However, such goals could also be pursued inside the prison estate.[53] Further, courses designed to educate and develop skills can assist in the pursuit of rehabilitation; this may be in order to remove the (perceived) need to commit crime in order to obtain money by improving prospects of entering employment, or alternatively to provide education in a broader sense to promote reflexive thinking on the part of the offender as to their motivation and decision to offend.[54]

Rehabilitation, at least on the correctional model, primarily concerns the attempt to nurture law-abiding habits among offenders by attempting to change attitudes and inclinations[55]—to this one might add efforts to change personal situations as regards housing, employment, skills, and cognitive behaviour. Ashworth notes that '[t]he term 'treatment' has often been used in this context ... as an allusion to the medical model in which the pathological state of the offender is diagnosed and treated by experts'.[56] This clearly adopts an individualized approach; the disposal is directly influenced by considerations of the offender's personal characteristics. The opposite approach, which as Ashworth notes is more aligned with the continental European approach, focuses upon reintegration into society.[57] While this at first blush might appear to be less ingrained with an individualistic approach than the correctional model, it still necessitates a consideration of the offender's circumstances. This approach may involve considerations of the offender's friends and family members, and

---

[52] For example, see s 174 of, and Sch 6 to, the Sentencing Act 2020 and the list of requirements which may be imposed as a part of a community order. These include alcohol and drug treatment, mental health treatment and rehabilitation activity requirements.

[53] A frequent criticism of short custodial sentences is that (particularly with early release and release on home detention curfew) it leaves insufficient time to complete courses while inside custody, see eg 'Learning and Skills for Offenders Serving Short Custodial Sentences' (Ofsted, January 2009) 5 <http://dera.ioe.ac.uk/338/1/Learning per cent20and per cent20skills per cent20for per cent20offenders per cent20serving per cent20short per cent20custodial per cent20sentences.pdf>, accessed 22 November 2021.

[54] There is perhaps here, an overlap with restorative justice and the concept of forcing an offender to face the reality of their offending as a method of promoting desistence. See Andrew Ashworth, 'Responsibilities, Rights and Restorative Justice' (2002) 42 British Journal of Criminology 578 and Ministry of Justice, Restorative Justice <https://www.gov.uk/government/collections/restorative-justice-action-plan> accessed 3 January 2022.

[55] Andrew Ashworth, 'Rehabilitation' in von Hirsch, Ashowrth, and Roberts (eds), (n 42) 2.
[56] ibid.
[57] ibid.

even the involvement in a discourse with what Ashworth terms 'stakeholders' in the offender's resettlement in the community.[58] This, too, involves tailoring the disposal to the particular offender, though, as suggested earlier, employs perhaps a wider interpretation of factors relevant to the decision. Ashworth notes that the resettlement model stems from a resurgence of criminological interest in desistence and resettlement, in an attempt to identify the conditions most favourable to an offender's desisting from offending. He notes that the focus is on 'dealing with the aftermath of the offence and the sentence so that the offender can be re-established as a law-abiding member of the community'. This, he states, is in contradistinction to the correctional model which places emphasis on responding to the individual's offending behaviour.[59] Regardless of whichever model is adopted, it is apparent that rehabilitation necessitates an individualized approach to the determination of sentence and that it is merely the parameters of the relevant considerations which differ.

Putting aside the lack of evidence of marginal deterrence, deterrence poses a greater challenge if one seeks to reconcile it with an individualistic approach to sentence.[60] It is necessary to distinguish between special and general deterrence. The former, in seeking to deter the individual from reoffending, adopts an individualized approach. The latter, however, focuses on deterring society from offending and so an individualist approach is difficult to read into general deterrence theory.

It is possible then, for the purposes of this discussion, to dismiss special deterrence rather swiftly. In focusing on the propensity of the individual to reoffend, special deterrence adopts an individualized approach, requiring an assessment of the individual and mandating the imposition of a penalty which achieves the crime control goals for that specific offender. In this way, the individualized approach focuses principally on the offender and their previous criminal history.[61] However, one might consider the view that special deterrence employs an individualized approach as somewhat stretching the definition as the thrust of much of

---

[58] Ashworth suggests that such individuals could also include victims, which inevitably introduces an overlap with restorative justice methods.
[59] Ashworth (n 55).
[60] See eg Anthony N Doob and Cheryl M Webster, 'Sentence Severity and Crime: Accepting the Null Hypothesis' (2003) 30 Crime and Justice 143.
[61] Ashworth and Kelly (n 22) 68.

the literature suggests that individualized justice tends to focus on more lenient punishments, or disposals which do not seek to punish at all.[62] Yet all that individualized justice requires, as noted earlier, is that the sentencing disposal is tailored to the individual offence and offender, with a focus upon the individual's characteristics. Where, for the recidivist offender (the most obvious example of when special deterrence would be employed as a purpose of sentencing)[63] the severity of a sentence is increased (within the bound set by proportionality) as a method of preventing the commission of further crime, an assessment of the offender's criminal history will have informed the decision to employ special deterrence as a purpose of sentencing and to what extent.

General deterrence on the other hand seeks through the imposition of severe penalties to deter the public at large (or a particular group of the public) from committing offences of the kind committed by the offender.[64] Is it possible to achieve general deterrence within an individualized justice framework? If, as established earlier, individualized justice requires consideration of the offence and the offender, the natural conclusion one may be drawn to is that general deterrence cannot be achieved by an individualistic approach as the focus is on the offence, to the exclusion of the offender. Warner stated that '[f]or general deterrence the individual offender does not matter'.[65] This logically follows the rationale underpinning general deterrence as a justification of punishment; the deterrent effect would be limited where considerations of the offender permit a deviation from such a sentence. For instance, allowing the existence of a mental disorder reducing culpability to permit a deviation from deterrent sentences could be argued to 'water down' their effect.[66] Some have acknowledged the argument that to impose deterrent sentences on, for instance, those with mental disorders reducing culpability[67] undermines

---

[62] It will be noted that almost all of the foregoing discussion surrounding individualized justice concerns measures in response to factors which would be considered to mitigate (or at least not aggravate) a sentence.
[63] Ashworth and Kelly (n 22) 68.
[64] ibid 68–69.
[65] Kate Warner, 'Theories of Sentencing: Punishment and the Deterrent Value of Sentencing, Sentencing: From Theory to Practice', Canberra, 8–9 February 2014, 5.
[66] The counter hypothesis would be that if reduced culpability is not taken into account, resulting in a reduction in the frequency with which general deterrence is employed as a rationale for sentencing, the public would see sentencing as unjust. This is an empirical claim which it is not appropriate to venture into here.
[67] See eg Warner, 'Theories of Sentencing' (n 65) 6.

the purpose, however the stronger argument goes the other way, namely that by imposing deterrent sentences on all, including those suffering from a mental disorder reducing culpability, the message communicated to the public is that there is little chance of avoiding condign punishment, as the courts will severely punish even those who it recognizes are less culpable.[68] In practice, the courts are unlikely to pursue such a policy as in a system grounded in mixed theory (as most Western systems are) as the likely result would be a disproportionate sentence which is likely to be in contravention of the principles underpinning the system.[69]

But is it correct to state that the individual offender does not matter in general deterrence theory? Consider an offence of possession of a prohibited firearm committed by the partner of a drug dealer. Where the offender allows the drug dealer to store a prohibited firearm at her address, through fear of violence, the decision as to whether to impose a deterrent sentence to 'send a message' to others in a similar position necessarily encompasses considerations of the individual offender. This is due to the need to consider the effectiveness of a general deterrent sentence and the class of people to whom the 'message' is being sent. Continuing the example, it is necessary to consider the circumstances of the offender in order to ascertain whether or not a general deterrence sentence is suitable. Therefore, Warner's claim that the individual is irrelevant may be questionable. However, if, in theory, general deterrence does permit punishment to be visited upon an innocent individual, as it permits a disproportionate punishment to be visited upon an offender of little or no culpability, is that fatal as regards a role for individualized justice? While considerations of the individual can be arguably encompassed within general deterrence theory, the question of whether or not individualized justice has a role to play in this context depends on the definition

---

[68] This echoes the principled objection to general deterrence as a rationale for sentencing, namely that it would in theory permit harsh treatment to be imposed upon an innocent individual if such treatment would deter others from committing such offences, see Ashworth and Kelly (n 22) 68–71 for a discussion.

[69] An example of such an approach can be seen in the cases concerning the possession of a prohibited firearm which is subject to a minimum sentence of five years' imprisonment (which the courts have noted are designed to achieve general deterrence, see *R. v Rehman* [2005] EWCA Crim 2056; [2006] 1 Cr App R (S) 77 at [4]). In cases where culpability is low or non-existent (as the offence is one of strict liability), the courts routinely disapply the minimum sentence, rejecting general deterrence as a purpose of sentencing. An examination of the case law reveals that such an approach is required when the minimum sentence would be disproportionate.

one adopts; if the prioritization of the offender's characteristics requires a consideration of what is best for the offender, then it can have no role in general deterrence theory. However, if it merely requires that the personal characteristics are prioritized, then it is arguable that there is a role for individualized justice to play. As this chapter has subscribed to the latter, it is suggested that individualized justice does in fact have a role to play here, though it is recognized that this is rather contentious.

There is support from this in practice. Certain jurisdictions have indicated that particular cases are inappropriate for deterrent sentences. In the Australian case of *Muldrock v The Queen*,[70] the Chief Justice noted that such a principle was 'well established' in relation to mentally disordered offenders. The court stated:

> A question will often arise as to the causal relation, if any, between an offender's mental illness and the commission of the offence. Such a question is less likely to arise in sentencing a mentally retarded offender because the lack of capacity to reason, as an ordinary person might, as to the wrongfulness of the conduct will, in most cases, substantially lessen the offender's moral culpability for the offence. The retributive effect and denunciatory aspect of a sentence that is appropriate to a person of ordinary capacity will often be inappropriate to the situation of a mentally retarded offender and to the needs of the community.

In *R. v Gomes Monteiro*,[71] the Lord Chief Justice underlined earlier guidance given by the Court of Appeal (Criminal Division) that:

> [g]iven the prevalence of knife crime among young persons, the youth court had to maintain a very sharp focus, if necessary through the use of more severe sentences, on preventing further offending by anyone apprehended for carrying a knife in a public place and to securing an overall reduction in the carrying of knives by young persons.

While underlining the need for deterrent sentences, this appears to invest courts with a degree of discretion when considering whether or not a

---

[70] [2011] HCA 39; (2011) 244 CLR 120 at [54].
[71] [2014] EWCA Crim 747; [2014] 2 Cr. App. R. (S.) 62.

particular case requires such a sentence. That there is a role for individualized justice in general deterrence theory is capable of further support by Parliament's approach to minimum sentences. The possession of a prohibited firearm for instance is subject to a five-year minimum sentence,[72] for the purposes of general deterrence.[73] In *R. v Rehman*[74] the court when considering the minimum sentence provision for an offence of possession of an offensive weapon said:

> The weapons, with which we are concerned, are ones in relation to which Parliament by [s 311] has signalled it was important that there should be imposed deterrent sentences. By 'deterrent sentences' we mean sentences that pay less attention to the personal circumstances of the offender and focus primarily upon the need for the courts to convey a message that an offender can expect to be dealt with more severely so as to deter others than he would be were it only his personal wrongdoing which the court had to consider.

Yet this minimum sentence is subject to an 'escape clause' allowing the court to disapply the minimum sentence provision where exceptional circumstances exist.[75] Typically the escape clause is applied in cases of low culpability[76] but it can include other factors such as guilty plea and matters of personal mitigation.[77] This forces a consideration of the individual features of the case as a gateway criterion to the imposition of a deterrent sentence. Therefore, as the court in *Rehman* noted, the offender's personal characteristics remain a relevant consideration. Take the example of an offender who suffers from a mental disorder. In sentencing for an offence concerning the use of a knife—an offence for which the

---

[72] See the Sentencing Act 2020 s 311.
[73] It is noteworthy that in setting a minimum sentence for the purposes of general deterrence, the exercise of individualization is performed by the judge in determining whether or not to disapply the minimum sentence and how severe the sentence ought to be (either above or below the minimum). The imposition of a deterrent sentence is at first *ex ante* as opposed to *ex post facto*, determined only by the offence itself.
[74] [2005] EWCA Crim 2056; [2006] 1 Cr App R (S) 77.
[75] Other instances of minimum sentence legislation in England and Wales use a seemingly wider 'unjust in all the circumstances' test for disapplication.
[76] For instance, where the offender has a mental disorder or where the offender had no *mens rea* in the context of a strict liability offence, see for example s 311 of the Sentencing Act 2020.
[77] HHJ Mark Lucraft QC (ed), *Archbold Criminal Pleading, Evidence and Practice 2022* (Sweet and Maxwell 2018) § 5A–75 et seq.

courts have consistently imposed deterrent sentences—the court may consider whether or not a deterrent sentence is appropriate, balancing the need to communicate to the wider public that severe sentences will be imposed for such offences against the presence of the mental disorder. If deterrence is appropriate, it may require a severe sentence in pursuit of those aims and the mental disorder may be relevant in determining how severe the sentence ought to be; if it is not, it will impose a sentence in accordance with one or more of the other sentencing principles. In both cases, the court will have considered the individual's characteristics of the individual (ie the mental disorder) to determine whether or not general deterrence is an appropriate aim to pursue, tailoring the sentence to the individual case.

Is this sufficient to bring sentences imposed in pursuit of general deterrence under the umbrella of individualized justice? It is arguable that this approach stretches the definition too far; individualized justice must require more than merely the fact of considering the circumstances of the case and imposing sentence. Otherwise, every system which did not arbitrarily impose sentences with no regard to the circumstances of each case could be said to subscribe to the concept of individualized justice.

While the Doob and Brodeur definition, discussed earlier, would appear to place general deterrence under the umbrella of individualized justice on the basis that it requires the court to select a primary rationale for sentencing and impose a sentence which meets that rationale, such a definition omits the focus on the offender which is so central to the concept. Without such a focus, the concept would be so general as to permit widespread disparity in sentencing, something which Doob and Brodeur described as '*anarchy*' and sought to avoid. Yet their second, preferred, definition did not achieve that aim. In a mixed theory system in which the court is able to select a primary rationale for sentencing from a wide range, disparity would result so as fundamentally to undermine confidence in the sentencing system.

Consideration of the offender's characteristics in determining first whether or not a general deterrent sentence is appropriate, and thereafter the severity of the sentence in pursuance of general deterrence are sufficient to identify an element of individualization within deterrence theory. It is accepted that it relies upon a rather weak account of the concept and the underlying rationale for deterrence has the ability to rather marginalize the effect of the individualization. That said, as argued earlier, a consideration of whether a sentence increased in the name of general deterrence is appropriate requires a consideration of factors which can fall within a wide definition of individualized justice. While much of the literature suggests a de-escalation of sentence severity in the name of individualized justice, the foregoing discussion does not appear to identify this as a pre-requisite. By prioritizing the offender's characteristics in order to determine the appropriate sentence, the sentence is individualized within the scope of the sentencing principles to which the system subscribes.

Judicial discretion

Some have opined that it requires *wide* judicial discretion[78] in order to enable a sentencing court to impose the sentence most appropriate to the individual facts of the case. However, this is of course a matter of degree; individualized justice is, like consistency, a vehicle which can be used to arrive at a principled sentence. It can operate with a narrow discretion afforded to sentencing judges, just as it can operate with a wide discretion. The extent to which the sentence is tailored depends upon the limits of the particular sentencing scheme and the sentencing disposals made available to a sentencing court by the legislature. While it therefore seems that a wide discretion is not a prerequisite, it certainly assists in the pursuit of individualized justice. In any event, a degree of discretion is absolutely necessary. Perhaps unsurprisingly then, the case for individualization (and a wide discretion) has traditionally been made by the judiciary.[79] The argument has however been made by academics too; for example, von Hirsch described the need for 'the widest discretion ... hampered by as few legal constraints as possible' in order to achieve individualization.[80] This of course places significant trust in those tasked to impose sentence.

---

[78] Arie Freiberg and Sarah Krasnostein, 'Statistics, Damn Statistics and Sentencing' (2011) 21 Journal of Judicial Administration 73.
[79] See eg Cyrus Tata, Nicola Burns, and Simon Halliday, 'Assisting and Advising the Sentencing Decision Process: The Pursuit of "Quality" in Pre-Sentence Reports' (2008) 48 British Journal of Criminology 835.
[80] von Hirsch (n 44) 27.

According to Freiberg and Krasnostein, individualization is shaped by a number of 'well-established' propositions, including:

(1) there being no single correct sentence;
(2) no two cases are the same; and
(3) sentencing cases are not precedents.[81]

These propositions would appear to complement rather than underpin the concept of individualized justice. If the core of individualized sentencing is to tailor the sentence to the unique facts of each case (encompassing both offence and offender), then at its most simplistic, all that would appear to be required is that the court has sufficient flexibility to impose what it considers to the be the appropriate sentence within the bounds of the particular sentencing regime; it is not necessary to have a wide range of sentencing disposals, simply the discretion to do what is appropriate within the confines of the particular system. This of course makes sense in theory, however in practice having a very narrow range of disposals (eg just the power to imprison or fine) might undermine the concept of individualized justice to the extent that it arguably could not be achieved, notwithstanding the apparent wide discretion afforded to sentencers. Accordingly, it appears that the concept rests on the discretion afforded to sentencing courts to reflect the individual circumstances of the offence and offender before the court. That is assisted by a wide range of sentencing disposals capable of meeting different purposes of punishment.

Other propositions, such as those advanced by Krasnostein and Freiberg, assist in the application and realization of individualized sentencing, but are not essential to it, at least in the abstract. Such propositions are desirable, however. A system of individualized justice which subscribed to the notion that there was a single correct sentence would be entirely unworkable in practice, inviting a significant increase in the number of appeals against sentence and flooding the appellate courts with cases. Further, such an approach would, in a system predicated upon judicial discretion, undermine the sentencing regime as it would be likely that the number of successful appeals against sentence would increase

---

[81] Freiberg and Krasnostein, 'Statistics, Damn Statistics and Sentencing' (n 78) 74.

sharply, suggesting that the inferior courts frequently make mistakes, mistakes many of which may be better described as a mere difference of opinion.

Similarly, the notion that no two cases are the same—a view held by many[82]—is not a prerequisite of individualized justice. As a concept it is capable of diverse interpretation, with its scope greatly dependent on the meaning of 'the same'. For example, 'the same' could refer to all factors in the case being identical, in which case it is axiomatic that no two cases are in fact the same. Alternatively, 'the same' could refer to a similarity between the legally relevant factors in a case, in which case a case may be 'the same' as another. The resolution of this issue is perhaps not determinative of whether it is complementary to individualized justice; the rationale for a sentencing system predicated upon the concept of individualized justice remains, whether or not one subscribes to the notion that no two cases are in fact 'the same'. The resolution of that question is more germane to the issue of methodology in that it goes to the process by which an appropriate sentence is arrived at. Sentencers will rely upon principles, guidance, and perhaps comparable cases; the fact that one considers that no two cases are in fact the same is not fatal to the use of comparable cases, it merely alters the way in which those cases are used. For example, a comparable case could be used to demonstrate the general approach to sentencing in a particular offence class, or the appropriate starting point for a particular offence. This would be in contrast to a system where it was accepted that it is possible for two cases be to be sufficiently similar so as to require the same or similar treatment, in which the comparable case might be relied on to demonstrate the propriety of a particular sentence in a particular case. That being said, the notion that no two cases are the same—taken literally—complements individualized justice as it underlines the complex nature of a sentencing exercise, involving different and often competing factors which must be weighed in order to determine the appropriate sentence. It therefore serves as a reminder of the need for a focus on individualized justice in order to deal most appropriately with each case. For this reason, the idea that no two

---

[82] For example, see Scottish Sentencing Council, 'About Sentencing' <https://www.scottishsentencingcouncil.org.uk/about-sentencing/introduction-to-sentencing/> accessed 17 December 2021.

cases are the same complements individualized justice, irrespective of one's interpretation of it.

The view that sentencing decisions are not precedents is prevalent throughout practice in England and Wales. The courts have regularly stated that cases decided on their own facts are of little or no utility.[83] This view is closely linked to the notion that no two cases are the same. In a move towards more principled sentencing, the Court of Appeal (Criminal Division) in England and Wales has sought to limit reliance upon cases which simply illustrate the 'going rate' for a particular offence in favour of reference to cases establishing or illustrating principles or offering broader guidance than merely what was decided in a particular case.[84] As will be explored later in this chapter, this marks a shift away from a focus upon inconsistency (or disparity) as traditionally understood to an approach consistent with the account of consistency given in Chapter 2.

A permissible range of sentencing decisions

A system adopting an individualized justice approach to sentence determination will necessarily assume that there is no correct, single sentence for a given offence. This is so for pragmatic reasons, such as the likely scale and attendant cost of appeals in a system which adopted strict proportionality, for principled reasons, such as legal certainty and for reasons of common sense, such as the recognition that in a human process with many variables, different sentencers are likely to arrive at different conclusions.[85] It is often claimed that sentencing is an art and not a science;[86] this appears to suggest that it is a question of judgment and that there is room for (reasonable) disagreement. If that is so, this

---

[83] See eg *Attorney General's Reference (Nos 26 and 27 of 2016)* [2016] EWCA Crim 613; [2014] 2 Cr App R (S) 45 at [35]; *R. v Dart* [2014] EWCA Crim 2158 at [24] and *R. v King* [2013] EWCA Crim. 1599; [2014] 1 Cr App R (S) 73 at [12].

[84] *R. v Thelwall* [2016] EWCA Crim 1755 at [22].

[85] See John Hogarth, *Sentencing as a Human Process* (University of Toronto Press 1971) 91 as to the differences in penal philosophies, effectiveness of different kinds of sentence and the importance of each of the purposes of sentencing among judges, evidenced by his study of Canadian magistrates.

[86] See eg *Attorney General's Reference (No 4 of 1989)* (1989) 11 Cr App R (S) 517 per Lord Lane CJ.

requires a rejection of a mathematical approach in favour of something more creative and (at least partially) subjective which inevitably leads to a divergence of outcome.[87] Moreover, a mathematical approach providing a narrower range—or perhaps even providing very precise results so as to avoid a range entirely—would be antithetical to the notion of individualization. Just as it is not possible to devise a sentencing guideline which applies to all offenders without the need for an 'escape clause' to avoid disproportionate results in unusual or difficult cases, similarly it is not possible (at present at least) to devise a mathematical approach to sentence determination that is able to recognize the 'key' factor(s) in a given case and give primacy to it in order to serve the aims of individualized justice. Sentencing remains a human process.

It will be recalled that the concept of a permissible range of sentences was introduced in Chapter 2 and is relied upon in the construction of consistency there established. This section of this chapter develops that concept with the context of an individualistic sentencing system.

A permissible range of sentences and the pursuit of principled sentencing

On a practical level, the rejection of the notion of a permissible range of sentences would be to bring a sentencing system to its knees by virtue of an unrelenting flood of appeals geared towards minor adjustments to sentencing quanta.[88] But the concept of a permissible range of sentences is well grounded in theory, too.

A sentencing system which affords sentencers any meaningful degree of discretion necessarily relies upon the existence of a range of sentences that are 'not wrong' for any given offence. This is so irrespective of the theory to which one subscribes. The widely held view is that because sentencing relies upon the exercise of judgment as opposed to the application

---

[87] The question of sentencing involving the exercise of discretion and the exercise of judgment is explored in more detail in Chapter 5.
[88] The practice of the Court of Appeal (Criminal Division) in England and Wales is not to 'tinker' with sentences, allowing appeals and Attorney General's references only where the court considers that it is necessary to affect a material difference in sentence. See Chapter 7 for an exposition of the court's approach to appeals against sentence.

of a mathematic equation or scientific formula,[89] there is no single, correct sentencing outcome in a given case, not least because the translation of legally relevant factors onto a scale of severity is an imprecise exercise. Limiting retributivists subscribe to the notion of a range of 'not undeserved' punishments,[90] on the basis that the concept is too imprecise to accurately identify the sentence.[91] Morris' position is that retributivism is a limiting principle, setting only the upper and lower bounds of the appropriate sentence. Within those bounds, he argues that crime prevention concerns determine the appropriate penalty, thereby establishing a range of 'not wrong' sentences.[92] Von Hirsch criticizes Morris' approach on the basis of censure; on utilitarian grounds, two similarly culpable offenders could receive different sentences within the range set, thereby impliedly conveying differing degrees of censure notwithstanding that the 'reprehensibleness' of their conduct is the same.[93]

Of the conflict between limiting and determining retributivism, von Hirsch asks 'limiting or determining for what purpose?',[94] suggesting that desert should be viewed as determining ordinal magnitudes but limiting in relation to cardinal dimensions of severity.[95] This too accepts that there is a range of sentences, however only in relation to the upper and lower limits for the offence. If desert is properly construed as partly limiting and partly defining, but desert is a vague concept which is 'poorly defined and understood',[96] then there is scope for a permissible range.[97] A 'traditional retributivist view of substantive commensurability' would however disagree with this notion as a pure retributivist considers there to be only one

---

[89] See eg *R. v Haining* [2016] EWCA Crim 854 at [26] and *R. v Price* [2016] EWCA Crim 1919 at [12].
[90] Frase (n 38) 119.
[91] Norval Morris, 'Punishment, Desert and Rehabilitation in Equal Justice Under the Law' (1977 US Government Printing Office) 158
[92] Andrew von Hirsch, *Past or Future Crimes: Deservedness and Dangerousness in the Sentencing of Criminals* (Manchester University Press 1986) 38.
[93] ibid 40.
[94] ibid 39.
[95] ibid 39.
[96] Mirko Bagaric 'Proportionality in Sentencing: Its Justification, Meaning and Role' (2000) 12(2) Current Issues in Criminal Justice 143.
[97] The range would presumably operate on narrower basis, however the justification for the existence of a range for the purposes of consistency remains the same: it is not possible to be so precise as to identify a single correct sentence.

appropriate sentence.[98] Yet, even those adopting a pure proportionality stance (thereby incorporating fewer considerations in the determination of offence seriousness and—arguably—producing a more precise result) appear to accept that the more precise result manifests itself as a narrower range, as opposed to a single sentence.[99] This is because, as von Hirsch accepts, proportionality does not furnish specific quanta of punishments (as it presupposes a 'heroic intuitionism' which is simply not borne out by reality).[100] A permissible range is therefore an inevitable feature of a system grounded in desert theory. As Krasnostein and Freiberg stated:

> Within a discretionary framework, [consistency of approach] assumes that sentences will only ever be 'reasonably consistent,' reflecting an acceptance that there is no correct sentence but rather a range of correct sentences, and that this is necessary if sentences are to be consistently proportionate.[101]

This view has support from others who, for example, consider that consistency means 'not uniform sentences' and that 'individual sentences will differ'.[102] Similarly, Tata and Hutton, in a study of the sentencing practices of ten Sheriffs in Scotland, commented that 'the concept of disparity is itself dependent on some notion of a 'normal' sentence from which the disparate sentence varies'.[103] Inherent in the notion of the 'normal' sentence is the existence of a range of sentences as opposed to a single correct sentence. Additionally, many other academics explicitly or implicitly recognize the existence of a permissible range (to a greater or lesser extent)[104]

---

[98] Anthony E Bottoms, 'Five Puzzles in von Hirsch's Theory of Punishment' in Andrew Ashworth and Martin Wasik (eds) *Fundamentals of Sentencing Theory: Essays in Honour of Andrew von Hirsch* (1998 Clarendon) 60.

[99] Paul Robinson, 'The A.L.I.'s Proposed Distributive Principle of "Limiting Retributivism": Does It Mean in Practice Anything Other than Pure Desert?' (2003) 7(3) Buffalo Criminal Law Review 10.

[100] See Andrew von Hirsch, 'Proportionality in the Philosophy of Punishment' (1992) 16 Crime and Justice 76 and Tonry (n 48) 356.

[101] Krasnostein and Freiberg, 'Pursuing Consistency in an Individualistic Sentencing Framework' (n 2) 271.

[102] Alec Samuels, 'Consistency in Sentencing', in Donald C Pennington and Sally Lloyd-Bostock (eds), *The Psychology of Sentencing: Approaches to Consistency and Disparity* (1987 Centre for Socio-Legal Studies) 66.

[103] Cyrus Tata and Neil Hutton, 'What "Rules" in Sentencing? Consistency and Disparity in the Absence of "Rules"' (1998) 26(3) International Journal of the Sociology of Law 339.

[104] See for example: John Raine and Elaine Dunstan, 'How Well do Sentencing Guidelines Work?: Equity, Proportionality and Consistency in the Determination of Fine Levels in the

and in fact, it is very difficult to find academic arguments to the contrary. The theory, and its limits, therefore appears to be relatively well settled. How does this operate in practice? The English courts have been unequivocal in endorsing the notion of a permissible range of sentences. In *Peters*,[105] Judge LJ stated in the context of the then recently enacted Criminal Justice Act 2003 Sch.21 (since repealed and re-enacted in the Sentencing Act 2020 Sch 21) governing the determination of the minimum term for the mandatory life sentence for murder: 'If, looked at overall, this Court takes the view that the end result fell within the appropriate range of sentence and the margin of judgment and discretion given to the sentencing judge ….'[106] More recently, in *R. v Khan*[107] the court stated that '[i]t is not for this court to interfere or to tinker with sentences when they are perhaps at the higher end of the permissible range'.

This approach is not exclusive to England and Wales; rather, it is shared by numerous jurisdictions who afford a varying degree of discretion to sentencing courts.[108]

The notion of a permissible range of sentences is vital to consistency in sentencing because it concerns one of the key questions to be addressed when applying the concept of consistency to a practical scenario: what constitutes 'like' treatment? A mere difference in sentences will therefore be insufficient to sustain a complaint as to the inappropriate length of a sentence; the length must therefore be sufficiently different so as to render it inappropriate. A sentence falling outside of the permissible

---

Magistrates' Courts of England and Wales' (2009) 48(1) The Howard Journal 13, which discusses inconsistency and disparity in terms of 'significant differences' in sentencing levels, the inference being that insignificant differences do not constitute disparity or inconsistency. Jose Pina-Sanchez and Robin Linacre, 'Enhancing Consistency in Sentencing: Exploring the Effects of Guidelines in England and Wales' (2014) 30 Journal of Quantitative Criminology 731, which proposes to measure consistency by reference to, *inter alia*, the extent to which sentences vary, thereby acknowledging the notion of a permissible range of sentences and James Spigelman, 'Consistency and Sentencing' (2008) 82(7) Australian Law Journal 450 in which the author states that 'within reasonable bounds, different judges can permissibly reach different conclusions', thereby endorsing the notion of a permissible range of sentences.

[105] [2005] EWCA Crim 605; [2005] 2 Cr App R (S) 101.
[106] [2005] EWCA Crim 605; [2005] 2 Cr App R (S) 101 at [9].
[107] [2016] EWCA Crim 125 at [17].
[108] See eg Tata and Hutton, 'What "Rules" in Sentencing?' (n 103) 351; the Supreme Court of New South Wales in *R. v Jurisic* [1998] NSWSC 423; the Supreme Court of Minnesota in *State v Evans* 311 N.W.2d 481 (Minn. 1981); and the High Court of Australia in *Lowe v The Queen* [1984] HCA 46 at [3].

range would be (by definition) disproportionate to the severity of the offence, and therefore incapable of justification and therefore unfair. A system committed to individualized justice therefore relies upon the notion of a permissible range of sentences. Without an acceptance of the notion of a permissible range of sentences, the concept of consistency becomes less about fairness and equality, and more about uniformity, which, as was established in Chapter 2, is an invitation to inconsistency.

The apparent tension between individualized justice and the concept of consistency

Are the two concepts actually in 'perennial conflict' as claimed by Krasnostein and Freiberg? Does individualized justice truly permit an 'anything goes' approach as suggested by Doob and Brodeur? The foregoing discussion suggests not.

In the 1830s, the Criminal Law Commissioners saw a need to reform sentencing and balance the need for individualization with the need for consistency,[109] identifying a tension between the two. The literature demonstrates that thinking has not advanced much in that regard since Victorian times; there is still a body of opinion which regards consistency and individualized justice as being inherently incompatible. Yet to posit these two concepts as requiring sentencers to balance conflicting demands is to misunderstand the premise of each.

Many accounts of consistency are premised on the basis that justice requires similar sentences be imposed on similarly culpable offenders committing similarly serious offences. Yet, as established in Chapter 2, this is insufficiently focused upon sentencing principles. Consistency does not require the same sentence to be imposed upon similarly culpable offenders convicted of offences of a similar gravity but that each sentence is imposed by a consistent application of sentencing principle. As this chapter has established, it is necessary, too, for individualized justice to operate within the confines of sentencing principles, enabling the

---

[109] Sir Leon Radzinowicz and Roger Hood, 'Judicial Discretion and Sentencing Standards: Victorian Attempts to Solve a Perennial Problem' (1979) 127(5) University of Pennsylvania Law Review 1288.

determination of sentence in a principled manner. If the key to both concepts is to allow sentencing principle to determine the sentence, the two concepts cannot be in conflict as claimed.

In a mixed system such as that prevailing in England and Wales, the permissible range of sentences is set by retributive theory and individualized justice operates within those bounds to determine a sentence appropriate for the individual on other considerations, including those deriving from consequentialist theory.[110] This is not an 'anything goes' approach to sentence but rather a highly principled approach to sentence.[111]

If, as suggested, individualized justice is inextricably linked to sentencing principles and theories of punishment, does the tension between individualized justice and consistency remain? If consistency is properly construed as being concerned not with the disposals of other 'similar' cases, but with the consistent operation of sentencing principle, then the apparent tension identified by the Victorian Criminal Law Commissioners, and Krasnostein and Freiberg, among others, falls away and it can be said that an individualized justice approach to sentence determination increases consistency. Structuring the discretion afforded to sentencers by strengthening the link between sentencing principle and the concept of individualized justice is more likely to produce a well-reasoned decision. If a decision taken in pursuit of individualized justice is underpinned by sentencing principle, then one could expect a greater degree of consistency in such cases, both so far as the decision to overtly pursue an individualized approach to sentence but also the degree to which the sentence ultimately imposed differs from the 'normal' sentence which could be expected in such a case. A body of case law may develop or Sentencing Council guidance may be created to distil or espouse some

---

[110] See eg Richard S Frase, 'Theories of Proportionality and Desert' in Joan Petersilia and Kevin R Reitz (eds), *The Oxford Handbook of Sentencing and Corrections* (OUP 2012) 131–49, 144, in which the author states: 'Instead, virtually all modern systems have adopted some version of limiting retributivism' and '[i]n some systems, retributive values define a range of allowable severity and available forms of punishment ... in choosing the particular form of punishment, courts consider offender characteristics, crime-control goals and other non-retributive factors'. It is submitted that this aptly describes the system in England and Wales; while the legislation provides for five purposes of sentencing, both retributive and consequentialist, primary legislation mandates that the severity of the sentence is driven by reference to offence seriousness, a retributive consideration. Thereafter, courts are required to apply Morris' parsimony principle and may take into account non-retributive factors.

[111] This fits neatly within the statutory scheme in force in England and Wales as described in Chapter 1.

principles or general rules as to the operation of a sentencer's discretion in this regard. For example, it might be said that an individualized justice approach to sentence is inappropriate in certain types of case, or that a particular type of sentence is, or is not, well-suited to consequentialist considerations. Over time, this structuring of discretion has the ability to promote consistency rather than undermine it, as some of the literature suggests.

A response to such a suggestion might well be that the fact that individualized justice interacts with the different theories of punishment differently creates a greater risk of inconsistency. This is so as the determination of sentence comes down to the individual sentencer's discretion: if individualized justice can be aligned to different principles which may rely on different factors, then there will be a lesser degree of consistency of sentencing principle, not more. Yet this criticism would only have traction where two different systems were being compared; this would give rise to different factors being taken into account. For example, identical robberies being sentenced by two different systems subscribing to two (even slightly) different schemes is likely to result in disparate outcomes. However, within a single system, such disparity would not arise as the principles to which sentencers make reference in the determination of sentence remain the same, and consequently, the decision ought to be consistent.[112]

This is well exemplified by the system adopted by England and Wales. Where proportionality sets the outer limits of the permissible range, say, two to five years for an offence of drug supply,[113] other considerations operate to determine sentence within that range. If within the two- to five-year range in the drugs supply example in the previous paragraph, any sentence could be said to be 'consistent', there remains the potential for a degree of disparity which would not be addressed

---

[112] This relies upon the definition of consistency discussed in Chapter 2; while s 57 of the Sentencing Act 2020 lists five purposes of sentences with no order of primacy, this proposition rests upon the notion of a permissible range of sentences and so where two judges may give primacy to different purposes of sentencing, providing the sentence falls within the permissible range for the offence, there would be no inconsistency.

[113] Two to five years is the category range for an offence of supplying a Class A drug contrary to s 4(3) of the Misuse of Drugs Act 1971 or possession with intent to supply a Class A drug, contrary to s 5(3) of the Misuse of Drugs Act 1971, under the Sentencing Council's *Drug Offences Definitive Guideline* (2021) (Category 4 significant role).

by the approach adopted in Chapter 2.[114] Individualized justice can add another layer to the equation, thus narrowing the scope of potential inconsistency, as the sentences within the permissible range are then subject to further scrutiny in order to determine where within the range the appropriate sentence is. Continuing with the drugs supply example, a two- to five-year range is wide; where an offender has, for example, a substance dependency and has dependent children and has made efforts to find employment, a sentence towards the bottom of the range would likely be merited by reference to those mitigating factors. Conversely, the absence of such factors is likely to receive a sentence towards the middle or top of the range. Such considerations fall squarely within the remit of individualized justice and thus, individualized justice operates as an additional level of scrutiny inside the outer limits set by the principle of proportionality, funnelling sentences in similar cases closer together.

Conclusion

This chapter has concluded that while individualized justice requires a sentence to be determined on the basis of the features of the offence and the offender, the focus is upon the individual. Adopting that interpretation of the concept, having considered the way in which individualized justice interacts with judicial discretion, it can be seen that individualized justice operates in conjunction with sentencing principles and therefore operates within a structured discretion. This rejects the suggestion made by some academics that individualized justice permits an 'anything goes' approach to sentence determination. By viewing individualized justice through the prism of sentencing principles, a sentence imposed in pursuit of individualized justice is one which accords with principle; it is the application of principle which permits the individualization. As such, the notion that a move towards consistency in sentencing undermines individualization can be dismissed; on the contrary, there is no tension between the two concepts.

---

[114] Save for where the alleged disparity is between co-defendants in the same case.

5
When is a sentencing decision 'discretionary' and how should that discretion be structured?

> ... the imposition of criminal penalties [is a] pre-eminently discretionary field.[1]

Introduction

This chapter takes the clarified conception of consistency and uses it as a critical tool in order to assess the relative effectiveness of commonly employed methods of structuring judicial discretion at sentencing. As O'Malley notes: 'For as long as discretion has existed, there has been an impulse to control it, and this has been particularly true in respect of the imposition of penalties.'[2] This chapter seeks to identify when a sentencing decision involves judicial discretion and to evaluate how that discretion structured.

The next task is to consider the concept of judicial discretion, at first more generally, and then in relation to sentencing specifically. That said, what this chapter seeks to do is discuss discretion as regards sentencing, nothing wider. As this work is concerned with consistency and the relative success of methods of structuring discretion, there would be little achieved by attempting that task without an understanding of what the

---

[1] Sir Thomas Bingham, 'The Discretion of the Judge' [1990] Denning Law Journal 27 cited in Colin Munro, 'Judicial Independence and Judicial Functions' in Colin Munro and Martin Wasik (eds), *Sentencing, Judicial Discretion and Training* (Sweet and Maxwell 1992) 26.

[2] Tom O'Malley 'Judgment and Calculation in the Selection of Sentence' (2017) 28(3) Criminal Law Forum 361–389, 374.

term means. It is therefore necessary to establish a model of judicial discretion for use in the later chapters.

What is judicial discretion?

Introduction

It is commonplace in modern legal systems for there to be widespread discretionary powers vested in a range of organizations and officials by the legislature.[3] Yet this is not a modern phenomenon. Galligan noted that:

> discretionary powers are not an innovation of the modern state since any system of authority relies on discretion in varying ways and degrees; the argument is only that in recent decades the quantity of discretion has increased to make it a more significant facet of state authority.[4]

Hawkins, for example, regards it as 'a central and inevitable part of the legal order'.[5] While one can perhaps conceive of an entirely discretionary system of law, in reality, a functioning and fair legal system requires rules creating institutions, empowering them to act and limiting the way in which they do so.[6]

According to Schneider, '[d]iscretion allows decision makers more easily to consult illegitimate considerations and does nothing to stop them making mistakes',[7] but can allow 'decisions to be tailored to the individual case ... [and] allows future decisions to be informed by past decisions following an evaluation of their success'.[8] In non-legal—plain English language—terms, 'discretion' has a wide definition, referring to

---

[3] Denis Galligan, *Discretionary Powers: A Legal Study of Official Discretion* (Clarendon Press 1986) 72.
[4] ibid 72. This view is shared by others, eg, Ronald Dworkin. See Ronald Dworkin, 'Judicial Discretion' (1963) 60(21) The Journal of Philosophy 624, 624; and Ronald Dworkin, 'The Model of Rules' (1967) 35 University of Chicago Law Review 14–46, 18.
[5] Keith Hawkins, 'The Uses of Legal Discretion: Perspectives from Law and Social Science' in Keith Hawkins (ed), *The Uses of Discretion* (Clarendon Press 1992) 11.
[6] Galligan, Discretionary Powers (n 3) 59.
[7] Carl E Schneider, 'Discretion and Rules' in Hawkins (ed), The Uses of Discretion (n 5) 68.
[8] ibid 67.

the jurisdiction to exercise a choice in respect of something.[9] There are, of course boundaries, in so far as the choices must be capable of selection (the discretion cannot be exercised in a sense that is an impossibility; choosing a red ball when the only options are a blue or green ball, for example), and one must have the jurisdiction to make such a choice (have the power or authority to make such a choice; choosing to sit in a first-class seat having purchased only a standard-class ticket, for example). Save for such basic constraints, in everyday usage of the term there appears to be little else to govern or guide the exercise of such a discretion.

Yet in law, discretion has a narrower and more exact meaning. There is, however, disagreement as to the precise definition. An appropriate starting point may well be a legal maxim *discretio est discernere per legem quid sit justum*—'discretion is to discern through law what is just'.[10] This provides an initial steer as to the meaning of 'discretion' and its limitations, suggesting first that judicial discretion is derived through (and therefore constrained by) law and secondly that the objective is to arrive at an outcome which is just (perhaps a synonym for 'fair', or 'appropriate', noting that those terms as perhaps equally as vague). It is possible to identify two distinct components to this definition, namely (i) the existence of discretion ('through law'); and (ii) the manner in which the discretion must be exercised ('discern ... what is just').

As will be demonstrated, writings on judicial discretion tend not to explicitly identify these two issues or approach them separately. By way of example, in his work on discretion Hart identified a key question as '[w]hat is discretion, or what is the exercise of discretion?'[11] seemingly not identifying a need to draw a distinction between what are, it appears, two very different questions. This chapter will suggest that a clearer and more coherent account of judicial discretion can be arrived at where a two-stage approach is adopted and accordingly will explore various definitions of judicial discretion by a consideration of those two key issues.

---

[9] For example, Dictionary.com provides as the first definition of 'discretion': 'the power or right to decide or act according to one's own judgment; freedom of judgment or choice', <http://www.dictionary.com/browse/discretion> accessed 1 January 2022.

[10] Of course, 'appropriate' may well be as vague as 'just', but it imports some notion of a standard or set of standards to which the decision maker should aspire.

[11] HLA Hart, 'Discretion' (2013) 127 Harvard Law Review 652, 652.

The scope of the endeavour

This section of the chapter is not concerned with the source of the discretionary power granted to judges, nor is it concerned with the Hart–Dworkin debate concerning the latter's 'right answers thesis' and various conceptions of law. This chapter undertakes the more modest task of identifying from the literature core features of judicial discretion to construct a working definition of judicial discretion to be employed in the later chapters for the purpose of examining the methods of structuring judicial discretion at sentencing. The difference between a jurisprudential and legal approach to the task of defining judicial discretion was noted by Hawkins who stated that legal philosophers have been more concerned with discretion's relationship with rules whereas lawyers have focused their attentions on the legal and public policy issues raised by the topic.[12] Hawkins also noted that social scientists have also been interested in the issue, however that that interest has been principally concerned with an understanding of how law may be translated into action.[13] This chapter adopts a hybrid approach.

This chapter will consider Hart's work on discretion[14] before turning to consider Dworkin and Raz's contributions to that debate. Reference will be made to other commentators, however it is noted that as the core of the Hart–Dworkin debate surrounds the disagreement as to the propriety of the positivist view of law as a social construct. As such, their discussions regarding judicial discretion are rather ancillary to the wider issue of the limits of the law and more general legal theory, rather than being principally concerned with a construction of a theoretically sound definition of judicial discretion. For this reason, the focus of this chapter will lie with the original discussions rather than the subsequent debates which have moved away from the issue with which this chapter is directly concerned.

Hart began his consideration of discretion by noting that the term may be 'hopelessly vague' and that its use in practice and academia is 'entirely haphazard'. He swiftly concluded that such a view could not endure as it

---

[12] Hawkins (n 5), 13.
[13] ibid 14
[14] This was, until 2013, principally contained in his 1972 Concept of Laws. However in 2013, the Harvard Law Review published a collection of essays introducing Hart's 'lost' essay on discretion, written in 1956.

was possible to identify a set of characteristics which it could be agreed exist in the 'standard case' of discretion.[15] Hart considered that discretion was a vital component of any legal system owing to society's ability to regulate the future being 'inherently limited by imperfect information and an imperfect understanding of aims'.[16] Raz identified three 'sources' of discretion requiring its existence. The first, 'vagueness', requires discretion because language and principles are vague, and discretion cannot be dispensed with in cases of vagueness where a court must render judgment.[17] The second renders discretion necessary as '[t]he law characteristically includes only incomplete indications as to their relative weight and leaves much to judicial discretion to be exercised in particular cases'.[18]

Dworkin identified three types of judicial discretion: two, in a 'weak' sense, referring to first, the need for judgment where a rule cannot be applied mechanistically; second, finality, in the sense that a decision is unreviewable; and a third, the 'strong' sense, to describe cases where judges are legally entitled to decide and in which there is no single correct decision. Dworkin uses this to frame the debate between himself and the positivists (principally, Hart) in order to refute their construction of the answer to the question 'what is the law?'[19] According to Hawkins, Goodin followed 'the same analytical line' as Dworkin and identified two further types of discretion, namely formal and informal (the former being where the options are explicitly written into a rule and the latter stemming from the vagueness of language).[20] Shiner criticized Dworkin's three types of discretion and particularly the examples used to justify it, claiming they fail to fit legal practice.[21] Such criticism accords with Hawkins' view noted earlier that philosophers and lawyers have approached the issue from different perspectives.

---

[15] Hart, 'Discretion' (n 11) 653. Hart gives three examples, namely rate-fixing by the ICC, the grant or refusal of specific performance by a court or the granting of a pardon or reprieve by the executive.
[16] Geoffrey C Shaw, 'HLA Hart's Lost Essay' (2013) 127 Harvard Law Review 666, 669.
[17] Joseph Raz, 'Legal Principles and the Limits of the Law' (1972) 81 The Yale Law Journal 823, 846. Hawkins (relying upon Denis Galligan's earlier work) partly shares this view as to the need for discretion stemming from the vagaries of language and law being 'fundamentally an interpretative exercise' and one involving 'people in interpretation and choice', see Hawkins (n 5) 11.
[18] ibid.
[19] Dworkin, 'The Model of Rules' (n 4) 16
[20] Hawkins (n 5) 14.
[21] Roger Shiner, 'Hart on Judicial Discretion' (2011) 5 Problemas 341.

Hart and Dworkin disagree as to whether judges have a discretion in hard cases in Dworkin's strong sense, yet this disagreement is derivative; Shapiro notes the 'clash' stems from 'very different theories about the nature of law'.[22] Accordingly, the following discussion seeks to identify core features which identify the existence and exercise of judicial discretion. It is not the intention of this chapter to resolve any dispute between the two on this issue. Rather, the literature will be surveyed to identify the most coherent, principled and practical definition of judicial discretion, to be employed later in the context of sentencing for the purposes of this work.

Raz considers that a discretion exists where there are available (as a matter of law) at least two possible outcomes and there exists the power vested in the judge to choose between them. Yet this is insufficient: for example, a judge choosing to make notes of legal submissions in a case with a blue pen rather than a red pen cannot sensibly fall within the label 'judicial discretion', despite being a choice between two legally correct decisions (there being no law against the use of blue or black pens). It would even be insufficient to import—as Raz does—a requirement that the outcome is 'correct'. To continue with the above example, the blue pen might be considered to be correct as red ink is conventionally reserved for noting errors or making comments on scripts. However, this choice between two coloured pens remains outwith the common understanding of the concept of judicial discretion. That is perhaps a silly example but it serves to illustrate that a tighter definition is needed. The issue of the exercise of discretion in a manner which is considered to be appropriate, or correct is considered later in this chapter.

Both Dworkin and Hawkins explicitly consider the extent to which discretion can vary: Dworkin in his 'strong' and 'weak' senses, and Hawkins in a more practical sense, commenting that it is 'difficult to contemplate the making of a legal decision that does not have at least a measure of discretion'.[23] While the latter is to take an obviously broad view of the

---

[22] Scott Shapiro, 'The Hart-Dworkin Debate: A Short Guide for the Perplexed' (2007) 77 Public Law and Legal Theory Working Paper Series, University of Michigan Law School, 17.
[23] Hawkins (n 5) 11.

concept, it serves at least to demonstrate that the question to consider is not binary, simply asking whether a court has a discretion, but also one of degree, considering the extent of the discretion. It is also one which necessitates a practical consideration as well as a theoretical one.

Summary of argument

The first part of this chapter contends that in order to construct a coherent account of judicial discretion, three issues must be considered: (i) the source of the power; (ii) how to identify its existence; and (iii) the manner in which the discretion must be exercised. This chapter will not concern itself with the question of the source of the discretionary power, as this will depend on the jurisdiction being considered, and particular sentencing issue at hand, and so will turn its attention only to the latter two points.

Further, it is contended that in considering the latter two points, it is possible to identify the following core features which must be present to identify the existence of judicial discretion:

(1) The decision maker is required to make a decision;
(2) There are principles guiding the making of that decision; and
(3) The proper application of those principles does not produce a single, obviously correct, result.

And the following features identify whether the discretion was properly exercised:

(1) It was not exercised in pursuit of personal whim or on an arbitrary or legally irrelevant basis;
(2) Its exercise was rational; and
(3) The choice made was, in the decision-maker's opinion, likely to bring about the most appropriate outcome.

It is contended that such a definition is both conceptually clear and workable in practice.

Identifying the existence of judicial discretion

Galligan noted that in a broad sense, discretion denotes an area of autonomy within which one's decisions are to some extent a matter of personal judgment.[24] Hart noted the need to avoid confusing a discretion with a choice, stating that the former was a 'near-synonym for practical wisdom or sagacity or prudence' and placed value in the notion of judgment, stating 'it is the power of discerning or distinguishing what in various fields is appropriate to be done and etymologically connected with the notion of discerning'.[25]

It appears clear that there is an evaluative component present in the concept of discretion, however Hart's reference to practical wisdom is perhaps questionable in light of Hood's consideration of the Australian concept of instinctive synthesis and the conclusion that the claim that all cases are unique must fail if reliance is placed upon intuition and experience-based sentencing.[26] Hart relies upon the example of a discreet person not simply remaining silent, but remaining silent when silence is called for, thereby suggesting some degree of experience necessary in the decision-making process. Yet this is to mix the common usage with the legal concept. It will be argued later in the chapter that the concept of judicial discretion does not require as a constituent part a degree of sagacity, wisdom, or experience. But such a discussion of experience is perhaps to place the cart before the horse; one must identify what discretion *is*, before espousing criteria by which it ought to be exercised and by whom. Hart argues that an appropriate starting point when considering the question of what discretion is, is to consider non-legal uses, suggesting that although to align the concept with the notion of choice is to fall into error, the two are related.

Dworkin recognizes this feature of judicial discretion where he identifies that there are two sources of judicial decision: rule and discretion.[27] The term discretion, opines Dworkin, is inappropriately used to mean that the judge must sometimes reach their decision by means other than

---

[24] Galligan (n 3) 8.
[25] Hart (n 11) 656.
[26] Roger Hood, *Sentencing in Magistrates' Courts: A Study of Variations of Policy* (Stevens and Sons 1962), cited in Andrew Ashworth, *Sentencing and Criminal Justice* (6th edn, CUP 2015) 50.
[27] Ronald Dworkin, 'Judicial Discretion' (1963) 60(21) The Journal of Philosophy 624.

the application of standards, that such standards sometimes leave them free to choose (the 'academics' view') and it is more accurate to describe a judge applying established principles (the 'layman's view').[28] This distinction is explored shortly. In later work, Dworkin argued that: '[t]he concept of discretion is at home in only one sort of context: when someone is in general charged with making decisions subject to standards set by a particular authority'.[29]

Hart also recognizes this fact, focusing upon the need to 'determine' or 'discern' the appropriate course of action to take.[30] He identifies three categories falling 'clearly ... within the agreed ambit of the term':[31]

(1) Express or avowed use of discretion (by administrative bodies or by courts);[32]
(2) Tacit or concealed discretion;[33] and
(3) Discretionary interface or dispensation from acknowledged rules.[34]

From this point, Hart, employs the non-legal example of a person hosting a dinner party faced with a decision between their best and second-best sets of cutlery. This, as noted by Shaw, was a 'classic application of Hart's analytical method'[35] examining the uses (both legal and non-legal) of the term. Hart considered that the dinner party host example presented features 'characteristic of discretion everywhere':

(1) There is no clear right or wrong and 'honest and sensible' persons may take different views;
(2) There is no clear definable aim (though a successful dinner party may be the stated aim, that encompasses numerous things at which the host is aiming);

---

[28] ibid 625.
[29] Dworkin (n 4) 32
[30] Hart (n 11) 656.
[31] Hart (n 11) 655.
[32] Examples given are licencing for carrying on a particular trade and sentencing in criminal cases.
[33] The two instances listed are interpretation of statutes and the use of precedent.
[34] The two instances listed are a reprieve or pardon and injunction against exercise of common law remedies.
[35] Shaw, 'HLA Hart's Lost Essay' (n 16) 696.

(3) The precise circumstances over which the decision will operate once it has been made are not known with any great degree of certainty;

(4) Within the vaguely defined aim of a successful dinner party, there are distinguishable constituent values or elements but there are no clear principles or rules determining the relative importance of these constituent values or, where they conflict, how compromise should be made between them;

(5) The decisions taken will not happily be called 'right' or 'wrong' but rather terms such as 'wise', 'sound' (but perhaps comparatives such as 'wiser', 'sounder', and 'better' are more appropriate); and

(6) If the decision is challenged there are two different ways in which a defence may characteristically be made of it: justification (ie explaining how the result was arrived at) and vindication (ie relying upon the success of the result of the decision taken).[36]

These features bear examination but first it is useful to examine the example chosen by Hart. The various decisions to be taken by a person hosting a dinner party may be better suited to the issue of the exercise of the discretion, rather than the identification of it; a choice between the best and second-best set of cutlery speak to the considerations surrounding the decision between the two rather than the features which make that choice a discretionary one. In this example, Hart's host is faced with a choice between two options, both of which appear (in the absence of further information) to be appropriate and fit for the stated purpose.

Now to consider the features identified by Hart which he considers illustrate discretion. The first, namely the absence of a clear right or wrong, is perhaps better expressed as the absence of a single, correct answer: Hart's expression of this feature is problematic as it places the focus upon the inability to identify right from wrong, yet this a product of his chosen example. To modify Hart's dinner party example, where three options were presented, namely the best cutlery set, the second-best set, or no cutlery at all, it would be rational to consider the third option as clearly wrong, and the first two as possible correct answers.[37]

---

[36] Hart (n 11) 659.
[37] Perhaps this would be better expressed as 'not wrong'; such would, as Shaw noted, probably find favour with Hart (and Henry Hart too), as 'Henry Hart went on to concede that ' "[r]ight

The question of which to choose then becomes one concerned with the exercise of the discretion rather than the existence of it and the existence of a discretion is not obviated by the existence of a clear wrong answer, or two answers which are clearly capable of being correct. Hart later appears to characterize this as the absence of a single correct answer,[38] and so it may be better to view this element in light of that unacknowledged modification (and the brief criticism contained in this paragraph). Dworkin's view on this point stems from the distinction that he draws between rules and principles. That will be explored later in this chapter in more detail in relation to the claim that for a discretion to exist there must exist principles guiding the decision. However, at this stage, it suffices to note that Dworkin considers that the application of a rule can determine the outcome of a case whereas a principle cannot. It follows that Dworkin regards a discretion to exist only where there is no single, clearly correct answer. Raz shares this view: 'a legal system which contains a rule that whenever the courts are faced

> with a case for which the law does not provide a uniquely correct solution they ought to refuse to render judgment [could exist]. In such a system there would be no judicial discretion.'[39]

---

means rationally justifiable by reasoning from settled or properly assumed premises," which harmonized with H. L. A. Hart's criterion for sound discretion', see Shaw (n 16) 713.

[38] Hart (n 11) 660. When constructing the account of judicial discretion which forms the basis of the discussion in this chapter, an earlier draft of this chapter had included 'the choice does not involve the application of a legal test', however during writing I realized that this was a red herring in so far as the identification of core features of judicial discretion. The application of a legal test, for instance the determination of an application to admit hearsay evidence under the Criminal Justice Act 2003 or the finding of 'dangerousness' pursuant to the Sentencing Act 2020 involves a binary choice and the application of a threshold; in fact, the determining feature in this regard is not that the court must apply a legal test, but that the proper application of principles produces an obviously correct result. For instance, the determination of a hearsay application involves the application of principles and case law, the proper application of which will produce a single, correct result. A judge making such a determination has to make an evaluative judgment, but it is not one which involves a true choice between various legitimate options as the application of the principles to the legal test produces only one legitimate result. This is reinforced by the way in which the Court of Appeal (Criminal Division) deals with such decisions on appeal and by contrast, the way it deals with decisions concerning sentence quantum on appeal.

[39] Joseph Raz, 'Legal Principles and the Limits of the Law' (1972) 81 The Yale Law Journal 823, 843 and 845.

The second, namely the absence of a clear definable aim, is somewhat curious. Can it be said that the presence of a clear definable aim can (or should) operate to obviate the existence of a discretion? In a sentencing system where the single aim is to punish, in pursuit of retributive proportionality (taking that as a clear definable aim that the sentence should be proportionate to the seriousness of the offence), can it credibly be said that the exercise in determining the length of sentence to be imposed for an offence is not a discretionary decision? Perhaps it is directed at the situation where there exist multiple (perhaps competing) aims, rather than appealing to the notion that the decision is to be made without direction. If so, this may be another feature operating as a proxy for complexity. This in fact speaks to the need for discretion, as Hart identifies (though not in this connection), namely the inability of society to adequately regulate the future.[40] Dworkin does not regard this to be a feature determinative of the existence of a discretion.

The third, namely that the precise outcome of the decision is not known with any degree of certainty, appears to be a proxy for the complex nature of the decision to be taken.[41] A simple choice, say between playing with a blue ball and a red ball which are otherwise identical, produces a definite result. Yet where the choice is complicated by other factors, say where one ball is larger than the other, or there are multiple persons of varying ages, physical capabilities, and skill intending to play with the ball, the outcome becomes less precise. Whether or not this feature is determinative of the existence of a discretion is unclear: Hart fails to justify why the outcome is linked to the existence of the discretion. And so perhaps this feature operates as a proxy for complexity, it being correlative with the existence of a discretionary decision but not causative. This returns us, again, to Hart's justification of the need for discretion, namely the inability to predict the future. Where outcomes are readily identifiable with a degree of certainty, it is possible to create rules prescribing the appropriate course of action. More complex scenarios would, it is suggested, be more likely to require a discretion owing to the inability to predict, accurately and comprehensively, the appropriate outcome in every instance, thereby preventing the creation of a rule. Again, Dworkin does not appear to regard this as a

---

[40] Shaw (n 16) 669.
[41] This in fact might be said about the second feature identified by Hart.

feature present in instances of judicial discretion, however Hawkins appears to, stating '[t]he particular way in which discretion may be exercised may not be predictable from the particular forms of rule'.[42]

The fourth, namely the absence of clear principles or rules guiding the importance of values comprising the decision, again might be viewed as a proxy for complexity, the issue being more complex to resolve (or at least resolve in an appropriate manner) in the absence of guidance. However, a better view may well be to place the emphasis on the inclusion of the qualifier 'clear'. If this is read as referring to principles or rules which resolve the decision, in other words the application of a principle or rule produces an obviously correct result, then Hart's point is more credible. Otherwise, it remains unclear as to why the absence of clear principles or rules leads to a decision involving the exercise of discretion. It may be premised upon the idea that such guidance is limiting and therefore the nature of the decision cannot be said to be truly discretionary. However, this is to adopt too rigid an approach. Can the presence of a rule or principle render an otherwise discretionary decision one not involving a discretion? Is the imposition of a sentence upon a criminal conviction not a discretionary exercise by virtue of it being governed by principles such as proportionality and parsimony? Hart perhaps contradicts himself here, as he identifies sentencing as a discretionary exercise earlier in the essay.[43] It seems that in fact the converse is true; the existence of principles or rules guiding the exercise of the decision is a constituent element of a discretionary decision. Without such guidance the exercise of the decision is unregulated and could permit a degree of arbitrariness, and inherent in the discretionary decision is some objective measure of appropriateness, which speaks to a set of governing rules or principles.

Dworkin had much to say in relation to this issue. He argued that '[t]he concept of discretion is at home in only one sort of context: when someone is in general charged with making decisions subject to standards set by a particular authority'.[44] Therefore, he states, it is appropriate to view discretion as the hole in the doughnut, existing only as 'an area left

---

[42] Hawkins (n 5) 36. The example given is where a rule seeks to limit a discretion to achieve a particular result; Hawkins suggests that this is not always successful.
[43] Hart (n 11) 655. This point could be rescued if it were argued that such principles are not sufficiently 'clear'.
[44] Dworkin (n 4) 32.

open by a surrounding belt of restriction.'[45] A variation of this metaphor is employed by Hawkins in his exposition of the uses of discretion.[46] Yet Dworkin focuses upon the relationship between rules and principles[47] as the importance that has for the wider discussion of the limits of the law rather than seeking to justify why a discretion must involve principles guiding the decision.

Dworkin discusses rules, which he describes as being 'exhaustive of "the law"'[48] and noted that where a case cannot be determined by the application of a rule (as none is appropriate, for example), the judge must decide the case by recourse to discretion. Dworkin describes this as 'reaching beyond the law for some other sort of standard to guide him in manufacturing a fresh legal rule or supplementing an old one'.[49]

While it is not necessary for the purpose of this discussion to enter into a jurisprudential discussion of the Dworkinian account of legal positivism and his conception of 'the law', the extent to which this work considers the nature of discretion is illuminating. He distinguishes rules from principles by appealing to their logical distinction. 'Rules are applicable in an all-or-nothing fashion. If the facts a rule stipulates are given, then either the rule is valid, in which case the answer it supplies must be accepted, or it is not, in which case it contributes nothing to the decision.'[50] A non-legal example is relied upon to demonstrate this, namely a game consisting of a rule which cannot be acknowledged but overridden. A principle on the other hand, Dworkin claims, 'does not even purport to set out conditions that make its application necessary. Rather, it states a reason that argues in one direction, but does not necessitate a particular decision.'[51] Dworkin also claims that unlike rules, principles carry a weight relative to one another, so that when they intersect the conflict can be resolved. Implicit in this statement is that rules do not, and cannot conflict. Dworkin states that if two rules conflict, one is not a valid rule.[52]

---

[45] ibid.
[46] Keith Hawkins, 'The Uses of Legal Discretion: Perspectives from Law and Social Science' in Keith Hawkins (ed), *The Uses of Discretion* (Clarendon Press 1992) 11.
[47] Dworkin uses the term 'principle' to mean 'a standard that is to be observed, not because it will advance or secure an economic, political, or social situation deemed desirable, but because it is a requirement of justice or fairness or some other dimension of morality', Dworkin (n 4), 23.
[48] ibid 17.
[49] ibid 17.
[50] ibid 25.
[51] ibid 25.
[52] ibid 27.

He disagrees with the positivist position that a rule can dictate a result whereas a principle cannot, stating that:

> [p]rinciples ... incline a decision one way, though not conclusively, and ... can dictate a result. If a judge believes that principles he is bound to recognize point in one direction and that principles pointing in the other direction, if any, are not of equal weight, then he must decide accordingly, just as he must follow what he believes to be a binding rule.[53]

This recognizes the evaluative nature of discretion, requiring a subjective but rational assessment of the governing principles when resolving the question. To permit a judge to act contrary to Dworkin's statement would be to permit irrational or unreasonable decisions which would not be conceptually (or legally) satisfactory.

Joseph Raz's writings on discretion similarly identified the need for principles to guide the exercise of discretion. Continuing to approach this issue via a two-stepped approach as outlined earlier, this speaks to both the existence of a discretion and its exercise. Raz stated: 'There are situations in which what ought legally to be done is determined directly by the application of various principles to the case ... The whole area of sentencing is governed almost exclusively by principles.'[54]

In a wider discussion, Raz identified two types of principles in the context of judicial discretion: substantive principles which dictate a goal to be pursued or a value to be protected, whereas principles of discretion guide discretion by stipulating what type of goals and values the judge may take into account in exercising the discretion.[55] In doing so, Raz considered that principles presuppose the existence of judicial discretion and direct and guide it.[56]

The fifth, namely preferring 'wise' or 'sound' to 'right' or 'wrong' overlaps with the first, rejecting the concept that the outcome of a discretionary decision can be right or wrong. As noted earlier, Hart later appears to modify this to a rejection of the notion that there is a single right answer. Hart suggests that the terms might be better used in a relative

---

[53] ibid 36.
[54] Raz, 'Legal Principles and the Limits of the Law' (n 39) 841.
[55] ibid 846.
[56] ibid 847.

sense, 'wise' becomes 'wiser', for example. This of course concerns the manner in which the discretion is exercised, rather than the identification of a discretion, it being directed at a value judgment as to which of the available options is best. This will be further considered later in the chapter.

The sixth, namely the way in which a defence may be mounted to a challenge of the decision taken, need not concern us here; Dworkin says nothing of this feature. It is difficult to envisage how the manner of the defence could be determinative of whether a discretion exists. In any event, this feature speaks more to the exercise of the discretion rather than existence of it and so need not be considered here. Hart later summarizes his view as follows. Discretion exists where 'there remains a choice to be made by the person to whom the discretion is authorized which is not determined by principles which may be formulated beforehand, although the factors which we must take into account and conscientiously weigh may themselves be identifiable'.[57] If the criticisms above are accepted, a hybrid account of the existence of judicial discretion can be constructed, comprising the following features: (i) the individual has a decision-making power conferred upon them; (ii) there is a choice to be made; and (iii) there is no obvious answer by the application of principles (though factors to consider when making the choice may be identifiable).

The manner in which the discretionary power must be exercised

As noted earlier, Hart discussed the use of more nuanced evaluative terms such as 'wise' (or 'wiser') and while this may, as has been suggested, overlap with the rejection of the notion that there might be a single, correct resolution to a discretionary decision, this is perhaps better viewed as Hart importing a degree of subjective judgment into the equation. This requires an evaluation not only of the available options in isolation—whether or not a particular option is permissible, for example, whether

---

[57] Hart (n 11) 661. The latter part of Hart's work on discretion considered the place discretion has in a legal system. That is not germane to this discussion and so nothing further will be said about it in this chapter. Shaw's essay on Hart's work on discretion considers this point in more detail, see Shaw (n 16).

a sharp knife or a teaspoon, or a plastic fork could be used to cut a piece of cheese—but an evaluation of each option relative to the others—which is the best option; for example, the teaspoon would be better than the plastic fork, and the sharp knife would be better than the teaspoon.[58] Dworkin speaks of judgment in terms of the reasonableness of the decision.[59] Implicit in much of Dworkin's writing on discretion is the notion that the decision-maker takes the decision on the basis that it is the most appropriate disposal of the case, or resolution of the issue.[60] It can be inferred that such judgment and reasonableness of the decision are linked to the application of the principles which Dworkin argues so strongly must be present for a discretion to exist. Raz, however, explicitly recognized the courts' duty to act 'as they think best'.[61] This clearly imports a subjective element to the exercise of discretion, as is no doubt obvious in an exercise which requires the decision-maker to apply standards to a situation to discern an appropriate outcome. As to the subjective element of this exercise, Dworkin notes that 'reasonable men may disagree'.[62] Dworkin disagreed with the positivist position that a rule can dictate a result whereas a principle cannot, stating that:

> [p]rinciples ... incline a decision one way, though not conclusively, and ... can dictate a result. If a judge believes that principles he is bound to recognize point in one direction and that principles pointing in the other direction, if any, are not of equal weight, then he must decide accordingly, just as he must follow what he believes to be a binding rule.[63]

For Dworkin therefore the decision must be reasonable; it would not be reasonable to take a decision having recognized the weight of the principles falls in the other direction.[64]

It is worth noting that the subjective element of discretion has been subject of criticism. Hawkins notes in his survey of writings on discretion that although the subjectivism can be invaluable in individualizing

---

[58] A fortiori the knife will be better than the fork.
[59] Dworkin (n 4) 37.
[60] ibid, eg at 34.
[61] Raz (n 39) 847.
[62] Dworkin (n 4) 37.
[63] ibid 36.
[64] See n 60 above and associated text.

the application of the law, it can also be the cause of inconsistency, which can be said to be arbitrary.[65] Hawkins notes that this criticism has been frequently made in sphere of criminal sentencing.[66] It is difficult to see that as fatal to the existence of discretion however, particularly in light of methods which may overcome such inconsistency and arbitrariness.

Shaw described Hart's construction of discretion as 'a special form of constrained, reasoned decision-making based on appeal to rational principles'.[67] This appears to import a value judgment (as noted earlier in relation to Hart's dinner party example) and is supported by Hart's reliance on the idea of wisdom and experience. However, this is perhaps better viewed as the foundation for establishing that judicial discretion is to discern an appropriate result to the exclusion of personal whim or caprice.[68] Such an approach has to be correct: to conceive of judicial discretion as involving a preference on the basis of one's personal whim would be to allow a judge to find in favour of one party on the basis that the judge preferred the presentation of counsel's arguments, or their dress, or the fact that they were friends or former colleagues, irrespective of the merit of each case. Hart relies on an example of a voter at the ballot box who may be exercising a discretion but, where they decide to vote for one candidate because of their personal like for them, that, so Hart says, would be a choice but not the exercise of discretion. In distancing discretion from merely that involving an indulgence of whim or desire, Hart focusses on the *quality* of the result of the decision, namely that it is an appropriate outcome to the scenario at hand. This serves an important purpose in identifying a discretion and when it is exercised and is underlined by Hart's demarcation between a choice and a discretion, best exemplified by Hart's example of a discrete person remaining silent when it is appropriate to do so, not merely remaining silent all of the time.[69]

---

[65] Hawkins (n 5) 15.
[66] ibid.
[67] Shaw (n 16) 668. As to rational decision theory, see Hawkins (n 5) 20 for a general overview.
[68] Hart (n 11) 656–57.
[69] It is perhaps important to note that while Shaw uses the term 'rational', Dworkin uses the term 'reasonable'. While in pure linguistic terms there may be a difference between the two, eg the former may allow for a consideration of the peculiarities of the decision maker—a mother choosing to save her child rather than twenty others, for instance, it appears that Dworkin uses the term reasonable in the public law sense, directed at an assessment of the public body's action and whether a reasonable authority could have arrived at the same decision, see Lord Harry Woolf, Sir Jeffrey L. Jowell QC, Catherine Donnelly, Ivan Hare QC, and Joanna Bell, *De Smith's Judicial Review* (8th edn, Sweet and Maxwell 2021) § 11–012 et seq.

Such a conception of discretion envisages three situations: (i) choosing an appropriate outcome out of numerous appropriate outcomes; (ii) choosing an appropriate outcome from numerous appropriate and inappropriate outcomes; and (iii) choosing the least inappropriate outcome out of numerous inappropriate outcomes. Take a non-legal example of affixing a framed picture to a wall. If the available means are via a hammer and a nail, an adhesive hook, a strip of sticky tape, and some chewing gum, in (i) above, the hammer and nail and the adhesive hook may be considered to be appropriate and therefore the sticky tape and chewing gum would not be viable options; in (ii) the sticky tape and chewing gum would be viable options (as this encompasses all means), but may not be considered to be appropriate means of affixing the frame to the wall; in (iii) the hammer and nail and adhesive hook would not be viable options, and the choice would be between the sticky tape and the chewing gum.

Would it be permissible in (i) and (ii) to choose the adhesive hook and in (iii) to choose the sticky tape? In Hart's writings, the concept of discretion appears to require a value judgment as to the 'best'[70] resolution of the case at hand, though he does not go so far as to state that the exercise of discretion is to choose the most appropriate outcome. It does, however, appear legitimate to read this into his writing and worked examples appear to demonstrate that this is an important component of discretion.

In the previous paragraph the word 'choose' was used to describe the court's decision between one outcome and another, yet Hart uses numerous examples to draw out the differences between 'choice' and 'discretion'. These examples seek to limit discretion to the exercise of a choice guided by principles or rules yet excludes decisions where there is only one 'sensible' option, or where convention or rules dictate the correct result. This, Hart professes, demonstrates that 'so much depends on the precise description of the choice with which the individual is faced'.[71] He states: 'It seems to me then that discretion occupies an intermediate place between choices dictated by purely personal or momentary whim and those which are made to give effect to clear methods of reaching clear aims or to conform to rules whose application to the particular case is

---

[70] The term 'best' is not defined and would have to be subjective if such a test were to be practicable in the real world.
[71] Hart (n 11) 658.

obvious.'[72] This lends credence to the point above regarding the absence of *clear* rules or principles guiding the exercise of discretion. Hart's discussion then returns to focus upon its existence and exercise in a legal context, considering the need for discretion by virtue of the 'human situation'.[73] Hart concluded that:

> [p]ending the evolution of rules, discretion must take its place because the area is really one where reasonable and honest men may differ, however well informed of the facts in particular cases.
>
> Hence, in such fields as these, the important matter, having diagnosed what it is that renders discretionary jurisdiction inevitable, is to identify what are the optimum conditions for the exercise of discretion, because where we cannot be sure of being right, we can at least do what we can to obtain the best conditions for decisions.[74]

In relation to the exercise of discretion, Raz states that 'judicial discretion is not arbitrary judgment. Courts are never allowed to act arbitrarily. Even when discretion is not limited or guided in any specific direction the courts are still legally bound to act as they think is best according to their beliefs and values.'[75]

Raz is therefore in agreement with Hart in relation to the exclusion of arbitrariness and the requirement that the discretion is exercised in a manner in which the decision-maker considers is the best resolution in the particular situation. Raz however made a stronger claim than Hart (who tended to focus upon the exercise of discretion involving a reasoned elaboration),[76] stating that:

> [a judge] has discretion when the law requires him to act on reasons which he thinks are correct, instead of imposing its own standards. When discretion is denied the law dictates which standards should be applied by all the judges. When discretion is allowed each judge is

---

[72] ibid 658.
[73] ibid 663.
[74] ibid 663.
[75] Raz (n 39) 847.
[76] Shaw (n 16) 713.

entitled to follow different reasons but he must believe that they are the best.[77]

So, we can see that there is broad agreement as to the fact that discretion must be exercised in a manner which is rational, reasoned and in pursuit of the 'best' outcome according to the purpose(s) of the exercise. Drawing the threads together, the key components of the exercise of discretion are that the decision must be taken:

(1) for reasons which the decision maker thinks are correct;
(2) by an application of the principles or standards which are required to be considered in the decision-making process;
(3) in a manner which is not arbitrary or in pursuit of personal whim; and
(4) having performed a comparative exercise between the various options (rather than an assessment of each in isolation).

The foregoing is, of course, a discussion of the general literature on discretion. Yet, many of these conclusions are echoed by the limited writings on judicial discretion in the context of sentencing. Building upon that general literature, Ashworth states:

> The purpose of discretion is certainly to allow the sentencer to select the sentence which he believes to be most appropriate in the individual case, considering both the facts of the case and any reports on the offender's character. The purpose of discretion is surely not to enable individual judges and magistrates to pursue personal sentencing preferences.[78]

This concerns both the exercise and the existence of discretion, identifying the need for a choice exercised in accordance with principles (making reference to proportionality, individualization and, obliquely, the purposes of sentencing in section 57 of the Sentencing Act 2020), the belief on the part of the sentencer that the resolution chosen is the 'best',

---

[77] Raz (n 39) 848.
[78] Andrew Ashworth, *Sentencing and Penal Policy* (Weidenfeld and Nicholson 1983) 69.

and the exclusion of arbitrariness. It is, therefore, in accordance with the conclusions drawn above.

Ashworth therefore joins Hart (and others) in the rejection of the existence of discretion where a decision may be taken on an arbitrary basis. This requires there to be some guidance as to the way in which the decision may be exercised, clearly acknowledging the need for rules or principles. Yet Ashworth builds upon the general position (the exclusion of arbitrariness and so on) to incorporate the notion that the outcome chosen in the exercise of the discretion is the one which the judge regards as most appropriate. This statement as to the purpose of discretion similarly rejects the notion of personal whim in favour of an approach which is informed by other sources. While not delving into the issue of the location of such sources, is it not clear that this speaks to sources of guidance such as principles by virtue of the references to factors concerned with the offence and the offender?

Ashworth further notes that there is a distinction to be drawn between a discretion to determine which policy to pursue, and how best to pursue that policy in an individual case, concluding that the arguments in favour of judicial discretion clearly go in favour of the latter, rather than the former.[79] The point here appears to be that it is for sentencers to exercise their discretion and impose a sentence (or package of sentences) which best pursues the policy aim as determined by the legislature.[80] This can be read as being in concert with Hart's requirement that the decision is not made in pursuit of the judge's personal opinion or 'whim'.

Such a view has historical support; it was the view taken by the Victorian Criminal Law Commissioners, who identified a lack of certainty as being problematic and leading to arbitrary sentences 'depending on peculiar notions of policy entertained by different individuals, or their firmness and resolution of mind'.[81] The Victorian

---

[79] ibid 69.

[80] Ashworth considers the current regime in England and Wales to be problematic. Under s 57 of the Sentencing Act 2020, there is a list of various (and conflicting) purposes of sentencing in the case of those aged eighteen+ at conviction. Some are retributive, some are consequentialist. The details of the operation of that section and the objections to it are not germane to the present discussion. For more, see Andrew Ashworth and Rory Kelly, *Sentencing and Criminal Justice* (7th edn, Bloomsbury 2021) 65 et seq.

[81] Sir Leon Radzinowicz and Roger Hood, 'Judicial Discretion and Sentencing Standards: Victorian Attempts to Solve a Perennial Problem' (1979) 127 University of Pennsylvania Law Review 1288, 1292.

Commissioners sought to limit the 'mischief' to the narrowest of margins, and thereby curtail judicial discretion: they proposed that sentence types were to be limited and that sentences had to fall within a minimum and maximum level.[82]

Conclusion

Bringing the various elements of this discussion together, the following propositions emerge: that the issue is most logically and clearly approached from considering two distinct questions, first the existence of a discretion and secondly, the way in which it must be exercised; that the long-standing disagreement between Hart and Dworkin, and as commented upon by numerous academics since, principally stemmed from the discussion of positivism and theories of law rather than a conception of judicial discretion in and of itself; as such the later debates do not add much by way of substance to *this enquiry* into judicial discretion; and that there is broad agreement as to the central tenets of what a theoretically sound conception of judicial discretion comprises, with vague disagreement around the edges.[83]

Proceeding on the above analysis, it is possible to construct a theoretically sound account of judicial discretion for the purposes of the analysis of Western sentencing and the focus upon England and Wales later in this work.[84] It is suggested that to answer the question 'what is judicial discretion?', one must consider two issues, each of which have three constituent parts. While it is accepted that there are competing accounts (though not substantially in conflict), the following is offered as a credible account of judicial discretion for the purposes of the examination of methods of limiting or structuring discretion. This chapter sought to identify and analyse Hart's and Dworkin's conceptions of judicial discretion, with additional commentary from, *inter alia*, Raz. Next, the commonalities of these three

---

[82] ibid 1293.
[83] As to this final point, it is noted that the comment on the Hart–Dworkin debates has furthered the overall debate regarding legal positivism, for instance, see Timothy AO Endicott, *Vagueness in Law* (OUP 2000), particularly chapter 4.
[84] This account does not purport to speak to the Hart–Dworkin debate on positivism, being constructed for its own purpose rather than as a part of a wider task of discerning the limits of the law.

dominant accounts were condensed into one, rationalized, account of judicial discretion. The account now put forward is based heavily on the agreement between Hart and Dworkin as to the nature of judicial discretion, borne out of their wider work on the limitations of the law and positivism.

It is therefore suggested that a discretion exists where the court is required to make a decision in circumstances where there are applicable rules and/or principles but where these rules and/or principles when properly applied allow for more than one result. This is to omit matters such as the exclusion of evidence, or the determination of an application to withdraw the case from the jury.[85] Moving on to the second limb, concerning the exercise of the discretion, a discretion is in fact exercised (and this is a determination *ex post facto*) where the decision was taken not in pursuit of personal opinion or on an arbitrary basis, but by virtue of a proper and reasonable application of the rules or principles. The account of judicial discretion proffered is therefore as follows.

Establishing that a discretion exists:

(1) the decision maker is required by law to make a decision;
(2) principles (or standards) exist which guide the making of the decision; and
(3) the proper application of those principles does not produce a single, obviously correct, result.

Establishing that the discretion was properly exercised:

(1) the decision was not taken in pursuit of personal whim or on an arbitrary or legally irrelevant basis;
(2) the decision was taken by an application of relevant principles;
(3) the exercise was rational; and
(4) the decision made was, in the decision-maker's opinion, likely to bring about the most appropriate outcome.

---

[85] The precise application of this definition to sentencing is considered later in this chapter.

The case for structured judicial discretion

Chapter 3 set out the current understanding of the realities of inconsistency in sentencing. While there may be some disagreement as to the extent of disparity, and the nature of the principal causes of it, the empirical literature is clear that unjustified disparate sentencing practices exist. Against that background, the need to promote greater consistency is manifest.

With unbridled discretion comes, as demonstrated by the literature earlier, a very real risk of unjustified disparity. The response therefore has to be to somehow exert some influence or control over the exercise of discretion in order to reduce the possibility of the impact of non-legally relevant factors impacting upon the outcome of the sentence. This could take many forms such as judicial education on diversity,[86] a reduction in the number of available sentencing disposals, or the creation of binding sentencing ranges. The extent to which such methods will impact upon the exercise of discretion will of course vary, and, perhaps, vary drastically.

The term 'control' is likely to be cause for concern for many, not least members of the judiciary who anecdotally value so dearly the discretion with which they are afforded. It also connotes a degree of oversight which does not necessarily follow from the desire to influence the exercise of the discretion. Instead, hereinafter, the term 'structure' will be used to mean a device designed to influence the way in which a discretion is exercised. All methods of influencing discretion in this way operate to provide some sort of structure to the decision-making process. Accordingly, the following paragraphs make the case for structured discretion as that response to the problems identified in the empirical literature discussed earlier.

To sentence in the absence of structure—or even in the absence of robust structure—is to invite inconsistency. Such can be seen from the empirical literature discussed above. Van Duyne described 'open problems' and 'well-defined problems', the former being one for which there was no objective test to ascertain whether the problem-solver's solution is the

---

[86] See eg Sonja B Starr and M Marit Rehavi, 'Mandatory Sentencing and Racial Disparity: Assessing the Role of Prosecutors and the Effects of Booker' (2013) 123(1) The Yale Law Journal 2.

correct one, the latter being one for which an objective test does exist. He continued to state that the task of imposing sentence for a criminal case 'is considered to be an open problem: the decision makers have no unambiguous criteria by which they can determine whether their decisions have been the correct ones. The only guideline is their conscience—their feelings of what constitutes a "fair" sentence.'[87] The absence of structure, to provide the unambiguous criteria by which decisions can be evaluated, inevitably produces uncertainty and, as demonstrated by the empirical studies discussed in Chapter 3, inconsistency. How then should judicial discretion be structured? This section begins with a simple proposition: methods of structuring discretion can be divided into one of two categories: (i) those which limit discretion and (ii) those which guide discretion. It moves on to consider the different devices used to structure discretion before drawing conclusions regarding the utility of those devices and their application to sentencing systems with different approaches and principles.

Methods of structuring discretion: Limiting or guiding?

This work uses the term 'structure' in relation to judicial discretion at sentencing to describe a legitimate measure which has influence over the exercise of that discretion. It is helpful to identify two types of structure, namely those which limit discretion, and those which guide it.[88] The term 'limit' is used here in its literal sense, to convey the concept of the measure acting to curtail or restrict the options available to the court in the exercise of its discretion. A simple example is that of a maximum sentence: where the law prescribes that a sentence for a particular offence may not exceed a particular level, that operates as an inviolable limit. The term 'guides' is

---

[87] Petrus van Duyne, 'Simple Decision Making' in Donald C. Pennington and Sally Lloyd-Bostock (eds) *The Psychology of Sentencing: Approaches to Consistency and Disparity* (Centre for Socio-Legal Studies 1987) 146.

[88] There appears to have been a tendency to shy away from the term 'limit' when considering methods employed by the courts and legislatures to set boundaries within which sentencing courts may exercise a discretion. It may be that this is a pragmatic attempt to avoid the overt acceptance of the notion that the courts and the legislature have employed (and continue to employ) methods to curtail the once almost limitless discretion enjoyed by sentencing courts in this jurisdiction. Irrespective of the reason for a tendency to avoid that term, this work will continue to use it.

used here also in its literal sense to connote a sense of informing the way in which the discretion should be exercised. This requires an extra step in the application of the measure of structure imposed on the exercise of discretion, namely a judgment on the part of the sentencer, to interpret the guiding measure. A basic example of that is the principle of proportionality; the sentence is told that a proportionate sentence is one which is commensurate with the seriousness of the offence, having regard to culpability and harm, but is left to determine how it applies to a particular offence and offender.

It is the simple hypothesis of this chapter, therefore, that there are broadly two methods of structuring discretion and that one can distinguish between these methods of structuring judicial discretion at sentencing by assessing the nature of the measure and whether it operates to limit, or (merely) to guide discretion. It is further suggested that an appropriate determinative feature of whether a measure is limiting or guiding is whether or not the measure is rules-based and therefore by its application produces an objectively definitive result. For example, in England and Wales the maximum sentence prescribed by law for the offence of theft would operate as a limiting method as it is rules-based: the rule being that no sentence in excess of seven years' imprisonment may lawfully be imposed.[89] A rule operates as absolute, defeating other considerations[90] and can be objectively said to produce a definitive, unambiguous result. To continue the theft example, where a judge feels an offence of theft is so serious that a sentence of ten years is merited, the rule, that is the maximum sentence, is inviolable: a sentence in excess of the maximum of seven years is not available.[91] The objective nature of the definitive result is key here as it needs to be capable of application without the additional subjective judgment of the sentencer in order to apply it to

---

[89] Theft Act 1968 s 7.
[90] Dworkin stated: 'Rules are applicable in an all-or- nothing fashion. If the facts a rule stipulates are given, then either the rule is valid, in which case the answer it supplies must be accepted, or it is not, in which case it contributes nothing to the decision.' See Ronald Dworkin, 'The Model of Rules' (1967) 35 University of Chicago Law Review 14–46, 25.
[91] Gardner discusses the application of a rule, and an 'absolute' rule, and what he calls Dworkin's view that rules are applicable in an all or nothing fashion was 'misleading'. In particular, the brief discussion of where two 'rules' conflict, and how that might be resolved, is of interest, although beyond the scope of this work. See John Gardner, 'Ashworth on Principles' in Lucia Zedner and Julian V Roberts (eds), *Principles and Values in Criminal Law and Criminal Justice: Essays in Honour of Andrew Ashworth* (OUP 2012) 13.

the situation at hand. The absence of judgment avoids any disagreement as to the result of the application of the rule.

By contrast, a guiding measure is not rules-based and therefore does not produce an objectively definitive result, nor does it limit the available options. In applying a guiding measure, it is not possible to discern a definitive result. Such measures are informative rather than determinative, requiring evaluation and judgment in order to apply them to a given case.

Perhaps it is simpler to describe the defining feature of a guiding measure as being of an evaluative nature, requiring the sentencer to exercise a degree of judgment in understanding its purpose and applying it to achieve its intended effect. For example, it is widely accepted that the principle of proportionality as understood in retributive theory is incapable of producing a definitive result when applied to an offence of theft. It might be possible to discern a range of sentences which might be permissible, but it is not possible to be definite about either the precise sentence that is proportionate, or even to be precise about the range; the available sentences are therefore not restricted but there is a discernible preference towards one or more of the available options. The key here is the amorphous nature of the guiding measure. It is contingent, to a degree, on subjective interpretation which is not present in the limiting category.

The principal task of a sentencing court is to determine the appropriate response to the transgressive behaviour which led to the conviction. That decision may (and in reality, must) be structured by the powers vested in the sentencing court and may be further structured by guidance as to the manner in which the decision should be made. It is helpful to conceive of this exercise as two concentric circles:[92] the outer circle defines the powers as prescribed by the law (ie the limiting measures); the inner circles define the principles and other guidance as to the exercise of the decision within the boundaries set by the outer circle (ie the guiding measures). It would be lawful to impose a sentence inside the outer circle but outside of the inner circle, contrary to the guiding measure.[93] As will be illustrated later in this chapter, such a result may well be correct.

---

[92] Although perhaps, given the many facets to sentencing law and the different range of measures used to structure discretion, the concentric circles are best conceived of as being irregular in shape, but with the same centre.
[93] The amorphous nature of guiding measures invariably requires a degree of flexibility to be present in the application of such measures. Whereas there is no flexibility in relation to the

Limiting measures

Methods of limiting discretion in England and Wales almost invariably come from primary legislation, however this is not a prerequisite, and one may find contrary examples in other jurisdictions. As noted earlier, one distinction between a rule and a principle in relation to the exercise of discretion is that a rule obligates a particular outcome whereas a principle merely seeks to inform as to the proper outcome. It is suggested that the following measures—a general list of measures, but constructed with an eye on the system in England and Wales[94]—can be classified as 'limiting' on the above analysis:

The range of penalties available: by primary legislation available penalties are prescribed by the law, making certain sentencing orders available to sentencing courts. This device has at least two constituent parts; first, the general range of sentencing orders, for example imprisonment, a fine, a community order, a behaviour order, and so on; and secondly, any restrictions placed upon the availability of those penalties by reference to certain factors such as the age of the offender, for example, in England and Wales, imprisonment is not available for a person aged under twenty-one at the date of conviction. This operates to limit the sentencing powers of the court by, in the case of the former, prescribing the penalties which may be imposed, and in the case of the latter, removing certain sentencing orders from the available list.

Maximum penalties: Primary legislation sets down maximum sentences for almost all offences.[95] For example, in England and Wales there is a maximum sentence of fourteen years' imprisonment for domestic burglary by virtue of the Theft Act 1968 section 9. Any sentence in excess of this limit would be unlawful. This requires the judge to impose a sentence not in excess of that maximum, or put another way, enables a judge to impose a sentence only within the limit.

---

limiting measures, those being absolute and inviolable (and most likely enforceable by law), guiding measures are capable of both dispute as to the appropriate result but also violation for exceptional cases. The latter point is explored later in this chapter.

[94] As such, the list ought to be capable of application to other jurisdictions, perhaps with some minor amendments.
[95] Certain common law offences have no maximum sentence; the sentence is therefore 'at large' and the in practice the maximum sentence is one of life imprisonment.

Minimum sentences: Primary legislation requires a sentence of a particular nature and length to be imposed in certain cases, for example a minimum of seven years' imprisonment for a third conviction for a drug trafficking offence.[96] This requires a judge to impose a sentence of not less than the prescribed amount. While the judge could omit to do so, either through forgetfulness or caprice (and in that sense it differs from the two previous categories) in theory this device of limiting judicial discretion remains appropriately classified as a rule as the law requires it to be applied and the non-application of it is therefore unlawful.

Combinations of sentences: Primary legislation in England and Wales prohibits the combination of certain penalties. For example, it is not permitted by law to impose a referral order and a youth rehabilitation order on a young offender.[97] Similarly, the common law prohibits the imposition of certain combinations of sentences, for instance the Court of Appeal (Criminal Division) has stated that a suspended sentence order and a sentence of immediate imprisonment may not be imposed together.[98]

Mandatory approach to sentencing: This final sub-category poses some difficulty. Measures which prescribe a particular approach to sentencing operate both as limiting but also guiding. Take for example, the duty to treat a particular factor as aggravating the seriousness of the offence. This can be placed within the limiting category by virtue of their effect, namely that a definitive result is produced (the aggravation of the offence) which operates as a limitation on the sentencing court's discretion (it has no option but to treat the factor as rendering the offence more serious than it would otherwise be but for the presence of the factor). The complication is that such a measure does not prescribe the result with any more precision. That can be resolved, however, by dividing the measure into two, the part which is limiting and the part which is merely guiding. The same can be said for statutory provisions which set down the sentencing scheme: section 63 of the Sentencing Act 2020 makes clear that proportionality is the guiding principle of sentencing in England and Wales (and concomitantly any derogation from this would be unlawful) but does not

---

[96] Where the requisite conditions are met, see Sentencing Act 2020 s 313.
[97] Sentencing Act 2020 s 89 (1) and (3)(b)(i).
[98] *R. v Sapiano* (1968) 52 Cr App R 674.

provide any further clarification as to how to translate that into a particular sentence in a particular case. It is therefore both limiting and guiding. Its application to sentencing generally is limiting, but its application to particular cases is merely guiding.

Guiding measures

Methods of guiding discretion may also come from hard law but are more likely to come from cases, as well as legislation, and quasi-legal sources such as sentencing guidelines, prosecutorial decision-making. It is suggested that the following measures—a general list but constructed with an eye on the system in England and Wales[99]—can be classified as guiding on the above analysis:

Sentencing guidelines: Sentencing guidelines vary: by way of example, different jurisdictions adopt different approaches to the binding nature of the guideline,[100] the style of the guideline,[101] the type of guideline,[102] and the type of disposal with which it deals.[103] However a common thread (generally) binding them together is the way in which they inform the determination of sentence. By an evaluative exercise, courts apply the guidelines which produce a range of appropriate sentences, or an indication of the appropriate sentence, in a particular case. This is therefore a measure which informs the determination of sentence without providing a definitive result.[104]

Approach to sentencing: This category forms the other side of the coin, so to speak, to the 'mandatory approach to sentencing' category listed in the 'Limiting measures' section earlier. Examples of such are so-called principles such as totality, parsimony, and proportionality. The

---

[99] As such, the list ought to be capable of application to other jurisdictions, perhaps with some minor amendments.
[100] For example, whether it is presumptive, like those in Ohio and Minnesota, or voluntary, like those in Virginia and Alaska.
[101] For example, whether it is narrative, like those in England and Wales and Delaware or numerical grid-based guidelines like those in Pennsylvania and the District of Columbia.
[102] For example, whether it is offence-specific or overarching.
[103] For example, whether a wide range of disposals are dealt with, like in England and Wales, or just determinate prison sentences, like in Virginia.
[104] This will be explored fully in the following chapters.

application of these concepts is incapable of being precise.[105] This, too, is an evaluative exercise designed to inform the decision as to what is the most appropriate sentence. While the application of such 'principles' produces a comparatively narrow range of permissible sentences, this is of course subjective and there will be disagreement regarding the precise range produced by applying those principles to a particular case. This category could also be said to incorporate overarching sentencing guidelines, such as those providing guidance as to the approach to sentencing generally, or to a particular area of sentencing.

Case law: The Court of Appeal (Criminal Division) in England and Wales, as an appellate court, provides both remedies in individual cases—for example by reducing a sentence it considers to be manifestly excessive—and guidance to other constitutions of the court, and lower courts, on matters pertaining to sentencing. Ashworth recently identified six categories of Court of Appeal (Criminal Division): (i) application and interpretation of definitive guidelines; (ii) assessing departures from definitive guidelines; (iii) creating or developing offence-specific guidance; (iv) creating or developing guidance on general principles (including sentencing procedure); (v) interpreting sentencing legislation; and (vi) 'common law' sentencing.[106] This guidance is again evaluative. As will be seen in the following chapters, however, the degree to which this guidance requires subjective interpretation can vary.[107]

Prosecutorial decision-making: While this element will vary significantly between jurisdiction, the central point remains the same; prosecutors (generally) have influence over the sentencing process through their decision-making power. Even where, as in England and Wales, the traditional role of the prosecutor at sentencing was almost non-existent, the decision to charge one offence or another (or accept a guilty plea to such) impacts upon the sentence to be imposed. This too has different dimensions and impacts by virtue of the maximum sentence which attached to the particular offence, availability of an ancillary order, or the existence

---

[105] For example, Norval Morris was a proponent of this view. See Richard S Frase, 'Sentencing Principles in Theory and Practice' (1997) 22 Crime & Justice 363, 368.

[106] Andrew Ashworth, 'The Evolution of English Sentencing Guidance in 2016' [2017] Criminal Law Review 507, 508.

[107] This will be explored fully in Chapter 7.

of any minimum or mandatory sentence.[108] There is of course a question surrounding both the intention (or inevitability) and the legitimacy of a prosecuting authority using its decision-making power to influence the sentence process.[109] This is not explored here, however, as it is outside of the scope of this work.

Conclusion

This chapter has sought to provide, from a consideration of major works on discretion, a definition of judicial discretion which is theoretically credible both in terms of its relationship to the general literature on the subject and to the nuances of the law and theory of sentencing. Adopting a two-staged approach, the account proffered considers how to identify the existence of a discretionary decision and then to identify whether the manner in which the discretion was exercised was appropriate. This provides a clear account of the concept which can be applied to the multitude of decisions which a sentencing court has to make to clearly identify whether a decision is one involving a discretion.

Thereafter, having considered the case for structuring judicial discretion, making reference to the review of the empirical literature in Chapter 3, it was determined that it is necessary to structure discretion in order to counter the risk of inconsistency. In exploring the various methods of structuring discretion, two broad categories were identified, namely limiting and guiding. This categorization will be used in later chapters, in conjunction with the account of discretion, to facilitate an analysis of the methods of structuring discretion and their relative success.

---

[108] As indicated in the previous sentence, the role of the prosecutor in England and Wales has changed. Prosecuting advocates are now an active part of the sentencing process, making submissions to the judge on the law, applicability of sentencing guidelines and even guideline categorization and appropriate sentence length. See eg The Prosecutor's Role in Sentencing, CPS Legal Guidance <https://www.cps.gov.uk/legal-guidance/sentencing-overview-general-princip les-and-mandatory-custodial-sentences> accessed 27 November 2017. For a brief comparative view, see Lyndon Harris, 'The Role of the Prosecutor at Sentencing' University of Oxford Faculty of Law Blog, 4 March 2016 <https://www.law.ox.ac.uk/centres-institutes/centre-criminology/ blog/2016/03/role-prosecutor-sentencing> accessed 1 January 2022.

[109] For a discussion in the Australian context, see John Willis, Some Aspects of the Prosecutor's Role at Sentencing, a paper given at the 'Prosecuting Justice Conference' hosted by the Australian Institute of Criminology in Melbourne, 18–19 April 1996 and subsequently revised.

6
Statutory methods of structuring judicial discretion at sentencing

'In the United Kingdom there has been very little legislative guidance on sentencing'[1]

Introduction

In the previous chapter, it was suggested that structuring judicial discretion at sentencing was the appropriate response to the manifest inconsistencies evidenced by the empirical literature. It was argued that methods of providing such structure can be grouped into either guiding or limiting measures, so characterized by their nature and effect upon the sentencing process. This chapter and the following three chapters consider the efficacy of the measures employed by the three main institutions responsible for promoting consistency in England and Wales: (i) Parliament; (ii) the Court of Appeal (Criminal Division) (CACD); and (iii) the Sentencing Council. While this domestic focus is naturally jurisdiction specific, it is hoped that lessons can be identified from the analysis that are applicable to other jurisdictions.

In essence this chapter considers two questions: first, whether and if so, to what extent, Parliament has provided in statute sufficient structure to the discretionary sentencing decisions of criminal courts, and second, whether further structure is necessary in order to pursue, and achieve, consistency as conceived of in Chapter 2. This chapter surveys the key

---

[1] Martin Wasik and Ken Pease, 'Discretion and Sentencing Reform: The Alternative' in Martin Wasik and Ken Pease (eds), *Sentencing Reform: Guidance or Guidelines?* (Manchester University Press 1987) 1.

provisions which operate to structure sentencers' discretion and considers both theoretical and practical strengths and weaknesses in light of the overarching pursuit of consistency. For reasons of space, the chapter does not seek to be exhaustive.

This chapter begins with a brief consideration of the sentencing scheme in England and Wales before exploring the main 'general' provisions concerned with determining the sentence for a criminal offence. Next, the chapter examines the sentencing orders which may be imposed for criminal offences by exploring the statutory maximum sentences and the availability of sentencing orders. The chapter then works its way through the conventional methodology adopted by the courts, namely to consider aggravating and mitigating factors and other factors reducing the seriousness of an offence or otherwise reducing the severity of a sentence (such as guilty plea), before concluding with an assessment of minimum and mandatory sentencing orders.

Parliament's role in providing structured discretion at sentencing

Legislatively structured judicial discretion

Constitutionally, Parliament determines its own role and the role of other actors in the provision of structure as regards the sentencing regime: Parliament created the CACD and the Sentencing Council and provided each with their powers.[2] The first point to note is that Parliament's (self-defined) role is not to provide a comprehensive scheme for regulating sentencing discretion: on the contrary, Parliament's involvement acknowledges that the Court of Appeal (Criminal Division) and the Sentencing Council have a significant role to play. In a civil law jurisdiction, where criminal codes are prevalent, the position is different. Yet in a common law jurisdiction, the comprehensive regime comes from multiple sources. That is of course not to say that either regime is incapable of

---

[2] See eg Criminal Appeal Act 1907 s 1; Criminal Appeal Act 1966 s 1; and Senior Courts Act 1981 s 2; and in relation to the Sentencing Council (and its predecessors), Crime and Disorder Act 1998 s 80 et seq; Criminal Justice Act 2003 s 167 et seq; and Coroners and Justice Act 2009 ss 118–124 and 127 et seq.

improvement; each has its merits. As will be seen in the following discussion, the Sentencing Act 2020 (the principal statute containing provisions concerning sentencing discretion in England and Wales) is deficient in a number of respects.

Radzinowicz and Hood considered the appointment of Criminal Law Commissioners who sought to 'bring order' to the confusion created by discretionary sentencing powers; the Commissioners attempted to provide a coherent and rational approach to equating the gravity of crimes with the severity of sentences and criticized the lack of certainty and identified this as leading to arbitrary sentences 'depending on the peculiar notions of policy entertained by different individuals'.[3] It will be noted that this conclusion is supported by the review of empirical literature in Chapter 3, and reached some considerable time before the academic studies evidenced the dangers of discretionary sentencing in the absence of structure. The Victorian Commissioners' reports spoke of injustice where aggravating factors were defined in law and observed that crimes which bore little resemblance to one another in terms of moral blameworthiness were routinely classed together without discrimination as to penal consequences. The problems of an inconsistent and incoherent legal framework in addition to the dangers of personal opinion and the 'human' factor in discretionary sentencing was therefore a major causes for concern to the Commissioners in their early reports in the 1830s. Many would observe the current system in England and Wales continues to suffer from those problems.

Thomas identified that the object of achieving harmony in sentencing, without destroying its essentially discretionary character, has occupied the attention of reformers inside and outside of Parliament for decades, noting that various methods of structuring discretion have been employed in the jurisdiction from the mid-1800s.[4] Indeed, various methods of structuring discretion have been utilized in the past 150 years, from minimum sentences in the mid-1800s[5] to systematic reviews of sentences

---

[3] Sir Leon Radzinowicz and Roger Hood, 'Judicial Discretion and Sentencing Standards: Victorian Attempts to Solve a Perennial Problem' (1979) 127 University of Pennsylvania Law Review 1288, 1292.

[4] David Thomas, *Constraints on Judgment: The Search for Structured Discretion in Sentencing, 1860–1910*, Institute of Criminology, Occasional Series No 4 (University of Cambridge Institute of Criminology 1979) 2.

[5] In 1861, the Offences against the Person Act 1861 s 61 abolished the death penalty for buggery and reduced the maximum sentence to one of penal servitude for life, with a minimum

at specified intervals.⁶ This response, at least in the mid to late 1800s, stemmed from a concern regarding disparity of sentence. Radzinowicz and Hood noted the various attempts to bring more order to the criminal law in the late 1800s, including proposed changes to maximum sentences yet reform was slow and disparity remained 'a stark reality'.⁷ Reliance was placed on a review conducted in 1895 of sentences imposed at the Central Criminal Court; the review detailed that the Common Serjeant would impose sentences of fourteen years for offences in which other judges at that court would routinely impose sentences of only twelve months to five years.⁸ Concern was also expressed by the press and groups such as the Howard Association.⁹ Thomas referenced the practice of flogging, which upon a judicial consultation exercise conducted by the Home Secretary in 1874 as to the potential extension of the power to impose flogging, revealed marked differences of opinion as to its ideal usage, success as a crime reduction tool and its efficacy.¹⁰ Thomas noted that its usage, as being 'reserved by general consent for the worst cases' was more likely to be a product of the individual judge's view rather than agreed criteria.¹¹ This echoes the custody threshold debate which has plagued sentencing legislation for decades.¹²

Similarly, Thomas noted that the greater difficulty of controlling the sentencing practices of quarter sessions (there being *circa* 5,000 magistrates at that time) than in the higher courts had been apparent to the Criminal Law Commissioners in 1843. The need to guide discretion had been realized then in their Seventh Report.¹³ Similarly, proposals

---

sentence of ten years' penal servitude. In 1891, the minimum sentence was repealed by the Penal Servitude Act 1891 s 1.

⁶ Home Office Memorandum (1899), Standard Sentences in Criminal Cases, cited in Thomas, *Constraints on Judgment* (n 4) 7.
⁷ Radzinowicz and Hood, 'Judicial Discretion and Sentencing Standards' (n 3) 1307.
⁸ ibid 1308.
⁹ ibid 1308.
¹⁰ Thomas (n 4) 8–9.
¹¹ Thomas (n 4) 9.
¹² See eg Julian V Roberts and Lyndon Harris, 'Reconceptualising the Custody Threshold in England and Wales' (2017) 28(3) Criminal Law Forum 477; Julian V Roberts and Lyndon Harris, 'Addressing the Problems of the Prison Estate: The Role of Sentencing Policy' (2017) 231 Prison Service Journal 8; Nicky Padfield, 'Time to Bury the Custody Threshold?' [2011] Criminal Law Review 593; and Lyndon Harris Andrew Ashworth, Antje du Bois-Pedain, et al, 'Academic Response to the Sentencing Council's Consultation Paper on the Draft Guideline for the Imposition of Community and Custodial Sentences' (2019) 1 Sentencing News 12.
¹³ Seventh Report of the Criminal Law Commissioners (1843) 99.

for recidivist premiums were discussed in Parliament in the mid to late 1800s. The Habitual Criminals Bill (1869)[14] contained a clause which, had it been enacted would have mandated a minimum of seven years' penal servitude to be imposed on an offender convicted of a third felony. There were proposals to extend this to subsequent convictions: Thomas referred to a speech in the House of Lords on the second reading of the Bill in which the Earl of Carnarvon supported in addition fourteen years for four convictions and twenty years for five or six convictions.[15] In the event the Bill was enacted without that provision.

There were suggestions that disparity resulted from the absence of principles in sentencing but a proposal for regular meetings of sentencers to discuss and agree upon a uniform standard of punishments for the most common offences; while this proposal in the event amounted to nothing, it can be seen as particularly pioneering and an early forerunner to both Judicial College[16] and a sentencing guidelines body.[17] Later moves to secure uniformity via legislation and the creation of a Royal Commission were unsuccessful.[18]

As the death penalty was abolished for an increasing number of offences and Parliament's interest in sentencing policy dwindled from the late nineteenth century onwards, the extent to which the courts had discretion at sentencing necessarily grew.[19] This growth of discretion continued throughout the twentieth century and has continued into the twenty-first. Munro and Wasik noted that this led to the courts filling that void and suggested that 'perhaps two generations of judges had become accustomed to think of sentencing policy as being entirely their own concern'.[20] High maximum sentences in conjunction with minimum sentences becoming 'virtually unknown',[21] led to the wide discretion with which judges were afforded in the twentieth century.

---

[14] This was later enacted as the Habitual Criminals Act 1869.
[15] HL Deb, 5 March 1869 vol 194 cc691–715 cited in Thomas (n 4) 15.
[16] The judicial body which is now responsible for the continued education and training of judges in England and Wales.
[17] Radzinowicz and Hood (n 3) 1319–20.
[18] ibid 1319–20.
[19] Colin Munro and Martin Wasik (eds), *Sentencing, Judicial Discretion and Training* (Sweet and Maxwell 1992) 26.
[20] ibid 26.
[21] ibid 26.

Politics

It can be seen, therefore, that albeit there has been some fluctuation, Parliament has steadily increased its involvement in regulating judicial discretion at sentencing. Perhaps somewhat paradoxically, discretion at sentencing grew. The increase in types of disposal afforded courts with an arsenal more broader than before, in conjunction with the demise of the minimum sentence. Sentencing courts were afforded a variety of options and little by way of restraint. Another aspect to consider in the expanse of Parliament's role is the politicization of sentencing. While this chapter does not propose to explore in any detail the extent to which politics impacted—and continues to impact—upon Parliament's role in structuring judicial discretion, one cannot explore the legislative landscape without acknowledging the role that populism and politics has played.

Law and order, once a cross-party issue without politicization, became a key topic on which elections were fought. For instance, policing matters were not generally considered to be of political concern until the 1970s.[22] Thatcher's Conservative Party (partly) ran its election campaign on a law and order platform. Once elected, her Government became the 'law and order party', instigating a rise in 'punitiveness' and a shift in the dialogue in the political rhetoric around tacking crime.[23] In the early 1990s, the landscape changed once more as Tony Blair became the leader of the Opposition and eventually took Labour into a landslide general election victory with the now-famous 'tough on crime, tough on the causes of crime' slogan. Since then, successive governments (both Conservative and the Liberal Democrat/Conservative coalition) have sought to wrestle this crown from the Labour Party, and in recent years there has been a number of what might be described as highly populist sentencing measures proposed or enacted.

So, from the 1980s, a slew of criminal justice legislation followed which dramatically altered the legislative landscape and the way in which sentencing courts could approach their task. From Acts in the 1980s

---

[22] Robert Reiner, 'Law-and-order politics', *The Guardian*, 22 December 2008 <https://www.theguardian.com/commentisfree/2008/dec/22/police-conservatives> accessed 28 May 2018.
[23] Stephen Farrell, Naomi Burke, and Colin Hay, 'Revisiting Margaret Thatcher's Law and Order Agenda: The Slow-burning Fuse of Punitiveness' (2016) 11(2) British Politics 205–231, 208.

providing the prosecution with the ability to 'appeal' against certain sentencing decisions[24] to providing purposes of sentencing,[25] the face of judicial discretion at sentencing in England and Wales dramatically changed. This increased politicization has impacted upon the view that Parliament has taken as to the need to intervene in the extent to which sentencing courts exercise their discretion.

Parliament's role in structuring discretion

As the quotation at the head of this chapter indicates, it was not until the creation of the Court of Criminal Appeal in 1907 that an appellate court expressly acknowledged its role in the provision of guidance on sentencing. As seen earlier, Parliament remained only moderately interested in sentencing policy in the first half of the twentieth century, with the focus on youth justice and expanding the types of sentencing order available to a court, rather than making further inroads into the discretion afforded to the judiciary. It had, however, enacted maximum and (some) minimum sentences, widened the range of sentencing options available to the court and created an appellate court with the capacity and authority to provide sentencing guidance. It had, in limited circumstances, sought to restrict judicial discretion in a greater way. For instance, section 40(2) of the Criminal Justice Act 1925 added to the discretionary power to disqualify an offender from driving under the Motor Car Act 1903 by imposing a mandatory period of twelve months' disqualification for offenders convicted of being drunk while in charge of a mechanically propelled vehicle. Additionally, section 17 of the Criminal Justice Act 1948 both prohibited the imprisonment of those under 17 and introduced a custody threshold (of sorts) providing that a court must only impose imprisonment on those aged under twenty-one where it was of the opinion that no other method of dealing with the offender was appropriate. A Private Members Bill (supported by the Howard League for Penal Reform) sought to extend that to adult offenders dealt with in the magistrates' courts.[26] This

---

[24] Criminal Justice Act 1988 ss 35 and 36.
[25] Sentencing Act 2020 s 57.
[26] JE Hall Williams, 'Statutes: The First Offenders Act 1958' (1959) 1 The Modern Law Review 41.

was perhaps Parliament's first real foray into structuring judicial discretion beyond the creation of certain mandatory sentences in the 1800s and the creation of different sentences which courts may impose. It's evident, therefore, that in the first sixty years of the twentieth century, Parliament only sought to limit judicial discretion sparingly and in very limited ways.

Has Parliament fulfilled its role, or is more needed? Parliament can be both proactive and reactive, though as will be seen, its contribution to the application of the sentencing regime is likely to be at either end of a scale of 'vague' to 'overly prescriptive', rather than occupying some intermediate ground. As discussed in the previous chapter, measures of structuring discretion may be categorized as either limiting or guiding, and typically the former will be blunt instruments with an inconsistent application or disparate results, whereas the latter will be vaguer and more reliant upon nuance and interpretation. As to Parliament's role, it has generally seen fit to provide an overarching structure (of types of penalty, maximum sentences, and so on) and to intervene in a limited number of specific cases only (such as the mandatory life sentence for murder and selected other mandatory or minimum sentences).

This was recognized in 2001 when the Halliday Report stated that it was Parliament's role to set down a framework for a sentencing regime.[27] By its nature, a framework may be described as skeletal and therefore reliant upon other actors to contribute to add 'flesh to the bones'. It is well accepted that Parliament has expected the appellate courts to intervene in matters of sentencing requiring guidance and clarification.[28] This was recognized by the scheme which observed that when considering how sentencing was 'supposed to work', the interested enquirer would need to consider the morass of legislation in addition to the decisions of the CACD and the Magistrates' Courts' Sentencing Guidelines (which were created by an informal group convened by the Magistrates' Association).[29] The report criticized the 'unnecessary rigidities' inherent in the scheme prevailing at the time, noting that a greater number of available sentencing orders would make the scheme less restrictive.[30]

---

[27] *Making Punishments Work: Report of a Review of the Sentencing Framework for England and Wales* (Home Office 2001) § 1.32.
[28] This will be expanded upon in the following chapter, however it is clear from the early 1900s that the court recognized this as its function and that Parliament had legislated to that effect.
[29] Home Office, *Making Punishments Work* (n 27) § 1.9.
[30] ibid 1.31.

This bolsters the claim that the examination of the extent to which discretion at sentencing is structured must extend beyond legislation, and that Parliament's role is to provide the general architecture of the sentencing scheme and to allow the courts (and now, the Sentencing Council) to fulfil their role as a provider of additional structure. What is clear, however, is that Parliament must provide—at least—the structure and the outer limits of the court's discretion; that it may, where is chooses to, expand its involvement in this exercise into areas formerly the preserve of the courts. Parliament is merely one actor in a tripartite effort to provide adequate structure to sentencing; this conjoined effort to provide adequate guidance is one which is entirely intentional.

Parliament therefore limits its role in this regard, requiring input from (principally) the CACD and latterly, a sentencing guidelines body, currently the Sentencing Council. This division of labour seems, in principle, appropriate given the respective expertise, ability to effect change and available resources.[31] There may be specific instances where Parliament could be said to have overstepped the mark, or conversely, to have failed to act where perhaps it ought, but in general, this work adopts the position that broadly, the division of labour as regards providing structured discretion is appropriate. Parliament's role is to provide the architecture of the scheme—a framework within which the other actors can work to provide additional guidance where required—but not intrude too far into the way in which a court should resolve particular cases.

It falls next to consider the way in which Parliament has provided such structure.

Provisions of general application

General

Sentencing in England and Wales is awash with primary and secondary legislation. Such is the proliferation of Parliamentary intervention in the

---

[31] For instance, as will be seen in the following chapters, it is more appropriate for a guidelines body to provide sentencing guidelines than the CACD (or, heaven forbid, Parliament) because of the resource implications of providing a guideline designed to replicate current practice but remove unjust disparity in sentencing decisions, yet it is more appropriate for Parliament to set the parameters of the court's sentencing powers given its constitutional role and the importance of such powers being democratically accountable.

sentencing process that between 1991 and 2022 (inclusive), there were at least twenty-four pieces of primary legislation making substantive changes to the sentencing process and affecting the exercise of judicial discretion.[32] Towards the end of that period came the commencement of the Sentencing Act 2020, a consolidation Act concerning sentencing procedure (but making no substantive policy changes). The consolidation (as many consolidation Bills) was the product of a Law Commission project;[33] during the project, the Law Commission identified that the primary legislation concerning sentencing procedure (therefore excluding offence-creating and penalty-setting provisions), a summary of which ran to over 1,300 pages.[34] Parliament is almost continuously amending the sentencing regime, but more importantly it demonstrates that Parliament finds the time (on an almost annual basis) to enact legislation affecting sentencing and judicial discretion. The importance of this is that there has therefore been ample opportunity to review the operation of structured discretion and make appropriate changes to increase its effectiveness.

As discussed earlier, statutory methods of structuring discretion may be limiting, or they may be guiding. The form of the method does not dictate its nature, but it is possible to say that a limiting measure, being rules-based, is naturally a rather blunt instrument with which Parliament seeks to influence the exercise of discretion at sentencing; and that by contrast, guiding measures are comparatively vague. As a result, the limiting measures tend to be rigid and guiding measures are more flexible. For example, a maximum sentence operates as a limiting measure,

---

[32] Criminal Justice Act 1991; Criminal Justice Act 1993; Drug Trafficking Act 1994; Criminal Appeal Act 1995; Crime (Sentences) Act 1997; Powers of Criminal Courts (Sentencing) Act 2000; Proceeds of Crime Act 2002; Criminal Justice Act 2003; Serious Organised Crime and Police Act 2005; Terrorism Act 2006; Criminal Justice and Immigration Act 2008; Coroners and Justice Act 2009; Legal Aid, Sentencing and Punishment of Offenders Act 2012; Offender Rehabilitation Act 2014; Serious Crime Act 2015; Criminal Justice and Courts Act 2015; Psychoactive Substances Act 2016; Armed Forces Act 2016; Assaults on Emergency Workers (Offences) Act 2018; Counter-Terrorism and Border Security Act 2019; Offensive Weapons Act 2019; Terrorism (Restriction of Early Release) Act 2020; Counter-Terrorism and Sentencing Act 2021; and Policing, Crime, Sentencing and Courts Act 2022.

[33] The Law Commission is the statutory independent body created by the Law Commissions Act 1965 to keep the law of England and Wales under review and to recommend reform where it is needed. The aim of the Commission is to ensure that the law is fair, modern, simple, and cost-effective.

[34] *Sentencing Law in England and Wales—Legislation Currently in Force*, Law Commission of England and Wales (Law Commission 2015).

prohibiting sentences in excess of the figure prescribed, whereas provisions mandating the treatment of particular factors as aggravating the seriousness of an offence are guiding, impacting upon discretion but providing no clarity as to the severity of the resultant sentence. As was briefly explored in the previous chapter, limiting measures tend to be statutory (though not always) as it is predominantly Parliament that has the ability to impose rules upon the exercise of discretion at sentencing. These typically take the form of hard limitations on sentencing powers but can take another form. In contrast, guiding measures tend to be statutory or non-statutory and, by their nature, are vague and take many forms.

This chapter will limit itself to courts of first instance and will not consider provisions applying *only* to appellate courts.

Principles underpinning the sentencing scheme in England and Wales

Perhaps the most appropriate starting point in a consideration of statutory methods of providing structure to discretion at sentencing is with the Sentencing Act 2020 sections 63 (assessment of seriousness), 204 (community order threshold), 230 (custody threshold), and 231 (principle of parsimony). Through these provisions, Parliament has provided guidance as to the approach to determining the nature and severity of sentence to be imposed. Section 230—commonly referred to as the 'custody threshold'[35]—acts as a limitation on the use of custodial sentences, prohibiting the imposition of a custodial sentence unless the offence (or the combination of the offence and any offences associated with it) was so serious that only a custodial sentence could be justified. Similarly, section 204—known as the 'community threshold'—serves the same purpose but in respect of community sanctions. Section 231 provides that any custodial sentence imposed must be for the shortest period which is commensurate with the seriousness of the offence. Finally, section 63 provides that that in assessing the seriousness of an offence, the court must consider the offender's culpability in committing the offence and any harm caused,

---

[35] See eg Padfield, 'Time to Bury the Custody Threshold?' (n 12) and Roberts and Harris (n 12).

intended to be caused, or might have foreseeably been caused. Section 63 adopts a traditional retributive account of offence seriousness and provides a theoretically clear and well-accepted approach to the determination of sentence.[36] The concept of offence seriousness therefore is at the core of the scheme; while section 63 'defines' offence seriousness, it does so by reference to two other concepts—harm and culpability—which themselves are not defined. How is one to assess seriousness? In this regard, it is instructive to view this aspect of structured discretion through von Hirsch's account of proportionality: ordinal proportionality requires that sentences should be proportionate to the severity of the offence(s), resulting in more serious offences receiving more severe penalties, whereas cardinal proportionality operates in a non-relative sense, setting the overall level of punishment. A sentencing system may therefore be cardinally disproportionate despite being ordinally proportionate.[37] A more culpable offence involving more harm is more serious than a lesser culpable offence involving less harm (ordinal proportionality), yet there is nothing in these provisions which assists with the question of cardinal proportionality, the anchoring point for the offence seriousness. The paucity of guidance is strongly suggestive of the fact that Parliament expects other actors to assist in providing guidance as to the application of these provisions. Without more, consistency of application is unobtainable, simply by virtue of the fact that the exercise is subjective.

As has been extensively discussed over the decades, retributivism prescribes that an offence be met with a disposal proportionate to the seriousness of the offending, serving as punishment for the wrongdoing in circumstances where the offender has society's disapprobation communicated to them.[38] Ashworth notes that '[c]ritics ... have called for a less prescriptive form of retributivism which recognises that the concept of proportionality cannot be made sufficiently precise to indicate rankings of offences and punishments'.[39] An alternative while remaining within a desert-based model—which would claim to be a solution to the

---

[36] There are many criticisms of retributive theory; for a brief overview, see Andrew Ashworth and Rory Kelly, *Sentencing and Criminal Justice* (7th edn, Bloomsbury 2021) 76 et seq.
[37] Rory Kelly, 'Reforming Maximum Sentences and Respecting Ordinal Proportionality' [2018] Criminal Law Review 450.
[38] Andreas von Hirsch, *Deserved Criminal Sentences* (Hart 2017) 17.
[39] Ashworth and Kelly (n 36) 77.

unobtainable ideal of retributivism as a defining principle—is limiting retributivism. This enables other principles to determine the appropriate disposal within the proportionate range set by desert.[40] Parliament has opted to modify the otherwise clearly retributive approach set out in sections 63, 230, and 231 (above), instead adopting limiting retributivism by enacting section 57 of the Sentencing Act 2020.

Through section 57, courts must have regard to five purposes of sentencing:

(1) the punishment of offenders;
(2) the reduction of crime (including its reduction by deterrence);
(3) the reform and rehabilitation of offenders;
(4) the protection of the public, and
(5) the making of reparation by offenders to persons affected by their offences.

This firmly establishes the system in England and Wales as a limiting retributivism model, with the purposes under section 57 operating to guide the determination of the appropriate disposal within the range of proportionate sentences determined by the seriousness of the offence.

There are, however, numerous problems in the application of section 57 and its interaction with the general provisions concerning the assessment of seriousness. It is these provisions which underpin the entire scheme and which are required to do much of the theoretical and practical work in the determination of sentence. Principally, the statute provides no guidance as to how the provision should be interpreted. First is that there is no hierarchy of purposes explicit or implied by the statute. One might suggest that the order in which the purposes appear implies a descending order of importance. This might be supported by the fact that punishment is the overriding aim of the scheme; such is clear from sections 63, 230, and 231 as discussed earlier. Yet this would be, at best, to strain principles of statutory interpretation,[41] or worse, to do no little

---

[40] ibid 78.
[41] Daniel Greenberg, *Craies on Legislation* (12th edn, Sweet and Maxwell 2020) 473 et seq.

violence to the statute.[42] Are sentencers to choose one (or more)? This was Ashworth's view when giving evidence to the House of Commons Justice Select Committee in relation to sentencing: 'because they are contradictory I think it is very difficult to pursue two of them in particular cases, and I think giving the court the choice rather than having a hierarchy of purposes is a mistake.'[43]

This, one can well imagine, permits (or even encourages) disparity; two closely similar cases may result in two wildly different sentences by virtue of the sentencing judges choosing different, competing purposes of sentencing. One may decide to pursue punishment and deterrence, imposing a harsh sentence of immediate custody, whereas another may choose to prioritize rehabilitation, imposing a community order. Parliament has offered no guidance as to how such a situation should be resolved.

Second, the purposes are not defined. Before a court determines which of the purposes of sentencing to pursue in a given case, it must first understand what is meant by each. Parliament has given no steer as to the meaning of, for instance, punishment.[44] Other enactments concerning sentencing use the same or similar terms; for example, a sentencing court has the power to make a reparation order. Section 109 of the Sentencing Act 2020, which makes provision for reparation orders, includes the rather circular definition: '(2) In this Chapter, references to making reparation for an offence are to making reparation for the offence otherwise than by the payment of compensation.'[45] In the absence of clear definitions of concepts which are central to the sentencing exercise, it is clear that Parliament envisages the courts either first instance courts or the CACD or the Sentencing Council, to offer assistance on

---

[42] A phrase relied upon by the courts when considering submissions in relation to statutory interpretation, see eg *R. (Gibson) v Secretary of State for Justice* [2018] UKSC 2; [2018] 1 WLR 629 at [20]

[43] Justice Committee, *Sixth Report Sentencing Guidelines and Parliament: Building a Bridge* HC 2008–2009, 715 at [49]. This view was repeated in Ashworth (n 36), 82.

[44] The same is true of the duty upon a court when imposing a community order; the court must impose a requirement for the purposes of punishment and/or impose a fine: Sentencing Act 2020 s 208(10) and (11). The statute does not define 'punishment' for this purpose and it is simply for the court to consider which requirement in the circumstances of the case satisfy that duty.

[45] It is correct to note that s 111 (further provision in relation to reparation orders) includes reference to 'work' which may be undertaken as part of a reparation order, but there is no further indication of what a reparation order may comprise.

such matters. One can well imagine two judges determining that two identical sentences serving different purposes in different cases, or perhaps even in the same case. In *Attorney General's Reference (R. v Singh)*,[46] the Court concluded that a judge erred in imposing as a requirement to a community order a 'rehabilitation activity requirement' and concluding that this met the statutory requirement that a requirement be imposed for the purposes of punishment. Thus, it seems that while this provision has an element of subjectivity to its application, there are limits to the reasonable range of conclusions to be drawn in each case.[47] The point is this: when such crucial interpretation is left to the subjective judgement of individual courts, there is a veritable invitation to inconsistency. While there has been criticism as to the ineffectiveness of provisions such as section 57,[48] such provisions are frequently referred to by courts and permit sentencers to impose different sentences and justify them by reference to whichever purpose they seek to pursue.

A recent example of this is *Attorney General's Reference (R. v Youngman)*[49] in which the offender had been convicted of misconduct in public office having taken prohibited items into a custodial institution following an inappropriate relationship with an inmate. She had provided a mobile telephone, a psychoactive substance (on three occasions), and letters of a sexual nature. When sentencing, the judge imposed twelve months' imprisonment suspended for two years, with 300 hours of unpaid work. The Attorney General sought leave to refer the sentence under the unduly lenient sentence scheme, under which the CACD could increase a sentence where they consider it to be 'unduly lenient'.[50] The Attorney General submitted that the offence called for a deterrent sentence and that the suspended sentence imposed was unduly lenient and should be increased. The court examined the judge's sentencing remarks,

---

[46] [2021] EWCA Crim 1426.
[47] Though perhaps this isn't as ill-considered as first appears. As was suggested in *R. v Williscroft* [1975] VR 292 at [300], 'No sentencing principle or factor is decisive in every case. The purposes of punishment vary from offender to offender and from crime to crime.'
[48] Ashworth and Kelly (n 36) 66–67.
[49] [2016] EWCA Crim 2224.
[50] For a summary of the unduly lenient sentence scheme, see Lyndon Harris 'Evaluating 30 Years of the Unduly Lenient Sentence Scheme: Attorney General's References 1988–2017' [2018] Criminal Law Review 370.

noting that the judge had considered a number of mitigating features and decided that an immediate custodial sentence was not necessary. The court concluded that the judge's conclusion was open to him, declined to find that the sentence was unduly lenient and accordingly refused the reference. Therefore, the risk of inconsistency is not just a theoretical possibility but a practical reality.

A recent independent report into the Sentencing Council suggested a sentencing guideline concerning what is now section 57 and argued that future sentencing guidelines (including offence-specific guidelines) should be informed by 'research evidence on consequences', given section 57 includes some consequentialist purposes.[51] This demonstrates a need for others to step in to provide additional guidance. It is unclear whether this was contemplated by Parliament, however as will become clear in the following chapters, it is clearly within the remit of both the CACD and the Sentencing Council to do so. Parliament should provide further guidance to aid a more consistent application of these provisions in a bid to curb the inconsistency which it is clear exists in practice at present.

Which sentences may be imposed for which offences?

Perhaps Parliament's most significant contribution to the structuring of discretion at sentencing is by prescribing the ways in which the state may respond to a criminal conviction. This is achieved by two principal means: (i) legislation setting the available penalties for particular offences; and (ii) the legislation creating the sentences which form part of a sentencing court's arsenal. To this should be added the limited role of the common law in both prescribing the availability of certain sentences, and in determining the nature and extent of sentences which may be imposed for certain offences.[52]

---

[51] Sir Anthony Bottoms and AR (Jo) Parsons, 'The Sentencing Council in 2017: A Report on Research to Advise on How the Sentencing Council Can Best Exercise Its Statutory Functions' (Office of the Sentencing Council 2017) 30 et seq.

[52] For instance, the Crown Court has an inherent jurisdiction to impose a sentence of imprisonment, subject to any limitations placed upon it by Parliament, see Senior Courts Act 1981 s 45 which expressly reserved the common law powers extant prior to the Act.

The maximum sentence available for particular offences

For all statutory offences (and some common law offences),[53] Parliament has set down a maximum sentence. This prescribes whether or not an offence is imprisonable, that is an offender convicted of that offence is liable to a term of imprisonment, the maximum length of any such imprisonment, and (usually) whether a fine may be imposed alongside any term of imprisonment. Where an offence is not imprisonable, the statute states that a fine is available, either by reference to an amount or by reference to a level on the 'standard scale'.[54] For those common law offences for which Parliament has not specifically prescribed a maximum sentence but instead designated that the sentence is 'at large', the maximum penalty is life imprisonment.[55]

Parliament therefore imposes limitations by restricting the ability to impose a level of sentence of a particular severity, thereby giving a steer as to its view as to the seriousness of offences and offence types. This is to be seen in conjunction with the provisions listed earlier concerning proportionality; here we see that maximum sentences perform both a limiting function (as described earlier) and a guiding function providing guidance as to the cardinally proportionate sentence (in concert with the general provisions already discussed). But is this sufficient?

The ability of maximum sentences to structure the sentencing decisions is recognized by scholars such as von Hirsch, who observed that such provisions may provide guidance as to the relative seriousness of offences of the same, or even different types.[56] This is acknowledged by the courts; for example the High Court of Australia has described them as 'guideposts'.[57] Kelly suggests that such comparisons—say, between

---

[53] For example, murder (see the Murder (Abolition of Death Penalty) Act 1965 s 1, manslaughter (see the Offences against the Person Act 1861 s 5) and conspiracy to defraud (see the Criminal Law Act 1977 s 3).
[54] See the Criminal Justice Act 1982 s 37.
[55] For example, perverting the course of justice (see Public Justice Offences incorporating the Charging Standard, CPS Legal Guidance, Crown Prosecution Service <https://www.cps.gov.uk/legal-guidance/public-justice-offences-incorporating-charging-standard> accessed 1 January 2022; and misconduct in public office (see Misconduct in public office, CPS Legal Guidance, Crown Prosecution Service <https://www.cps.gov.uk/legal-guidance/misconduct-public-office> accessed 1 January 2022). This is so unless the Sentencing Act 2020 s 223 applies, which limits the maximum penalty to two years where it is not otherwise limited or expressed to be life imprisonment.
[56] Andreas von Hirsch, 'Proportionality in the Philosophy of Punishment' (1992) 16 Crime and Justice 55, 77.
[57] *Muldrock v The Queen* [2011] HCA 39; (2011) 244 CLR 120, at [27].

rape which has a maximum sentence of life imprisonment and theft which has a maximum sentence of seven years—allow one to conclude that the maximum sentence for offence X is too low when compared with the maximum sentences for offences Y and Z.[58] This is of course relative rather than absolute; the latter would presume that offences Y and Z had cardinally proportionate maximum sentences. Yet such comparisons may inform the disposal of individual cases: what level of sentence should a (comparatively) high seriousness theft receive as compared with a (comparatively) low seriousness rape? While such comparisons may inform the disposal of a case (the rape should receive a more severe sentence than the theft, or vice versa), such guidance is unhelpfully vague. Kelly suggests—in the context of reforms of maximum sentences—that comparison is not a replacement for consideration of why our views as to the gravity of an offence have changed, but an aid to it.[59] Kelly subtly suggests that this is perhaps an idealistic view; perhaps such comparisons *ought* to be an aid to such an analysis, but in a climate where criminal justice policy is increasingly politicized, reforms to maximum sentences (rare as they are) are brought about in an *ad hoc* manner without wholesale review, can any weight be placed upon maximum sentences? Such scepticism would seem to be justified.

Can maximum sentences offer any other guidance? In (comparatively) high seriousness cases, the common law was clear that judges may compare the 'most serious example of the offence' against the case for which they must impose sentence in order to inform them as to how serious the instant offence is for the purpose of imposing sentence.[60] Accordingly, the maximum sentence may provide some guidance in the form of providing an anchoring point for cardinal proportionality. Yet this, too, is problematic. First, there is the obvious issue of subjectivity; when is a case in the

---

[58] Rory Kelly, 'Reforming Maximum Sentences and Respecting Ordinal Proportionality' [2018] Criminal Law Review 450.
[59] *Muldrock v The Queen* [2011] HCA 39; (2011) 244 CLR 120, at [27].
[60] See eg *R. v Pinto* [2006] EWCA Crim 749; [2006] 2 Cr App R (S) 87. This has been refined over time and the generally understood position now appears to be that the maximum sentence is not reserved for the most serious example of the offence, but that it is necessary to consider the worst type of offence which comes before the court and ask themselves whether the particular case they are dealing with comes within the broad band of that type. For more detail, see HHJ Lucraft QC (ed), *Archbold Criminal Pleading, Evidence and Practice 2022* (Sweet and Maxwell 2021) § 5A–649 et seq.

bracket of the most serious cases of its type? Is this based on experience (in which case it is almost infinitely variable, depending on a number of factors), is it an exercise in conceiving of the worst possible case, or a hybrid of the two? If based on experience (in whole or in part), then the criticisms of an approach akin to that of 'instinctive synthesis'—the process by which all relevant factors are simultaneously evaluated by the sentencing judge favoured in Australia[61]—must surely apply. Irrespective of one's view of the propriety of instinctive synthesis as an approach to sentence, even the most ardent defender of instinctive synthesis accepts that further guidance than mere 'intuition' is needed: 'A sentence can only be the product of human judgment, based on all the facts of the case, the judge's experience, the data derived from comparable sentences and the guidelines and principles authoritatively laid down in statutes and authoritative judgments.'[62] Similar considerations apply if the exercise is performed by imagining the fictional 'worst case'; individuals will inevitably concoct different factual scenarios of varying seriousness which will be said to be 'the worst', and so the attendant problems of individualization exist. Further, the concept of a bracket of 'the worst' types of case to come before the courts is surely fluid: the worst case is only the worst case until a case arises which is worse still. Not only may this be influenced by one's experiences as a practitioner or a judge[63] but is subject to change.

A further complication is that maximum sentences fail to keep pace with change caused by non-legal factors. Take drug supply as an example; changes in the purity of drugs sold on the street will vary the seriousness of the band of worst cases likely to come before the courts. Perhaps a simpler example is that of acquisitive crime. Changes in the value of money, both as a result of inflation but also the relative health of the economy, constantly adjust where the theft of £100 falls on the scale of seriousness for the offence of theft.

---

[61] For a brief discussion of instinctive synthesis, see Arie Freiberg and Sarah Krasnostein, 'Pursuing Consistency in an Individualistic Sentencing Framework: If You Know Where You're Going, How Do You Know When You've Got There?' (2013) 76 Law and Contemporary Problems 265, 268.
[62] *Markarian v The Queen* [2005] H.C.A. 25; (2005) 228 CLR 357, at [52] (High Court of Australia).
[63] Which of itself is another source of guidance in addition to the maximum sentence provided by Parliament, it is right to note.

But even supposing that there was unanimity as to the 'worst' type of case likely to come before the courts, there remains the significant hurdle of applying that to the instant case to the sentenced. This is reliant on the individual's assessment of the seriousness of the offence in light of the worst-case example thought of. As has already been considered, the assessment of seriousness by reference to retributive proportionality is an imprecise concept which lends itself to inconsistency when reliance is placed upon the very limited guidance given by Parliament in section 63 of the Sentencing Act 2020.

Even if one considers that the challenges outlined in the preceding paragraphs could be overcome, that is based on the significant assumption that the maxima provided by Parliament are correct relative to one another in a cardinally proportionate fashion. The strongest claim that can therefore be made is that maximum sentences provided by Parliament *may* be able to provide *some* guidance as to the imposition of sentences. It seems as though such guidance is of limited utility.

In its 1978 report, *Sentences of Imprisonment*, the Advisory Council on the Penal System conducted an extensive review into the structure of maximum sentences, its terms of reference being to assess the extent to which the structure and level of maximum sentences operate as a guide to sentencing practice.[64] The report advocated a two-tier system of sentencing, reducing the maximum for the majority of cases for a particular offence, but allowing sentences in excess of that maximum for exceptionally grave cases.

The report attracted criticism from scholars. One such critic regarded its major flaw to exist in the assumption, which as at the heart of the Report, that maximum penalties have any great relevance to the sentences actually imposed.[65] Wasik and Pease suggest that it is generally accepted that maximum sentences are irrelevant to the control of judicial sentencing.[66] This seems somewhat of an overstatement, given the inescapable limiting effect of maxima on judicial discretion; did the

---

[64] Advisory Council on the Penal System, *Sentences of Imprisonment: A Review of Maximum Penalties* (Home Office 1978).
[65] J.E. Hall Williams, 'The Advisory Council Report: Sentences of Imprisonment' (1978) 18(4) British Journal of Criminology 396.
[66] Martin Wasik, 'Time to Repeal the Firearms Minimum Sentence Provision' [2017] Criminal Law Review 203.

reduction of the maximum sentence for theft from ten to seven years not impact upon judicial decision making, for example?[67] Perhaps the better point is that maxima cannot adequately structure sentencing discretion or provide meaningful guidance as to the determination of sentence. Maximum sentences thus serve a dual purpose. They have a guiding effect upon the court's discretion, operating as an indication of seriousness by providing guidance as to the cardinally proportionate sentence; this is in conjunction with the 'seriousness' provisions which provide for a framework within which to assess the ordinally proportionate sentence. They also have a limiting effect, acting as an inviolable limit beyond which a sentence for a single offence may not go. It is notable however that while this places constraint on the discretion of the court in cases of (relative) high seriousness (thereby impacting upon the sentence to be imposed) all other cases beneath the highest level of seriousness are left without much by way of guidance. Considering the provisions together, as one must, it appears that the Parliament has provided guidance as to the proportionate sentence. Yet this assessment remains vague and subjective. For example, how serious is a serious robbery? How culpable is offence X when considered against offence Y? How near to the maximum sentence should the sentence be? The statutes therefore provide an overarching but limited structure, yet this is perhaps symptomatic of the fact that the concept of proportionality is considered to be imprecise.[68] Again, more is needed from the other actors at play.

Availability of sentencing orders

Aside from continuing to make imprisonment an available sentence,[69] Parliament has created various types of sentences and orders on

---

[67] While it certainly limited the discretion to impose sentences of between seven and ten years, the answer to the empirical question, did sentencers interpret the change as a change in cardinal proportionality, is unknown.
[68] Most notably by Norval Morris. See Richard S Frase 'Theories of Proportionality and Desert' in Joan Petersilia and Kevin R Reitz (eds), *The Oxford Handbook of Sentencing and Corrections* (OUP 2012) 134, for a consideration of proportionality in retributive and non-retributive theories.
[69] As noted above, the Crown Court has an inherent jurisdiction to impose imprisonment; the magistrates' courts have a limited power to impose imprisonment by virtue of s 32 of the Magistrates' Courts Act 1980.

conviction.[70] There has been a proliferation of sentences and ancillary orders over the past twenty-five years or so, providing courts with a wider range of orders which may be imposed in consequence of a conviction. Whereas in the Victorian era, available sentences included execution by hanging, imprisonment, and transportation (to one of the British colonies),[71] in the twenty-first century, a sentencing court's arsenal now includes a range of community penalties with requirements variously designed to effect rehabilitation, treatment and punishment,[72] a multitude of 'ancillary orders' principally designed to prevent further offending,[73] and orders of a compensatory nature.[74]

This clearly impacts upon a court's discretion at sentencing by providing sentencing courts with a wide array of options—wider than ever before—spanning various purposes of sentencing.[75] Parliament has, however, limited the availability of certain orders, thereby curtailing the otherwise extremely wide discretion created by the sheer number of orders which may be made following a conviction for a criminal offence. Examples of this include by limiting the availability of particular orders to

---

[70] The distinction between a 'sentence' and an 'order' available on conviction is somewhat unclear. It stems from the Criminal Appeal Act 1968 s 50 which provides a right of appeal against a 'sentence'. There appears to have been some concern regarding so-called ancillary orders and their designation as 'sentences'; the avoidance of such a label relieves sentencing courts from the limitations of the criminal hearsay rules and the prohibition on retroactive penalties, see Lucraft, *Archbold Criminal Pleading, Evidence and Practice 2022* (n 60) § 5A–912.

[71] When the colonies refused to accept prisoners in 1853, sentences of transportation were converted into sentences of hard labour. See Victorian Prisons and Punishments, British Library, 14 October 2009 <https://www.bl.uk/victorian-britain/articles/victorian-prisons-and-punishments> accessed 1 January 2022.

[72] For example, the community order which is a non-custodial sentence enabling the court to impose one or more 'requirements' which must be completed or adhered to during the currency of the order, see the Sentencing Act 2020 ss 200–220.

[73] For example, the sexual harm prevention order which is a behaviour order which imposes limitations on the behaviour of a person convicted of certain offences such as to not be in the sole company of a child, or to only use devices capable of accessing the internet which have the ability to retain browsing history and not to delete that history, see the Sentencing Act 2020 ss 343–358, the criminal behaviour order which is an order which places prohibitions on the behaviour of a person who has engaged in behaviour that caused or was likely to cause harassment, alarm or distress to any person where it will help in preventing the offender from engaging in such behaviour, see the Sentencing Act 2020 ss 330–342, and the forfeiture of any item which relates to a drug trafficking offence, see the Misuse of Drugs Act 1971 s 27.

[74] For example, the compensation order which is designed to compensate victims of injury or loss in cases where the issue of liability is simple, see the Sentencing Act 2020 ss 133–146, and the statutory surcharge which is a financial order designed to recoup funds to finance victim support services, see the Sentencing Act 2020 ss 42–43.

[75] A discussion of the statutory purposes of sentencing follows later in this chapter.

cases in which there is a conviction for a particular offence.[76] By adopting such an approach, Parliament has structured, by way of limitation, the discretion afforded to sentencing courts. However, this is not so for a large number of sentencing orders. For instance, (for an adult) a community order is available where the offence is imprisonable; a criminal behaviour order[77] is available upon conviction for any criminal offence. The same is true of a restraining order,[78] an order for forfeiture of a vehicle,[79] a compensation order,[80] and numerous others.

Even with the limitation placed on the discretion given to sentencing courts by virtue of constraints on availability of certain sentencing orders, there remains a significant discretion as to whether an order should be imposed in a particular case, and if so, in what form. Wasik and Pease noted that despite the influx of legislative provisions and available sentences in the 1980s, there was very little guidance on their appropriate use.[81] The availability of sentences can limit the court's discretion and can do so in a meaningful way, for example making imprisonment unavailable for a particular offence. In some circumstances, however, the availability provides little guidance, for instance where the sentencing range is wide and/or the test for imposition devoid of substance providing guidance on whether the order should be imposed (such as a conditional discharge which may be imposed where it is 'inexpedient to impose punishment'),[82] or where there is no guidance as to the contents of the order (such as community order or sexual harm prevention order).[83]

---

[76] For example, sentences for 'dangerous' offenders are available only following conviction for an offence listed in Schs 18 and 19 to the Sentencing Act 2020 (extended sentences and life sentences, respectively); sexual harm prevention orders are available only following conviction for an offence listed in Sch 3 or 5 to the Sexual Offences Act 2003

[77] See (n 73) above.
[78] Sentencing Act 2020 ss 359–364.
[79] Sentencing Act 2020 ss 152–161.
[80] See (n 74).
[81] Wasik and Pease, *Sentencing Reform* (n 1). This remains the case today: for example, in 2018, the Sentencing Council had to issue a guidance note to sentencers and authors of pre-sentence reports in an attempt to 'correct' the misuse of suspended sentence orders, see Sentencing Council of England and Wales, Chairman's letter to sentencers on imposition of community and custodial sentences, 24 April 2018, <https://www.sentencingcouncil.org.uk/news/item/chairmans-letter-to-sentencers-on-imposition-of-community-and-custodial-sentences/> accessed 1 January 2022.
[82] Sentencing Act 2020 s 80.
[83] Where the court must impose conditions or requirements.

Availability of orders can therefore only ever provide limited guidance as to the exercise of discretion.

Tests for imposing sentencing orders

With the exception of sentences of immediate and suspended custody which will be dealt with shortly, almost all sentencing orders have conditions which must be satisfied prior to their imposition. The 'dangerousness' test for the imposition of an extended determinate sentence or a life sentence under the Sentencing Act 2020 is one such example which requires the court to be satisfied that the offender poses a significant risk of serious harm to members of the public by the commission of further specified offences (specified offences being those listed in Schedule 19 to the Sentencing Act 2020).[84] A further example is the 'necessity' test before a sexual harm prevention order is imposed which requires that the court is satisfied that the order is necessary for the purpose of protecting the public or any particular members of the public from sexual harm from the defendant or protecting children or vulnerable adults generally (or any particular children or vulnerable adults) from sexual harm from the defendant outside of the United Kingdom.[85]

While such tests provide a more concrete steer as to the type of case in which Parliament intended such orders to be imposed, there is a comparative lack of clarity in relation to other orders. For instance, in relation to a suspended sentence order Parliament has provided no guidance as to when such an order should be imposed. Section 277 of the Sentencing Act 2020 states:

(1) This section applies where, in dealing with an offender for an offence, a court passes a sentence of imprisonment.

---

[84] See the Sentencing Act 2020 ss 279 and 285 in respect of those aged twenty-one or over at the date of conviction. For a discussion of the dangerousness regime, see Lyndon Harris and Sebastian Walker, 'Difficulties with Dangerousness: The Timing of the Assessment of Risk—Part 1' [2018] Criminal Law Review 695 and Lyndon Harris and Sebastian Walker, 'Difficulties with Dangerousness: Determining the Appropriate Sentence—Part 2' [2018] Criminal Law Review 782.

[85] See the Sentencing Act 2020 s 346(2)(b).

(2) A suspended sentence order (see section 286) is available in relation to that sentence if the term of the sentence of imprisonment is—
  (a) at least 14 days, but
  (b) not more than 2 years.

Section 286 provides:

(1) A suspended sentence order is an order providing that a sentence of imprisonment or detention in a young offender institution in respect of an offence is not to take effect unless—
  (a) an activation event occurs, and
  (b) a court having power to do so subsequently orders under paragraph 13 of Schedule 16 that the sentence is to take effect.
(2) A suspended sentence order may also specify one or more available community requirements with which the offender must comply during the supervision period.
(3) An activation event occurs if the offender—
  (a) commits another offence in the United Kingdom during the operational period (whether or not punishable with imprisonment), or
  (b) during the supervision period, contravenes any community requirement imposed by the order.

Not only is there no test which must be satisfied before imposition (merely that where imprisonment of between fourteen days and two years, inclusive, is imposed, a suspended sentence order *may* be imposed), but there is no statutory guidance as to when it may be appropriate to impose such an order. It is right to note, however, that the opening words of the provision (requiring the court to have decided to impose a custodial sentence) operate to limit the court's discretion in making a suspended sentence order available only in those prescribed circumstances. Here it is clear that Parliament's intention is for the courts to interpret the provision and self-regulate; the role of the CACD will be explored in the next chapter, but it is evident that Parliament considers there to be a demarcation between matters on which it should provide guidance, and those on which it is for another actor to do so. When compared with the previous regime providing suspended terms of imprisonment (which employed an 'exceptional circumstances' test), it is clear the intention was that a greater number of orders would be imposed.

The same is true of the imposition of fines. There is some debate as to whether the power to impose a fine on conviction on indictment lies in the inherent jurisdiction of the Crown Court (eg it is not in debate that a fine could be imposed for a common law offence), the penalty setting provision of an offence (eg where statute states that an offence carries a term of imprisonment or a fine or both), or in the Sentencing Act 2020 section 120 (discretionary power to impose a fine save where certain mandatory sentences apply). It is, however, perfectly clear that Parliament has, in the provision prescribing the power to impose a fine on indictment, provided no guidance as to when such a sentence is appropriate.[86] Again, it appears clear that the view taken is that it is for the courts to self-regulate in this area.

It is possible therefore, to identify two variables: (i) availability (whether Parliament has, in creating a power to impose an order, set down when it is available, or *ceteris paribus,* the disposal is available in all cases); and (ii) test for imposition (whether or not Parliament has, in creating the power to impose an order, prescribed one or more conditions which must be satisfied before the order may be imposed).

The result is differing degrees of vagueness in the statutory provisions. Availability of orders is comparatively simple. Where Parliament has provided that particular orders are available only in particular cases, that operates as a limitation on courts' discretion; where it has not so provided, the discretion is unbridled. The existence of tests for imposition of such orders is perhaps more problematic. Where there is no test, the court is left to look elsewhere for guidance, otherwise

---

[86] The magistrates' court, a creature of statute, appears to derive its power to impose a fine from the penalty setting provisions, see the Criminal Justice Act 1982 s 37. Section 37 refers to a standard scale of fine levels (each ascribed a monetary value) and states that where a penalty setting provision refers to liability to a fine or a fine no greater than a particular level, the reference to a level is to the corresponding level in the standard scale.

STRUCTURING DISCRETION THROUGH PARLIAMENT 169

one is left with personal judgment as to what is appropriate. Where there is a test, the test invariably provides only limited guidance. For instance, what is meant by a 'significant' risk? When does *mere* harm become 'serious' harm? When is an order 'necessary'? Such tests are, it is suggested, necessarily vague. This provides sufficient flexibility to sentencing courts enabling their application to appropriate cases, without being overly inclusive or unnecessarily restrictive. This utilization of loose language clearly envisages an important role for the courts to play in shaping the boundaries of the statute, intended to provide the courts with the degree of discretion they determine necessary. In this way, there is a degree of self-regulation envisaged by Parliament afforded to the courts.

Earlier in this work, it was suggested that at sentencing, the application of a legal test is not an exercise in discretion as the proper application of principles applicable to the question (eg of whether or not an offender is 'dangerous', or whether or not a sexual harm prevention order is necessary) produces a single, correct result.[87] Such tests do not therefore involve the exercise of discretion (there being no discretion if the application of principles produces a single, correct result). Instead, the provisions operate to constrain the exercise of discretion, making a test capable or incapable of being imposed in a particular case. To take a common example, where the court is faced with the sentencing exercise of an offender convicted of an offence specified in Schedule 18 or 19 to the Sentencing Act 2020, it must consider whether the offender is 'dangerous'. Where it applies the test—whether there is a significant risk of serious harm to members of the public by the commission of the offender of further specified offences, for which Parliament has provided limited guidance as to the interpretation—it may impose an extended sentence. In this way, the test operates to limit the discretion of the court, making the order available only for dangerous offenders. However, the court may still decline to do so as the order is discretionary, not mandatory. A court may decide not to impose an extended sentence where other, less coercive, measures will achieve the same purpose of public

---

[87] See Chapter 5.

protection.[88] This serves as an example of the tripartite provision of guidance and structured discretion: Parliament provides the framework and the general policy intention and leaves the details and specific application to the courts (and sometimes the Sentencing Council).

Aggravation and mitigation

The following discussion proceeds on the basis that sentencers in England and Wales approach sentencing decisions not as their Australian counterparts—simultaneously assessing the seriousness of the offence and weighing the aggravating and mitigating factors in an instinctive fashion[89]—but by a step by step methodology which begins with assessing the harm and culpability inherent in the offence and then, at a second stage, factoring in aggravating and mitigating factors.

Aggravating and mitigating factors can be divided into two categories; those which are mandated by statute and those which are not. This chapter concerns itself only with those Parliament has prescribed to have an aggravating or mitigating effect. This category represents a device used to structure discretion which is comparatively minor when considered against other statutory methods of structuring discretion.[90] There are eight provisions which operate as statutory aggravating factors.

Where an offence was committed while the offender was on bail, the seriousness of the offence will be aggravated by virtue of the Sentencing Act 2020 section 64.[91] Section 66 of the Sentencing Act 2020 requires that where a court finds that an offence was racially or religiously aggravated, or that immediately before, during, or immediately after the offence, the

---

[88] For a recent example, see *R. v Bourke* [2017] EWCA Crim 2150; [2018] 1 Cr App R (S) 42. See also Harris and Walker, 'Difficulties with Dangerousness' (n 84).

[89] For consideration of the concept of instinctive synthesis, see Mirko Bagaric, Richard Edney, and Theo Alexander, *Sentencing in Australia* (Thomson Reuters 2017) 35–50.

[90] It is submitted that the statutory aggravating factors are factors which, if present in a given case, would be unreasonable not to consider increase the seriousness of the offence.

[91] Ashworth and Kelly note that this is a re-statement of a principle which has long been recognized, see Ashworth and Kelly (n 36) 147. They argue that the presence of this factor neither increases the harm caused by the offence nor the culpability of the offender, suggesting that instead, it is capable of justification on the basis of it being an act of defiance of the court or a breach of trust, though one might consider the dual breach of duty (to not commit a criminal offence, to which all citizens are subject, and the additional duty imposed in the agreement to grant bail) constitutes increased culpability.

offender demonstrated hostility based on the victim's (presumed or actual) sexuality or disability or the fact they are (presumed or actually) transgender. Sections 68, 71, and 72 of the Sentencing Act 2020 require that certain features are treated as aggravating the seriousness of specific offences (contained with the respective pieces of legislation).[92] Where an offence has a 'terrorist connection', the court must treat that as an aggravating factor,[93] something which the court would probably do anyway. Finally, there is section 65 of the Sentencing Act 2020 which requires a court to treat previous convictions as aggravating the seriousness of the offence.

In relation to the parts of section 66 concerning disability, transgender identity, or sexual orientation, what may be crudely described as 'general' statutory aggravating factors, it is suggested that the impact has thus far been minimal. A search of legal databases (utilizing no date range) reveals eleven cases which mention the duty concerning race and religion,[94] and twelve which mention the duty concerning disability, sexual orientation, or transgender identity. These are, of course, appellate proceedings only but perhaps indicate the extent to which the provisions are explicitly referenced in proceedings. The important point, however, is that the provisions provide no guidance as to the extent to which the sentence should be increased to reflect the aggravating factor(s). The sentencer has, by this point, decided on the proportionate range of sentences having assessed the seriousness of the offence as required by statute, for example two to four years' custody, and has identified a starting point within that range. It is then necessary to consider the extent of the aggravation (and/or mitigation) and the effect that should have on the proportionate sentence. The only statutory guidance given to sentencers in this endeavour is by virtue of the maximum sentence which provides an upper limit on the sentence which may be imposed, otherwise the sentencer is left to seek guidance from other sources. Again however, this appears to be a

---

[92] Supply of controlled drugs or psychoactive substance near school or involving a child, or the assault or battery of a person exercising the functions of an emergency worker.
[93] Sentencing Act 2020 s 69.
[94] This search concerns the duty under the previous iteration of this part of section 66 (formerly s 145 of the Criminal Justice Act 2003), as the duty under section 66 was only enacted in 2020 and thus it may skew the results to search for section 66 alone. One of the results for s 145 was a civil case in which reference was made to s 145 in the context of linked criminal proceedings.

conscious and principled decision concerning the respective roles of the three main actors in structuring sentencing discretion.[95]

In relation to mitigation, there exists a general provision in section 77 of the Sentencing Act 2020 which serves multiple purposes.[96] Subsection (1) clarifies that the common law power to mitigate a sentence by reference to any factor it considers to be relevant is unaffected by, for example, the provisions pertaining to the imposition of fines, community sentences, and custodial sentences. Subsection (2) permits a court to impose a community order in a case which, save for the factor(s) considered to reduce the seriousness of the offence, crossed the custody threshold. Unsurprisingly, it does not provide a methodology to determine the extent of the reduction for the identified mitigating factor(s). As with the aggravating factors, the sentencer is therefore left to determine the extent to which the mitigating factor reduces the sentence from the starting point alighted upon earlier in the process with any assistance from the CACD or Sentencing Council.

Mitigation and the assessment of its effect upon a sentence is necessarily a rather fluid concept; it calls into question the fundamental approach of the sentencer. As Hough and Jacobson note, a key question is whether justice is best served by sentencing the offence or the offender.[97] Their empirical study identified six overlapping categories of personal mitigation, though it was noted that the categorization was somewhat arbitrary. This speaks to the complex and amorphous nature of mitigation as a concept. They identified at least thirty-six factors of personal mitigation which were present in their sample of 162 sentencing decisions; against that background, it is notable that the statute does not designate which factors have (or even may have) a mitigating effect,[98] nor does it provide guidance as to the approach to determine the effect of such factors on the sentence or the extent to which mitigation could or should alter a sentence.[99]

---

[95] As to which, see (n 455) and *Making Punishments Work: Report of a review of the sentencing framework for England and Wales* (Home Office 2001) § 1.32.
[96] Sentencing Act 2020 s 77(3) will be dealt with later in this chapter.
[97] Mike Hough and Jessica Jacobson, 'Personal Mitigation: An empirical analysis in England and Wales' in Julian V Roberts (ed), *Mitigation and Aggravation at Sentencing* (CUP 2012) 146.
[98] Save for those dealt with in the next section.
[99] Interestingly, an Australian practitioner text identified over 100 aggravating and mitigating factors: see Bagaric, Edney, and Alexander, *Sentencing in Australia* (n 89) 44.

The position is therefore worse—assuming that an absence of guidance is a negative—than with aggravating factors as the statute merely provides in section 77 that the court *may* reduce a sentence for factors it regards as mitigating. The risk of disparity, both inter- and intra-courts is therefore manifest in the absence of statutory guidance. Hough and Jacobson note the 'considerable discretion' which sentencers are afforded in this regard.[100] They note: 'in according significance to certain aggravating or mitigating factors, sentencers are (implicitly) prioritizing certain sentencing rationales over others'.[101] Ashworth and Kelly's criticism of the way in which Parliament has legislated for the purposes of sentencing under the Sentencing Act 2020 section 57 affords sentencers the ability to determine policy and invites inconsistency could be said to apply to mitigation too.[102] Certain factors are more contentious than others. For example, as Padfield notes, one judge might determine that intoxication is an aggravating factor in the commission of an offence whereas another might consider it (on the same facts) to be a mitigating factor.[103] A prominent example which gained attention by the press in England and Wales concerned a case of sexual activity with a child in which it was said by the prosecutor at first instance the fact that the victim, a fourteen-year-old child, had initiated the sexual activity operated to reduce the seriousness of the offence.[104] When referred to the CACD by the Attorney General under the unduly lenient sentence scheme, the court regarded such an approach as an error of judgement and stated that that fact was an aggravating factor.[105]

Young and King, in a comparative piece considering problems arising from different factors at sentencing, note that in lieu of guidance as to mitigation (among other things) judges have to rely on other sources of guidance.[106] Courts are therefore unaided by the statutory regime and

---

[100] Hough and Jacobson, 'Personal Mitigation' (n 97) 156.
[101] ibid 156.
[102] Ashworth and Kelly (n 36) 66–67.
[103] Nicola Padfield, 'Intoxication as a Sentencing Factor: Aggravation or Mitigation?' in Roberts, *Mitigation and Aggravation at Sentencing* (n 97) 81–101.
[104] 'Lawyer who called 13-year-old 'predatory' is barred from sex offence cases', *The Telegraph*, 7 August 2013 <https://www.telegraph.co.uk/news/uknews/crime/10228621/Lawyer-who-called-13-year-old-predatory-is-barred-from-sex-offence-cases.html> accessed 1 January 2022.
[105] *Attorney General's Reference (No 53 of 2013)* [2013] EWCA Crim 2544; [2014] 2 Cr App R (S) 1.
[106] Warren Young and Andrea King, 'Addressing problematic sentencing factors in the development of guidelines' in Roberts (n 97) 211.

the question of whether and to what extent a sentence should be modified for aggravating or mitigating factors returns them to a combination of the 'seriousness' provisions, the maximum sentence for the given offence, and their own intuition; yet each of these sources provides little (if any) accurate guidance in this context. This aspect of the discretionary decision appears to be particularly prone to inconsistency of approach and outcome.

Other factors operating to reduce the severity of a sentence

There are three other factors which may operate to reduce the severity of a sentence: (i) providing information to the authorities regarding other offences; (ii) pleading guilty; and (iii) the mere existence of a number of offences, a cumulative sentence for which would render the overall penalty disproportionate. These will be dealt with briefly in turn.

The first two are non-retributive factors which are generally accepted to be legitimate to the determination of the severity of the penalty imposed for a criminal offence. Slobogin notes (in the context of plea bargaining) that such factors are problematic for desert theorists as they routinely result in disproportionate punishments.[107] Frase notes that this extends beyond the guilty plea and into other forms of cooperation and restitution.[108]

However, in a system such as that prevailing in England and Wales, those factors can be amply justified on the basis that the offender is cooperating with the state in relation to their offence (plea) and other offence(s) (assisting the prosecution). It is accepted that the state should respond to such cooperation. A slightly less positive view of such factors is that they both constitute transactions between offender and the state, with the state 'buying' the cooperation (which results in cost savings in

---

[107] See eg Christopher Slobogin, 'Plea Bargaining and the Substantive and Procedural Goals of Criminal Justice: From Retribution and Adversarialism to Preventive Justice and Hybrid-Inquisitorialism' (2015) William & Mary Law Review, Vanderbilt Public Law Research Paper No 15-4, 4.

[108] Richard S Frase 'Theories of Proportionality and Desert' in Petersilia and Reitz (eds), *The Oxford Handbook of Sentencing and Corrections* (n 68) 134.

STRUCTURING DISCRETION THROUGH PARLIAMENT 175

terms of the investigation and prosecution of offences in addition to the wider social benefits). Slobogin explicitly notes, in the context of US plea bargaining, that efficiency becomes the primary concern; this is a view which can support either interpretation of the rationale for the discount in sentence. The view that the enterprise is transactional is supported by the Sentencing Council's 2017 *Reduction in Sentence for a Guilty Plea* which makes clear that a reduction in sentence for a guilty plea and remorse are divorced from one another, and that the benefits of pleading guilty to an offence are the reduction in cost, the avoidance of witnesses and victims having to give evidence at court, and the reduction of the impact of the offence on victims.[109] There are some, however, who remain of the view that a guilty plea does indicate remorse and that remorse is a factor which underpins the justification of a discount in sentence upon a plea of guilty.[110]

Assisting the prosecution

There are two routes by which the severity of a sentence can be mitigated by virtue of information provided to the prosecuting authorities: one is a create of statute, the other is a creation of the common law. They serve principally the same purpose but for obvious reasons this chapter will concern itself only with the former.[111]

The Serious Organised Crime and Police Act 2005 (SOCPA) created a statutory scheme whereby an offender who pleaded guilty may enter into a written agreement with a prosecutor under which they would assist or offer to assist the investigator or prosecutor. This has since been repealed and re-enacted (see Sentencing Act 2020 section 74 and sections 387–392). In consideration for that assistance, the court might take that into account in determining what sentence to

---

[109] Sentencing Council, *Reduction in Sentence for a Guilty Plea Definitive Guideline* (Office of the Sentencing Council 2017) 4.
[110] Fiona Leverick, 'Sentence Discounting for Guilty Pleas: An Argument for Certainty over Discretion' [2014] Criminal Law Review 338, 338.
[111] For a discussion of the two regimes see Lucraft (n 60) § 5A-107 and the decisions in *R. v A* [1999] 1 Cr App R (S) 52 and *R. v P; R. v Blackburn* [2007] EWCA Crim 2290; [2008] 2 All ER 684.

pass on the offender, often granting a substantial reduction in the severity of a sentence. The scheme is not confined to offenders who provided assistance in relation to crimes in which they were participants or accessories.[112]

The statute offers no assistance as to the manner in which the sentence may be mitigated (can it merely change the severity of a penalty, or the nature of it too?), the methodology which ought to be followed, nor the extent to which the sentence ought to be reduced. In this way, this factor is similar to the assessment of aggravating factors noted earlier, and similar observations about the dearth of guidance so as to achieve an appropriate, and consistent result apply. The courts are once more forced to look to the CACD and the Sentencing Council for further assistance.

Guilty plea

The reduction in sentence for a guilty plea is a mandatory factor which reduces the severity of a sentence. By virtue of section 73 of the Sentencing Act 2020:

> The court must take into account the following matters—
> (a) the stage in the proceedings for the offence at which the offender indicated the intention to plead guilty, and
> (b) the circumstances in which the indication was given.[113]

But Parliament has provided no guidance as to the extent to which a guilty plea should be reflected in the sentence: it is unclear how the various stages at which a plea may be entered should impact the sentence imposed, similarly it is unclear the circumstances which may be relevant

---

[112] *R. v P; R. v Blackburn* [2007] EWCA Crim 2290; [2008] 2 All ER 684; and more recently, *Re Loughlin* [2017] UKSC 63; [2017] 1 WLR 3963.

[113] Interestingly, this is in stark contrast to Scotland. Leverick notes that '[i]n England and Wales, sentencers are required to start from the presumption that a discount will be awarded, whereas in Scotland there now exists a presumption against a discount unless there are convincing reasons to justify it'. See Fiona Leverick, 'Sentence Discounting for Guilty Pleas: An Argument for Certainty over Discretion' [2014] Criminal Law Review 338, 338.

to the issue, and the nature and extent of the reduction. This absence of guidance from Parliament clearly risks of inconsistency.[114] Simply following the statute (excluding non-statutory guidance for the time being), a court may award any discount upon a plea of guilty.[115] Although this point applies to, for example, the discount for providing assistance to the prosecution, and to aggravation and mitigation, the risk of disparity is more pronounced in the context of guilty pleas. This is due to the sheer scale of the guilty plea as a factor reducing the severity of a sentence, both in terms of its frequency and the extent of the reduction.[116]

Totality and multiple offences

The sentencing of multiple offences should not be overlooked. In their recent work on multiple offences, Roberts, Ryberg, and de Keiser note that the Sentencing Council estimate that 40 per cent of sentencing decisions involve multiple offences.[117] Additionally, Jareborg regards the sentencing of the multiple offences as 'the most complicated topic in criminal law'.[118] With such complexity and prevalence, the need for structure in the discretionary decision-making of sentencing courts is all the more important. The sentencing of an offender for multiple offences requires a careful calibration of differing, perhaps overlapping offences with inevitably varying degrees of seriousness. It is generally accepted in England and Wales that adopting an approach of establishing the proportionate sentences for each individual offence cumulating them may produce a result which is disproportionate to the entirety of the offending. For example, ten rapes each worth, individually, ten years' imprisonment will not be met with 100 years' imprisonment. Roberts, Ryberg, and de Keiser

---

[114] See earlier in relation to the wider application of Ashworth and Kelly's criticism of s 57 of the Sentencing Act 2020.
[115] Subject to the mandatory sentences for which Sentencing Act 2020 s 73 is modified.
[116] The coalition government (2010–2015) explored permitting reductions of up to 50 per cent (up from 33 per cent) though they were later dropped: 'Ken Clarke forced to abandon 50% sentence cuts for guilty pleas', *The Guardian*, 21 June 2011 <https://www.theguardian.com/law/2011/jun/20/ken-clarke-abandon-sentence-cuts> accessed 1 January 2022.
[117] Julian V Roberts, Jesper Ryberg, and Jan W de Keiser, 'Sentencing the Multiple Offender: Setting the Stage' in Julian V Roberts, Jesper Ryberg, and Jan W de Keiser (eds), *Sentencing Multiple Crimes* (OUP 2017) 1.
[118] Nils Jareborg, 'Why Bulk Discounts in Sentencing?' in Andrew Ashworth and Martin Wasik (eds), *Fundamentals of Sentencing Theory: Essays in Honour of Andrew von Hirsch* (Clarendon Press 1998) 57

note that the result would be simplistic sentencing policy which would see a 'crushing' prison sentence imposed.[119]

This is where the principle of totality comes into play; totality provides that in a multiple offence case it may be necessary to reduce the total of the otherwise proportionate sentences imposed on the individual offences to ensure overall proportionality with the totality of the offending. While beautifully simple, its application in practice (and, too, its theoretical justification) is devilishly complex.[120] So, how to calculate the seriousness of multiple offences? Recourse must be made to the general principles concerning the determination of seriousness. Yet, (perhaps unsurprisingly) the vagueness of proportionality in relation to a single offence is compounded when considering multiple offences. For example, if the proportionate range for offence A is two to four years, and the proportionate range for offence B is eighteen months to three years, then range is widened from eighteen months or two years, to two years six months.

Parliament recognizes (though does not define) the principle of totality in section 77(3) and (5) of the Sentencing Act 2020, which state:

(3) Nothing in any of the basis of opinion provisions prevents a court—
  (a) from mitigating any penalty included in an offender's sentence by taking into account any other penalty included in that sentence, and
  (b) in the case of an offender who is convicted of one or more other offences, from mitigating the offender's sentence by applying any rule of law as to the totality of sentences.

...

(5) In this section 'basis of opinion provision' means any of the following—
  (a) section 30 or 33 (pre-sentence reports and other requirements);
  (b) section 124, 125 or 126 (fixing of fine);

---

[119] Roberts, Ryberg, and de Keiser, 'Sentencing the Multiple Offender' (n 117) 3.
[120] This depends on the basis on which the principle is sought to be defendant. Roberts, Ryberg, and de Keiser note that for desert theorists, two bases have been advanced. First, overall proportionality, namely that no number of less serious offences can be as serious as a single incident of an offence of a more serious type. Secondly, the concept of mercy or humanity. See Roberts, Ryberg, and de Keiser (n 117) 6–9.

(c) section 179, 180 or 186(3) to (9) (exercise of power to impose youth rehabilitation order, with or without intensive supervision and surveillance or fostering, and other requirements);
(d) section 204 or 208(3) to (9) (exercise of power to impose community order, and community requirements);
(e) section 230, 231 or 232 (imposing custodial sentences).

It can be seen that the concept is not defined and there is no indication as to how this 'rule of law' should be applied. The court is left to consider other avenues for guidance as to whether, and if so, the extent to which, a sentence should be reduced to account for the principle of totality.

Minimum and mandatory sentences

Minimum and mandatory sentencing provisions—requiring the imposition of a particular sentence type or type and length—operate as a limiting measure upon the discretion generally afforded to sentencing courts by prescribing that certain cases are disposed of in a particular fashion. In some cases, discretion is removed entirely, in others it is merely constrained. There are three variables: (i) the nature of the sentence; (ii) the severity of the sentence; and (iii) whether there exists what might be termed an 'escape clause' which enables the court to avoid imposing the sentence ordinarily required by the statute.

It is helpful to place the statutory provisions which mandate the imposition of a particular sentence into two categories: (i) where the nature and length of the sentence is mandated by the statute ('minimum sentences'); and (ii) where the nature of the sentence is mandated by the statute 'mandatory sentences'). It is possible to subdivide the second category into those orders which include an escape clause and those which do not.

Minimum sentences

There are five provisions imposing minimum sentence requirements for a range of offences currently in force in England and Wales that fall into the description of 'minimum sentences' above.[121] The provisions require the imposition of a sentence of a prescribed nature (custody) for a prescribed period (from four months to seven years, depending on the provision, the plea, and the age of the offender).

These provisions can be sub-divided once more: there are provisions which apply to single offences, in other words where a conviction for a single offence is sufficient to attract the minimum sentence, and there are those which apply to repeat offenders, that is where the offender is convicted of an offence in circumstance where they have a previous conviction for a relevant offence at the time of the commission of the new offence. Falling into the former category are offences of possession of prohibited firearms, possession of a bladed article in a public place, threatening with a bladed article in a public place or on school premises, threatening with an offensive weapon in a public place.[122] Falling into the latter category are third domestic burglary, a third Class A drug trafficking offence, possession of an offensive weapon in a public place where the offender has previously been convicted of a relevant offence, and possession of a bladed article or offensive weapon on school premises where the offender has been previously convicted of a relevant offence.[123]

The objection to such minimum sentences in a proportionality based system is that, by design, they require the imposition of a disproportionate sentence. Where a minimum sentence applies, there are three potential scenarios: (i) the proportionate sentence exceeds the minimum; (ii) the proportionate sentence is equal to the minimum; and (iii) the proportionate sentence is beneath the minimum. In the first and second scenarios, the minimum is therefore ineffective, not (in theory) having any impact upon the determination of the proportionate sentence. Only in the third scenario does the minimum have such an impact, and that impact is to require the imposition of a sentence in excess of that which is proportionate. Minimum sentences therefore undermine the principle of proportionality and in a manner adverse to the offender.

---

[121] That figure is correct at 1 January 2022. There is another minimum sentence provision in relation to the possession of corrosive fluid which is enacted but not yet brought into force and others proposed at the time of writing.

[122] Sentencing Act 2020 s 311 (prohibited weapons); and s 312 (threatening with bladed article or offensive weapon).

[123] Sentencing Act 2020 s 313 (repeat Class A drug-trafficking offence); and s 314 (repeat domestic burglary offence); s 315 (repeat offence involving weapon or bladed article).

Now turning to the details, the regimes vary slightly in their operation. For instance, the majority permit a reduction in sentence for a guilty plea (to a figure not less than 80 per cent of the required sentence length), however the prohibited weapon minimum sentence does not permit a reduction for a guilty plea and the bladed articles and offensive weapons minimum sentence permit any sentence to be imposed where a sixteen or seventeen year old pleads guilty to such an offence.[124] This causes problems for proportionality; accepting that for a limiting retributivist, a guilty plea is a factor which operates to mitigate sentence severity,[125] limiting the discretion of the sentencer to reflect the fact of a guilty plea may produce a disproportionately severe sentence. Where otherwise an offender may receive a discount of 33 per cent, the limiting nature of this element of the minimum sentence regime may reduce that to a very small percentage indeed.[126] While there may be consistency with offences of the same type and with co-defendants convicted of the same offence, the approach taken by Parliament creates inconsistency between those convicted of these offences and those who plead guilty, and those who plead guilty to these offences and those who plead guilty to other offences.

Another crucial difference was that while all of the minimum sentence provisions included an escape clause, the statutory test differed. The majority required the presence of 'particular circumstances' which would make the imposition of the minimum sentence unjust before the court is released from the obligation to impose the required sentence; however, the prohibited weapons minimum sentences require the presence of 'exceptional circumstances'. Neither exceptional nor particular circumstances making the imposition of the sentence unjust were defined by the statute. Wasik notes that in addition to the difference in language, each has been construed differently by the courts, with the latter being interpreted to be a more stringent test.[127]

---

[124] See the Sentencing Act 2020 ss 73 and 312.
[125] For example, see Hough and Jacobson (n 97) 43.
[126] For instance, a guilty plea in a case to which the three-year minimum sentence for a third domestic burglary may result in a discount of *circa* seven months.
[127] Martin Wasik, 'Time to Repeal the Firearms Minimum Sentence Provision?' [2017] Criminal Law Review 302. Amendments brought into force on 28 June 2022 by the Policing, Crime, Sentencing and Courts Act 2022 standardized the 'escape clause' tests across the minimum sentence provisions, each now adopting the 'exceptional circumstances' formulation. 'Exceptional' remains undefined.

Further, there is significant variance between the minimum sentences when the level of the required sentence is considered as a proportion of the maximum sentence. Some offences which attract the minimum sentence under Sentencing Act 2020 section 313 have maximum sentences of life imprisonment, whereas some have a maximum of fourteen years' imprisonment.[128] This of course makes the imposition of a minimum seven-year sentence inconsistent dependent upon the offence of conviction. By contrast, the bladed article and offensive weapons minimum sentences (encompassing both the 'single offence' provisions and the 'repeat offender' provisions) all apply to offences carrying a maximum of four years' imprisonment. The minimum sentence of six months for an adult therefore represents 12.5 per cent of the maximum sentence (out of step with the 50 per cent figure for some of the Class A drugs provisions). Here, however, there is no distinction between the 'single offence' and 'repeat offender' provisions.[129] The three-year minimum sentence for a third domestic burglary offence operates at just over 21 per cent of the maximum sentence of fourteen years. This is, again, inconsistent with the others. This very brief exposition of the inconsistencies among the various minimum sentences reveals that the provisions present challenges—to say the least—for a proportionate approach to sentencing.[130] That causes, in consequence inconsistency inter- and intra-offences and inter- and intra-individual cases.

Returning to the thrust of this chapter, minimum sentences provide some structure to the court's discretion at sentencing by limiting the range of sentences which are available to it. Wasik noted the decision of the Canadian Supreme Court in *Nur* held that:

> mandatory minimum sentences ... function as a blunt instrument that may deprive courts of the ability to tailor proportionate sentences [and]

---

[128] See Sentencing Act 2020 s 313 and Proceeds of Crime Act 2002 Sch 2 para.1.
[129] This chapter does not explore potential justification for such disparity however *prima facie* it appears that it is not capable of justification.
[130] One might consider that in fact, minimum sentences operate as a correction to cardinal proportionality in that Parliament has told the courts how serious particular offences are. The better view appears to be that minimum sentence provisions trump the principle of proportionality as the principles of sentencing in s 57 of the Sentencing Act 2020 are disapplied to minimum sentence provisions (see s 57(3) and s 399 of the Sentencing Act 2020).

they may, in extreme cases, impose unjust sentences, because they shift the focus from the offender during the sentencing process in a way that violates the principle of proportionality.[131]

Mandatory sentences

Mandatory sentences—those which prescribe the imposition of a particular sentence type—exist at various levels in the hierarchy of disposals available to a sentencing court. These sentences fall into one of three categories: first, those for which the imposition of the sentence is mandatory where the relevant conditions (objectively assessed) are met; secondly those for which the imposition of the sentence is mandatory where the relevant conditions (objectively and subjectively assessed) are met; and thirdly, those where the sentence is mandatory where the relevant conditions are met subject to an 'escape clause' to prevent manifestly unjust results.

The mandatory life sentence for murder is the only sentence which falls into the first category. Where an offender is convicted of murder, the only sentence available is one of life.[132] The sentencer has no discretion as to the nature of the sentence but may determine the length of the minimum term imposed in conjunction with the sentence.[133] Before 2003, the trial judge would suggest a minimum term to be imposed alongside the mandatory life sentence. This would then be reviewed by the Lord Chief Justice, before passing to the Home Secretary who would finally impose the sentence. Following a challenge to the lawfulness of political actors involving themselves in the determination of specific criminal cases, Parliament enacted Schedule 21 to the Criminal Justice Act 2003 (since repealed and re-enacted, happily, as Schedule 21 to the Sentencing Act 2020) which set out a sentencing guideline of sorts for murder cases. The Schedule provided a series of 'starting points' which

---

[131] [2015] 1 RCS 773 at [44], cited in Wasik, 'Time to Repeal the Firearms Minimum Sentence Provision?' (n 127) 206.

[132] The nature of the sentence is determined by the age of the offender at conviction and/or sentence, see Lyndon Harris, 'Age of Offender and Availability of Sentences' in *Thomas' Sentencing Referencer* 2022 (Sweet and Maxwell 2021) § 71.

[133] See Murder (Abolition of Death Penalty) Act 1965 s 1 and Sentencing Act 2020 ss 259, 275, and 321, and Sch 21.

would 'normally' apply to cases of a type described in each paragraph. One view is that this increased the discretion afforded to sentencing judges as they have the final determination of the minimum term to be imposed, though one would be forgiven for considering Schedule 21 to be Parliament overstepping the mark by providing a sentencing guideline in all but name, albeit a rather rudimentary guideline at that.

Into the second category falls the discretionary life sentence for dangerous offenders, the special custodial sentence for offenders of particular concern, the special terrorism sentence, and the referral order.[134] It is unnecessary to delve into the details of each order; suffice it to say that each relies not upon a discretion but on a judgement as to an aspect of the order. All require a determination of the seriousness of the offence (as to which see earlier in this chapter) prior to its imposition to determine whether the custody threshold is crossed, and if so, the appropriate length of the custodial sentence. Upon the resolution of that determination, the order is either mandatory or does not apply.[135]

Into the final category falls the 'two strikes' life sentence which requires a determination of the seriousness of the offence to determine whether the provision applies to a particular case but is also subject to an 'escape clause' whereby the court is released from its obligation to impose the sentence where it considers that do to so would be unjust.[136] This provision can require a life sentence to be imposed where neither the previous offence nor the new offence warrant, on proportionality grounds, a life sentence and even in circumstances where neither offence carry life as a maximum.[137] This is a significant limitation of discretion. While it would be entirely possible for a court to determine in such a case that it would be unjust to do so and apply the escape clause, it cannot have been Parliament's intention that that would be the approach in every case. If that were the intention it would have been simple to draft an exclusion

---

[134] With the exception of the referral order, one might note the label given to these orders in the context of the aforementioned politicization of sentencing.

[135] See the Sentencing Act 2020 ss 258, 274, 285 ('dangerousness life'); ss 252A, 265, 278 (offenders of particular concern); ss 268A and 282A (serious terrorism sentence) and s 83 (referral order).

[136] See the Sentencing Act 2020 ss 273 and 283 (and a similar historic provision still in force, Powers of Criminal Courts (Sentencing) Act 2000 s 109).

[137] *Attorney General's Reference (No.27 of 2013) (R. v Burinskas)* [2014] EWCA Crim 334; [2014] 2 Cr App R (S) 45. [2014] 2 Cr App R (S) 45 at [8].

for those offences to which the provision applies not having life as a maximum sentence.

Another provision worthy of mention is sections 233–248 of the Sentencing Act 2020 which prescribes the length of a detention and training order (DTO) to be imposed on an offender aged ten to seventeen years at conviction.[138] The section provides that the length of a DTO must be one of the following: four, six eight, ten, twelve, eighteen, and twenty-four months. The effect of this is to remove a degree of the court's discretion. At the lower end of seriousness, this is of little consequence as there it is generally accepted that proportionality is not precise as to differentiate with any appreciable degree of accuracy between four months and five months. However, at the upper end, the difference is greater. If a court decided that twenty-four months was too much, but eighteen was too little, then the lower amount must be imposed.[139] The purpose of these specified periods is administrative rather than borne of any desire to limit the discretion of the court, however. This is because as a youth sentence of detention involving 'training' (which addresses, *inter alia*, anger management, relationship issues, education and work), the sentence includes the provision of set programmes. Accordingly, an *ad hoc* approach to the time an offender spends in custody is potentially disruptive to the delivery of the 'training'.

The mandatory orders limit or remove discretion from the court in determining the nature of the disposal. In some cases, this requires the imposition of a life sentence when it may not have otherwise been imposed on proportionality grounds. However, most of the provisions are concerned with public protection and the mandatory sentence has the effect of overriding the dominance of the principle of proportionality. Even in this situation, the penal element of the sentence is subject to ordinary proportionality principles, with the court determining the length of the minimum term of the life sentence, or the determinate term of the offender of particular concern order or serious terrorism sentence, and the nature of the sentence dictated by Parliament prescribes a particular

---

[138] The statute provides that the order is available for those aged ten to seventeen but availability for those aged ten to eleven is contingent upon an order made by the Secretary of State which has not yet been made, and availability for those aged twelve to fourteen is contingent on a finding of the court that the offender is a 'persistent offender'.

[139] David A Thomas, 'Detention and Training Orders' (2000) 4(7) Sentencing News 9.

release provision. The court is therefore provided with a degree of structure, by virtue of the duty to impose a sentence of a particular type, but the severity of the sentence remains at their discretion. This relies upon the general provisions relating to offence seriousness which, as noted earlier, provide insufficient guidance so as to consistency achieve a proportionate outcome. Thus, this sub-category provides, for a narrow class of offence, a mandated sentence type (with attendant release provisions), removing the element of discretion as to the nature of sentence. In practice, this will have little or no effect for some offences (eg murder and serious sexual, violence, or terrorism offences) and in some cases, a significant impact (eg comparatively low seriousness offences which receive a public protection sentence on the basis of the conviction offence and/or criminal history, rather than the individual circumstances of the offence and offender). It follows, therefore, that mandatory sentences of this nature remove the element of individualization and treat a class of offenders as homogenous when otherwise, the sentences imposed may be quite different.

There are also provisions which include a duty to consider making a particular order, or to explain why a particular order was not made, and other orders such as financial orders which are mandatory upon conviction. For reasons of space and due to the limited effect they have upon the overall sentencing decision, these are not considered in this chapter.

Conclusion

The extent to which judicial discretion is structured by Parliament in England and Wales

There are numerous statutory provisions which structure judicial discretion. This chapter has reviewed the principal provisions in England and Wales, across the different stages of the sentencing decision as undertaken by sentencing courts. This has included such considerations as the initial assessment of the seriousness of the offence, any amendment to that initial assessment by reference to the aggravating and mitigating factors, and the effect of the increasingly prevalent mandatory and minimum sentences.

It is clear from this review that the statutory provisions tend to fall into one of two categories. Some provisions are general in nature, providing limited guidance on the exercise of discretion, such as those concerning the principles of sentencing and the assessment of seriousness. Whereas others are very prescriptive, limiting the exercise of discretion which has the ability to produce absurd results (usually) at the lower end of the spectrum of seriousness. Examples of the latter might be low seriousness offences attracting a minimum sentence (such as under section 311 of the Sentencing Act 2020 which applies to strict liability offences) or a mandatory sentence (such as an offence of murder where it is a true mercy killing[140] or where there is an oblique intention to cause serious harm[141]).

It is also clear that while these provisions, whether prescriptive or general in nature, assist in answering the questions mentioned at the beginning of the chapter—whether to punish and if so, how much?—the assistance provided is insufficient. None of the provisions discussed earlier, in isolation nor in concert, operate to provide a structure to the sentencing court's decision as to what disposal(s) to impose upon a person convicted of a criminal offence which is sufficient to ensure consistency: more structure is needed.

Parliament's role in structuring discretion

Parliament—with its sovereign power—has defined its own role as regards the extent to which it legislates in relation to the exercise of judicial discretion and created other bodies to assist in the provision of guidance as to the determination of sentence and therefore structuring judicial discretion at sentencing. Traditionally, it has limited itself to providing the outer limits of sentencing powers and left the details and the way in which those powers are to be exercised to the courts. This has, as demonstrated, changed over the latter part of the twentieth century and into the early part of the twenty-first century. Parliament has seen fit to legislate in areas where before it would have been considered inappropriate to do so. The landscape is now cluttered with many procedural provisions which

---

[140] See eg *R. v Inglis* [2010] EWCA Crim 2637; [2011] 1 WLR 1110.
[141] See eg *R. v Woolin* [1999] 1 AC 82; [1998] 3 WLR 382.

operate to restrict or otherwise structure the discretion which a sentencing court is afforded. This is done in overt ways such as mandatory sentences but also by more subtle devices such as principles and purposes of sentencing which operate to guide (rather than require or dictate) action on the part of the sentencer. It is clear that Parliament's role is only one piece of the puzzle.

Lessons to be learned

What broader lessons can be learned? It appears that the English experience is that the provisions fall into one of two categories, and that when analysed, they provide either insufficient guidance and assistance as to the task of imposing an appropriate sentence on their own, or, conversely, they are too prescriptive and result in a loss of individualization, adopting a 'broad brush' approach based on a small number of case/offender characteristics. And so, the overarching conclusion to draw—at least at this interim stage—is that Parliament alone has not provided sufficient structure to effectively promote consistency in sentencing. More nuance is required and Parliament seemingly cannot provide that. The position may be different in civil law jurisdictions of course, with criminal codes typically providing far more by way of detail and prescription; the pitfalls identified in the English approach ought to sound a warning to common law and civil law jurisdictions alike when considering legislative measures designed to achieve consistency.

7
Structuring judicial discretion through the Court of Appeal (Criminal Division)

Given the looseness of the statutory framework for the exercise of sentencing discretion, any hope of achieving consistent sentencing practices depends on the ability of the judiciary to regulate itself.[1]

Introduction

In addition to Parliament, the Court of Appeal (Criminal Division) (CACD) was, for almost the entirety of the twentieth century, the only other institution responsible for producing guidance on sentencing and structuring the discretionary sentencing decisions of first instance courts.[2] The court's involvement in the structuring of judicial discretion at sentencing has varied over time, dependent on both the legislative scheme within which it must operate and the court's attitudes towards its role as an appellate court.[3]

This chapter explores the court's role in this regard, considering how the court acts to structure discretion and assessing the relative

---

[1] David Thomas, 'Judicial Discretion' in Lorraine Gelsthorpe and Nicola Padfield (eds), *Exercising Discretion Decision Making in the Criminal Justice System and Beyond* (Routledge 2011).

[2] The Divisional Court has played a minor role in dealing with sentencing appeals on the grounds that a sentence imposed by the magistrates' court was oppressive, harsh, or '*Wednesbury*' unreasonable (ie so far outside the range of the normal sentence so as to involve an error of law). See eg *R. v St Albans Crown Court ex parte Cinnamond* [1981] QB 480; [1981] 2 WLR 681.

[3] Of course, there is an element of those in the senior positions in the CACD having influence over policy and direction of the court on this (and other) issues, however this is not explored in this work.

effectiveness of each method employed. Beginning with a consideration of the history of a criminal appellate court, the chapter explores the development of the court's powers and how that shaped its attitude to its role as a court of review. Next, the chapter considers the different methods the CACD employs to structure judicial discretion. An analysis of these methods feeds into a consideration of the political pressures of the early to mid-2000s to establish a sentencing guidelines body to achieve greater consistency, among other things, in the sentencing system in England and Wales. The chapter then concludes by considering whether or not the combination of Parliament and the CACD's involvement in the structuring of discretion is sufficient to achieve consistency at sentencing, or whether other methods (such as sentencing guidelines) are required to meet that important aim. From this consideration of England and Wales, strengths and weaknesses are identified such that lessons can be learned for other jurisdictions.

History

Legislative history of a criminal appellate court

The origins of the CACD lie in the Court of Criminal Appeal. The Criminal Appeal Act 1907 brought about the creation of a specific criminal appellate court to which offenders convicted on indictment had a right to apply for leave to appeal conviction and/or sentence for the first time.

Prior to 1907, there existed the Court for Crown Cases Reserved, a court which heard only cases concerning points of law and to which referral from assize courts or quarter sessions was discretionary only.[4] Handler noted that at the time there was a commonly held belief that review of criminal trials should be sparing and that the Court for Crown Cases Reserved had no power to review sentences until in 1892 the Council of Judges passed a resolution in favour of establishing an appeal

---

[4] Crown Cases Act 1848. For more information about the Court for Crown Cases Reserved, see Phil Handler, 'The Court for Crown Cases Reserved 1848–1908'xyz 29(1) Law and History Review 259–88.

court with a power to review sentences.⁵ Brand and Getzler observed that at this time, 'consistency took second place to pragmatism in judicial minds', and that despite the 1892 proposal, no reform was forthcoming and the widespread inconsistencies continued into the twentieth century.⁶ Discretion at sentencing was wide and there was a 'distrust of generalising principles'.⁷

Concerns regarding miscarriages of justice led to the 1907 Act and the creation of the Court of Criminal Appeal. There are various accounts as to the catalyst for this significant change. One such account surrounds the case of Adolf Beck. In 1897 Beck (also identified as a John Smith who had been convicted of similar offences) was convicted of a series of frauds committed against women. A previous medical examination of Smith revealed he had been circumcised, whereas a later examination of Beck revealed that he had not. Beck was released but three years later was again convicted of similar offences. A contemporaneous arrest of Smith exonerated Beck and he was awarded compensation. An inquiry found major faults and press coverage reported disquiet among the public.⁸ Another such case was that of George Edalji who was convicted of the eighth of the 'Great Wyrley Outrages' (a series of livestock mutilations) after anonymous letters were circulated claiming George Edalji was responsible. The Edalji family had previously received abusive letters, and the Chief Constable of Staffordshire Police believed that George Edalji was responsible for those letters and the anonymous letters seemingly incriminating himself in the livestock offences. He received seven years' imprisonment but was released after approximately three years, with no explanation or pardon. He sought to clear his name (as he could not otherwise continue to practise as a solicitor) after his release and gained the assistance of Sir Arthur Conan Doyle, of Sherlock Holmes fame. Edalji's case gained notoriety and a special committee convened by the Home Secretary cleared

---

⁵ ibid 267.
⁶ Paul Brand and Joshua Getzler, *Judges and Judging in the History of the Common Law and Civil Law: From Antiquity to Modern Times* (CUP 2012) 155.
⁷ ibid 147.
⁸ Sir Leon Radzinowicz and Roger Hood, 'Judicial Discretion and Sentencing Standards: Victorian Attempts to Solve a Perennial Problem' (1979) 127 University of Pennsylvania Law Review 1288, 1334–36.

him of the mutilations but did not clear him of the letter-writing. Edalji was given a free pardon but was not compensated.[9]

These cases helped shape public opinion about the British justice system and led to the creation of the Court of Criminal Appeal. Handler stated that the court 'came to occupy a central position in the criminal justice system and viewed as an indispensable safeguard against injustice'.[10] Though much of the focus was on conviction appeals, this was a dramatic change for sentencing.

For the first time, there was a right to apply for leave to appeal against any sentence imposed following a conviction on indictment (save for any sentence which was fixed by law).[11] The Act gave the court the power to 'quash the sentence passed at the trial, and pass such other sentence warranted in law by the verdict (whether more or less severe)' in circumstances where the court thought 'a different sentence should have been passed'.[12] This gave the court a significant degree of power, both to reduce but also to increase sentences on appeal.

In relation to the role of the court, Pease and Wasik noted that '[a]t least since 1909 that Court has accepted as part of its legitimate function 'the revision of sentences … to harmonise the views of those who pass them and so ensure that varying punishments are not awarded for the same amount of guiltiness' (Woodman, 1909).'[13]

This suggests that the court took it upon itself to address the concerns of the public and the judiciary as to the inconsistent sentencing practices reportedly prevailing at that time. This prompted the court to proffer in effect two methods of structuring discretion, revision of sentences (thereby informing the particular first instance court of its 'error') and to set down 'a few' basic sentencing principles.[14] Few sentences were

---

[9] The Open University, 'George Edalji', <http://www.open.ac.uk/researchprojects/makingbritain/content/george-edalji> accessed 4 May 2022.

[10] Handler, 'The Court for Crown Cases Reserved 1848–1908' (n 4) 287.

[11] This is a defined term and remains in the current law, referring only to the mandatory life sentence for murder.

[12] Criminal Appeal Act 1907 s 4(3). Prior to its enactment, there was debate in Parliament concerning an amendment to remove the power to increase sentences, with some MPs opining that the power would operate as a deterrent to appeal one's sentence and that it was not a 'fair way of dealing with prisoners', HC Deb 29 July 1907 vol 179 cc663. The amendment was voted down ninety-one votes to forty-four.

[13] Martin Wasik and Ken Pease, 'Discretion and Sentencing Reform: The Alternatives' in Martin Wasik and Ken Pease (eds), *Sentencing Reform: Guidance or Guidelines?* (Manchester University Press 1987) 2.

[14] Thomas, 'Judicial Discretion' (n 1) 64.

STRUCTURING DISCRETION THROUGH THE CACD 193

appealed (perhaps because of the risk of an increased sentence)[15] and the court's impact upon sentencing was said to be limited.[16] Thomas noted that few sentencing decisions of the Court of Criminal Appeal were reported[17] and there was 'little interest among the judges who sat in the court in the idea of developing principles or guidelines on sentencing for judges in the lower courts'.[18]

The Criminal Appeal Act 1966 abolished the Court of Criminal Appeal, created the Court of Appeal (Criminal Division), transferred jurisdiction to hear criminal appeals from the former to the latter, and merged the two courts, to create a Court of Appeal with a civil and a criminal division.[19] The powers of the CACD largely replicated those vested in the Court of Criminal Appeal, save for the newly inserted prohibition on 'treating the defendant more severely' than they had been treated at first instance, effectively removing the power to increase a sentence on an appeal. This led to an increase in the number of appeals, bearing out (perhaps) the suspicions of the Donovan Committee regarding the power to increase sentences acting as a deterrent to meritorious appeals.[20]

The powers of the court have remained the same since. The lack of interest in the development of jurisprudence on sentencing continued into the 1960s when, so Thomas suggests, the interest in the use of the CACD as a means of promoting consistent sentencing practices grew.[21] Thomas attributes this to a number of factors including an increased academic interest in criminal law generally and more specifically sentencing reports began to appear in journals.[22] At this juncture it is necessary to

---

[15] This led to the enactment of s 4(2) of the Criminal Appeal Act 1966, and its subsequent re-enactment in s 11(3) of the Criminal Appeal 1968 Act which placed a limitation on the power to increase a sentence on an appeal against sentence. This stemmed from the Report of the Interdepartmental Committee on the Court of Criminal Appeal ('The Donovan Committee') (August 1965, Cmnd 2755) para 204 and the concern that the broad power to increase sentences was acting to deter the right of appeal being exercised in meritorious cases.
[16] Thomas (n 1) 64.
[17] These came in the form of 'rudimentary' reports in the Criminal Law Review from 1954 onwards. See ibid 65.
[18] ibid 65.
[19] A single Court of Appeal had been created in 1873 by the Judicature Act 1873, however this court could only hear appeals in civil cases.
[20] After the imposition of the restriction, the number of applications for leave predictably grew: from the mid-2,000s in 1963–1965, to 4,403 in 1966, 5,798 in 1967, and 7,898 in 1968. Figures taken from John R Spencer, *Jackson's Machinery of Justice* (8th edn, CUP 1989), 208, figure 5.
[21] Thomas (n 1) 65.
[22] Thomas (n 1) 65.

note Thomas' important work in his analysis of the sentencing decisions of the CACD from 1962 to 1969.[23] After Thomas' many articles, chapters, and books on the practice of sentencing and, in particular, on the practice of the CACD in relation to sentencing, references to appellate sentencing decisions both in the CACD and at first instance became commonplace. The inception of practitioner texts in relation to sentencing such as *Current Sentencing Practice* (Thomas) and latterly *Banks on Sentence* (Banks) in addition to the *Criminal Appeal Reports (Sentencing)* cemented sentencing as a topic in its own right; as Thomas notes, an interest in the principles and practices of sentencing, once considered to be inappropriate, is now encouraged.[24]

This change in the perception of, and interest in, sentencing is responsible for the CACD's increased involvement in the structuring of judicial discretion. To a degree, the courts are self-regulating. The shift from, for example, it being considered to be inappropriate to cite previous sentencing decisions of the CACD[25] to it being positively encouraged stemmed from judicial practice at the CACD and fed down to the first instance courts. The CACD therefore drove a change in its role. This coincided with an increase in Parliament's interest and involvement in sentencing and legislating to structure judicial discretion.[26] As noted in the previous chapter, Parliament legislated to provide a greater number of sentencing powers, creating new thresholds for the imposition of custodial sentences and latterly the creation of provisions setting out principles and purposes.

This, as was suggested in the previous chapter, envisaged the CACD playing a more active role in the structuring of judicial discretion. Fortunately, the CACD did so. By way of example, *Archbold 2018* listed in its sentencing guidelines supplement a section reproducing a list of cases originally produced by the Sentencing Guidelines Council which it considered to provide guidance on either sentencing principles or in relation to offences in the previous thirty years. There were cases listed under some sixty-nine topics spanning two-and-a-half pages. This clearly

---

[23] David Thomas, *Principles of Sentencing* (Heinemann 1970).
[24] Thomas (n 1) 65.
[25] See eg *R. v Rees* [1978] Criminal Law Review 298, 299 for an example of this practice where the court commented that 'keeping sentences in step was a matter for judges, not for counsel'.
[26] As to which, see the previous chapter.

demonstrates the CACD's engagement with the issue and its role in providing guidance and structured discretion at sentencing.

Ashworth and Kelly noted that the CACD began to give guideline judgments in the 1980s, though this was relatively rare and covered only a small number of offences by the late 1990s.[27] The Crime and Disorder Act 1998 sections 80 and 81 introduced the Sentencing Advisory Panel which would draft guidelines, conduct a consultation exercise, and then revise them and advise the CACD on the form such guidelines should take, and simultaneously limited the CACD's ability to give guideline judgments to areas on which it had received guidance from the Sentencing Advisory Panel. This issue will be explored fully in the following chapter. However, for present purposes it suffices to observe that it was seen as necessary to limit the CACD's ability to issue guideline judgments in light of the creation of the Sentencing Advisory Panel but that Parliament had seen the continued need for such sentencing guidance and addition structure to the discretionary sentencing decision.

This section has sought to illustrate the way in which the CACD's role (and its attitude) evolved from its inception in 1907 to the latter parts of the twentieth century and the early parts of the twenty-first century; it is clear that the CACD has taken on the role ascribed to it by Parliament (as identified in the previous chapter), namely to provide additional structure around the more skeletal sentencing framework provided by the legislation. It now falls to consider the way in which the CACD fulfils this role and provides such guidance and structure and its efficacy.

The types of guidance given by the Court of Appeal (Criminal Division)

The power of precedent

The term 'guidance' in the context of sentencing is now generally understood to refer to a judgment of a higher court made in respect of an

---

[27] Andrew Ashworth and Rory Kelly, *Sentencing and Criminal Justice* (7th edn, Bloomsbury 2021) 17; Rosemary Pattenden, *English Criminal Appeals 1844–1944: Appeals against Conviction and Sentence in England and Wales* (Clarendon Press 1996) 270.

individual case in which the court uses the case to enunciate principles or make statements or observations of more general application.[28] This guidance has been an increasingly common feature of sentencing law in England and Wales. But what is its status?

In *Young v Bristol Aeroplane Company, Limited*,[29] the court held that the Court of Appeal is bound to follow its own decisions except where (i) there are two conflicting decisions; (ii) a decision of its own which, though not expressly overruled, cannot, in its opinion, stand with a decision of the House of Lords (or the Supreme Court); and (iii) a decision of its own where the court is satisfied that the decision was given *per incuriam*. The CACD provides guidance to other constitutions of the court and to lower courts on a range of issues relevant to sentencing. This, in conjunction with the doctrine of *stare decisis*—to stand by things already decided—generally requires lower courts to follow decisions of higher courts, and today's court to follow yesterday's court of an equal level. According to the US Supreme Court, *stare decisis* 'promotes the evenhanded, predictable, and consistent development of legal principles, fosters reliance on judicial decisions, and contributes to the actual and perceived integrity of the judicial process'[30] and though not an 'not an inexorable command',[31] it is 'a principle of policy and not a mechanical formula of adherence to the latest decision'.[32] There has been dispute as to the flexibility of the rule; in *Lewis v Attorney General of Jamaica*[33] Lord Hoffman was, for example, particularly critical of the majority opinion of the Judicial Board of the Privy Council in circumstances where the Board had reversed the decision of the Court of Appeal of Jamaica, declining to follow two earlier decisions of the Privy Council, stating that '[i]f the Board feels able to depart from a previous decision simply because its members on a given occasion have a "doctrinal disposition to come out differently", the rule of law itself will be damaged and there will be no stability in the administration of justice in the Caribbean'.[34] For present

---

[28] Martin Wasik and Ken Pease, 'Discretion and Sentencing Reform: The Alternatives' in Martin Wasik and Ken Pease (eds), *Sentencing Reform: Guidance or Guidelines?* (Manchester University Press 1987) 2.
[29] [1944] KB 718.
[30] *Payne v Tennessee* (1991) 501 US 808, 827.
[31] *Payne v Tennessee* (1991) 501 US 808, 828.
[32] *Helvering v Hallock* (1940) 309 US 106, 119.
[33] [2001] 2 AC 50; [2000] 3 WLR 1785.
[34] [2001] 2 AC 50; [2000] 3 WLR 1785, 90.

purposes it is sufficient to note that decisions of the CACD providing guidance will be followed by lower courts and, in the case of subsequent constitutions of the CACD, will be followed unless one of the exceptions identified in *Young* exists. The constitution of the court—including the number of judges and their relative seniority, position, or perceived expertise—has the ability to influence the weight given by lower courts and practitioners to a particular decision. For instance, a decision of a five-judge court presided over by the Lord Chief Justice[35] is going to be considered to be a more authoritative decision than that of a two-judge court in which the judgment was given by a circuit judge sitting with a puisne judge.[36] There is room for debate on whether, *de jure*, that is correct (though not in this work), however as a matter of practice it is clear that the impact of a decision is influenced by the constitution of the court. The power of the CACD to influence decisions of lower courts is therefore manifest. It stands as a very strong influence upon the practice of the Crown Court (but less so in respect of the magistrates' courts, given the type of case which comes before it).

While there may be an academic argument as to the jurisdiction to provide such guidance and the status of such guidance, the practice of the court in giving guidance has been adopted for some considerable time and continues unchallenged. Decisions of the CACD providing such guidance are routinely cited in first instance and appellate courts and are treated as binding.[37] As is explored later in the chapter, this guidance can take many forms and operates to limit and guide the exercise of judicial discretion at sentencing.

In a recent review of English and Welsh sentencing guidance, Ashworth considered the relationship between what he described as the two primary sources of sentencing guidance, the Sentencing Council of England

---

[35] For example, as was the case in *R. v Forbes* [2016] EWCA Crim 1388; [2017] 1 WLR 53.
[36] A judge of the High Court.
[37] In brief, the argument would be that the court's responsibility is to determine the case before it and any comments which purport to be guidance for future cases (and therefore not part of the *ratio decidendi*) are *obiter dicta* and do not have to be followed by lower or future courts under the doctrine of *stare decisis*. A recent example of courts effectively legislating through *obiter* is *Ivey v Genting Casinos UK Ltd (t/a Crockfords Club)* [2017] UKSC 67; [2018] AC 391, a civil case involving cheating in which the Supreme Court stated that the subjective element of the test for dishonesty in criminal law in *R. v Ghosh* [1982] QB 1053 did not correctly represent the law and that directions in cases where dishonesty was in issue should not accord with *Ghosh*.

and Wales and the CACD.[38] In so doing, he identified six main classes of case coming before the CACD following a review of the reported decisions in the Criminal Appeal Reports (Sentencing). They were:

(1) application and interpretation of definitive guidelines;
(2) assessing departures from definitive guidelines;
(3) creating or developing offence-specific guidance;
(4) creating or developing guidance on general principles (including sentencing procedure and 'policy' cases);
(5) interpreting sentencing legislation;
(6) 'common law' sentencing (by which Ashworth refers to offences for which the Sentencing Council has not issued a definitive guideline).

Ashworth notes that the first two categories recognize the increased prominence of the sentencing guidelines but that the third and fourth categories demonstrate the power of the CACD to create guidelines and issue guidance in order to 'fill in gaps' left by the definitive guidelines.[39]

At this juncture it is worth noting that the present inquiry is narrower than that which Ashworth undertook in his article; while he considered each of the six categories he identified, this chapter will explore only relevant to the CACD's role in structuring judicial discretion. Decisions of the CACD which, for instance, interpret the wording of a statute may not always involve guidance or structure in relation to a discretionary sentencing decision. It will be recalled that in Chapter 5 it was posited that a discretionary sentencing decision existed where:

(1) the decision maker is required by law to make a decision;
(2) principles (or standards) exist which guide the making of the decision; and

---

[38] Andrew Ashworth, 'The Evolution of English Sentencing Guidance in 2016' [2017] Criminal Law Review 507.
[39] This represents something of an expansion from the four categories Ashworth and Kelly have identified (originally in an earlier edition of *Sentencing and Criminal Justice*: see now Ashworth and Kelly (n 27), 27 et seq. This point is also made by O'Malley, who additionally notes that this extends to interpreting and amplifying sentencing guidelines: Tom O'Malley, 'Judgment and Calculation in the Selection of Sentence' (2017) 28(3) Criminal Law Forum 361, 388.

STRUCTURING DISCRETION THROUGH THE CACD   199

(3) the proper application of those principles does not produce a single, obviously correct, result.[40]

Accordingly, cases which, for instance, concern a decision which does not meet this test (the obvious example being the determination of dangerousness under the Sentencing Act 2020, which is clearly an exercise in judgment producing a correct answer following the proper application of the relevant principles) will not feature in the discussion contained in this chapter.

For the purposes of the present inquiry, it is convenient to modify Ashworth's six categories, and to consider the role of the CACD in providing guidance and structured discretion under the following headings:

(1) General principles of sentencing (eg the meaning of totality, or when a sentence may be legitimately increased to account for the fact it is particularly prevalent in the local area)
(2) Offences
   (i) Guidance as to approach of sentence in cases where there is no guideline (eg 'The following factors are particularly relevant to the assessment of seriousness: (a) the nature of the threat; (b) the credibility of the threat...')
   (ii) Review of sentence imposed in specific case (where there is or is not a guideline) (eg where the court considers whether a sentence is manifestly excessive
   (iii) Traditional guideline judgment (eg A category 1 offence will attract a sentence of between three and five years)
(3) Interpretation
   (i) Of terms of sentencing guidelines (eg the meaning of 'vulnerable victim')
   (ii) Of statutory provisions (eg the interaction of particular legislative provisions or the meaning or effect of a particular phrase or provision)

---

[40] That chapter also argued for a four-part test to establishing whether or a not a discretionary decision was taken in a proper manner. That is not reproduced here as it is not relevant to the point at hand.

(4) Procedure (eg the approach to dangerousness, the procedure to be followed in cases in which a mental health disposal may be relevant, or the interaction between minimum sentence provisions and the sentencing guidelines).

Principles of sentencing and other general concepts

The provision of guidance on general principles is a challenging task. As has already been noted, limiting rather than guiding methods of providing structure to the discretionary sentencing decision are easier to interpret and apply. The same is true when the CACD attempts to provide guidance on amorphous topics such as general principles. It is far easier to say 'the sentencing range in a case such as [X] is five to ten years'. It is more difficult to describe the intricacies of a principle in a way which is both clear and easy to apply but not so heavily caveated that it becomes meaningless. This element of the CACD's guidance is therefore one which has had a varied impact upon the practices of lower courts.

As was demonstrated in the previous chapter, the statutory regime has set down numerous principles of sentencing such as the principle of offence seriousness, encapsulating the concept of retributive proportionality, modified by prescribed purposes of sentencing thereby creating a limiting retributivism model. Additionally, there are provisions which require adherence to the principle of parsimony, a recognition of the principle of totality, and the acknowledgement of a hierarchy of sentencing disposals. Yet as was noted in that chapter, Parliament legislates in such a way as to be seemingly inviting (or at least envisaging) the courts to amplify such provisions where it considers it to be necessary.

Here it is necessary to note that the term 'principle' is used in a rather looser sense than may be expected, intending to capture concepts at sentencing which are generally relevant to the sentencing exercise. It is used, for example, in a manner which encompasses rules, doctrines, and concepts. Gardner notes that Ashworth—a strong proponent of principles in the criminal law and in sentencing—speaks of principles, contrasting them with rules, doctrines, values, and policies, but he does not define what a principle is.[41] For present purposes therefore, this chapter speaks of principles in the wider sense than merely referring to principles such as proportionality and parsimony and instead includes totality (which appears to be a rule of law),[42] the concept of prevalence of an offence in a particular locality as an aggravating factor, and the relevance of release arrangements to the determination of sentence.[43]

In *R. v Bondzie*[44] the court gave guidance as to the manner in which the prevalence of a particular offence type in a particular locality could aggravate the seriousness of an offence, in the context of a drugs offence to which the Sentencing Council's *Drug Offences Definitive Guideline (2012)* applied:

10 Sentencing levels set in guidelines such as the Drugs Guideline take account of collective social harm. In the case of drugs supply this will cover the detrimental impact of drug dealing activities upon communities. Accordingly offenders should normally be sentenced by straightforward application of the guidelines without aggravation for the fact that their activity contributes to a harmful social effect upon a neighbourhood or community. It is not open to the judge to increase sentence for prevalence in ordinary circumstances or in response to his own personal view that there is 'too much of this sort of thing going on in this area'.

11 First, there must be evidence provided to the court by a responsible body or by a senior police officer. Secondly, that evidence must be before the court in the specific case being considered with the relevant statements or reports having been made available to the Crown and defence in good time so that meaningful

---

[41] John Gardner, 'Ashworth on Principles' in Lucia Zedner and Julian V Roberts (eds), *Principles and Values in Criminal Law and Criminal Justice: Essays in Honour of Andrew Ashworth* (OUP 2012) 4.
[42] Sentencing Act 2020 s 77(3).
[43] To borrow the words of Lord Atkin in *Liversidge v Anderson* [1942] AC 206 at 243, one might think that this is to adopt a 'Humpty Dumpty method of the construction' of the meaning of words; however, it allows this chapter to deal with concepts which apply generally to sentencing hearings in one section, rather than split across several. This is convenient for the purposes of the present inquiry.
[44] [2016] EWCA Crim 552; [2016] 1 WLR 3004.

representations about that material can be made. Even if such material is provided, a judge will only be entitled to treat prevalence as an aggravating factor if:
a) he is satisfied that the level of harm caused in a particular locality is significantly higher than that caused elsewhere (and thus already inherent in the guideline levels);
b) that the circumstances can properly be described as exceptional; and
c) that it is just and proportionate to increase sentence for such a factor in the particular case before him.

It is clear therefore, that a court should be hesitant before aggravating a sentence by reason of prevalence. Judges will be only too well aware of the types of harm which are caused by drug dealing and will not be assisted by statements of the obvious. Only if the evidence placed before the court demonstrates a level of harm which clearly exceeds the well understood consequences of drug dealing by a significant margin should courts be prepared to reflect this in sentence. If judges do so, they must clearly state when sentencing that they are doing so.[45]

This guidance goes to both procedure and substance. It is both guiding and limiting; the procedural aspect (concerning the receipt of evidence etc, phrased in definitive language) operates as a limiting measure requiring the court to receive evidence, whereas the 'exceptional circumstances' threshold is guiding, with a wide discretion clearly resting with the judge with little by way of assistance from the court as to the type of case in which the threshold might be passed. In addition to the overarching points made in relation to the extent to which a sentence might be increased to account for its prevalence, the court is also commenting upon the sentencing guidelines. The court makes clear that there is an element to which the factor is accounted for in the drugs guideline and therefore a new approach to sentencing in this area is required.

This is an issue on which the CACD has been inconsistent (at least, prior to *Bondzie*). The Sentencing Guidelines Council's *Overarching*

---

[45] [2016] EWCA Crim 552; [2016] 1 WLR 3004 at [10] and [11].

Principles: Seriousness Definitive Guideline (2004) (no longer in force)[46] required supporting evidence for an increase in sentence length based on the prevalence of the offence. However, the CACD in *R. v Stockdale*[47] questioned the propriety of that approach and, more importantly, suggested that a judge was entitled to increase the sentence to account for the prevalence of the offence based on his or her own local knowledge. While such comments were *obiter* (and there was a statutory duty to have regard to the guideline),[48] this was clearly likely to result in inconsistent practice. This is, in fact, what resulted, with a number of other cases on the issue taking different approaches.[49] That is particularly so, given that the guidelines were a new creation and the precise relationship between the CACD and the guidelines council was still being established.

The status of the guidance offered in *Bondzie* is that of *obiter*, but powerful *obiter*. This power comes from the constitution of the court, the decision being a judgment of a senior Lord Justice of Appeal and the Chair of the Sentencing Council, on a topic which required a strong judgment to bring clarity to the issue. In this instance, the CACD delivered such clear, strong guidance as was necessary, effectively overruling the cases to the contrary (though perhaps only as a matter of practice but not law).

Offences: Guidance on the approach to sentencing

Guidance in relation to specific offences can be divided into two categories: (a) guidance as to the general approach in cases for which there is no existing guidance; and (b) a review of the sentence(s) imposed in a particular case.

Taking them in order, the court has from time to time provided general guidance as to the approach to cases for which there is no extant

---

[46] At para 1.39.
[47] [2005] EWCA Crim 1582 at [15].
[48] Criminal Justice Act 2003 s 172.
[49] See eg *R. v Oosthuizen* [2005] EWCA Crim 1978; [2006] 1 Cr App R (S) 73; *R. v Racman* [2014] EWCA Crim 2133; [2015] 1 Cr App R (S) 18 and *R. v Tatomir* [2015] EWCA Crim 2167; [2016] Criminal Law Review 503.

guidance. This involves the court, in a descriptive manner, setting out the way it suggests courts should approach the sentencing exercise. For instance, in R. v McKay[50] the court gave guidance regarding the factors that might be relevant when assessing the appropriate sentence in a case of arson:

> 18 ... We agree with the judge that there is a dearth of relevant authority to provide guidance.
>
> 19 It seems to us that in setting sentence the sorts of considerations that might be relevant (without wishing to set out an exhaustive list) would include the following: (i) whether the arson was committed recklessly or intentionally; (ii) the amount of time that the risk continued for; (iii) whether there were medical or mental health issues which played a part in the setting of the fire; (iv) whether there were other aspects of personal mitigation to be taken into account; (v) the nature and level of the risk posed by the fire to life and property; (vi) the extent of any damage actually caused to property and/or to person's health; (vii) the conduct of a defendant upon realising that a fire had started; and (viii), importantly, whether the fire was connected to some other unlawful activity and whether that was pursued for personal gain or otherwise.[51]

This guidance is descriptive as opposed to numerical and guiding as opposed to limiting. It is suggestive of a qualitative assessment on the part of the sentencer but gives no indication of any relative hierarchy of importance; the existence or extent of any limitation on the effect of the presence of any of the listed considerations; the manner in which the presence of the listed considerations should be assessed; or the effect of the presence of the listed considerations (some manifestly being solely mitigating factors for example). Further, the listed is heavily caveated: 'without wishing to set out an exhaustive list'. The guidance acknowledges its incompleteness and that it merely provides a checklist of considerations which may be relevant to sentencing in cases of arson (an offence which involves a wide range of offence

---

[50] [2017] EWCA Crim 2299; [2018] 1 Cr App R (S) 36.
[51] R. v McKay [2017] EWCA Crim 2299; [2018] 1 Cr App R (S) 36, at [18] and [19].

seriousness[52]).[53] Finally, with guidance of this nature, it is likely that much of it will be obvious: for example, the risk posed will be relevant to the assessment of the seriousness of the offence of arson. That doesn't act to extinguish its utility—it is useful to have that statement of guidance—but it perhaps diminishes it somewhat, as examples may tend towards the obvious rather than the unusual.

A further example of such guidance is the decision of the CACD in R. v Tunney[54] in relation to an offence of perverting the course of justice in circumstances where evidence is concealed or false alibis are provided:

> In our judgment the sentence which is appropriate for offences of this nature depends effectively on three matters. Two of those were referred to by the judgment of this court in Rayworth [2004] 1 Cr. App. R. (S.) 75 in which two-and-a-half years were upheld on a plea for perverting the course of justice. The particular factors which the court must have regard to are, first, the seriousness of the substantive offence to which the perverting of the course of justice relates. Here the offence in question, murder/manslaughter, was at the most serious end of the spectrum. The second matter which the court must have regard to is the degree of persistence in the conduct in question by the offender. Here there was a degree of persistence, although ultimately the appellant ceased to persist in his lies. Thirdly, one must consider the effect of the attempt to pervert the course of justice on the course of justice itself. Here it was unsuccessful. Nonetheless, the substantive offence of murder or manslaughter could scarcely have been more serious.[55]

The court provides factors which, it states, the court must have regard to, thereby providing a framework for the assessment of the seriousness of the offence. Again, it does not provide a methodology or metric by which the impact or importance of those factors are to be evaluated and the same observations as made in relation to McKay above apply.

The provision of loose guidance requiring qualitative assessment on the part of individual sentencers as a method of structuring discretion at

---

[52] R. v McKay (case comment) [2018] Criminal Law Review 492.
[53] This is not to be critical; the court has a difficult task and does not want to bind the hands of a future court, or unduly constrict first instance courts.
[54] [2006] EWCA Crim 2066; [2007] 1 Cr App R (S) 91.
[55] [2006] EWCA Crim 2066; [2007] 1 Cr App R (S) 91 at [10].

sentencing is a move in the direction of more consistent sentencing, but it is of limited utility: there is no guidance as to the means of weighing the particular factors, or indeed whether (as with the guidelines issued by the Sentencing Council)[56] some factors are to be given more prominence than others. In fact, one might consider that the guidance given here is merely stating the obvious factors of relevance and therefore provides little by way of structure at all for the majority of cases or sentencers. Additionally, what of the factors not listed? Are they worth less than those listed by the Court? If so, why? If not, how useful is the limited guidance provided?

Offences: Reviewing sentences in specific cases

The second category of offence-based structured discretion provided by the CACD is by virtue of appellate review. That is to say, the 'ordinary' cases which come to the CACD which raise no point of principle but require the court to determine whether a sentence is manifestly excessive or wrong in principle. In these cases, the court provides guidance by virtue of a statement as to the propriety of the sentence(s) imposed by the first instance court and any alteration to it. These cases are either appeals against sentence or Attorney General's references.

Appeals against sentence by the defendant are not as of right but by virtue of permission given by a judge having reviewed the papers in the case. 'Appeals' is therefore perhaps the wrong term, yet this is a convenient label for present purposes. If an application is refused, and no further action is taken by the defendant, nothing further occurs. However, such a defendant may renew their application, thereby forcing a full hearing before the full court, at which the full court may give leave and hear the substantive appeal or refuse leave.[57] If the Registrar of Criminal Appeals considers there to be merit in an application, the Criminal Appeal Office

---

[56] As to which see the following chapter.
[57] If leave is refused, the defendant is exposed to a 'loss of time direction' under Criminal Appeal Act 1968 s 29, which has the effect of disqualifying a number of days from being credited against the sentence.

has identified a legal error, or where there is a degree of urgency due to the length of the sentence or personal characteristics of the applicant, the application can be referred to the full court for a hearing.[58] Otherwise, in cases where permission is given, there will be a full hearing. Section 11(3) of the Criminal Appeal Act 1968 provides the court's powers on an appeal against sentence:

> On an appeal against sentence the Court of Appeal, if they consider that the appellant should be sentenced differently for an offence for which he was dealt with by the court below may—
> (a) quash any sentence or order which is the subject of the appeal; and
> (b) in place of it pass such sentence or make such order as they think appropriate for the case and as the court below had power to pass or make when dealing with him for the offence;
> but the Court shall so exercise their powers under this subsection that, taking the case as a whole, the appellant is not more severely dealt with on appeal than he was dealt with by the court below.[59]

At a full hearing, the practice of the court has been to consider two tests in the determination of such appeals: is the sentence (i) manifestly excessive or (ii) wrong in principle? This test has developed from the common law and was an attempt by the CACD to impose a more tangible test upon the broad discretionary power granted by section 11(3) quoted earlier. Indeed, David Thomas described this as the CACD placing limitations upon its 'broad powers'.[60] Manifestly excessive has been interpreted in a common-sense fashion to mean more than merely excessive, thus creating a seemingly high bar. The CACD has said that it will not 'tinker' with sentences.[61] Here, there may be

---

[58] Alix Beldam and Susan Holdham, *Court of Appeal Criminal Division: A Practitioners' Guide* (2nd edn, Sweet and Maxwell 2018) § 5-087.
[59] Criminal Appeal Act 1968 s 11(3).
[60] David Thomas, *Principles of Sentencing* (Heineman 1970) xlvii.
[61] See eg *R. v Planken* [2017] EWCA Crim 1807; [2018] 1 Cr App R (S) 24, *R. v Khan (Mohammed Gulnawaz)* [2016] EWCA Crim 125 and *R. v Leader* [2014] EWCA Crim 300. For older examples dating back to the 1960s, see David Thomas, *Principles of Sentencing* (Heineman 1970) xlix.

a disconnect with the rhetoric and reality; anecdotally, Crown Court judges have criticized the CACD for tinkering with sentences, often a claim made when the CACD makes a small adjustment to the sentence. Such a measure of whether the CACD has 'tinkered' or not is misconceived, however. If a Crown Court judge imposes a sentence of thirty-two months, and on appeal, the CACD decide the upper limit of the proportionate range is thirty months, then a reduction will be necessary, and may only be one of two months. Further research on this point would be needed before any conclusions could be drawn. In practice then, the court ought only to intervene when the sentence falls outwith the permissible range of sentences; the court is a court of review, and appeals are not *de novo* sentencing hearings.[62]

An Attorney General's reference enables the Attorney to ask the CACD to increase a sentence he or she thinks is unduly lenient. The process is as follows. Under Criminal Justice Act 1988 Part IV, the Attorney General may, in cases of indictable only offences and certain limited triable either way cases, apply for permission to refer sentences which he or she considers to be unduly lenient. The court then may give or refuse leave; in cases where leave is granted, it then considers whether or not the sentence is unduly lenient, and if it is, it then considers whether or not to increase the sentence. Section 36 of the Criminal Justice Act 1988 provides:

(1) If it appears to the Attorney General—
    (a) that the sentencing of a person in a proceeding in the Crown Court has been unduly lenient; and
    (b) that the case is one to which this Part of this Act applies,
    he may, with the leave of the Court of Appeal, refer the case to them for them to review the sentencing of that person; and on such a reference the Court of Appeal may—
    quash any sentence passed on him in the proceeding; and
    in place of it pass such sentence as they think appropriate for the case and as the court below had power to pass when dealing with him.

---

[62] As is the case from the magistrates' courts to the Crown Court.

This test is different to the test which applies to defence appeals against sentence, by virtue of the 'unduly lenient' requirement, and the two tests are not directly equivalent; the CACD has suggested that the test for increasing a sentence is high one:

> It cannot, we are confident, have been the intention of Parliament to subject defendants to the risk of having their sentences increased—with all the anxiety that that naturally gives rise to—merely because in the opinion of this Court the sentence was less than this Court would have imposed.[63]

Further, a plain English approach to construction of the two terms would suggest that in an appeal against sentence, the error must be *manifest*: that speaks not to the degree of the error but of its discernibility; it must be obvious. By contrast, in an Attorney General's reference, the sentence must be *unduly* lenient: that speaks to the degree to which it is below that which other sentencers would have imposed; the sentence must be more than just lenient.

Through these two processes, the court can give guidance and structure to the discretionary sentencing determination via three methods: (i) a declarative judgment, in other words, stating that the sentence imposed was or was not within the permissible range; (ii) a range-setting judgment, that is, in addition to (i), describing the permissible range in the individual case; and (iii) a limiting judgment, in addition to (i), identifying one end of the permissible range.[64]

---

[63] *Attorney General's Reference (No 4 of 1989)* 11 Cr App R (S) 517 per Lord Lane.

[64] It will be recalled that the description of the sentencing scheme in England and Wales, namely a limiting retributivism model which sees desert set the outer limits of the proportionate sentence with other considerations governing the decision as to where within that range the final sentence falls. Earlier in this work it was said that it is not possible to identify a single correct sentence for a particular offence. Here, I contrast 'correct' with 'not wrong' to represent the view that when an individual court imposes a sentence, they think it is 'correct', ie the most appropriate disposal of the case. For instance, with a permissible sentencing range of two to four years, and in accordance with s 57 of the Sentencing Act 2020, the court considers that a deterrent sentence should be imposed, a sentence towards the top of the range is merited. Where the appeal court considers that a deterrent sentence is not merited but that the sentence imposed was within the permissible range of two to four years, the court should not intervene. In such circumstances, the sentence is not wrong but perhaps not 'correct'. An example of the court expressly acknowledging that they would have imposed a different sentence to that imposed at first instance but, in light of the sentence imposed not being outwith the permissible range of sentences, the appeal would be dismissed can be seen in *R. v Quick* [2017] EWCA Crim 66; [2017] 1 Cr App R (S) 54 where the court accepted that a suspended sentence order could have been imposed but that the

It is possible to identify three types of judgment in this category: (i) a declarative judgment, (ii) a range-setting judgment, and (iii) a limiting judgment.[65] The vast majority of cases fall within the first band, namely the declarative judgment in which the court states that the sentence was or was not manifestly excessive or wrong in principle and declines to provide any further guidance, merely, in the case of a successful appeal, reducing the sentencing accordingly. The CACD routinely dismisses appeals (after a discussion) by holding that the sentence was, or was not, manifestly excessive. In the case of the former, the sentence will be reduced accordingly. This provides no indication of (i) the width of the permissible range of sentences for the offence(s) subject to appeal; (ii) the location of the sentence(s) within or without that range; or (iii) whether or not the CACD felt that the sentence imposed was the correct sentence (as opposed to merely not being wrong).[66] While this may provide feedback to the specific judge whose decision is subject to review, it provides little guidance to others; while one may infer from the new sentence imposed the rough location of the range (substituting a sentence of seven years for one of two years suggests the judge erred in a gross manner), this is imprecise and wide open to error. As this is the most common device used by the CACD, its lack of utility is only compounded by its inefficacy as a device to provide guidance and structure discretion.

Rarely, the court will provide a range-setting judgment. An example is the decision of the court in *Attorney General's Reference (No 16 of 2014) (R. v Gill)*, involving an offence of 'one-punch' manslaughter, in which Treacy LJ stated: 'It seems to us that after a trial, taking account of all the circumstances, including the offender's age and his offending on bail and during the period of a suspended sentence, a sentence of the

---

immediate custodial sentence imposed by the sentencing judge was not manifestly excessive. The court may not increase the sentence or alter it so that the defendant is treated more severely than at the Crown Court.

[65] The following paragraphs provide examples of these devices evidenced by decisions from the CACD, with a description of the prevalence of the practice. The assessment of the prevalence of the device is based on a qualitative assessment of the published case law from the CACD in sentencing cases from 2011 to present, however support for these conclusions can be found in Lyndon Harris and Sebastian Walker (eds), *Current Sentencing Practice* (Sweet and Maxwell 2021).

[66] As to which see the discussion above in relation to 'not wrong' sentences.

STRUCTURING DISCRETION THROUGH THE CACD   211

order of six to seven years would have been appropriate.'[67] A slight variation on this range-setting judgment is where the court provides comment as to the location of the sentence in the range when dismissing the appeal. The court may, for instance, note that a sentence imposed is 'severe but not manifestly excessive' (or a variation thereof).[68] This provides guidance in the form of an indication that the sentence was towards the top of the sentencing range for the particular offence. Another example would be where the court acknowledges that a different (typically lower) sentence would have fallen within the permissible range, but that the sentence imposed did not exceed the range and so the appeal will fail. The case of *Quick*, referred to earlier, provides a particularly complex example of this, where the court observed:

> We appreciate that a suspended sentence could have been imposed in this case, and we would observe that it would have been of assistance if the recorder had directly referred to that part of the guidelines which sets out the stepped approach to this issue, and stated his reasons for deciding that a suspended sentence could not be justified. However, we do not consider that the imposition of an immediate sentence of imprisonment was outwith the reasonable range of sentences open to the recorder, particularly bearing in mind that the appellant had been convicted after a trial and had persisted in his denial of the offence to the author of the pre-sentence report. In these circumstances, we consider that the sentence was justified, and we dismiss the appeal.[69]

While this does in fact provide a steer as to the range, it is, once more, of limited utility as it neither expresses the upper or lower limits of the range, nor does it identify the location of the sentence imposed in that range. The case of *Quick* provides an additional complication; although the imposition of a suspended sentence order is certainly a discretionary

---

[67] [2014] EWCA Crim 956 at [31]. There is now a Sentencing Council *Manslaughter Offences Definitive Guideline* which has replaced this type of decision in cases of manslaughter.
[68] See eg *R. v AP* [2018] EWCA Crim 1701; *R. v Price* [2018] EWCA Crim 1528; *R. v Smith* [2018] EWCA Crim 1621; and *R. v Jones* [2018] EWCA Crim 1499. And for examples of this as a practice in older cases, see *R. v Hatfield* [2009] EWCA Crim 1589; *R. v Maka* [2005] EWCA Crim 3365; [2006] 2 Cr App R (S) 14; *R. v Simmons* (1995) 16 Cr App R (S) 801 and *R. v Freeman* (1989) 11 Cr App R (S) 398.
[69] [2017] EWCA Crim 66; [2017] 1 Cr App R (S) 54 at [9].

sentencing decision (it not really having a legal test for imposition, for one thing), the ability to change the nature of the sentence from immediate to non-immediate custody does not fit comfortably within the hierarchy of sentencing options available to a court. While an offender may well prefer a twelve-month suspended sentence to a three-month immediate sentence, the process by which a suspended sentence must be imposed—determination of the period of custody by reference to the severity of the offence, and only then a consideration of whether or not it can be suspended—rather conflicts with that view.[70]

Finally, the court may provide a limiting judgment, indicating that the appropriate sentence in a given case should or not have exceeded a particular level. A recent example can be seen in *R. v Moriaty*[71] in which the court considered that a sentence of four years' imprisonment imposed for breach of a criminal behaviour order and failing to provide a non-intimate sample was manifestly excessive and 'should have been no more than 40 months'.[72] Use of this device remains comparatively rare, however.[73]

Such devices provide assistance to judges and practitioners who are able to compare future cases with comparable facts to the CACD case and infer from the judgment the likely range in their case. Such an exercise is naturally imprecise, involving subjective assessments of the factors present in both cases and a computation of their effect on the new case. Each differs in its utility but all are limited. The first, the declarative judgment, provides almost no guidance or structure, merely stating that a sentence was or was not manifestly excessive. Additionally, this very limited utility is compounded by the high frequency with which this device is used by the CACD. The second, a range-setting judgment is perhaps the most useful, particularly

---

[70] See the Sentencing Act 2020 s 286 et seq. (formerly Criminal Justice Act 2003 s 189) and the Sentencing Council's *Imposition of Community and Custodial Sentences Definitive Guideline*. Additionally, support for the notion that a suspended sentence is always less severe than an immediate custodial sentences comes from the decision of a five-judge court in *R. v Thompson* [2018] EWCA Crim 639; [2018] 2 Cr App R (S) 19 in which the court placed emphasis on the time spent in custody (not merely the time liable to recall) in the context of Criminal Appeal Act 1968 s 11(3).
[71] [2018] EWCA Crim 1590.
[72] [2018] EWCA Crim 1590 at [19].
[73] Other examples include *R. v Wright and Bing* [2017] EWCA Crim 1195 and *R. v Foster* [2015] EWCA Crim 916; [2015] 2 Cr App R (S) 45.

STRUCTURING DISCRETION THROUGH THE CACD   213

when it is accompanied by a comment as to the location of the sentence imposed relative to the range. When unaccompanied, it provides little steer as to how the process of determining sentence was in error and where the sentence imposed fell within the permissible range. Regrettably, this is fairly uncommon. It therefore has a minimal impact upon the structure of the sentencing decision. The third, the limiting judgment, is useful but less so than the range-setting judgment as it provides an incomplete view of the proportionate sentencing range and therefore there remains a degree of interpretation and guesswork in the determination of the proportionate range. It is used comparatively rarely, however, and therefore as a structural device, its impact on the structure of the discretionary sentencing decision is limited.

A further point, however, is that cases which facilitate a comparison with other factual scenarios fly in the face of the conception of consistency advanced in Chapter 2; it will be recalled that there it was argued that such an exercise (in pursuit of establishing whether or not a particular sentence is 'consistent', or as an aid in determining the appropriate sentence in a given case) proceeds on the fallacious basis that the case with which the comparison is being made is 'correct'. It was subsequently argued that it is necessary to concentrate on the consistent application of principle in order to pursue consistency in a more accurate and conceptually sound manner. Accordingly, though many may find the rough comparison with a 'like' case useful, this type of guidance or structure proffered by the CACD can only be of limited utility.

Offences: Traditional guideline judgment

Another method of structuring judicial discretion employed by the CACD is through the traditional guideline judgment. The court surveys previous case law and seeks to provide guidance on a particular topic, either relying upon the experience of the members of the particular constitution of the court or a special court of consisting of members with experience of the particular area in question may be convened. The CACD is supported by the Criminal Appeal Office, a small team of lawyers directed by the Registrar of Criminal Appeals who conduct research in relation to the cases coming before the court. A recent example of this can be seen in *R. v Smith*[74] in which the Lord Chief Justice expressly referenced the fact that the Criminal Appeal Office had been tasked with researching sentencing levels in cases of parents or guardians killing their children.[75] The time for in-depth research is limited, however, given the workload of the court and the pressure on resources.[76]

Although traditional guideline judgments are now rare, as the Sentencing Council has issued guidelines for the major and most frequent criminal offences to come before sentencing courts, the CACD has, on occasion, seen a need to step in and 'fill' a perceived gap. A recent example of this is in *Attorney General's Reference (R. v Kahar); R. v Ziamani*.[77] The court considered a number of otherwise unconnected appeals and applications along with a reference by the Attorney General under the unduly lenient sentence scheme following convictions for offences of preparation of terrorist acts.[78] The court provided a lengthy and comprehensive judgment setting out guidance on the factors which would be relevant in such cases, particular issues which might arise in the sentencing of such cases, considerations of the type of offender which would typically fall to be sentenced for such an offence, and, crucially for this point, a sentencing guideline. The guideline identified six levels covering a wide range of offence seriousness. The court provided descriptions of conduct (supplemented by examples of real cases) which would fall into each category, along with a sentencing range (eg five to ten years) and an indication of the nature of that sentence (eg whether determinate or indeterminate).

This particular example is comprehensive, perhaps as comprehensive as a Sentencing Council guideline,[79] providing detailed guidance in addition to the sentencing levels and broad descriptions of conduct which falls within each category. It is not as nuanced as a Sentencing Council guideline (there being no detailed list of factors that would place an offence in a particular category, just a broad description). Similarly, there is no clear methodology (there being no step-by-step process for determining the

---

[74] [2017] EWCA Crim 1174; [2017] 2 Cr App R (S) 42.
[75] At [82] and [84].
[76] *The Lord Chief Justice's Report 2016* (Judicial Office 2016), 14.
[77] [2016] EWCA Crim 568; [2016] 2 Cr App R (S) 32.
[78] Contrary to s 5 of the Terrorism Act 2006.
[79] As to which see Chapter 8.

category, for instance) like a sentencing guideline. However, it provides very clear guidance to sentencers; though guiding (rather than limiting) in nature as it requires the sentencer to engage with the guideline and interpret the descriptive categories, the doctrine of *stare decisis* means that in practice the guideline will be followed.

While there could be improvements in terms of the pursuit of consistency, it appears to be specific and clear enough that the scope for inconsistency therefore comes largely from a sentence misinterpreting or misapplying the guideline. This therefore operates as an effective way of structuring the sentencing decision so as to bring about both consistency of approach and outcome. The efficacy of the guideline judgment, however, rests upon the extent to which it can provide clarity, not just in terms of broad sentencing ranges but in relation to the methodology to be applied, the relevance and importance of particular factors, and any special features that an offence or offence type has which merits a different approach from normal. It will be noted, however, that this relies upon judges and practitioners being aware of the decision, which may in some cases limit its effectiveness. There is a role for judicial education, here too. The Judicial College, which is responsible for the delivery of judicial training, is able to draw to the attention of judges (of all levels) particular decisions and their effect.[80]

Another example would be the decision of the CACD in R. v Aramah,[81] generally accepted as the first guideline judgment. The Lord Chief Justice provided (then) comprehensive guidance on drugs offences, setting out factors and sentencing ranges for a variety of offences.

Interpretation: Terms in sentencing guidelines

In recent years, the CACD has given far more consideration to the interpretation and application (beyond that in a specific case) of the sentencing guidelines. Consideration of a couple of cases will illustrate the way in which the CACD has provided guidance and structure to the

---

[80] This can be achieved through training courses or via the delivery of newsletters or bulletins ensuring that members of the judiciary are aware of the latest developments relevant to the area(s) in which they sit.
[81] R. v Aramah (1983) 76 Cr App R 190.

discretionary sentencing decision in relation to the application of sentencing guidelines.

First, consider the Sentencing Council's *Sexual Offences Definitive Guideline*. A commonly listed aggravating feature is that the offence involved an abuse of trust.[82] As is standard practice, the guideline omits to provide guidance as to what amounts to 'abuse' and who would be considered to be in a position of 'trust'. In *R. v Forbes*[83] the court stated:

> 16 It is evident from the appeals that one issue that has caused difficulty is 'abuse of trust' as an express aggravating factor and as used in respect of culpability extensively in the Definitive Guideline.
>
> 17 Whilst we understand that in the colloquial sense the children's parents would have trusted a cousin, other relation or a ... to behave properly towards their young children, the phrase 'abuse of trust', as used in the guideline, connotes something rather more than that. The mere fact of association or the fact that one sibling is older than another does not necessarily amount to breach of trust in this context. The observations in [54] of H should be read in this light.
>
> 18 The phrase plainly includes a relationship such as that which exists between a pupil and a teacher ..., a priest and children in a school for those from disturbed backgrounds ... or a scoutmaster and boys in his charge .... It may also include parental or quasi-parental relationships or arise from an ad hoc situation, for example, where a late night taxi driver takes a lone female fare. What is necessary is a close-examination of the facts and clear justification given if abuse of trust is to be found.[84]

The court appears to provide some limitations on the application of the term 'abuse of trust' but does so in a non-binding manner; by providing a non-exhaustive list (at paragraph [18]) of the types of scenarios which would 'plainly' fall within the term, the court proffers an illustrative list which future sentencers can then use and apply. Without being

---

[82] See for example the guideline for offences of rape of a child under thirteen, at page 29.
[83] [2016] EWCA Crim 1388; [2017] 1 WLR 53.
[84] At [16]–[18]. The quoted passage has been edited to remove references to the specific cases under consideration by the court so as to aid comprehension.

prescriptive, the court structures the discretionary decision as to whether a particular case falls within the term used in the guideline. This has obvious benefits, such as the narrowing of the term, and the use of an illustrative list plainly aids interpretation and application, as more information is provided to the sentencer as to what is meant by the term. This approach, however, retains the breadth of discretion afforded to sentencing courts by doing so in a manner which is guiding rather than limiting. The drawbacks, on the other hand, are also manifest. The illustrative list contains the 'obvious' types of case which consist of abuse of trust, and so the court has not drawn the outer limits of the term, merely the core, leaving open the possibility for future guidance when sentencers apply this guidance to cases which fall on or around the outer limits of what (the court thinks) was meant by the term.

A second illustration would be the term 'injury which is less serious in the context of the offence' in the *Assault Offences Definitive Guideline* which indicates that an offence consists of lesser harm (rather than greater harm) for the purposes of determining the offence category.[85] A point often taken on appeal is whether or not a particular offence was correctly categorized as one consisting of greater harm by virtue of the injury not being one which can properly be said to be less serious in the context of the offence.[86] The court, in *R. v Smith (Christopher)*[87] observed:

14. First, with regard to the injury, the question is whether the injury was serious 'in the context of the offence'. It is axiomatic that all violence within the context of a s.18 offence is serious, but some violence is more serious than others. The purpose behind the words 'which is serious in the context of the offence' in the guidelines is to distinguish between that level of violence which is inherent or par in a standard s.18 offence and that which will, by definition, go beyond what may be viewed as par for the course. In our view, given that there is such a marked disparity in the starting point between Categories 1 and 2, the sorts of harm and violence which will justify placing a case within Category 1 must be

---

[85] See eg the s 18 wounding or causing GBH with intent guideline at p 4.
[86] See for example *R. v Beaumont* [2015] EWCA Crim 2334; [2016] 1 Cr App R (S) 58 and *R. v Thompson* [2015] EWCA Crim 1575; [2016] 1 Cr App R (S) 26.
[87] [2015] EWCA Crim 1482; [2016] 1 Cr App R (S) 8.

significantly above the serious level of harm which is normal for the purpose of s.18.[88]

By explaining the purpose of the use of that term in the guideline, sentencers are instructed as to the focus of the exercise and the way to approach the assessment of the injury in question. This context aids comprehension of the terms in the guideline and goes some way to address the lack of guidance on such points in the guidelines themselves. Again, this requires a qualitative assessment and the structure provided by the court is guiding as opposed to limiting; it is instructive of the way in which the court ought to resolve the issue, rather than being determinative. Such is inevitable in an exercise which requires the qualitative assessment of something which relies heavily on interpretation.

The court's efforts in providing guidance and structure in relation to terms used in sentencing guidelines result in greater consistency in the application of the guideline: it is clear, for example, from *R. v Thompson*[89] that a bite resulting a portion of flesh being removed from above the victim's eyebrow is unlikely to be properly considered to be an injury which is serious in the context of the offence. The Sentencing Council revised the *Assault Offences Definitive Guideline* in 2021, removing the factor 'injury serious in the context of the offence' and replacing it with '[p]articularly grave or life-threatening injury caused'. This is perhaps in recognition of the difficulty with the concept of an injury being 'serious' in the context of an offence which requires a serious injury. But in any event, the example still stands; the CACD had seen the need to step in and provide assistance on a particular term of a sentencing guideline which was perceived to be causing difficulties, or at least was potentially leading to a less than desired degree of consistency. The CACD is well placed to make this assessment of course; it (or the Criminal Appeal Office) sees all the applications made for permission to appeal against sentence, and can therefore identify particular issues which are raised frequently, thus

---

[88] At [14].
[89] [2015] EWCA Crim 1575; [2016] 1 Cr App R (S) 26.

indicating that an issue regarding consistency may exist among the Bar or bench.[90]

The guidance given by the CACD in such cases is however, limited in that it requires the application of what is, at most, rather loose guidance, to different factual scenarios. In certain cases, this will be comparatively easy and will result in greater consistency of application of the guideline (which ought to result in greater consistent of outcome, *ceteris paribus*);[91] whereas in others, perhaps where the case to be decided falls towards the limits of, of even beyond, the guidance given by the court. Again, therefore, such guidance is of limited use. The impact of such guidance, though useful, is therefore limited: it can cater in a general sense to what might be termed the 'run of the mill' cases, for example the typical burglary, or typical assault, but will necessarily struggle with providing guidance (detailed or otherwise) on more unusual features or factual scenarios.

Interpretation: Statutory provisions

Sometimes, the CACD provides guidance on the interpretation of statutory provisions (or parts thereof). While not all of these decisions will fall into the category of structuring judicial discretion, some will. Those falling within the definition will be decisions interpreting a provision of a statute which conveys a discretion. Ashworth, in his review of English and Welsh sentencing guidance, proffered two examples:[92] first, the approach to the five statutory starting points which normally apply to offences of murder contingent on their particular features,[93] and second, the approach to 'exceptional circumstances' in relation to the mandatory

---

[90] If the interpretation of the same phrase in a guideline, or same statutory provision features as a ground of appeal against sentence time and time again, then it rather indicates that there is (at least the perception) of a lack of consistency or an error in its application at first instance.
[91] As to which see Chapter 2.
[92] Andrew Ashworth, 'The Evolution of English Sentencing Guidance in 2016' [2017] Criminal Law Review 507, 517. He also provides two further examples in relation to the determination of dangerousness for the purposes of the availability of extended determinate sentences and life sentences under the Criminal Justice Act 2003 (now contained in the Sentencing Act 2020), however these can be discounted as the dangerousness test fails the metric to determine whether a decision at sentencing is a discretionary decision, as set out earlier in this work. As the dangerousness test is the application of a legal test, with a binary outcome, for the purposes of this work it is not a discretionary decision.
[93] See Sch 21 to the Sentencing Act 2020.

minimum sentence for a specified firearms offence.[94] There are other examples but these two are undoubtedly the best, not least because each encompasses a significant discretion and there is a vast body of case law providing such guidance.

Taking Schedule 21 to the Sentencing Act 2020 first, there are a series of decisions interpreting the provisions, many of which occurred, as is perhaps to be expected, shortly after the coming into force of the new regime. Since then, there have been periodic advancements in the application and understanding of the schedule. A couple of examples will suffice.

Paragraph 5A of Schedule 21 to the Criminal Justice Act 2003 (now paragraph 4 of Schedule 21 to the Sentencing Act 2020) provides for a twenty-five-year starting point which is 'normally' the starting point for offences of murder in which the offender (aged eighteen or over at the time of the offence) took a knife or other weapon to the scene intending to (i) commit any offence, or have it available to us as a weapon and used the knife or other weapon when committing the murder. The application of the provision therefore largely turns on the interpretation of the term 'took a knife or other weapon to the scene'.

In *R. v Kelly*[95] the court cautioned against a literal interpretation of the provision, relying upon the potential injustice which would result, demonstrated by two examples:

> 12. If a man makes up his mind to kill his partner and walks back to their home, and there picks up a knife in the kitchen and kills her with the knife, he will not have taken the knife to the scene. On the face of it this offence would not fall within para.5A. If a man in exactly the same frame of mind walks home and buys a knife on the way and kills his partner in the kitchen in exactly the same circumstances, then on the face of it para.5A would apply. We doubt whether anyone would believe that justice would be represented by the assessment of the starting point for respective minimum terms for each of these defendants at 15 years and 25 years respectively.

---

[94] See s 311 of the Sentencing Act 2020 which requires the imposition of a minimum five-year custodial sentence (or in the case of an offender aged sixteen to seventeen at conviction, a three-year sentence) unless there are 'exceptional circumstances' which exist which would justify not doing so.
[95] [2011] EWCA Crim 1462; [2012] 1 WLR 5.

The culpability levels are the same: the consequences are similarly catastrophic. Yet, unless examined in the context of the decisions of this Court about the way in which the provisions of Sch.21 should be approached, a literal interpretation of [para.4] might produce this disparate result.

13. The second of these examples forcefully underlines that [para.4] is not confined to murders committed with the use of a knife which has been taken out onto and used on the streets. It does not follow that a murder committed with a knife in the offender's home, or for that matter in the victim's house, automatically falls outside the ambit of para.5A.

14. Further problems arise in the context of what is meant by 'the scene'. If the victim is in the kitchen, and the defendant takes a knife from a drawer and kills him or her, for the purposes of [para.4] that knife was not taken 'to the scene'. If in the same example the kitchen is at one end of the living room with no partition between the two, the victim is in the living room and the defendant takes a knife from the kitchen drawer and kills her, then again for the purposes of [para.4] this knife was not 'taken to the scene'. The situation will be additionally complicated if one of the doors in the premises through which the assailant went with the knife had been open, or closed, or locked. The present group of cases demonstrates the difficulties.[96]

This guidance instructs sentencers to guard against too strict an approach which would, it was said, lead to injustice. The guidance, however, stopped short of providing more concrete instruction, thereby preserving a significant degree of discretion in the interpretation and application of the provision.

There were a number of cases which followed and the guidance in *Kelly* was developed in *R. v Dillon*,[97] another case involving paragraph 4 in which the court reviewed the authorities and attempted to provide clearer guidance as to the application of the provision:

---

[96] [2011] EWCA Crim 1462; [2012] 1 WLR 5 at [12].
[97] [2015] EWCA Crim 3; [2015] 1 Cr App R (S) 62.

32. We consider that the following emerges from the cases cited to us:
    (a) a knife taken from a kitchen to another part of the same flat or house, including a balcony (Senechko), will not normally be regarded as having been taken to the scene, even if a door is forced open (Kelly);
    (b) conversely, if the knife is taken out of the house or flat into the street (Bowers), or into another part of the premises (Balraj Singh), or on to a landing outside a flat (Folley), it will normally be regarded as having been taken to the scene; and
    (c) however, a starting point is not the same thing as a finishing point. The judgment in Kelly emphasises the importance, in cases of similar culpability, of avoiding major differences in sentence based on fine distinctions. As the Lord Chief Justice observed by way of example in the passage cited above, to make a distinction of 10 years in the minimum term between the case of a man who kills his partner with a knife from the kitchen of their home and a man who kills his partner with a knife which he bought on the way home would not represent justice in anyone's assessment. If a case is only just within [para.4], because a knife was taken from a kitchen and used to inflict a fatal wound a short distance outside the door of the flat or house, this principle may well lead to a minimum term of less than 25 years (Bowers, Balraj Singh).

This attempt at collating the relevant decisions of the CACD and attempting to identify a consistent and coherent approach provides sentencers with a more tangible piece of guidance; it provides statements of the 'normal' interpretation and application while retaining the necessary discretion (and as intended by Parliament). One can certainly criticize paragraph 4 for its lack of clarity and potential for creating a bright line in circumstances where nuance is key. This guidance is therefore all the more important as it seeks to avoid such inconsistency by the imposition of some structure to the discretionary decision. It enables the CACD to control (to a limited degree) the cases to which courts and practitioners refer to when seeking guidance on a particular topic, informing them as to the way in which those decisions ought to be interpreted. This identification of a general rule (set out in paragraphs (a) and (b) above) provide a clear starting point for a sentencer, adding context to the sparse words of paragraph 4. As with the example of *Smith (Christopher)*, this device is capable of providing great assistance. An explanation of the purpose underlying a word, phrase, or provision in circumstances where the guidance cannot (or should not) be prescriptive such that the sentencer is required to interpret and apply it enables the individual to adopt a purposive approach and is likely to result in a more accurate outcome (as compared with no such guidance).

There is therefore now a more common approach to the interpretation of paragraph 4. The focus upon the crossing of the threshold between the property and other communal/public areas seems clear, but it remains an incoherent policy if rigidly applied: if X stabs their neighbour who has stepped momentarily across the threshold into X's property, X has not taken the knife to the scene, but if X step's momentarily across the threshold, they have taken the knife to the scene. The need to retain some discretion is therefore manifest, which necessarily limits the efficacy of the guidance and the degree to which consistency is produced.

The second example is another which has plagued the courts. The minimum sentence for certain firearms offences includes a provision which allows the court to 'disapply' the minimum sentence provisions where exceptional circumstances exist which in the court's view justify not imposing the minimum sentence ('the escape clause').[98] In *R. v Rehman; R. v Wood*[99] the court considered the interpretation of section 51A of the Firearms Act 1968 (now section 311 of the Sentencing Act 2020) and, in particular, the meaning of the term 'exceptional circumstances' in relation to the escape clause. The court observed:

> 11.... A holistic approach is needed. There will be cases where there is one single striking feature, which relates either to the offence or the offender, which causes that case to fall within the requirement of exceptional circumstances. There can be other cases where no single

---

[98] See s 51A of the Firearms Act 1968 and s 29 of the Violent Crime Reduction Act 2006 and now, s 311 of the Sentencing Act 2020.
[99] [2005] EWCA Crim 2056; [2006] 1 Cr App R (S) 77.

factor by itself will amount to exceptional circumstances, but the collective impact of all the relevant circumstances truly makes the case exceptional.[100]

This guidance assists the court in so far as it instructs the court that the approach to the determination is one considering all the circumstances and arriving at a balanced conclusion, rather than considering each factor in isolation. This provides structure to the decision-making process by adding some consistency to the way in which the decision is approached. However, it is notable that the court does not engage with the issue of how to determine whether a factor is 'exceptional', or the types of factor which may or may not be 'exceptional'. Later decisions of the CACD engaged with this issue, however they have done so on a fact-specific basis, deliberately not limiting future constitutions of the court. Reliance was placed on the fact that no two cases are the same and that the CACD could only give general guidance in relation to this issue.[101] Nevertheless, the case law developed. For instance, in *R. v Edwards*[102] the CACD emphasized that strong personal mitigation on its own was unlikely to be sufficient to amount to exceptional circumstances; in *R. v Boateng*[103] the CACD found that a genuine absence of knowledge of the contents of a bag subsequently found to contain a firearm and ammunition could amount to an exceptional circumstance; in *R. v Zehkov*[104] the CACD found that a Bulgarian lorry driver who, when driving in the United Kingdom was found to be in possession of a stun gun in circumstances where he genuinely did not know that possession of such items were illegal amounted to an exceptional circumstance. Hitherto, the guidance was sporadic and to be found in multiple decisions of the Court.

More recently, the CACD reviewed the authorities to provide some further holistic guidance. In *R. v Nancarrow*[105] the court held that:

---

[100] [2005] EWCA Crim 2056; [2006] 1 Cr App R (S) 77 at [11].
[101] For example, see *R. v Tuka* [2017] EWCA Crim 2210 at [12] and *Attorney General's Reference (R. v Parish)* [2017] EWCA Crim 2064. at [34].
[102] [2006] EWCA Crim 2833; [2007] 1 Cr App R (S) 111.
[103] [2011] EWCA Crim 861; [2011] 2 Cr App R (S) 104.
[104] [2013] EWCA Crim 1656; [2014] 1 Cr App R (S) 69.
[105] [2019] EWCA Crim 470; [2019] 2 Cr App R (S) 4.

STRUCTURING DISCRETION THROUGH THE CACD 225

(1) the purpose of the mandatory minimum term is to act as a deterrent;
(2) circumstances are exceptional if to impose five years' imprisonment would amount to an arbitrary and disproportionate sentence;
(3) it is important that the courts do not undermine the intention of Parliament by accepting too readily that the circumstances of a particular offence or offender are exceptional and that to justify the disapplication of the five-year minimum, the circumstances of the case have to be truly exceptional;
(4) it is necessary to look at all the circumstances of the case together, taking a holistic approach; it is not appropriate to look at each circumstance separately and conclude that, taken alone, it does not constitute an exceptional circumstance; further, that there may be cases where no single factor by itself will amount to exceptional circumstances, but the collective impact of all the relevant circumstances makes the case exceptional;
(5) the court should always have regard, among other things, to the four questions set out in R. v Avis[106]—namely:
  (a) what sort of weapon was involved?
  (b) what use, if any, was made of it?
  (c) with what intention did the defendant possess it?
  (d) what is the defendant's record?
(6) the reference in the section to the circumstances of the offender is important and it is relevant that an offender is unfit to serve a five-year sentence or that such a sentence may have a significantly adverse effect on their health;
(7) each case is fact-specific and the application of the principles dependent on the particular circumstances of each individual case; limited assistance is to be gained from referring the court to decisions in cases involving facts that are not materially identical;
(8) unless the judge is clearly wrong in identifying exceptional circumstances where they do not exist or clearly wrong in not

---

[106] [1998] 2 Cr App R (S) 178.

identifying exceptional circumstances where they do exist, the Court of Appeal (Criminal Division) will not readily interfere.[107]

Through this decision, while on one view the guidance remains general in its nature and preserves a great deal of discretion (in particular see item (8)), the CACD provides clear, intelligible, easily accessible guidance on this complex and nuanced topic. It brings together (and analyses) the existing guidance and presents—almost in the form of a guideline—the key principles to which a sentencing court ought to have regard when considering a case to which section 311 applies. As a method of structuring judicial discretion at sentencing, the CACD in interpreting provisions of statute is able to impact effectively upon the approach to sentencing in cases where the particular statutory provision applies.

What is evident, however, is that given the understandable reluctance to be overly prescriptive (which risks inadvertent egression into judicial discretion and potentially 'bright line' distinctions), the guidance remains fairly general in nature and is often iterative. The court may, over a period of time, develop existing guidance as new issues emerge and thinking advances. This is of course a strength, as the court can react to developments, though as will be discussed shortly, it is reactive rather than proactive.

Sentencing procedure

The final category concerns cases in which the court provides structure or guidance as to the application of sentencing procedure. Such decisions falling to be determined by a sentencing judge typically fall short of the account of judicial discretion as proffered in Chapter 5 on the basis that they do not involve the application of principles or standards (perhaps requiring the exercise of judicial judgment) or because the application of such principles or standards produces a single, correct result.

---

[107] Lyndon Harris and Sebastian Walker, *Sentencing Principles, Procedure and Practice* (2nd edn, Sweet and Maxwell 2021) 531.

This would preclude decisions such as the determination of dangerousness within the meaning of the Sentencing Act 2020, as this produces an obviously correct result: the offender is, or is not, dangerous and the court will not entertain a submission that the permissible range of sentencing outcomes straddles this threshold. By contrast, in theory at least, the custody threshold—the fictional line between cases which are, and are not, serious enough to warrant a custodial sentence—is a discretionary decision. The distinction between those two examples is the existence of a scale in the case of the latter which does not exist in the case of the former. Imagine a scale from 1 to 10, where the custody threshold sits at 4; as the determination of seriousness is not so precise that one can pinpoint the single point on the scale where a given offence falls, the range may, in theory, straddle the custody threshold, notwithstanding the fact that the decision appears to be binary. The focus on the binary decision is a red herring; the result of the binary question in this instance is a result of the determination of the non-binary question (where is the offence on the scale of seriousness?). In the case of the determination of dangerousness, no such scale exists and the choice is binary. It is therefore not a discretionary decision.

One example of a discretionary decision pertaining to sentencing procedure is the extent to which sentencing decisions should be explained. Section 52 of the Sentencing Act 2020 states:

(1) A court passing sentence on an offender has the duties in subsections (2) and (3).
(2) The court must state in open court, in ordinary language and in general terms, the court's reasons for deciding on the sentence.
(3) The court must explain to the offender in ordinary language—
   (a) the effect of the sentence,
   (b) the effects of non-compliance with any order that the offender is required to comply with and that forms part of the sentence,
   (c) any power of the court to vary or review any order that forms part of the sentence, and
   (d) the effects of failure to pay a fine, if the sentence consists of or includes a fine.

In *Attorney General's Reference (No 96 of 2009) (R. v F)*[108] where there was concern over the ability of the offender to follow proceedings, the CACD held that the judge had been entitled to keep sentencing remarks (in accordance with section 52) short and to have reduced them to writing, but that they should have been delivered in open court. Section 52 is plainly open to interpretation as to the level of detail a judge is bound to provide; here the CACD provided guidance as to the extent to which the remarks could be abbreviated, but that the requirement to deliver them in open court was inviolable. More recently, in *R. v Chin-Charles*,[109] the Court has sought to restrict the length of sentencing remarks, having formed the view that first instance courts have taken the terms of section 52 and the previous judicial guidance on the topic too literally. The Court set out features which should, and which should not, generally feature in first instance sentencing remarks. This guidance provides some, limited, structure to this aspect of sentencing procedure though makes clear that it is an exercise of judgment as to the extent to which, for example, the remarks might be abbreviated. A similar example is seen in *R. v Bourke*[110] in which the court commented that it would have been 'of assistance' had the judge dealt with the suitability of a determinate sentence in circumstances where the judge had found the offender to be 'dangerous' within the meaning of the Criminal Justice Act 2003 (now the Sentencing Act 2020).[111] This, again, provides an indication of the way in which such decisions should be approached. This is both guiding, in that it presents as non-binding, but is also in fact a polite but clear instruction that this is the way in which matters should be approached.

Limitations on the CACD's ability to provide guidance and structure

The limitation of the CACD's ability to provide guidance and structure is well-rehearsed. The Halliday Report, in 2001, noted that although the CACD had been developing guideline judgments since the 1980s, many

---

[108] [2010] EWCA Crim 350.
[109] [2019] EWCA Crim 1140; [2020] 1 Cr App R (S) 6.
[110] [2017] EWCA Crim 2150; [2018] 1 Cr App R (S) 42.
[111] At [41] and [42].

gaps remained.[112] Additionally, the report noted that guideline judgments were not particularly accessible to the public, something it considered was particularly problematic. Notwithstanding the CACD's unique position to provide guidance on sentencing, given its position at (effectively) the apex of appellate courts for sentencing decisions with great experience and knowledge of its membership, the Halliday Report noted that the membership was not particularly 'broad'.[113] Additionally, the usual arguments may be made as to why the CACD is perhaps not the most appropriate body to devise and issue guidelines and guidance; the CACD has a high case load[114] and thus may be ill-equipped to produce guidelines or guidance in most cases; it has an inability to conduct research and collect data[115] and the fact that it may deal with a particular topic only when an appropriate case comes before it.

Each of these raises particular issues. In relation to the workload of the CACD, the Lord Chief Justice reported in 2016 that despite a slight decline in number of cases received, the workload had in fact increased owing to the fact that the cases coming before the court were more complex than previously.[116] There was already a high volume of cases outstanding in the Crown Court (the first instance trial court in England and Wales) prior to the COVID-19 pandemic. That rose considerably as a result of court closures and additional restrictions on court business. The CACD has continued to dispose of cases at a similar rate to that pre-pandemic, and thus, its case load remains the same, but with a greater number of outstanding cases.[117] This inevitably places a strain on the court and its staff with attendant pressures to hear cases and hand down judgments promptly so as to reduce (or limit) any delays. In turn, there is little if any time for additional, lengthy research prior to the writing and handing down of a guideline or guidance judgment. This has been recognized by other jurisdictions: in Victoria, Australia, a report of the

---

[112] John Halliday, 'Making Punishments Work: A Review of the Sentencing Framework for England & Wales' (Home Office 2001) 54.
[113] ibid 56.
[114] Judiciary of England and Wales, *The Lord Chief Justice's Report 2016* (Judicial Press Office 2016) 6.
[115] Sentencing Commission Working Group, *Sentencing Guidelines in England and Wales: An Evolutionary Approach* (Ministry of Justice 2008) 41.
[116] Judiciary of England and Wales, *The Lord Chief Justice's Report 2016* (n 114) 4, 6.
[117] Judiciary of England and Wales, *The Lord Chief Justice's Report 2021* (Judicial Press Office 2021) 4.

Sentencing Advisory Council noted that reliance on an appellate court to issue guidance 'places a responsibility on the court and institutional parties to invest time and resources into monitoring systematic issues'.[118]

The CACD, like all courts, is restricted in the cases that comes before it. If it appears that a guideline judgment on a particular offence or set of offences, or guidance on a particular topic is desirable, the court must wait for a case to come before it which raises the point.[119] Young and King note that appellate guidance tends to be confined to the more serious offences and atypical cases, arguing that such guidance can 'only ever be a partial answer to the inconsistency problem'.[120]

The 'suite' of guidelines which an appellate court can therefore provide is only ever going to be incomplete. This limitation is twofold: not only can an appeal court not control the cases coming before it but it cannot plan for issuing guideline judgments. For instance, if two cases came before the court the same month raising two issues on which it was desirable to issue guideline judgments, that places a strain on the court's resource.

Moreover, the guidelines which are able to be issued by an appellate court are not tested, or at least not tested in any robust or controlled manner. They may be subject to informal discussions with others but can in no way tested and revised in a manner similar to that adopted by the Sentencing Council (as to which, see Chapter 8). Finally, the composition of the court, the way in which it is staffed and funded is to operate as an appellate court and not as a *quasi*-guidelines body.

An additional point relates to the propriety of the CACD giving guideline judgments. Although this has long been recognized at common law,[121] there is perhaps a question over the propriety of the court purporting to give such guidance. A court's jurisdiction is to decide the case before it; the judgment of the court comprises of the ratio decidendi—the rationale for the decision—and *obiter dicta*—words said 'by the way', that is, they could be removed from the judgment and the

---

[118] Sentencing Advisory Council, *Sentencing Guidance in Victoria: Report* (Sentencing Advisory Council 2016) 145.
[119] Warren Young and Andrea King, 'The Origins and Evolution of Sentencing Guidelines: A Comparison of England and Wales and New Zealand' in Andrew Ashworth and Julian Roberts (eds), *Sentencing Guidelines* (OUP 2013) 204; O'Malley, 'Judgment and Calculation in the Selection of Sentence' (n 39) 378.
[120] ibid 204.
[121] See eg Ashworth and Kelly (n 27) 28 and Crime and Disorder Act 1998 s 80.

STRUCTURING DISCRETION THROUGH THE CACD   231

same decision still be reached. The former is binding whereas the latter is merely persuasive for future cases. It might be argued therefore, that comments as to future cases can only ever properly be considered to be *obiter*; views as to the way in which future courts should approach the determination of sentence are not necessary for determining the sentence in the instant case. Therefore, the guidance provided by the CACD is only ever persuasive. In practice, even if such guidance is merely *obiter*, it will be followed, not least because it is persuasive and authoritative.[122] The point has been acknowledged by the Australian High Court[123] and Ashworth.[124] Whether or not this argument is correct, it would at least seem arguable and therefore it raises a question as to the propriety of such guidance.[125] In practice, however, this point appears to be overlooked in England and Wales.

These points taken together ought not to be read as criticism of the CACD in discharging its function in providing guidance and structure in sentencing; on the contrary, it is evident that the court provides useful and effective structure and guidance despite the challenges which have been identified in the preceding paragraphs. These points do, however, question the suitability of the CACD as the sole (or even primary) provider of structure and guidance.

Conclusion

This chapter has sought to survey the current provision of sentencing structure and guidance by the CACD. Through a systematic analysis of the decisions of the CACD, it has been demonstrated that the CACD provides structure and guidance to the discretionary sentencing decision through

---

[122] Support for this might be taken from the first guideline case, *R. v Aramah* (1983) 76 Cr App R 190, in which the Lord Chief Justice stated: 'All these are matters which we have to take into consideration, but before we deal with this particular case, it may be of assistance if we make some general observations about the level of sentences for drug offences, since our list, as will have been observed, is entirely composed of such crimes.'

[123] *Wong v The Queen* [2001] HCA 64 at [147] per Kirby J.

[124] Ashworth and Kelly (n 27) 29.

[125] An alternative argument would be that such guidance is part of the ratio as it forms the basis of the court's assessment of seriousness, ie it is necessary to set out the various levels in order to determine the one to which the instant offence falls within. This point would need further work and it is not for this work to embark upon such a task. It is merely sufficient to raise the question of the basis on which such guidance is given.

a variety of means, with varying degrees of efficacy. In some cases, as with general principles and general approach to sentencing, the court has provided structure by guiding comments, at a rather vague and high level. These require more input from the recipient of the guidance than more prescriptive forms of structure. While this preserves the wide discretion afforded to sentencers, which in theory enables courts the 'freedom' to achieve consistency,[126] the loose structure leaves greater scope for error or inappropriate or inadvertent departure. In other cases, the court has provided more concrete guidance such as the more traditional guideline judgment. While this still requires a degree of engagement from the sentencing judge (with the inevitable risk of inconsistency), this provides a greater degree of structure, albeit the applicability of such guidance is necessarily restricted.

The different means of providing such structure results in varying degrees of structure and consistency. In giving such guidance, the CACD plays the role envisaged by Parliament. Yet there remain barriers to the effective and efficient provision of such structure and guidance; as explored in this chapter, the CACD is not equipped to conduct research and obtain and interpret data. Similarly, the ability of the court to provide structure and guidance where necessary is severely limited by the fact it may only deal with the cases which come before it and it has no influence over that case load. Additionally, there is a question surrounding the legitimacy of the provision of such guidance.

It is important to consider the provision of guidance by the CACD in the context of the account of consistency proffered in Chapter 2. A focus upon principles and their proper and consistent application does not naturally lend itself to much of the guidance given by the court. Where the judgment in an appeal against sentence or Attorney General's reference states that a particular sentence was too high or too low, the focus is likely to be on the outcome and not (or not necessarily) on the approach to determining the sentence. The provision of guidance regarding the

---

[126] As defined in Chapter 2. As to the wide discretion, this is clearly an historical feature of the sentencing system in England and Wales. O'Malley notes the need for prescriptive guidance is jurisdiction specific and as will be seen in Chapter 8, the guidelines scheme adopted in this jurisdiction respects and reflects that culture of sentencing being a discretionary field of law. See Tom O'Malley, 'Living without Guidelines' in Andrew Ashworth and Julian V Roberts (eds), *Sentencing Guidelines: Exploring the English Model* (OUP 2013) 227.

approach to the determination of sentence remains limited and is outweighed by the many appeals in which the court indicates the appropriate outcome only. While this is not a criticism, it is a material factor in the assessment of the provision of structure to the discretionary sentencing decision: the role of the CACD can only be to contribute to, rather than to lead, the provision of guidance.

Taken together, the combination of the CACD and Parliament is an insufficient means of providing structure to the sentencing decision: more is required. There is an insufficient degree of consistency achieved through the provision of structure given by these two institutions. The CACD performs an important function in the provision of guidance and structure which is effective in influencing the approach of sentencing courts to the determination of sentence. It can 'fill the gaps', provide interim guidance or identify issues in a broad manner, however, the inescapable reality is that the CACD is limited in its effectiveness as a provider of structure at sentencing and this is due to the difficulty of a subject so inherently amorphous and fact-specific.

8
Structuring discretion through sentencing guidelines: Do the Sentencing Council's guidelines promote greater consistency?

In recent years, many jurisdictions have introduced reforms designed to restrict and guide judicial discretion at sentencing ... however formal guidelines are the most promising and well-studied innovation.[1]

Introduction

There can be no doubt that sentencing guidelines have revolutionized sentencing in England and Wales. But have they achieved their primary aim: to promote consistency in sentencing?

It will be recalled that this work has adopted a definition of consistency which focuses upon the application of principles, rather than a more traditional account of the concept which looks to compare outcomes to measure consistency. It was argued in Chapter 2 that this produced a purer, more theoretically sound conception of consistency. Accordingly, in testing the efficacy of the Sentencing Council's guidelines as a means of promoting greater consistency in sentencing, the following definition is used:

---

[1] Julian V Roberts and Wei Pei, 'Structuring Judicial Discretion in China: Exploring the 2014 Sentencing Guidelines' (2016) 27 Criminal Law Forum 3, 1–2.

Achieving consistency in sentencing requires sentences to be determined only by the application of established principles, having regard to legally relevant factors, in a manner which follows an established fair procedure.

In a principally retributive framework, this entails the production of a range of sentences proportionate to the seriousness of the offence. A particular sentence within the range can then be chosen with reference to other established principles, secondary to proportionality, and imposed following an established fair procedure.

In exploring whether the Sentencing Council's guidelines do promote greater consistency in sentencing, this chapter is broken down into five parts: first, there are some brief introductory remarks about the Sentencing Council and its guidelines. Secondly, the chapter considers the requisite features of sentencing guidance which is designed to structure judicial discretion as a means of promoting greater consistency. Thirdly, the guidelines produced by the Sentencing Council are examined in detail against what has been argued to be the fundamental features of sentencing guidance. Fourthly, the chapter considers the degree of constraint guidelines impose upon a sentencing court. Fifthly, the empirical research and the extent it has explored the Sentencing Council's success in promoting greater consistency is examined. Finally, the chapter draws conclusions as to whether the Sentencing Council's guidelines achieve their stated aim, namely to promote greater consistency in sentencing.

The Sentencing Council's guidelines

Background

It is unnecessary for the purposes of this analysis to provide 'chapter and verse' on the history of the Sentencing Council, the way in which it produces its sentencing guidelines, the Sentencing Council's composition or indeed the history of sentencing guidance in England and Wales leading to the creation of the Sentencing Council and the current approach to structuring judicial discretion at sentencing.

For present purposes, it suffices to note the following:

(1) The Sentencing Council identifies a multi-step process for their workflow:
   (i) Priorities (identifying work plan priorities);
   (ii) Research (policy and legal investigations are carried out and a draft guideline is produced, including evaluating current sentencing practice);
   (iii) Scoping paper (preliminary draft setting out various options to be discussed by the Council);
   (iv) Skeleton guideline (including road testing of the preliminary draft);
   (v) Revision (the Council discusses the draft guideline and agree a broad structure for the consultation);
   (vi) Consultation (usually a 12-week period during which statutory consultees and members of the public are invited to comment on the proposed documents);
   (vii) Responses (analysis of responses and revision of the draft guideline);
   (viii) Publication (guideline issued and judicial training is offered); and
   (ix) Monitoring (the operation of the guideline, once in force, is monitored).
(2) The Sentencing Council is supported by an office of staff including researchers and economists.
(3) Prior to producing sentencing guidelines, research as to current practice is undertaken and factored into the composition of the guideline.
(4) Draft guidelines are subject to public consultation and 'road testing' with sentencers and practitioners.
(5) As a default, the Sentencing Council's guidelines are generally anticipated to be neutral in their effect upon the prison population.[2]
(6) The Sentencing Council is made up of judicial and non-judicial members, with the former being in the majority.

---

[2] Lord Justice Colman Treacy, 'Letter to the Editor' [2016] Criminal Law Review 489, 490.

(7) The Sentencing Council's aim of promoting consistency in sentencing focusses upon consistency of approach.

The Sentencing Council's guidelines can be placed into one of two categories: (i) offence-specific guidelines and (ii) overarching guidelines. The former all adopt the same format with the same step-by-step process for the determination of sentence; the latter are more descriptive but do not adopt an identical format. The approach taken by both is explored in detail below.

Should the reader wish to explore these topics further, reference should in the first instance be made to work by Ashworth and Kelly, and Ashworth and Roberts regarding the history of guidelines and the establishment of the Sentencing Council and its predecessor bodies[3] and Bottoms and Parsons and the Sentencing Council itself as to the methodology employed by the Sentencing Council.[4]

The constituent elements of sentencing guidance

Before considering whether the Sentencing Council's guidelines do in fact promote consistency as defined in Chapter 2, it is necessary to consider what characteristics a guideline must have in order to achieve that aim. Two distinct qualities are necessary: guidelines must (i) contain substantive guidance and (ii) constrain the court's exercise of its discretion.

Dealing with the first, what is meant by 'substantive guidance'? In essence, it must inform as to the way in which sentencing is to be approached, in contrast to merely dictating without explanation. It would, for instance, provide little to no guidance if the guideline merely stated

---

[3] Andrew Ashworth and Rory Kelly, *Sentencing and Criminal Justice* (7th edn, Bloomsbury 2021) 17–18; Andrew Ashworth and Julian V Roberts, 'The Evolution of Sentencing Policy and Practice in England and Wales, 2003–2015' (2016) 45(1) Crime and Justice 307; and Andrew Ashworth and Julian V Roberts, 'The Origins and Nature of the Sentencing Guidelines in England and Wales' in Andrew Ashworth and Julian V Roberts (eds), *Sentencing Guidelines: Exploring the English Model* (OUP 2013) 2–15.

[4] Sir Anthony Bottoms and AR (Jo) Parsons, 'The Sentencing Council in 2017: A Report on Research to Advise on How the Sentencing Council Can Best Exercise its Statutory Functions' (Sentencing Council, 2018) 7; and Sentencing Council of England and Wales, 'About the Sentencing Council' <https://www.sentencingcouncil.org.uk/sentencing-and-the-council/about-the-sentencing-council/> accessed 1 January 2022.

what the guiding principle was, without further explanation: such would leave the sentencer alone in the task of determining its substance and how it ought to be applied. The Scottish Sentencing Council's *Definitive Guideline on Principles and Purposes of Sentencing (2018)* provides a useful example; it purports to provide guidance as to the approach to sentence, but for instance, merely states:

1. Sentences in Scotland must be fair and proportionate.
2. This principle requires that:
   - all relevant factors of a case must be considered including the seriousness of the offence, the impact on the victim and others affected by the case, and the circumstances of the offender;
   - sentences should be no more severe than is necessary to achieve the appropriate purposes of sentencing in each case;
   - reasons for sentencing decisions must be stated as clearly and openly as circumstances permit;
   - sentencing decisions must be made lawfully and sentencers must have regard to any sentencing guidelines which are applicable;
   - people should be treated equally, without discrimination; and
   - sentencing decisions should treat similar cases in a similar way, assisting consistency and predictability.[5]

This is representative of the approach taken by the guideline and is, one is bound to observe, practically devoid of guidance: while the guiding principle (is it one, or two?) is stated, there is insufficient detail to enable a court to apply it with any degree of consistency.[6] One is left wondering what a 'fair and proportionate' sentence is and how to achieve such a result. Put simply, the accompanying text contains assertion without explanation—that is insufficient to meaningfully promote consistency.

So far as treating 'similar cases in a similar way'—potentially crucial for consistency—the guideline defines 'similar' as follows: 'In the context of sentencing, "similar" means having features or factors in common.

---

[5] Scottish Sentencing Council, *Definitive Guideline on Principles and Purposes of Sentencing* (Scottish Sentencing Council 2018) 11.
[6] Lyndon Harris, Rory Kelly, Julian V Roberts, and Leila Tai, 'A Response to Scottish Sentencing Council's Consultation on the Principles and Purposes of Sentencing Draft Guideline' (2017) 3 Sentencing News 9–13, 10.

The aim of individual guidelines will be to identify where cases should be treated as similar. Treating cases similarly does not mean that similar cases should be dealt with in exactly the same way.'[7] This is little more than a dictionary definition and does not assist in the application of the principle(s) of fairness and proportionality. It is true that there is *some* guidance: it is clear that sentences must be fair and proportionate, but the explanation of that is vague at best, referring to concepts without further elaboration or definition. The only conclusion one may draw is that it is highly unlikely that this guideline will promote greater consistency in a meaningful way as the risk of disparate understanding and application of the terms used is significant.

Thus, a requirement that a guideline contains substantive guidance requires detail as to what underlies the principle described and how it is to be applied. The more detail, the greater the likelihood that the principle will be understood and its application will be consistent.[8]

Compare that with guidance from the Sentencing Council as to the principle of totality:

> The principle of totality comprises two elements:
> 1. All courts, when sentencing for more than a single offence, should pass a total sentence which reflects all the offending behaviour before it and is just and proportionate. This is so whether the sentences are structured as concurrent or consecutive. Therefore, concurrent sentences will ordinarily be longer than a single sentence for a single offence.
> 2. It is usually impossible to arrive at a just and proportionate sentence for multiple offending simply by adding together notional single sentences. It is necessary to address the offending behaviour, together with the factors personal to the offender as a whole.[9]

The guideline begins to explain the principle and provides further detail about how it is to be applied in practice. What follows (though not

---

[7] ibid 3.
[8] Of course, the substance of the principle and an assessment of its propriety is a separate issue altogether.
[9] Sentencing Council, *Offences Taken into Consideration and Totality Definitive Guideline (2012)* (Office of the Sentencing Council 2012) 5.

reproduced here, for reasons of space) is detailed guidance as to the use of concurrent and consecutive sentences, and examples of the proper application of the principle in various different scenarios. This provides a degree of substantive guidance as to the principle and crucially its application, enabling a user to better understand the principle and its proper application.

That position should not be overstated, however; the principle of totality remains insufficiently defined (eg principle 2 is particularly vague) to produce a meaningful degree of consistency, though perhaps this is understandable given the amorphous nature of the concept. That said, it is axiomatic that the use of examples in conjunction with a narrative explanation of the principle makes it more likely that users will understand how to apply the principle than if the guideline includes just a bare statement of the principle. This guideline provides substantive guidance which promotes consistency, albeit more could perhaps be achieved.

The second requirement, that the guideline imposes some constraint upon the sentencer, is equally important. Without this, the efficacy of a guideline is likely to be limited. A non-binding guideline leaves the decision *whether* to apply it to the individual and therefore the risk of inconsistent use of the guideline is manifest. An absence of constraint provides no control and no method of enforcement: advisory guidelines may be ignored (and may tend to be vaguer in their guidance due to the advisory nature) and defendants are likely to have little recourse in the appellate courts as a result. The Gage report argued for guidelines to be presumptively binding, noting that a balance must be struck between preserving discretion to avoid injustice and a high(er) degree of constraint to produce 'the necessary consistency'.[10] A minority of the working party felt that the constraint did not need to be as extreme as argued by the majority; their major fear was unjust sentences caused by insufficient discretion to 'do justice'.

It is necessary for guidelines to be binding, therefore. Without such a presumption, the application of guidelines is unpredictable, and it follows that the degree of consistency achieved will be lower than under a presumptively binding scheme. But does the lack of flexibility limit the

---

[10] Sentencing Commission Working Group, *Sentencing Guidelines in England and Wales: An Evolutionary Approach* (Ministry of Justice 2008) paras 7.14–7.21.

ability to individualize a sentence? If so, this would be incompatible with the argument presented in Chapter 4, namely that a conception of consistency based on principles relies upon and is congruent with individualization and accordingly there is a need for a degree of flexibility in structured sentencing discretion. As was demonstrated in Chapter 6, inflexible rules tend to produce inconsistency. The balance is therefore between constraint and flexibility. Too much constraint and the nature of the guideline becomes directing, rather than guiding. Too much flexibility and the guideline will produce insufficient consistency. This issue is discussed at length later in this chapter, when the current regime is examined in detail.

Through these two characteristics—substance and constraint—guidelines will promote greater consistency and accordingly, these two elements are vital to any guideline regime intending to promote consistency.

The Sentencing Council's offence-specific guidelines

General

The Sentencing Council's offence-specific guidelines are designed to assist with the application of the principle of proportionality and seek to promote consistency as regards the assessment of the seriousness of the offence in question. The format of all offence-specific guidelines is narrative, in stark contrast to the US 'grid' style guidelines. O'Malley considers the narrative nature of the guidelines to facilitate a more nuanced judicial evaluation of key factors.[11] As will be seen, the greater degree of flexibility certainly requires greater judicial involvement in the process. The form of the offence-specific guidelines is as follows:

Step 1 (entitled 'determining the offence category') concerns retributively significant factors which are structured into numerous categories.[12] The list of factors deemed to be relevant to the assessment

---

[11] Tom O'Malley, 'Judgment and Calculation in the Selection of Sentence' (2017) 28(3) Criminal Law Forum 361–389, 377.

[12] Some guidelines divide Step 1 into 'higher' and 'lower' culpability and 'greater' and 'lesser' harm, whereas others adopt an approach which sees multiple levels of each.

of the culpability and harm present in an offence at Step 1 is exhaustive; only those factors listed may be considered for the determination of culpability and harm at Step 1. This provides a high degree of constraint over the assessment of the seriousness of the offence at Step 1; it allows the Sentencing Council, in devising its guideline, to control the application of the guideline more accurately as the risk of inconsistency is limited to incorrect interpretations of the guideline (rather than reference to other factors which are not listed).

The assessment of culpability and harm is in effect a two-dimensional matrix involving various categories of each depicted by numbers or letters (eg Culpability A, or Harm 2). Step 2 (entitled 'starting point and category range') contains a table, displaying various categories, and users perform a similar task to that required of a mileage chart, using the culpability and harm categories produced by the analysis at Step 1 to identify the appropriate cell in the table. Each cell contains a starting point and a category range.

Step 2 also contains a non-exhaustive list of factors which aggravate and mitigate the seriousness of the offence. Reference to these factors allows for movement from the category starting point. These factors appear to be either those which most commonly arise in cases of the offences in question (eg location and timing of offence for an offence of assault) or those which are of general relevance to the assessment of seriousness (eg presence of previous convictions). Some have argued for factors in guidelines to be exhaustive,[13] however this argument is misplaced; such a prescriptive approach would risk excluding a factor which may be relevant to sentence, thereby limiting the ability of the court to impose a proportionate sentence. This would undermine the efficacy of the guidelines as it would render the guidelines of utility in only those cases which include common features of such an offence without any unusual features. The decision to make Step 2 non-exhaustive allows for an appropriate balance between keeping the guidelines at a manageable length (obviating the need to identify every possible factor of relevance, however infrequently

---

[13] See eg Mandeep K Dhami, 'Sentencing Guidelines in England and Wales: A Missed Opportunity?' (2013) (76) Law and Contemporary Problems 289–307, 294.

relied upon, and providing sufficient guidance as to the factors commonly warranting a movement from the starting point).[14]

Bottoms and Parsons criticized the Sentencing Council for its approach to the construction of Step 2 of the guidelines, recommending that caution is exercised to ensure the inclusion of mitigating factors which correspond to aggravating factors. An example is given of 'leading role' as an aggravating factor in a group offence, but playing a minor role is not listed as a mitigating factor. While there may be some specific circumstances where the point has purchase, as a general point this observation seems problematic. The presence of a factor may be aggravating but its absence does not necessarily constitute mitigation; for instance, the use of a weapon may be aggravating but the absence of a weapon is not mitigating. Such an approach is to undermine the 'baseline' offence upon which the starting points are based. For example, an offence of robbery does not require the use of a weapon, and so, it would be nonsensical to have the use of a weapon as a factor increasing seriousness, but the absence of a weapon as a factor reducing seriousness: there would be no coherent 'base' offence, as it would neither assume the use of a weapon nor assume its absence. It is far more logical to have the factors informed by the elements of the offence[15] and thus, where the offence does not require the use of weapon, that factor increases seriousness but its absence does not reduce it, as the 'base' offence is the offence of robbery without a weapon. Thus, the Bottoms and Parsons approach to have factors increasing seriousness without corresponding factors reducing seriousness is sound where the factor operates on a scale (such as the extent of the role played by the defendant) but does not withstand scrutiny where the factor is binary (such as the use of a weapon).

Additionally, as Step 2 is non-exhaustive, the sentencer is not prohibited from taking account of a factor not listed, in appropriate circumstances. This however risks inconsistency as it relies upon the

---

[14] There is research to demonstrate that sentencers consider guidelines to be too long in their current form and that overly long documents are likely to be under-utilized. See ibid 299.

[15] It is beyond the scope of this work to make this argument in detail, however it is suggested that there ought to be a greater focus upon the elements of the offence when constructing a sentencing guideline; for instance, where an offence is a conduct crime, there should be more emphasis on intention, whereas a result crime should have a greater emphasis on the harm caused. From this, a more coherent and theoretically sound approach to determining the offence seriousness—which, it is suggested must be informed by the offence—can be constructed.

identification and quantification of non-listed factors by the advocates or the court. It therefore appears particularly important that Step 2 lists as many of the commonly occurring or usually relevant factors as possible (while maintaining a concise and useable length). One option for the Sentencing Council would be for guidelines to describe the 'baseline' offence expressly; for example, an assault without the use of a weapon (thereby prohibiting taking account of the *absence* of a weapon).

Step 3 onwards (depending on the particular guideline) concerns other adjustments to the sentence, such as reductions for a guilty plea, totality, time spent on remand, and other steps which the sentencing court *must* take, such as explaining the reasons for the sentence imposed. By employing this same step-by-step format, the Sentencing Council ensures a consistent approach across each offence type. This also ensures that adjustments to sentence are made at the same stage in every case; with reductions for assistance to the prosecution and for a guilty plea, the stage at which the discount is applied can have an effect on the outcome.[16]

There are two key structural devices utilized in the Sentencing Council guidelines. First, the listing of the relevant factors, and secondly, the division between Step 1 and Step 2, and the prescribed methodology.

Listing (even non-exhaustively) factors undoubtedly provides some substantive guidance; by bringing them to the attention of the sentencer, the Sentencing Council has identified factors which, if present, ought to be taken into account. Further, although this may be obvious, by placing them into, for example, higher, medium, and lower harm or culpability categories, this provides substantive guidance as to the importance and relative weight that each should be afforded. This is a device designed to address ordinal proportionality directly. These factors produce an offence category (with starting point and category range) which ought to be of great assistance to sentencers, and ought to produce consistency of approach (and, indeed, outcome). This device is useful as it narrows the range of sentences which will be considered to be proportionate for a particular offence, based on the factors present. For example, in cases of causing grievous bodily harm with intent, every offence involving an injury which is not grave or life threatening will fall into harm Category 3. That will produce a sentencing range of two to seven years (that being

---

[16] See eg *R. v RB* [2020] EWCA Crim 643; [2021] 1 Cr App R (S) 1.

the bottom of the Category 3C range to the top of Category 3A range) rather than a range of a non-custodial sentence to life imprisonment (that being the range of available sentences).

The second structural device is particularly important, yet it is one which has received relatively little discussion. As regards the division between the factors to be considered at Steps 1 and 2, the guidelines suggest that Step 1 contains consideration of factors relevant to culpability and harm, and Step 2 concerns aggravating and mitigating factors. In fact, a better view is that Step 1 contains *primary* factors driving the severity of a sentence, in other words, those which are most influential in that determination, and Step 2 to contain factors of secondary importance. For example, the *Assault Offences Definitive Guideline* for causing grievous bodily harm with intent lists the nature and extent of the injury, whether the attack was sustained, planned, or premeditated, and whether a weapon was used (and if so whether it was 'highly dangerous'), at Step 1; at Step 2, the domestic context of the offence, whether the victim was an emergency worker performing the functions of such at the time of the offence, and whether the offender is a primary or sole carer for dependent relatives are listed. Thus, it can be seen that the Step 1 factors are closely related to the elements of the offence and the conduct and harm which the offence is designed to prohibit, whereas at Step 2, the factors are significant in the determination of the appropriate sentence, but less closely related to the offence and thus are less influential to the resultant sentence. This also illustrates that the factors at Step 2 are not exclusively retributively significant (in contrast to Step 1).

The process required by the offence-specific guidelines is linear (Step 1, then Step 2, and so on) and so departures from the broad structure (intended or inadvertent) ought to be manifest; for instance, if the court does not apply Step 1 and consider the factors which illustrate the various levels of harm and culpability relevant to the particular offence in question, in favour of a different approach. Due to the duty to follow sentencing guidelines (Sentencing Act 2020 section 59) it will be rare that a case is sentenced otherwise than in accordance with the approach provided by the guideline, not least because the Sentencing Council's step by step methodology follows (and develops upon) the approach to the assessment of seriousness set out in Sentencing Act 2020 section 63. Therefore, even where a guideline is not explicitly being complied with, the looser

DO GUIDELINES PROMOTE GREATER CONSISTENCY? 247

approach required by the Sentencing Act 2020 should provide a degree of consistency of approach, notwithstanding an absence of consistency of outcome ensured by following the guideline. The guideline provides far greater detail and therefore a greater degree of constraint.

An ancillary issue, noted at the outset of this chapter, is that the Sentencing Council's guidelines are generally intended to be 'neutral' as regards the prison population, thereby continuing with current sentencing practice and maintaining current sentencing levels. There are exceptions to this (eg where the Sentencing Council expressly stated they wished to reduce levels for so-called drug mules in the 2012 *Drug Offences Definitive Guideline*). A broader question that has hitherto not been considered in detail is whether it is appropriate (in the current regime or in a modified regime) for the Sentencing Council to have what is akin to a policy-making role (like the Court of Appeal (Criminal Division) (CACD)) in the determination of sentencing levels, passing in effect a (moral?) judgment on the level of penalties imposed for particular offences. For reasons of lack of space, this is not considered in this work (save to a very limited extent in Chapter 9), however it is a question which ought to be considered. Recently, the Sentencing Council embarked upon a consultation as to its future, asking what its priorities should be in the coming five years. In its response, the Sentencing Council stated that it did not feel that a policy role was within its remit.[17] Should the Sentencing Council have a policy role to comment or influence sentencing levels or broader sentencing policy? If so, what test should be met, or what arguments must be satisfied before a guideline makes such a significant substantive change?

Interpreting offence-specific guidelines

The interpretation of terms used in offence-specific guidelines risks inconsistency; two different judges may reasonably arrive at a different conclusion as to whether a particular factor justifies moving outside of the category range, just as they may arrive at different conclusions as to the

---

[17] Sentencing Council, 'What Next for the Sentencing Council? Response to Consultation, (Office of the Sentencing Council) 14.

presence of a factor listed at Step 1. To use an example referred to earlier, what, for instance, is a 'highly dangerous weapon'?

While Step 1 is prescriptive in its form, there remains a degree of flexibility as the terms used at Step 1 are not defined, nor are they accompanied by illustrative examples. The product is therefore a highly prescriptive process which produces an outcome. Although this is more likely than not to produce a more consistent outcome, is open to abuse and error in its subjective interpretation. For example, what is meant by 'grave injury' in the *Assault Offences Definitive Guideline*? The guideline provides no definition and therefore the sentencer is left to apply that term to the facts of the offence before them according to their own view. Where one might consider, for example, an attack in which four blows were delivered to be an offence involving a 'sustained or repeated assault on the same victim' (a Step 1 factor indicating greater harm in the 2010 Assault Offences Definitive Guideline), others may not. The Court of Appeal (Criminal Division) discussed this in *R. v Smith (Christopher)*,[18] observing at [18]:

> Thirdly, was the assault sustained or repeated, again as required by the guidelines? The phrases 'sustained' and 'repeated' may imply different things. An assault may be sustained because it continued over the course of a significant period of time, even though it did not necessarily involve a substantial number of blows. An assault may be repeated because it involves multiple blows over a short period of time. In one sense, the present case involves a repeated offence in that there were two blows, though only one of them was charged under s.18. We have doubts whether a difference between one blow and two blows could justify moving the starting point from a Category 2 (six-year) level to a Category 1 (12-year) level. If this were so, there would be very few attacks that were not Category 1. The concept of sustained or repeated, in our view, imports some degree of persistent repetition. These concepts must be read in the light of the major difference in starting point between the two categories. In order for a sentence to be compliant with the test of proportionality, the facts warranting the higher sentence should reflect the difference in the guidelines. In our judgement, two blows, one of which is not said to amount to a s.18 offence, would not

---

[18] [2015] EWCA Crim 1482; [2016] 1 Cr App R (S) 8.

at least normally amount to a sustained or repeated assault. We do not wish to be more specific or precise than this because we acknowledge that each case will entail a very fact-specific assessment.

A further example is provided by the case of *R. v Teklu*[19] (a case concerning a sexual assault committed on the street in circumstances where the offender approached a female student who was walking home at night). The CACD concluded that the term 'significant' as regards the culpability factor 'significant degree of planning' in the *Sexual Offences Definitive Guideline* was not an 'absolute concept', rather whether the factor applied was contextual. While there may be absolute consistency of approach (in a broad sense), this approach to the guidelines clearly creates a risk of their disparate application, leading to inconsistent approaches and outcomes.

The Sentencing Council could provide guidance on such factors. Illustrative examples may provide outer limits of such factors which inform and constrain (in a soft sense) the application of these factors. This is more likely to result in consistency of approach and outcome if the term used in the guideline is defined (or at least amplified) in the same document, rather than waiting for the CACD to consider the issue in an appropriate case and provide some guidance. It is also more likely that the term is given its intended meaning. This would provide greater consistency. There are, no doubt, challenges to such an enterprise. Though as was demonstrated in the previous chapter, the CACD has begun to provide such guidance. The risk, of course, in waiting for the CACD to provide such guidance is (i) that there is a delay between the guideline coming into force and the CACD providing such guidance, and (ii) the CACD arrive at a conclusion that is different to the intention of the Sentencing Council.

In 2019, the Sentencing Council issued supplementary guidance on what it termed 'expanded definitions', that is, terms used at Step 2 in the offence-specific guidelines in respect of which it sought to provide additional guidance as to the interpretation.[20] The Sentencing Council had

---

[19] [2017] EWCA Crim 1477; [2018] 1 Cr App R (S) 12.
[20] Sentencing Council, 'General Guideline: Overarching Principles' (Office of the Sentencing Council 2019).

concluded that it would be unhelpful to provide further guidance on Step 1 factors as those factors are tailored to each specific guideline; by contrast, . That may be a missed opportunity: if this is a function that the CACD can properly fulfil, why can the Sentencing Council not perform that function? Surely, one would think, as the author of the guideline, it would be better placed to provide guidance on the scope of Step 1 factors. Additionally, of course, it has the time and (some) resource to dedicate to researching the way in which particular factors are interpreted or misinterpreted, an advantage the CACD does not have. Further, as identified earlier, Step 1 factors exert a greater degree of influence over the sentencing outcome, this is likely to have a greater positive impact on the search for consistency—and if an economic case needed to be made for such an approach, it would likely result in fewer (or narrower) appeals to the CACD.

Moving on to Step 2, the offence-specific guidelines do not 'weight' the factors set out at Step 2, nor do they provide a standardized approach to assessing the weight to be properly accorded to such factors. Some have suggested that the Sentencing Council should provide such guidance.[21] It could be said that the *Reduction in Sentence for a Guilty Plea* guideline (which provides a percentage figure by which the sentence ought to be reduced) is an example of how this can work in practice. Yet this argument is misconceived as a guilty plea, as a factor reducing sentence, is *sui generis*. It is neither an offence nor offender-related factor; instead a guilty plea is transactional, predicated upon the (largely) measurable effect a plea has on proceedings (eg avoiding trial preparation or a witness coming to court). By contrast, whether the offender has previous convictions is not so easily objectively quantifiable in terms of its seriousness and the impact it ought to have on sentence as the principle by which to assess this is more amorphous. That said, it is clear that the subjective weighting of aggravating and mitigating factors presents a problem for consistency. Jacobson and Hough found that there was significant variation in the way in which sentencers applied factors relevant to personal mitigation and concluded that there should be guidance from the Sentencing Guidelines

---

[21] See Dhami, 'Sentencing Guidelines in England and Wales' (n 13) and Jose Pina-Sanchez and Robin Linacre, 'Enhancing Consistency in Sentencing: Exploring the Effects of Guidelines in England and Wales' (2014) 30(4) Journal of Quantitative Criminology 731–748, 733.

Council (then the relevant guidelines body) on the principles of personal mitigation relevant to sentence.[22]

While one could operate a crude measure by reference to the number of convictions and offences,[23] such would be woefully inadequate, being blind to the circumstances of the offender (eg is the offending increasing or decreasing in seriousness, are the number of convictions and offences significant for a person of the offender's age or has there been a gap in offending prior to the instant offence and so on), or the offence (eg are the offences related to the offence in question and do they show a pattern of offending), or the overall circumstances. It is therefore the case that such Step 2 factors cannot be quantified in the abstract; it is conceivable that the same factor might be aggravating in one set of proceedings, neutral in another and mitigating in another, for example the presence of a previous conviction for burglary. What might be possible, however, is to provide guidance on the way in which such an exercise is to be undertaken; this could take the form of indicating limits (maximum and minimum increases or decreases) and listing considerations which are relevant to each factor. To some degree, this is achieved by the expanded explanations. For instance, the guidance on previous convictions provides:

1. Previous convictions are considered at step two in the Council's offence-specific guidelines.
2. The primary significance of previous convictions (including convictions in other jurisdictions) is the extent to which they indicate trends in offending behaviour and possibly the offender's response to earlier sentences.
3. Previous convictions are normally relevant to the current offence when they are of a similar type.
4. Previous convictions of a type different from the current offence may be relevant where they are an indication of persistent offending or escalation and/or a failure to comply with previous court orders.

---

[22] Jessica Jacobson and Mike Hough, *Mitigation: The Role of Personal Factors in Sentencing* (Prison Reform Trust 2007) <http://www.prisonreformtrust.org.uk/uploads/documents/FINALFINALmitigation%20-%20small.pdf> accessed 1 January 2022.
[23] Such as that employed by some US sentencing grids.

5. Numerous and frequent previous convictions might indicate an underlying problem (for example, an addiction) that could be addressed more effectively in the community and will not necessarily indicate that a custodial sentence is necessary.
6. If the offender received a non-custodial disposal for the previous offence, a court should not necessarily move to a custodial sentence for the fresh offence.
7. In cases involving significant persistent offending, the community and custody thresholds may be crossed even though the current offence normally warrants a lesser sentence. If a custodial sentence is imposed it should be proportionate and kept to the necessary minimum.
8. The aggravating effect of relevant previous convictions reduces with the passage of time; older convictions are less relevant to the offender's culpability for the current offence and less likely to be predictive of future offending.
9. Where the previous offence is particularly old it will normally have little relevance for the current sentencing exercise.
10. The court should consider the time gap since the previous conviction and the reason for it. Where there has been a significant gap between previous and current convictions or a reduction in the frequency of offending this may indicate that the offender has made attempts to desist from offending in which case the aggravating effect of the previous offending will diminish.
11. Where the current offence is significantly less serious than the previous conviction (suggesting a decline in the gravity of offending), the previous conviction may carry less weight.
12. When considering the totality of previous offending a court should take a rounded view of the previous crimes and not simply aggregate the individual offences.
13. Where information is available on the context of previous offending this may assist the court in assessing the relevance of that prior offending to the current offence.[24]

---

[24] Sentencing Council, *General Guideline: Overarching Principles* (Office of the Sentencing Council 2019).

This guidance is particularly important as it limited the wide discretion previously afforded to sentencers, ensuring a more consistent approach to the determination of this particular factor. As such, the expanded explanations provide important additional guidance for sentencers which, on a qualitative analysis, will produce a more consistent approach (and thus a more consistent outcome). The success of the 'expanded explanations' however depends upon the substance of the additional guidance; where, for example, it is limited to the obvious, the impact will clearly be marginal. For instance, in relation to the concept of 'planning' an offence, the following additional guidance is now provided:

- Evidence of planning normally indicates a higher level of intention and pre-meditation which increases the level of culpability.
- Planning may be inferred from the scale and sophistication of the offending and/or role of the offender
- The greater the degree of planning the greater the culpability.[25]

In reality, this provides little further structure by way of guidance. The first is obvious from its inclusion in the offence-specific guideline; the third explains that the factor is relevant to culpability and again, is obvious from the offence-specific guideline and one's common sense. The second does provide some assistance, obvious though it is. What is lacking is assistance in determining when offending behaviour ought to be considered to include a significant degree of planning. Illustrative examples would no doubt assist, to provide examples of scenarios which are, and are not, intended to fall within the term.

In assessing the extent to which the Sentencing Council's offence-specific guidelines contain substantive guidance, it is helpful to consider one of the guidelines in detail. The following paragraphs consider the guideline for the commonly prosecuted offence of robbery.

Robbery Offences Definitive Guideline (2016)

The *Robbery Offences Definitive Guideline* ('the robbery guideline') is a typical example of an offence specific guideline, containing within it

[25] ibid.

three guidelines: (i) street and less sophisticated commercial robbery; (ii) professionally planned commercial robbery; and (iii) robbery in a dwelling. The first point to note, therefore, is that the sentencer has to decide which guideline to apply; this is something which is not typical of Sentencing Council guidelines which usually consist of a single guideline per statutory offence. There is only one offence of robbery contained in section 8 of the Theft Act 1968 and thus with the three guidelines available, the offence charged will not assist. This situation can be contrasted with other Sentencing Council guidelines such as the burglary offences guideline which contains three guidelines, (dwelling, non-dwelling and aggravated burglary); which guideline applies is clear from the indictment, as there are two offences of burglary, burglary and aggravated burglary, but in the case of the former, whether the offence is one of dwelling burglary must be stated on the indictment.[26] The decision as to which applies should therefore be determined prior to sentence and not open to interpretation. In the case of robbery, courts are often faced with the submissions as to whether a robbery is less sophisticated or professionally planned. The CACD has commented that the guideline provides little by way of assistance to sentencers who are required to determine which guideline applies:

> 14 The two kinds of robbery which were discussed in this case are defined to some extent in the sentencing guidelines. A street or less sophisticated commercial robbery, is said to refer to robberies committed in public places including those in taxis or involving public transport. It also refers to unsophisticated robberies within commercial premises or targeting commercial goods or money. A professionally planned commercial robbery is said to refer to robberies involving a significant degree of planning, sophistication or organisation.
>
> ...
>
> 16 In this court's view, this robbery sits on the line between two types of robbery which we have described. We conclude that we are not greatly helped by the guidelines.[27]

---

[26] His Honour Judge Mark Lucraft QC (ed), *Archbold Criminal Pleading, Evidence and Practice 2022* (Sweet and Maxwell 2021) § 21-110.
[27] *R. v Noel* [2017] EWCA Crim 782; [2018] 1 Cr App R (S) 5.

DO GUIDELINES PROMOTE GREATER CONSISTENCY? 255

The risk of inconsistency here is manifest; if courts are unclear as to which guideline should be applied in particular circumstances, then the guideline does little to ensure consistency of approach, let alone consistency of outcome.[28] However, it is right to note that this is not an issue which extends beyond the offence of robbery.

The following paragraphs consider the street and less sophisticated commercial robbery guideline ('street robbery guideline') as a suitable example through which to examine the contents of an offence specific guideline.

Step 1

The exhaustive list of factors requires the sentencer to determine, for instance, whether the offence involved the 'use of a weapon to inflict violence'. This requires consideration of the meaning of 'weapon' and 'use of a weapon' and 'violence'. While it is clear that a shod foot is a weapon (or perhaps more accurately, a weapon equivalent) in the context of assault offences (by virtue of CACD guidance),[29] the same is not as clear in the case of robbery offences; further, it is unclear whether the offender showing the victim that they are in possession of a weapon is 'using' a weapon; and finally, there is no guidance as to the meaning of 'violence' and whether a simple assault (without a battery) is sufficient. Similarly, in relation to harm, it will be for the court to determine whether there is 'serious' harm caused, with no guidance as to whether

---

[28] Another criticism, particularly in relation to the robbery guideline, is that the single offence of robbery encompassing a wide range of criminal behaviour creates a difficult sentencing exercise in many cases. While the SC has sought to identify different types of robbery offence, it forces the sentencing court to make the decision as to which to apply. Separate offences would force the CPS to choose which offence it charged. It is however right to recognize that this may serve to shift the responsibility (and cause of inconsistency) from the court to the CPS. In the SC's consultation in relation to the robbery guideline, the issue of the distinction between different types of robbery was not the subject of any specific questions, Sentencing Council, *Robbery Guideline: Consultation* (Office of the Sentencing Council 2014).

[29] See eg *R. v Waters and Others* [2021] EWCA Crim 1356. In addition to the point being made in this paragraph, it is worth noting that there is a great degree of importance surrounding the factors chosen for inclusion in a guideline and the phrasing of that factor. For instance, 'shod foot' as a weapon equivalent accords with common sense, however, there is a difference between a foot wearing a shoe with a cloth upper as compared with a shoe with a leather upper and steel toe cap. Additionally, if the use of the shod foot is spontaneous, this appears to be a harm factors, whereas if it is deliberate, it may be a culpability factor. Further, there is a legitimate question as to whether the true factor is the use of a kick (as a means of inflicting greater harm than with, ceteris paribus, a punch) rather than the fact the kick is delivered by a shod foot.

that is to be interpreted in the context of a robbery offence, or whether this is to be interpreted in accordance with the case law on offences against the person, to refer to grievous bodily harm. The presence or absence of a single factor can, for example, determine the difference between a starting point of five years and eight years, or two years and four years. The risk of inconsistency here is relatively high in terms of outcome; while there is a degree of consistency of approach in so far as the court will have adopted the same methodology for the determination of sentence, the opportunity for disparate outcomes is manifest, from the very first stage of the guideline as there is heavy reliance upon the interpretation. This underlines the need for the definition of consistency to combine both procedural and substantive elements, with a focus on both approach and outcome.

Step 2
Formerly, there was, no guidance as to the interpretation of particular terms, such as 'significant planning' or 'prolonged nature of the event' used at Step 2. This was perhaps designed to preserve discretion and the ability to do justice to the individual. However, it gave rise to a real risk of inconsistency. As noted earlier, in 2019 the Sentencing Council provided additional guidance on some Step 2 factors. Certain factors (including 'significant planning' but not 'prolonged nature of event') are followed by additional text. For instance, following 'significant planning' now appears:

- 'Evidence of planning normally indicates a higher level of intention and pre-meditation which increases the level of culpability.
- Planning may be inferred from the scale and sophistication of the offending and/or the role of the offender.
- The greater the degree of planning the greater the culpability.'

The first and third bullet points merely serve to justify the inclusion of this factor as an aggravating factor, however the second does provide substantive guidance. It illustrates how a sentencer may determine whether this factor is present and therefore must be seen as an advancement (albeit a small advancement) in the search for consistency. Thus, while the current approach may promote consistency, further structure in the form of illustrative examples is likely to be even more effective. While the previous approach of not providing such additional guidance may have been designed to afford greater discretion to the courts, the conclusion must be that provided insufficient guidance.

The question then is which approach is to be preferred? That must depend on one's view of consistency. There appear to be, broadly, two camps: first, that a consistent approach may legitimately result in disparate applications of the guideline and accordingly no guidance ought to be given (the point made by Ashworth); or secondly, that consistency of approach requires more than mere observance of the process, and therefore further guidance should be given. The CACD clearly, as discussed above and in the previous chapter, regard the latter to be preferable. That too was the position advocated in Chapter 2: consistency predominantly means the consistent application of principle. An absence of guidance on points such as this should not be regarded as satisfactory.

The current position remains unsatisfactory, however. No Step 1 factors have additional guidance provided by the Sentencing Council and only some Step 2 factors have this additional guidance. Of those Step 2 factors that do, the guidance is inconsistent (in that it varies from substantive guidance on when a factor might be present to a mere explanation of how the factor might be relevant) and thus, the level of additional guidance varies, with the likely result that some factors will see a greater degree of consistency in their application than others. Finally, no guidance is given on the weighting of Step 2 factors, however this risk of inconsistency is perhaps tempered somewhat by the fact that the use of category ranges suggests that a relatively modest adjustment (within the category range) is likely to be made at Step 2 (as compared with Step 1 which generally appears to feature more significant factors). This is indicated by the following words included in the guideline at Step 2: 'In some cases, having considered these factors, it may be appropriate to move outside the identified category range.' One might conceive of an approach which sought to provide a percentage increase for each factor; for instance, an increase of 10 to 25 per cent for the offender having played a leading role in the group. Yet this would risk being overly prescriptive and unduly limiting the court's discretion: such factors are contextual and their impact (both in terms of the importance of the factor to a case but also the strength of the factor) can vary significantly. Additionally, a single factor is unlikely to be determinative of the appropriate sentence, and thus, it appears difficult to conceive of an approach that would place a numerical figure on particular factors but also would be both meaningful in terms of the structure provided and a positive step in terms of promoting consistency without unduly limiting discretion. The ranges provided would have to be sufficiently wide to cater for the majority of cases which would of course limit the effect of the guidance; alternatively, this element of the guideline could be subject to a discretion to depart from it. The former would suffer from a lack of substantive guidance whereas the latter would suffer from a lack of constraint. Accordingly, the status quo appears to be the appropriate approach. One further option would be to indicate, for instance, that Step 2 factors should not result in a change in the nature of the sentence, for instance, from non-custody to custody. But this would not provide substantive guidance for the majority of cases.

Conclusion

The offence-specific guidelines, exemplified by the robbery guideline, balance affording the sentencer with discretion with constraining the extent to which the exercise is subjective. The offence range in the guideline for street robbery extends from a community order to twelve years. This wide range enables a sentencer impose a proportionate sentence, with a strong indication as to where in that range the offence should be. The categorization of offences, with starting points and ranges, provides a clear and strong structure, however this is compromised by the reliance upon the subjective interpretation of the terms used in the guideline.

The Sentencing Council's overarching guidelines

The need for substantive guidance

The overarching guidelines do not each adopt the same format as one another. While they are all narrative, with descriptions of concepts and principles, the approach differs from guideline to guideline. What does remain constant, however, is that each guideline contains an explanation of the relevant principle (sometimes with reference to the primary law) followed by illustrative examples demonstrating the proper approach and outcome. For example, the *Imposition of Community and Custodial Sentences Definitive Guideline (2017)* contains a section on the imposition of suspended sentence orders. Following an explanation of the law (the statutory test to be imposed and the procedure to be followed), there is a table containing factors which the guideline states would tend towards a sentence either being suspended or not being suspended. Further, the *Totality Definitive Guideline (2016)* provides illustrative examples of cases in which a concurrent sentence would be imposed, and cases in which a consecutive sentence would be imposed.

This combination does provide substantive guidance, enabling sentencers to understand the wider object of the principle in question and to see the circumstances in which it is to be applied, and the way in which it is to be applied. This would appear highly likely to have a positive effect upon consistency: guidelines are not tick box exercises but require input from the sentencer as to the underlying principles at play and their relevance to the sentencing exercise at hand. The examples provide an illustration of the application of the principle. Perhaps a rather crude example would be attempting to put together a piece of flat-pack furniture with and without the instruction guide and pictorial explanations. One is more likely to achieve the correct result with the illustrations.

There are multiple overarching guidelines on topics as diverse as offence seriousness,[30] allocation[31] (ie which level of court in which a particular case to be heard), domestic abuse,[32] imposition of custodial and community sentences,[33] and the approach to sentencing children and young persons.[34] Therefore the overarching guidelines provide guidance on sentencing principles (both the principle of proportionality and the purposes of sentencing) as well as more practical tasks such determining

---

[30] Sentencing Guidelines Council, *Overarching Principles: Seriousness Definitive Guideline* (Sentencing Guidelines Council 2004).
[31] Sentencing Council, *Allocation Definitive Guideline* (Office of the Sentencing Council 2016).
[32] Sentencing Council, *Domestic Abuse Definitive Guideline* (Office of the Sentencing Council 2018).
[33] Sentencing Council, *Imposition of Community and Custodial Sentences Definitive Guideline* (Office of the Sentencing Council 2017).
[34] Sentencing Council, *Children and Young Persons Definitive Guideline* (Office of the Sentencing Council 2017).

the venue for a trial and the approach to imposing a suspended sentence order. Each of these primarily concern the *approach* to sentencing rather than particular outcomes (though as is obvious, the former informs the latter). For instance, the children and young persons guideline provides material as to the factors which will be relevant when considering a sentence to be imposed on a person aged under eighteen (and indeed sentencing a young adult for an offence committed when under eighteen). This, naturally, makes empirical research into the effect of overarching guidelines more challenging as the output is not as easily measured. The Sentencing Council does not provide guidance on the imposition of preventive orders and other collateral consequences (save for in the domestic abuse guideline, where the basic operation of the restraining order regime is provided). It is unclear why this is so. One could debate whether or not such orders are part of the 'sentence' of the court (the legislation broadly considers that they are), but irrespective of that, as demonstrated in Chapter 7, it is clear that there is a need for guidance. Should that guidance be provided by the Sentencing Council? That question is not to be resolved in this work, however there appears to me to be a strong argument to answer in the affirmative.

Allen's 2016 review of the Sentencing Council and its guidelines suggested that some users found the offence-specific guidelines complex and elaborate, recommending that consideration is given to the production of more overarching guidelines to alleviate the volume of material in the offence-specific guidelines.[35] It is difficult to see how the offence-specific guidelines could be simplified. Additionally, there would be a legitimate concern that removing material from offence specific guidelines and placing it in overarching guidelines would result in sentencers approaching the offence-specific guidelines in a way which was unthinking and superficial. Indeed, Bottoms and Parsons' research revealed that 'while [sentencers] will of course read and absorb overarching guidelines when they are first promulgated, most will not regularly refer to them thereafter'.[36] Whether this is true is an empirical question which is as yet unanswered.

---

[35] Rob Allen, *The Sentencing Council for England and Wales: Brake or Accelerator on the Use of Prison?* (Transform Justice 2016) 10.
[36] Sir Anthony Bottoms and AR (Jo) Parsons, 'The Sentencing Council in 2017: A Report on Research to Advise on How the Sentencing Council Can Best Exercise its Statutory Functions' (Office of the Sentencing Council 2017) 14.

Interpretation of overarching guidelines

The interpretation of overarching guidelines presents similar challenges to those identified with offence-specific guidelines. As the overarching guidelines describe and expand upon principles and other factors of sentencing, there is heavy reliance upon the accurate interpretation and application of those principles to particular cases. Some guidelines, such as the *Totality Guideline*, provide examples of the application of the principles. For instance, when making provision for the imposition of concurrent sentences, the guideline provides:

Concurrent sentences will ordinarily be appropriate where
a) offences arise out of the same incident or facts.
Examples include:
- a single incident of dangerous driving resulting in injuries to multiple victims;[37]
- robbery with a weapon where the weapon offence is ancillary to the robbery and is not distinct and independent of it;[38]
- fraud and associated forgery;
- separate counts of supplying different types of drugs of the same class as part of the same transaction.[39]

This provides additional guidance to the sentencer to assist in the application of the rule which is described in the abstract ('Concurrent sentences will ordinarily be appropriate where ... offences arise out of the same incident or facts'). In the absence of a definition of the 'same incident or facts', illustrative examples provide additional guidance as to the application of the principle, thereby increasing the likelihood of consistency of approach and outcome. This implicitly limits or structures the application of the principle by drawing to the attention of the sentencer factors which are particularly relevant and also encouraging the sentencer to consider whether the case at hand is congruent with the

---

[37] *R. v Lawrence* (1989) 11 Cr App R (S) 580 (footnote in source material).
[38] *R. v Poulton and Celaire* [2002] EWCA Crim 2487; *Attorney General's Reference Nos 21 & 22 of 2003* [2003] EWCA Crim 3089 (footnote in source material).
[39] Sentencing Council, *Offences Taken into Consideration and Totality Definitive Guideline* (Office of the Sentencing Council 2012) 6.

given example. This operates in a similar way to principles of statutory interpretation, where for instance, a list in a statute preceded by the word 'includes' (or something similar) is to be interpreted, thereby structuring the exercise of discretion.[40] It is notable that this guidance is in stark contrast to the more opaque wording in relation to the principle of totality discussed earlier in this chapter.

In everyday language, where the definition of a word is not fully or properly understood, its use may be inconsistent or inaccurate. The same applies to terms used in guidelines. Where terms are misunderstood, their application is more likely to result in the incorrect application of the principle or concept referred to in the guideline. Using the above example, where 'same incident or facts' is misunderstood or insufficiently defined, there is a risk that a concurrent sentence will be imposed in a circumstance where the Sentencing Council intended consecutive sentences to be imposed. The result being a clear inconsistent approach and outcome.

Reduction in Sentence for a Guilty plea Definitive Guideline (2017)

The Sentencing Council's *Reduction in Sentence for a Guilty Plea Definitive Guideline* ('the guilty plea guideline') came into force in 2017 and regulates the discounts which are made to sentences in recognition of a plea of guilty. The guideline therefore applies to all cases in which a guilty plea is entered.[41] In one sense, the guilty plea guideline is *sui generis*; whereas the offence-specific guidelines feature sentencing starting points and ranges defining the suggested sentencing outcome, the overarching guidelines (almost without exception) leave the user with a little more work to do.

---

[40] *Bennion, Bailey and Norbury on Statutory Interpretation* (8th edn, Lexis Nexis 2020) § 18.3.

[41] And, arguably, some in which no plea of guilty is entered; see *R. v Markham and Edwards* [2017] EWCA Crim 739; [2017] 2 Cr App R (S) 30 where one-sixth credit for pleading guilty was given to an offender who was convicted after a trial in circumstances where the offender had admitted killing 'with murderous intent'. The court held that medical evidence and advice of leading counsel as to the availability of medical defences to murder was necessary prior to pleading guilty and that in fact the reason that the offender had not pleaded guilty was in fact the supportive medical evidence which was subsequently successfully challenged at the trial resulting in a conviction.

Both are descriptive in nature requiring a qualitative assessment on the part of the user as outlined above. The guilty plea guideline, in that regard, is different as it requires a qualitative assessment but then *does* provide numerical reductions which are to be deducted from the sentence which would otherwise be imposed. Notwithstanding this difference, it provides a useful example with which to consider the effectiveness of overarching guidelines, not least because it is likely to be the most commonly used overarching guideline (and, one might speculate, the most commonly used guideline of all).

The guilty plea guideline operates in conjunction with section 73 of the Sentencing Act 2020 which requires the court to take account of the stage in proceedings at which the offender indicated an intention to plead guilty and the circumstances in which that indication was given. In contrast the many mandatory aggravating factors,[42] guilty plea is the only mandatory *mitigating* factor.[43]

Key principles
The first substantive section concerns 'key principles'; this in essence explains the rationale for the reduction in sentence for a guilty plea, citing the reduction in impact of the offence(s) on victims, the avoidance of a trial (and the attendant cost saving), and the avoidance of requiring victims and witnesses to attend court and give evidence. This section also explains the staggered approach (as to which, see later in the chapter) to making reductions to sentences for guilty pleas (pleas produce benefits and earlier pleas produce greater benefits) and a list of factors which should not be taken into account in determining the appropriate reduction. These include admissions at interview and the strength of the prosecution's case. This section also clarifies that the guilty plea guideline applies only to punitive elements of a sentence and not to ancillary orders, which tend to have a consequentialist purpose.[44]

---

[42] See ss 64–72 of the Sentencing Act 2020.
[43] Under s 74 of the Sentencing Act 2020 the court *may* make a reduction to reflect any assistance given to the prosecution.
[44] The express exclusion of driving disqualification could be said to be at odds with the common law position that driving disqualifications serve both a punitive and preventive purpose, however.

The inclusion of the rationale for making reductions provides background and an explanation for the content of the guideline.[45] This is in contrast to the approach the Sentencing Council has taken with other guidelines where the content of the guideline is justified in the consultation paper (or response to consultation paper) rather than in the guideline itself. By providing this explanation, the guideline provides context to the approach taken and the principles underpinning the guideline, but one might wonder how this assists the sentencer? The guideline requires a qualitative assessment of, for instance, the point in time at which the offender pleaded guilty (and the concomitant benefits derived as a result) in order to determine the appropriate reduction to the sentence that would otherwise be imposed; this context is important and enables sentencers to make a more informed, principled, and nuanced decision that is inevitably more consistent with the underlying principles.

This does appear to assist with making the decision as to the reduction of sentence as the guideline affords sentencers with a degree of discretion; it therefore follows that information as to the *reason* for the reduction in sentence enables a sentencer to make a more informed assessment in the cases which do not fall 'squarely' into a particular description, or those in which an exception is said to apply. That is more likely than not to be in accordance with the intentions of the Sentencing Council and therefore it follows that not only does this aspect structure the discretionary decision as to the appropriate sentence, but in doing so, it is more likely than not that there will be inter-judge consistency as a result of the guideline.

The approach

The next section of the guideline prescribes the approach to be taken in determining the reduction. There are five steps which the guideline states must be followed in sequence;[46] this is key to the promotion of consistency for two reasons. First, it ensures a consistent approach in a broad

---

[45] It is worth noting that this was the third iteration of this guideline and there had previously been issues with some sentencers wishing to withhold (or reduce) a discount for offenders caught 'red-handed'. This may explain the expanded guideline and inclusion of detailed rationale.

[46] 1. Determine the appropriate sentence before a reduction for a guilty plea in accordance with any offence-specific guideline; 2. Determine the appropriate reduction in accordance with the guilty plea guideline; 3. State the amount of the reduction; 4. Apply the reduction to the sentence; 5. Follow any further steps in any applicable offence-specific guideline.

sense of the term. Secondly, taking the steps in a different order can result in different outcomes. For example, taking a starting point of ten years, making a reduction of 25 per cent for the guilty plea, and then making a reduction for one year spent subject to electronically monitored bail,[47] produces a sentence of seventy-eight months, whereas taking a starting point of ten years, making a reduction for one year spent subject to electronically monitored bail, and then making a 25 per cent reduction for the guilty plea produces a sentence of eighty-one months. The consistency of approach ensured by an application of the guideline therefore directly impacts consistency of outcome in this instance.

Determining the level of reduction
The guideline states the level of reduction is indexed to the stage in proceedings at which the guilty plea was indicated. There follows a description of each of those stages, with a degree of discretion as to what the 'first stage of proceedings' is and therefore what reduction applies. Additionally, there is a degree of discretion as to the level of the reduction. The guideline provides that a plea indicated at the first stage should attract a reduction of one-third, but when entered after that stage, it should attract a reduction between 10 and 25 per cent. That provides the court with a discretion to determine the figure in accordance with the principles underpinning the guideline, as discussed above. There is, therefore, a loose structure within which a sentencer may move. The illustration of the principles underpinning the guideline (for example, the description of how the first stage of proceedings would 'normally' be interpreted) encourages sentencers (i) to think closely about whether the case before them truly fits that description, and if not, why not; (ii) to give reasons if not adopting the 'normal' approach; and (iii) places a 'soft' limitation on the interpretation of the guideline, encouraging interpretations consistent with the illustrative examples, rather than permitting wild departures.

Applying the reduction
The section concerning the application of the reduction includes an explanation of some statutory law (such as the limitations on sentencing

---

[47] Sentencing Act 2020 s 325.

powers in magistrates' courts) as well as guidance from the Sentencing Council about the application (such as the fact that the court can apply a reduction by changing the nature of the sentence). The examples provided illustrate the way in which the Sentencing Council intended the guideline to be applied, thereby influencing the sentencer's application of the guideline in a similar way to the 'soft' limits of the category ranges. As is noted elsewhere in this chapter, the reliance on subjective interpretation here creates an obvious risk of inconsistency of outcome, however the risk is limited by the exposition of the underlying rationale and examples provided.

Exceptions

The guideline provides for a number of exceptions to the general guidance contained earlier in the guideline. This, again, includes a mixture of descriptions of the statutory law (such as the minimum sentence provisions and the extent to which that could be reduced in respect of a guilty plea) and guidance (such as the approach where circumstances exist which may be unreasonable to expect a plea to be indicated sooner than in fact it was).[48] This guidance is, again, general in nature leaving the sentencer to determine whether the exceptions apply and therefore the extent to which the remainder of the guideline should be applied. The focus is therefore overwhelmingly on the consistency of approach. The result is that a greater degree of consistency of outcome could be achieved, if the Sentencing Council wanted to adopt a different, more detailed approach as to the explanation of the various exceptions.

Appendices

The guilty plea guideline also features three appendices, each containing a flow chart illustrating the process to be adopted in cases of summary only, triable either way, and indictable-only offences. The flow charts bring together, albeit at a high level, the various the steps of the process prescribed by statute law and the guideline. This is clearly designed to ensure consistency of approach by controlling the steps taken by the court. Providing a sentencer follows the guideline as required, sentencers will adopt the same

---

[48] For instance, where psychiatric evidence was necessary to afford leading counsel to provide advice as to the availability of a medical defence in a case of intentional killing.

methodology of determining the appropriate reduction, thus ensuring (at a high level) consistency of approach.

Conclusion

The guilty plea guideline combines guidance from the Sentencing Council and summaries of primary law (both statute and case law) to prescribe a clear methodology for the determination of sentence, with guidance as to the way in which the guilty plea guideline interacts with any relevant offence-specific guideline. There remains a degree of discretion as to the discount actually applied, arising from the interpretation of terms used in the guideline, which impacts upon (i) the decision as to the point in proceedings at which the plea was indicated, (ii) the reduction to be made, and (iii) whether one or more of the listed exceptions apply.

Additionally, the guideline does not define when a plea is 'indicated' or 'further assistance necessary' in relation to the exceptions. This creates an obvious risk of inconsistency and demonstrates both the Sentencing Council's view that sentencers need to retain a degree of discretion so as to ensure justice is done, but also that there remains a role for the CACD in interpreting and amplifying their guidelines. And the CACD had clearly seen a need to provide further guidance and structure, through many decisions on this topic.[49] Roberts and Bradford found a high level of compliance with the previous guilty plea guideline and that judicial interpretation remained a relevant factor in the application of the guideline.[50] This provides strong evidence that the guideline contained substantive

---

[49] For instance, the CACD has given guidance on the timing of the indication of the plea, see *R. v Plaku* [2021] EWCA Crim 568; [2021] 4 WLR 82. There are a number of fact-specific decisions which provide guidance on the proper reduction to be made, see eg *R. v Creathorne* [2014] EWCA Crim 500; [2014] 2 Cr App R(S) 48 (amnesia causing delay in plea indication); *R. v Woods* [2020] EWCA Crim 84 (further advice needed before plea); *R. v Kovali* [2013] EWCA Crim 1056; [2014] 1 Cr App R (S) 33 (expert advice as to breach of duty required in case of manslaughter); *R. v Ball* [2019] EWCA Crim 1260 (it is the indication rather than entering the plea that is pertinent); *R. v Hardy* [2020] EWCA Crim 398; [2020] 2 Cr App R (S) 37 (indication given in defence statement but plea entered at PTPH); *R. v James* [2011] EWCA Crim 2630 (plea to a lesser count); *R. v Reid* [2017] EWCA Crim 1523; [2018] 1 Cr App R (S) 8 (the method of communicating the intention to plead); *R. v Dalton* [2021] EWCA Crim 160 (abuse of process arguments and subsequent guilty pleas); and *R. v Carter* [2021] EWCA Crim 667 (plea after initial trial date but before revised trial date).

[50] Julian V Roberts and Ben Bradford, 'Sentence Reductions for a Guilty Plea in England and Wales: Exploring New Empirical Trends' (2015) 12(2) Journal of Empirical Legal Studies 187.

guidance. The new guideline—based on its predecessor—develops that guidance.

Do the Sentencing Council's guidelines contain substantive guidance?

This section has considered the extent to which the Sentencing Council's guidelines—both overarching and offence specific—contain substantive guidance. The foregoing establishes that (i) each contain substantive guidance; (ii) through a variety of devices, the guidelines assist the court in its determination of sentence by structuring the sentencing decision in such a way that judicial discretion remains; and (iii) the process is informed by a consistent approach to the key questions a sentencer must consider. It now falls to consider the extent to which the Sentencing Council's guidelines constrain a sentencer's discretion.

The degree of constraint provided by the guidelines regime

Duty to 'follow' sentencing guidelines

The Sentencing Act 2020 sections 59–60 regulates a sentencing court's relationship with the Sentencing Council's guidelines. The 2020 Act provided for a 'tighter' relationship between sentencing court and sentencing guidelines; previously, there was a duty to 'have regard' to the guidelines, however with the creation of the Sentencing Council came the seemingly more prescriptively worded duty to 'follow' sentencing guidelines. Sections 59 and 60 provide:

s.59(1) Every court—
(a) must, in sentencing an offender, follow any sentencing guidelines which are relevant to the offender's case, and
(b) must, in exercising any other function relating to the sentencing of offenders, follow any sentencing guidelines which are relevant to the exercise of the function,

unless the court is satisfied that it would be contrary to the interests of justice to do so.

...

s.60(1) This section applies where—
(a) a court is deciding what sentence to impose on an offender for an offence, and
(b) offence-specific guidelines have been issued in relation to the offence.

(2) The principal guidelines duty includes a duty to impose on the offender, in accordance with the offence-specific guidelines, a sentence which is within the offence range.

(3) Subsection (2) is subject to—
(a) section 73 (reduction in sentences for guilty pleas),
(b) sections 74, 387 and 388 (assistance by offenders: reduction or review of sentence) and any other rule of law by virtue of which an offender may receive a discounted sentence in consequence of assistance given (or offered to be given) by the offender to the prosecutor or investigator of an offence, and
(c) any rule of law as to the totality of sentences.

(4) If the offence-specific guidelines describe different seriousness categories—
(a) the principal guidelines duty also includes a duty to decide which of the categories most resembles the offender's case in order to identify the sentencing starting point in the offence range, but
(b) nothing in this section imposes on the court a separate duty to impose a sentence which is within the category range.

(5) Subsection (4) does not apply if the court is of the opinion that, for the purpose of identifying the sentence within the offence range which is the appropriate starting point, none of the categories sufficiently resembles the offender's case.

A court must 'follow' a relevant sentencing guideline unless it is contrary to the interests of justice to do so. This requires careful consideration. First, there will be offences to which the guideline expressly applies. Offence-specific guidelines state on their first page to which offences that particular guideline applies: sometimes that is a single offence (eg grievous bodily harm with intent contrary to section 18 of the Offences against the Person Act 1861) and sometimes that there are multiple offences (eg fraud contrary to section 1 of the Fraud Act 2006, false accounting contrary to section 17 of the Theft Act 1968 and conspiracy to defraud contrary to common law). Secondly, there are inchoate offences such as attempts to commit substantive offences or offences of conspiracy to commit a substantive offence to which guidelines for the substantive offences have been held to apply by common law.[51] Thirdly, there are analogous guidelines, where a court considers that although not directly applicable, a guideline may provide assistance (eg in blackmail cases, depending on the nature[52]).[53] There is therefore a need for flexibility in the application of offence-specific guidelines to account for these differing circumstances.

Having determined that a guideline applies or may be relevant to the sentencing exercise at hand, the duty in section 59 (1) is a duty to 'follow'[54] it. The sentencer is therefore required to apply its contents. In the case of an offence specific guideline, section 59(1) states this requires the court to determine into which of the described categories the offence falls (ie Steps 1 and 2), though this clearly also means to following the other steps in the guideline; in the case of an overarching guideline, it clearly means to apply whichever sections are relevant, though section 59 makes no provision for it. Roberts concluded that the new duty to follow guidelines would create a heightened expectation that a court would impose a sentence consistent with the sentencing guidelines.[55] This has been borne out by the data: in 2011 the Sentencing Council conducted research into compliance rates, finding that only 2 per cent of sentences

---

[51] *R. v Laverick* [2015] EWCA Crim 1059; [2015] 2 Cr App R (S) 62 and *Attorney General's Reference (R. v Agolini and Others)* [2017] EWCA Crim 173.
[52] *R. v Murphy* [2019] EWCA Crim 438.
[53] *R. v Lewis* [2012] EWCA Crim 1071.
[54] Although, the former duty, a duty to 'have regard', is in my view practically indistinguishable from the new 'duty to follow'.
[55] Julian V Roberts, 'Sentencing Guidelines in England and Wales: A Review of Recent Developments' (2010) 82 Centre for Crime and Justice Studies 41, 42.

were outside of the offence range, in other words the court had not followed the guideline.[56]

Where the court considers it would be contrary to the interests of justice to do so, the court is released from its obligation to follow the guideline. Strictly this appears to no longer require the sentencer to follow the process, though it may be that the departure in fact comes in the form of departing from the figures provided at Step 2 of the offence-specific guidelines, rather than departing from the process and approach. Roberts notes that this combination of forceful language ('follow') and the interests of justice test focus the court's attention on the relevance of a particular guideline.[57] Additionally, it focuses the court's mind on the utility of the guideline: while, for example, the assault guideline will be relevant to an assault case, it may not provide much assistance where the facts of the offence are so unusual, or it is evident that the guideline was not drafted intending to cater for such a set of facts. The use of the phrase 'interests of justice' suggests a high threshold, demonstrating an intention of Parliament for departures to be rare.[58]

The Sentencing Council have previously described this as requiring 'substantial and compelling reasons' for departing from a guideline.[59] The limiting effect of the duty to follow provision is therefore entirely dependent upon the breadth of the range which in turn is influenced (but not dictated) by the statutory maximum sentence. Many offences involve a wide range of seriousness and therefore the offence ranges tend to be wide, although often not extending to the statutory maximum sentence. The use of wide offence ranges narrows the scope for the court to have to rely on the 'escape clause' in section 59 (1), not following the guideline on the basis that the court is of the view that it is in the interests of justice not to do so. It is therefore no surprise that compliance rates are high.

---

[56] Sentencing Council, *Crown Court Sentencing Survey Experimental Statistics* (Office of the Sentencing Council 2011) 3.
[57] Roberts, 'Sentencing Guidelines in England and Wales' (n 55) 42.
[58] Andrew Ashworth, 'Coroners and Justice Act 2009: Sentencing Guidelines and the Sentencing Council' [2010] Criminal Law Review 389–401, 394.
[59] Sentencing Council, 'Sentencing guidelines and the Sentencing Council' Available at <https://www.sentencingcouncil.org.uk/wp-content/uploads/Presentation_-_for_researchers_and_academics.pdf> accessed 29 December 2021.

Bottoms and Parsons note that compliance rates are 'frequently over 90 per cent' and 'not very meaningful'.[60] Given the wide ranges, the high compliance rate is expected and their conclusion as to its meaning is sound. They reject an alternative approach of measuring compliance by category range (rather than offence range) by reference to the fact that the category is determined prior to the later adjustment by reference to the aggravating and mitigating factors (and Step 3 et seq). Both points appear to be misconceived. First, the high compliance rate is meaningful because it illustrates the usage of the guideline and the extent to which the guidelines are capable of catering for the full range of offences coming before the courts within a particular offence type. A 90 per cent compliance rate—that is, 90 per cent of sentencing decisions result in a sentence within the offence range—suggests that the guidelines cater for 90 per cent of offences coming before the courts. That is a highly relevant statistic (and one which the Sentencing Council should arguably make more of). Inverting that, if the statistic was that the guidelines could not cater for 90 per cent of cases, then it would seem reasonable to conclude that the guidelines were deficient in some way. To cater for 90 per cent of cases seems like a prerequisite—though not a hallmark—for success. Secondly, Bottoms and Parsons are correct to reject the alternative approach of measuring compliance by category range, but only because category range alone is insufficient. Data as to the percentage of cases which are placed into each category at Step 2 do not inform us as to the success of the guideline without knowing where the eventual sentence is located within the offence range. This requires further data collection of course, but the rejection of the notion of measuring compliance by reference to guideline category as a measure of success seems premature.

A consequence of guidelines has been that the nature of appeals to the CACD has changed. Formerly, a large number of appeals would be put on the broad ground that the sentence was manifestly excessive; now, there is a large number put on the basis that the judge chose the incorrect guideline category. Not only does this bring the CACD into a prominent position in relation to 'policing' compliance with the guideline, but it

---

[60] Bottoms and Parsons, 'The Sentencing Council in 2017' (n 36) 12.

underlines the importance of the category range (rather than the offence range).

Offence range versus Category range

It is obvious that section 59 significantly softens the duty upon the court to 'follow' a guideline.[61] A court is required, in following a guideline, to impose a sentence within the offence range—that is the range provided by all categories—not the category range. For an offence of rape that the court has determined falls within category 2A (starting point ten years, range nine to thirteen years), the duty is only to impose a sentence between four and fifteen years.

One can therefore see why Ashworth described the duty as 'pitifully loose'.[62] Despite the seemingly prescriptive process which the court must adopt, including the exhaustive list of factors at Step 1, when the court reaches the stage at which it must impose sentence, the obligation is significantly less prescriptive. The duty is therefore one mostly directed at form rather than substance: the guidelines appear to be predominantly concerned with the observance of the process rather than the outcome. This accords with the Sentencing Council's agreed statement at its first meeting that the Sentencing Council will 'promote a clear, fair and consistent *approach* to sentencing' (emphasis added).[63] Of course it is right to observe, as noted in Chapter 2, that greater consistency of approach is likely to lead to greater consistency of outcome; if sentencers are adopting the uniform process, referring to the same factors at Step 1, and beginning with the same starting points, the likelihood of movement from those starting points to a point which renders the sentence disproportionate to the seriousness of the offence is clearly reduced.

Step 1 of the offence-specific guidelines is more influential on the eventual sentence as it provides the greatest degree of guidance by narrowing

---

[61] This was first noted by Ashworth, describing the duty to follow as having been 'diluted' by other provisions in the Act: Ashworth, 'Coroners and Justice Act 2009' (n 58) 394.
[62] ibid 395.
[63] Sentencing Council, *Minutes of Meeting of the Sentencing Council, 22–23 April 2010*, para 9.2. Available at <https://www.sentencingcouncil.org.uk/wp-content/uploads/web_22_23-04-2010.pdf> accessed 29 December 2021.

down the range of proportionate sentences from the offence range down to the category range. Thereafter, at Step 2, the determination of the degree of movement from the starting point (either within or without the category range) is unlikely to be significant given the secondary importance of the factors listed at Step 2, as argued earlier.

Although the duty under section 59 (1) is only to impose a sentence within the offence range—not within the category range—the category ranges provide soft limits beyond which it is unusual for a sentencer to venture, thereby providing an additional degree of constraint. This is because the onus is upon the court to find, at Step 2, factors to justify moving outside of the category range (whether up or down), notwithstanding the absence of a duty upon the court to impose a sentence within the category range unless a certain test is met. This would appear to prey upon common sense; if the court has a duty to follow the guideline and to determine (where possible) the category into which an offence falls, and where the category includes a starting point and a range of sentences for offences within that category, then to move beyond the category range must be justified by reference to factors at Step 2 (or any other relevant factors). Without such justification, it would be unreasonable to impose a sentence outside of that category range. This structure therefore encourages the imposition of sentences within the category range, though it does not require it. The product is therefore far greater consistency of outcome.

Empirical literature

The preceding paragraphs have presented a picture of limited efficacy; despite the highly prescriptive nature of the duty and of Step 1 of the offence specific guidelines, Step 2 and the (recently reduced but still subsisting) risk of differing interpretations places a limitation on the effect the guidelines can have on sentencing consistency. The overarching guidelines rely heavily upon interpretation and application, which has an attendant risk of inconsistency. This risk, however, is mitigated by the illustrative examples which constrain the application of the broad principles described by the guideline and encourage application of the principles in a manner consistent with the examples provided. Concomitantly, those without such examples contain a greater risk of inconsistency.

It is well recognized by the courts that the Sentencing Council's primary objective is to promote greater consistency in sentencing.[64] Academics have explored the content and structure of the guidelines and concluded that improvements can be made to the guidelines regime. A qualitative assessment can only take this exploration so far, however. Ultimately, the question of whether the Sentencing Council's guidelines have improved consistency is to be answered through empirical research. Such research is limited at present.

For instance, Pina-Sanchez and Linacre found that after the introduction of the Assault guideline, variation decreased (ie there was an improvement in consistency) which was partly attributable to the implementation of the new guideline.[65] There are limits to what the empirical literature can tell us about the efficacy of guidelines, however. Pina-Sanchez and Linacre also explored inter-court consistency and the application of aggravating and mitigating factors and, although they found limited evidence of inconsistency, this was partly due to the limitations of the data; for instance they were unable to assess inter-judge disparity and had to exclude thirty-eight of forty-seven sentencing factors.[66]

More recently, the Sentencing Council has conducted research in relation to the drugs offences guideline. This was considered in Chapter 3, but in short, the study was able to control for a greater number of factors than had previously been controlled for. It concluded that although (in relation to England and Wales) the disparity was less than had previously been found, there was still a degree of inconsistency present attributable to both sex and ethnicity. A main driver of the research was the fact that the Sentencing Council is revising its drugs guideline and it considered it necessary to identify areas in which the guideline ought to be improved.

---

[64] See eg *Attorney General's Reference (R. v NC)* [2016] EWCA Crim 1141 and *Attorney General's Reference (R. v Kahar); R. v Kahar* [2016] EWCA Crim 568; [2016] 2 Cr App R (S) 32.

[65] Jose Pina-Sanchez and Robin Linacre, 'Enhancing Consistency in Sentencing: Exploring the Effects of Guidelines in England and Wales' (2014) 30(4) Journal of Quantitative Criminology 731.

[66] Jose Pina-Sanchez and Robin Linacre, 'Sentence Consistency in England and Wales: Evidence from the Crown Court Sentencing Survey' (2013) 53(6) The British Journal of Criminology 1118;

This is clearly an important aspect to the Council's work. It is important for at least two reasons. First, it is vital that the true position as regards inconsistency (and the source of it) is known: without such knowledge, it is not possible to look beyond the theoretical to the practical. Secondly, it enables the Sentencing Council to make necessary amendments to its current guidelines, and learn from past mistakes to enable higher quality guidelines in the future. Most recently, the Sentencing Council conducted an assessment of three of its offence-specific guidelines.[67] In summary, the research found that 'for domestic burglary and supply/ possession with intent to supply a controlled drug, there is some evidence of an increase in consistency following the introduction of these guidelines. However, for theft from a shop or stall, no increase in consistency was observed.'[68] This is particularly important. It illustrates that following the introduction of the domestic burglary and drug supply guidelines, consistency in sentencing increased. The Council accepts that it is difficult to measure consistency in sentencing and that there are challenges in attributing the results to the guidelines themselves.[69] Against the background of the literature discussed in Chapter 3—much of which in the United Kingdom pre-dates the guidelines era—this is very strong evidence that sentencing guidelines have a positive effect on sentencing consistency, however, the findings in relation to the theft guideline will be of some concern, no doubt. It is right to note, however, that in its research papers on consistency, the Sentencing Council has unequivocally stated that its efforts to increase consistency should be viewed as efforts to improve consistency of approach, that is, how the guidelines are applied. Importantly, this research has not considered the effect (if any) of the offence-specific guidelines on the severity of sentencing outcomes. Therefore, while this is important research that informs the understanding of the search for greater consistency, it is limited by virtue of the Sentencing Council's definition of consistency (which is far narrower than that adopted in this work) and thus the scope of the research.

---

[67] Domestic burglary, supply/possession with intent to supply a controlled drug and theft from a shop/stall. Sentencing Council, *The Impact of Three Guidelines on Consistency in Sentencing* (Office of the Sentencing Council 2021).
[68] ibid 4.
[69] ibid 6.

Additionally, there are problems in assessing consistency purely through an empirical lens. In a scheme predominantly reliant on a principle which is widely regarded to be imprecise, analysis of data exploring consistency can only be approximate; if the right result is imprecise, measuring it accurately is fraught with difficulties. As the Sentencing Council itself accepts that 'whilst we know that variation in outcomes does not necessarily mean an inconsistent approach, we can assume that where there are more consistent outcomes there are likely to be more consistent approaches'.[70] Moreover, an analysis of sentence lengths based on the presence of case characteristics recorded in the Crown Court Sentencing Survey (CCSS) can only show consistency of sentence in cases where a particular factor was found to be present; it cannot show results in sufficient detail to be able to assess whether a particular offence received a sentence which was consistent with the applicable principles, rather it can only show the extent to which it was consistent with other offences with the same factors. For instance, if all Category 1 grievous bodily harm with intent offences (category range nine to sixteen years) received sentences of twenty years, that would be consistent, but not in accordance with the principle of proportionality. Further, the CCSS data spans from 2010 to 2015 and thus there is a narrow window of data which can be analysed. For the purposes of pre- and post-guideline analysis, this further limits the work that can be done. Thus, empirical literature—at present—cannot materially inform the consideration of consistency in sentencing where the definition of consistency adopted focuses on the application of principle.

As such, the empirical literature is an imperfect means through which to study consistency as conceived of in this work. The absence of a theoretical framework as regards the principles upon which the imposition is founded renders studies such as those based on CCSS data of limited utility.

Conclusion

This chapter has sought to examine the Sentencing Council and the way in which it provides structure to the discretionary sentencing decision.

---

[70] ibid 9–10.

It has been argued that there are two requisite components to sentencing guidelines which effectively promote consistency: (i) substantive guidance and (ii) constraint. In considering both the overarching and offence-specific sentencing guidelines, this chapter has sought to expose the strengths and weaknesses of the guidelines, identifying the extent to which the guidelines regime provides substantive guidance and operates as a constraint on judicial discretion.

While, it is clear that the Sentencing Council's guidelines do provide substantive guidance to assist in the pursuit of consistency of sentencing, there are elements which could be improved upon, not least the provision of further guidance and structure surrounding the elements of the process which rely upon the subjective interpretation of the sentencer. The guidelines are concerned with a consistent approach to the application of sentencing principles. Most notably this is the principle of retributive proportionality, with the structure delivered primarily (though not exclusively) through the offence-specific guidelines. Additionally, the overarching principles provide substantive guidance as to other principles and concepts which are relevant to the sentencing decision. That the substantive guidance has a positive impact upon the pursuit of consistency in sentence is supported by empirical research.

The issue of constraint is perhaps slightly more contentious. At the creation of the Sentencing Council, Ashworth noted the limited effect of duty imposed on sentencers:

> The whole idea of guidelines has been undermined. The purpose of guidelines is to steer judges along particular channels but the new legislation is destructive because it hardly binds judges at all. It is possible that the new legislation will lead to the sort of idiosyncratic sentencing that used to cause people such worry. It depends on how tightly the court of appeal polices things, but under the new statute as we now have it, that is a possibility.[71]

This work has not found that cautionary view to be made out by the operation of the guideline. The degree of discretion afforded to sentencers

---

[71] Amelia Hill, 'Judges given free rein by "pitifully loose" sentencing law' *The Guardian*, 5 April 2010, <https://www.theguardian.com/uk/2010/apr/05/judges-sentencing-andrew-ashworth> accessed 29 December 2021.

does not appear to be an error by Parliament and the Sentencing Council; it is intentional. As Roberts and Rafferty (two members of the Council) noted: 'the guidelines in England and Wales promote consistency by prescribing a sequence of steps for courts to follow, while also allowing a significant degree of discretion.'[72] But does it strike the correct balance? On one view, the guidelines are insufficient to secure a desirable degree of consistency as the 'work' done at Step 1 is capable of being undone at Step 2 and the loose duty (effected by the wide offence ranges) renders the 'steer' provided gentle at best. The contrary view would be that the balance is well struck between being overly prescriptive and retaining an appropriate degree of discretion. The guidelines feature a high level of constraint at certain parts: for instance, the duty to follow provides a high degree of constraint as there is a high threshold to meet before the guidelines may be departed from, and the flexibility is necessary to allow for necessary individualization.

This chapter has concluded that there *is* a sufficient degree of constraint to have a positive effect on the pursuit of consistency. Of course, it could be more constraining, however that would undermine the need for individualization, as explored in Chapter 4. Certainly, there are measures which could be adopted to provide more substantive guidance to better promote consistency: it is quite clear that the scope for subjective/disparate interpretations of particular terms used in the guidelines provides scope for inconsistency. While this question is one which requires further empirical research, and therefore to a degree, the jury is still out, this chapter has found that there is strong prima facie evidence that the Sentencing Council's guidelines do promote consistency of sentencing as defined in Chapter 2.

---

[72] Julian V Roberts and Anne Rafferty, 'Sentencing Guidelines in England and Wales: Exploring the New Format' [2011] Criminal Law Review 681, 682.

9
Achieving consistency in sentencing

Defining sentencing disparity as a situation in which similar offenders are treated differently or different offenders are treated the same is overly simplistic.[1]

Introduction

Consistency is widely regarded as a necessary component for a fair sentencing system. It is often described as the requirement to treat like cases alike, yet the simplicity of that maxim belies the complexity of a sentencers' task. What actually *is* consistency? How can it be achieved? And what lessons can be learned from the way in which the system in England and Wales has sought to promote consistency? This work has sought to answer those questions.

An examination of the system in England and Wales provides other jurisdictions the opportunity to learn lessons from a developed sentencing system which has had guideline judgments for some forty years, and a guidelines system for almost twenty years. As is clear, the sentencing scheme in force in England and Wales is a form of limiting retributivism. The governing principle is that of retributive proportionality, the application of which produces a range of proportionate sentences (as retributivism is accepted to be an imprecise concept). Within this range, there are other principles at play, including consequentialist considerations, which operate to inform the determination of the eventual sentence. Thus, jurisdictions which share some of these characteristics can benefit from the English experience—good and bad—in their search to

---

[1] Cassia Spohn, *How Do Judges Decide? The Search for Fairness and Justice in Punishment* (2nd edn, Sage 2008) 130.

better promote consistency. Further, Parliament, the Court of Appeal (Criminal Division) (CACD) and the Sentencing Council in England and Wales can learn lessons from this analysis; what is and is not effective, what is problematic, and in particular areas in which guidance is needed but lacking.

What is consistency in sentencing and what theoretical and practical problems does it pose?

Chapter 2 examined the concept of consistency. First it was argued that a lack of clarity surrounding the concept prevented it from being used as a critical tool to evaluate the efficacy of any sentencing system in its pursuit of consistency. In particular, this hampered the analysis of the sentencing system in England and Wales in its overt desire to be more consistent in the name of fairness. Secondly, it was argued that a normatively sound definition of consistency had to comprise both substantive and procedural elements and focus upon the application of established sentencing principles. In England and Wales, this would first require the consistent application of the principle of retributive proportionality to produce in each sentencing exercise a range of proportionate sentences (though this could of course be substituted for another dominant principle as the particular jurisdiction required). Thereafter, it would require the consistent application of the purposes of sentencing (as prescribed by parliament) to determine where within the proportionate range a particular sentence ought to fall in a particular case. Additionally, Chapter 2 argued that a consistent sentence was one determined by the application of a fair and established procedure, though this is not something reserved exclusively to the concept of consistency, of course.

In arriving at this definition, the notion of 'treating like cases alike' was rejected for two principal reasons. First, there is a lack of clarity, in particular as to what 'like' and 'alike' mean. Secondly, the methodology it encouraged appears to envisage a comparison between one case and another (or others), an approach which it was argued was flawed as it proceeds on the unverified (and perhaps unverifiable) basis that the case(s) with which the comparison is made is correctly decided. Instead, a definition which seeks conformity with established principles in a manner which is theoretically sound and both substantively and procedurally fair is to be preferred.

As retributive proportionality is an imprecise concept, sentences determined by the prescribed procedure and which fall within the permissible sentencing range (ie those which are 'not wrong', to use Morris' formulation) will conform to both the substantive and procedural elements of the definition of consistency advocated. If a sentence is consistent with the governing principles and is imposed in a procedurally fair manner, it satisfies the requirement for consistency.

Does consistency pose a problem in practice, however? Chapter 3 examined the empirical literature in the field, concluding that there was strong, coherent evidence of inconsistency in sentencing. Although the literature provided various possible explanations as to the source of the inconsistency (eg racial bias, gender bias, and geographical variation in crime rate), no single source is conclusively provided by the literature in the field as the sole or primary culprit. What was clear from the literature, however, was that it is judicial discretion which permits (or perhaps encourages) the inconsistent application of sentencing principles as discretion introduces the need for subjective interpretations of principles and subjective applications of those principles to individual cases.

Can consistency be reconciled with the concept of individualized justice?

The concept of individualized justice was then considered in Chapter 4. While the dominant view is that consistency and individualized justice are irreconcilable, it was argued that this is based on a misconception of the concept of consistency and that if the account proffered in Chapter 2 were adopted, consistency and individualized justice may be reconciled. Individualized justice requires that the determination of sentence ought to consider both the features of the offence and the offender, but placing a particular emphasis upon the characteristics of the individual.

It was suggested that a conception of consistency which placed an emphasis upon the proper—and therefore consistent—application of principle would, in fact, accord with an individualized approach to sentencing. This involved a rejection of the notion that individualization permits an 'anything goes' approach to sentencing, in favour of what was argued to be the better view, namely that individualization pays respect to sentencing principles; in fact, there is a strong argument that the limiting retributivist model operative in England and Wales not only permits but arguably encourages an individualized approach to sentencing. While the eventual sentence must be proportionate, that concept is imprecise and produces a range of sentences which are acceptable; therefore a sentence may be individualized by reference to other factors (defined in section 57 of the Sentencing Act 2020) which determine where in the proportionate range the eventual sentence falls.

What is a discretionary sentencing decision and how may such decisions be structured?

It is evident that where the sentencing process involves the subjective interpretation of a principle, there is a risk that different individuals will arrive at different conclusions. That does not automatically produce an inconsistent result, but it makes inconsistency *prima facie* more likely. Accordingly, Chapter 5 considered the concept of judicial discretion and how it may be structured so as to limit the risk of inconsistency.

First, it was necessary to identify where discretion exists in sentencing. The concept of discretion was analysed and it was argued that a discretion exists where:

(1) the decision-maker is required by law to make a decision;
(2) principles (or standards) exist which guide the making of the decision; and
(3) the proper application of those principles does not produce a single, obviously correct, result.

Thereafter, it is necessary to determine whether a discretion has been properly exercised. It was argued that where:

(1) the decision was not taken in pursuit of personal whim or on an arbitrary or legally irrelevant basis;
(2) the decision was taken by an application of relevant principles;

(3) the exercise was rational; and
(4) the decision made was, in the decision-maker's opinion, likely to bring about the most appropriate outcome,

the discretion was properly exercised.

This enabled the identification of the decisions in the field of sentencing which are properly labelled 'discretionary' decisions. Thereafter, the chapter considered different methods of structuring discretion, distinguishing between limiting and guiding measures. It was argued that limiting measures tended to be blunt tools which prescribe specific outcomes, requiring the sentencer to apply the limiting measure to the case in question without much by way of analysis or judgment. By contrast, it was argued that guiding measures are evaluative in nature and require qualitative engagement by the sentencer who performs a more nuanced task.

How effectively does the system in England and Wales promote consistency?

This section seeks to bring together the analysis of the three institutions who provide that structure, Parliament, the CACD, and the Sentencing Council, and considers the efficacy of their combined efforts in promoting consistency in sentencing. Using England and Wales as a case study, it is possible to identify strengths and weaknesses in perhaps the most advanced narrative guidelines system currently in force. From this, lessons can be learned, both for improvements domestically and abroad, based on the analysis of the successes and failures of the English experience.

The extent of the structure currently provided

Parliament provides the foundations of the sentencing scheme in England and Wales but as Chapter 6 established, it provides little more by way of guidance. For decades, it was the CACD who provided additional structure and guidance as explored in Chapter 7, however much of that structure is now provided by the Sentencing Council. Can any one of the three institutions provide the requisite level of structure on its own, within the current scheme? The previous three chapters strongly conclude that they cannot.

The structure provided by Parliament comes in the form of the identification of general principles and the limitations it places on the sentencing courts' powers. Chapter 6 concluded that this structure is insufficient to achieve any meaningful degree of consistency; the provisions are either guiding measures of a general nature and lack sufficient detail to provide any substantive guidance as to the application of the applicable sentencing principles, or they are limiting measures which are insufficiently flexible to enable the requisite individualization needed to ensure the sentence imposed is in accordance with the principles underpinning the scheme. One exception to this is parliament's attempt at substantive guidance as to the application of the principle of proportionality in cases of murder in the form of Schedule 21 to the Sentencing Act 2020. As Chapter 6 explored, although Schedule 21 does provide more substantive guidance as to the principle of proportionality than other legislative provisions, this piece of legislation has been subject to plenty of academic criticism regarding the 'loose adherence' paid to Schedule 21 and the lack of discussion in the passage of the Bill.[2] Additionally, it has been the subject of much comment by the CACD; in *R. v Peters* the court observed: 'Broad guidance will produce sentencing consistency, but precisely because the circumstances of the offence and the offender vary, and may vary widely, an individual sentencing decision appropriate for the unique circumstances of each case is required.'[3]

Chapter 7 concluded that the structure provided by Schedule 21 is insufficient and that it has been necessary for the CACD to provide additional guidance. If that is correct, and it is neither practicable nor pragmatic for parliament to provide the requisite guidance (either in the case of murder or for all aspects of sentencing), the irresistible conclusion appears to be that Parliament cannot provide adequate structure on its own.

---

[2] See eg George Mawhinney, 'Sentencing Murders Done for Gain: The Court of Appeal and Schedule 21' (2015) 3 Sentencing News 8–11 and Barry Mitchell, 'Identifying and Punishing the More Serious Murders' [2016] Criminal Law Review 467.

[3] [2005] EWCA Crim 605; [2005] 2 Cr App R (S) 101 at [3].

As was described in Chapter 7, sentencing practice evolves in an iterative fashion, principally through the continual development of sentencing jurisprudence through the decisions of the CACD. That chapter concluded that the CACD provided structure to the sentencing decision in numerous ways, including through the guideline judgment which it pioneered in the 1970s. The structure currently provided by the CACD—though positive in its effect upon the pursuit of consistency—is insufficient either in isolation or in conjunction with Parliament. In particular, the analysis suggested that the guidance provided by the CACD as to the determination of sentence severity is too vague and too *ad hoc* to achieve the desired degree of consistency. Chapter 7 aimed to provide a comprehensive analysis of the many forms of guidance proffered by the CACD, concluding that the mainstay of the CACD's guidance—reviews of sentence—does not provide detailed, substantive guidance as to the application of the principle of proportionality. Quite simply, the effect of simply informing whether a particular sentence is too low, too high, or just right is not an efficient nor effective means of exerting influence over the wider sentencing system. Accordingly, the other forms of guidance vary in the form, level of detail, and degree of constraint provided.

This lack of detail is perhaps understandable, though, and one should not mistake this conclusion for criticism. The primary function of an appeal against sentence is to determine the issue(s) presented by the case before the court; the provision of guidance for future cases is a latent aim only. Further still, the CACD is limited by the cases which come before it as to the guidance which it can provide. Finally, Chapter 7 concluded that general guidance given by the CACD is prone to subjective (and therefore inaccurate and inconsistent) interpretation and application. This is particularly so in the case of guidance as to the application of the principle of proportionality (ie whether a sentence is too long or too short). The chapter concluded that the structure provided by Parliament and the CACD was insufficient to effectively promote consistency, but that the CACD performs a vital role, nonetheless.

With insufficient structure provided by Parliament and the CACD, one must look to the Sentencing Council. The Sentencing Council has now assumed the role of the primary provider of guidance and structure of the decision to impose sentence. As Chapter 8 concluded, the Sentencing Council's guidelines provide more detailed guidance than that which had previously been provided by the CACD and this increased detail brings about a high degree of consistency, albeit there is more guidance that could be given. Chapter 8 established that the Sentencing Council's guidelines do provide substantive guidance in a form which imposes an appropriate level of constraint upon sentencing courts. Elements of the guidelines which risked (or encouraged) inconsistency were identified; these particularly included parts of the guideline which require the subjective interpretation of words and phrases in respect of which there is no further substantive guidance and which can impact in a significant way on the guideline categorization and therefore the eventual sentence. Notwithstanding these deficiencies, Chapter 8 concluded that the guidelines do promote consistency in a meaningful way.

Chapters 6, 7, and 8 examined the way in which the sentencing scheme in England and Wales provides structure to the discretionary sentencing decision as a means of promoting consistency. It is clear that no one institution alone can provide the requisite degree of structure to promote greater consistency in sentencing effectively and efficiently. In concert, however, the conclusion of this latter part of the work is clear: the combined structure provided by the three institutions does promote consistency in an effective way and is likely to produce a high degree of consistency in practice.

The division of labour

Parliament, the CACD, and the Sentencing Council all provide structure concerning the application of the principles underpinning the sentencing system. Parliament's role in this regard is principally to prescribe the core principles which underpin the scheme; it has (seemingly deliberately) not expanded upon them, instead explicitly recognizing that the CACD and the Sentencing Council will amplify the principles and develop further guidance.[4] Parliament has offered some structure as to the application of

---

[4] For instance, Parliament placed (and later removed) a limitation on the CACD's ability to produce a guideline judgment, and expressly required the SC to produce a guideline on the principle of totality and the reduction in sentence for a guilty plea. See the Crime and Disorder Act 1998 ss 80–81 and the Coroners and Justice Act 2009 s 120(3).

the principle of proportionality, though this remains vague. For instance, the creation of limitations on a sentencing court's power by the imposition of maximum and minimum sentences provides a broad steer as to what Parliament considers to be a proportionate sentence for a particular offence. As was noted in Chapter 6 however, as the maximum sentences tend to be high causing the sentencing ranges to be wide, the guidance provided is loose at best.

Having set down the broad limits of the scheme, generally speaking, Parliament leaves the courts' discretion relatively untouched (merely providing for a maximum sentence and the general sentencing powers). On occasion, however, it has intervened where (it can be inferred) it considers that the courts are not imposing appropriate sentences. Examples include Schedule 21 (discussed earlier), altering maximum sentences and creating minimum and mandatory sentences. Aside from these relatively rare legislative interventions, Parliament's role is clearly one concerning the prescription of sentencing powers and overarching principles rather than detailed guidance as to the practice of sentencing—though it is right to note that recent legislative changes and policy proposals have tended to have the appearance of politics rather than principle.

It then falls to either the CACD or the Sentencing Council (or a both) to provide such further guidance as is necessary to promote consistency. It is evident that the Sentencing Council has largely replaced the CACD (which had previously replaced Parliament) as the primary provider of guidance as to the principles to be applied by sentencing courts. This is evidenced not just by the Sentencing Council's output but also by the fact that where there is existing CACD guidance, the creation of an Sentencing Council guideline on that topic supersedes that guidance.[5] The CACD has clearly recognized this transfer of responsibility and has altered its approach to providing structure to the sentencing decision. While it continues to consider appeals against sentence, such appeals now typically revolve around the application of

---

[5] For instance, see *R. v Webbe* [2001] EWCA Crim 1217; [2002] 1 Cr App R (S) 22 (handling stolen goods), *R. v Saw* [2009] EWCA Crim 1; [2009] 2 Cr App R (S) 54 (domestic burglary) and *Attorney General's Reference (R. v Kahar)*; *R. v Ziamani* [2016] EWCA Crim 568; [2016] 2 Cr App R (S) 32 (terrorism).

the guidelines and appeals against sentence do not provide guidance in the way they used to. Formerly, practitioners would appear in the CACD and refer to multiple cases which (they would submit) demonstrated support for their contention that the sentence in question was too high, too low, or neither. These were not guideline cases but cases said to be illustrative of the CACD's approach to the determination of sentence in previous, similar, cases. With the introduction of guidelines, this has changed and the court has commented that the citation of such cases 'is generally of no assistance'.[6]

As such, for offences where there is Sentencing Council guideline, the CACD's role has morphed into providing guidance on the application of the guideline (interpreting terms and clarifying any misunderstandings that may have developed in practice). This represents a significant change in the practice of the CACD; it now acts in concert with the Sentencing Council, supporting its work and amplifying the Sentencing Council's guidance where necessary. Although guidelines are not to be interpreted as though they were a statute, the CACD has adopted a similar role to that which it takes with statutory provisions,[7] providing guidance as to their meaning and application. The CACD has continued to provide guidance separate from the Sentencing Council, however. In cases where there is no Sentencing Council guideline in existence at the time, the CACD has provided guidance regarding the approach to sentencing.[8]

In producing its guidelines, the Sentencing Council relies heavily on the past decisions of the CACD. The default position for the Sentencing Council is to replicate current practice,[9] with deviations from this—what might be described as 'policy change'—rare. The Sentencing Council is concerned with the regularization of practice

---

[6] *R. v Thelwall* [2016] EWCA Crim 1755; [2017] Criminal Law Review 240 at [21].
[7] *R. v Robinson* [2015] EWCA Crim 1839; [2016] 1 Cr App R (S) 35.
[8] For example, in cases of arson see *R. v McKay* [2017] EWCA Crim 2299; [2018] 1 Cr App R (S) 36 (prior to the criminal damage guideline), *R. v Webbe* [2001] EWCA Crim 1217; [2002] 1 Cr App R (S) 22 (prior to the theft guideline), and *Attorney General's Reference (R. v Kahar); R. v Ziamani* [2016] EWCA Crim 568; [2016] 2 Cr App R (S) 32 (prior to the terrorism guideline).
[9] See eg Sentencing Council, *Theft Offences Guideline Assessment* (Office of the Sentencing Council 2019) 1, <https://www.sentencingcouncil.org.uk/wp-content/uploads/Theft-report-FINAL-web.pdf> accessed 29 December 2021 and Julian V Roberts and Andrew Ashworth, 'Evolution of Sentencing Policy in England and Wales 2003–2015' (2016) 45(1) Crime and Justice 307, 339.

and is not principally concerned with sentencing levels or the prison population (in so far as they might be regarded as too high, too low, or just right). Instead, this remains the domain of the CACD who continue to hear appeals against sentence and adjudicate upon the application of the Sentencing Council's guidelines. There is perhaps no better example of this than the Sentencing Council's *Sexual Offences Definitive Guideline (2014)*. The levels contained in the guideline represented a marked increase on the levels contained within the earlier *Sexual Offences Definitive Guideline (2007)*, however this was not an example of the Sentencing Council performing a 'policy' role in deciding to increase the levels as it considered them to be too low. Rather, the levels had been increased to reflect how current practice had evolved since the creation of the 2007 guideline. This was something explicitly stated by the Sentencing Council at the time of the production of the 2014 guideline.[10] This creates a clear picture of harmony between the two institutions, each complimenting the other's work and marking a clear delineation between the CACD's 'policy' role and Sentencing Council's pursuit of consistency.

The system clearly relies upon each institution to perform a distinct role. Although the current system has developed somewhat organically, there is a clear tripartite approach to the provision of structuring sentencing discretion. Parliament provides the foundations for the scheme, prescribing the general principles and imputing some limitations on the powers of the sentencing courts. Thereafter, the Sentencing Council provides substantive guidance, this is principally in relation to the application of the principle of retributive proportionality in order to assist courts in determining the appropriate length of sentence. The CACD provides any additional guidance as is necessary to assist in the use of the Sentencing Council's guidelines and additionally, further guidance in relation to topics not the subject of Sentencing Council guidelines. While the picture is one of a functioning system providing structure to effectively promote consistency in sentencing, could more be achieved?

---

[10] Sentencing Council, *Sexual Offences Response to Consultation* (Office of the Sentencing Council 2014) 19–20.

How could the current regime in England and Wales be improved upon?

Insufficient flexibility

Although the risk of inconsistency stems predominantly from insufficient structure and too much judicial discretion and flexibility, there is one area in which the pursuit of consistency requires *greater* flexibility. It will be recalled that in Chapter 6, there was criticism of the use of minimum and mandatory sentences which limit the exercise of judicial discretion as a means of imposing a proportionate sentence. Chapter 6 described these devices as 'blunt' tools which, because of their highly prescriptive nature, cannot achieve the form of consistency advocated for in this work. This is because minimum and mandatory sentences place an inappropriate emphasis on consistency of outcome as opposed to the finely balanced determination of a proportionate sentence achieved through a consistent approach and application of sentencing principles which requires individualization. Such provisions treat cases which are not alike as if they were, resulting in disproportionate sentences or otherwise complicating the sentencing process, taking the sentencers' focus away from the primary task of imposing a proportionate sentence. The complete reliance upon the CACD and the Sentencing Council to provide this type of structure would produce greater consistency in sentencing and in a more principled manner. Chapter 6 was clear in its conclusion: minimum and mandatory sentences are antithetical to consistency.

Although Chapter 6 was clear that the structure provided is insufficient as a means of achieving an account of consistency focused upon the proper application of sentencing principles, the combination of the CACD and the Sentencing Council obviate the need for Parliament to take any major remedial action. While there could be improvements made on a theoretical level to the sentencing system in England and Wales, it appears that the scheme is clear enough as to the principle on which it is founded. Within the regime, therefore (with the exception of mandatory and minimum sentences as discussed earlier) improvements to promote consistency are to be made elsewhere.

More substantive guidance

As identified in Chapter 8, the Sentencing Council could provide more detailed guidance on specific terms used in their offence-specific guidelines, and more illustrative examples could be used in the overarching guidelines when describing principles and their proper application. Currently, the former is partially fulfilled by the CACD where it may make a broad statement about the meaning of the term in the guideline or simply determine the issue but confine its comments to the case before it. Accordingly, this guidance produced by the CACD is of varying assistance and arises only when the CACD is presented with a suitable case raising an issue, where the CACD is minded to provide guidance and is in fact able to do so.[11] Additionally, on a practical level, further detail contained within guidelines is more likely to be brought to the attention of the sentencing judge than if reference has to be made to a Sentencing Council guideline and CACD authorities.

It seems proper that greater substantive guidance is given by the Sentencing Council; not only is the Sentencing Council the body specifically given responsibility for promoting consistency in sentencing, but who is better placed to define a term used in a Sentencing Council guideline? The question as to which terms require expansion is trickier. A starting point may be to take the terms which the CACD has interpreted, on the basis that it has considered that greater guidance is necessary. Thereafter, the Sentencing Council may have to be more proactive and attempt to identify those terms which may be more commonly applied (or misapplied) or predict which terms require greater detail.

Moreover, while the factors listed at Step 1 of the offence-specific guidelines are weighted (in the sense they are placed into categories, greater, medium lesser, etc), the factors at Step 2 are not. As argued in Chapter 8, this creates a real risk of inconsistency and undermines the guidance provided by Step 1. Accordingly, real consideration ought to be given to the provision of further guidance as to the application of the factors listed at Step 2 of the offence-specific guidelines. Whether an approach which seeks to weight these factors proves to be too prescriptive,

---

[11] It may be that the issue raised is one which requires further research and is not suited to guidance delivered through a judgment.

or whether an approach which seeks to guide the approach to the (case-by-case) weighting of these factors proves to be insufficiently detailed remains to be seen. Certainly, there are challenges to such an endeavour.

The conclusion is surely that a sufficient degree of constraint and substantive guidance provided for by the current guidelines regime, in conjunction with the CACD's decisions. That was the clear conclusion of Chapter 8 and is supported by empirical research. Chapter 8 did, however, conclude that further guidance is likely to produce a higher degree of consistency. Chapter 8 identified elements of the offence-specific guidelines and the overarching guidelines which could benefit from more detailed guidance and greater structure and it is likely that a further positive effect on consistency would be seen as a result.

Would this further structure limit flexibility? As concluded in Chapter 8, there is an appropriate degree of constraint imposed by the Sentencing Council's guidelines regime. While the duty to 'follow' appears highly prescriptive and limiting, it has sufficient flexibility built into it (particularly at Step 2) to allow a sentencer to impose the sentence he or she considers proportionate. The guidelines regime assists the sentencer by encouraging them to consider the appropriate sentence in a structured way, rendering a proportionate sentence more likely.

What role for the CACD?

With the Sentencing Council the predominant provider of guidance, what role is left for the CACD? It is readily apparent that the expertise and skill within the CACD ought to continue to be put to good use through the provision of substantive guidance on an *ad hoc* basis. As the Sentencing Council is better equipped to provide substantive guidance than the CACD, this should be restricted to instances of interpreting guidelines or providing guidance in areas which the Sentencing Council has yet not produced substantive guidance. In due course, the Sentencing Council can consider the CACD's decisions and determine whether to produce guidance of its own. If it does, that guidance can replace the guidance provided by the CACD, in the same manner as described earlier.

Additionally, there is clearly a continuing role for the CACD in the form of appellate review as to the application of the guidelines. By

ACHIEVING CONSISTENCY IN SENTENCING 295

hearing appeals against sentence and providing a 'steer' as to whether the application was correct or incorrect, the CACD has a direct impact upon the application of the principle of proportionality in so far as the level of sentences is concerned. This respects what has become the loose delineation of responsibility, between the provision of substantive structure by the Sentencing Council to produce consistency and the supervision of the levels of sentences by the CACD. Finally, this process is cyclical, as when the Sentencing Council come to review and revise the guidelines, the practice of the CACD will be taken into account as the Sentencing Council's approach is to replicate current practice rather than to adopt a policy-making role as regards sentencing levels. The CACD therefore retains a central (albeit less visible) role.

The CACD ought to continue to provide guidance in areas where the Sentencing Council has not and that the symbiotic relationship between the Sentencing Council and CACD should continue. One would expect, however, that over time as the Sentencing Council moves towards completing its programme of work, the role of the CACD will involve providing fewer traditional guideline judgments and involve a greater amount of guidance which is complementary to existing Sentencing Council guidelines.

Lessons for other jurisdictions

And so that brings the discussion to the important topic of the wider lessons than can be learned from the English and Welsh efforts of structuring discretion to better achieve consistency in sentencing. What follows is a number of broad points that can be taken from the foregoing discussion, predicated on the definition of consistency adopted in Chapter 2.

The need for a clear principle/principles

One. It is important to understand that while the early parts of this work are agnostic to the principle or principles to which a particular sentencing system subscribes, what has been demonstrated is the need for a clear theoretical basis for the particular system being considered. Without a clear principle or number of principles at the heart of a scheme, there can be no realistic hope of achieving consistency as efforts will fail at the first hurdle: 'consistent with what?' A scheme seeking consistency without a clear theoretical basis would be, to adopt Alice's approach to her journey as set out in the quote in the introduction to this work:

> 'Would you tell me, please, which way I ought to go from here?'
> 'That depends a good deal on where you want to get to,' said the Cat.
> 'I don't much care where,' said Alice.
> 'Then it doesn't matter which way you go,' said the Cat.
> '—so long as I get SOMEWHERE,' Alice added as an explanation.
> 'Oh, you're sure to do that,' said the Cat, 'if you only walk long enough.'[12]

If the aim of a system is to arrive at a consistent sentence but the system does not much care for the destination, then it will be extremely difficult to identify with any accuracy the route which should be taken. Thus, the absence of a clear principle or set of clear principles renders the search for consistency a fruitless exercise. And so, the first lesson—obvious as it may be—is that a sentencing scheme must identify its underlying theoretical basis, both in a broad sentence (eg retributive proportionality) but also in a narrower sense (eg ordinal and cardinal proportionality).

It follows, from the foregoing analysis, that a legislature is well placed to articulate these broad, central, principles in legislation; although this hasn't been discussed in this work, it is likely to be considered that this is most appropriate given the way in which Western democracies operate and the requirement for widespread overarching policy decisions to be taken by democratically elected officials.

The need for further guidance in addition to the legislative scheme

Two. It is important that a scheme has an additional institution to provide additional, more specific, structure and guidance. This may be an

---

[12] Lewis Carroll, *Alice in Wonderland* (Macmillan and Co, 1866).

ACHIEVING CONSISTENCY IN SENTENCING 297

appellate court, which can 'flesh out' the broad principles promulgated by the legislature; however, it may also be a guidelines body given the authority to create sentencing guidelines. It may also involve a combination of the two; although the English and Welsh system has developed iteratively, with the Sentencing Council taking some responsibility for sentencing guidance from the CACD, it appears that this system of shared responsibility in fact works very well indeed. The Sentencing Council provides the substantive, primary guidance and the CACD 'fills the gaps' and provides *ad hoc*, and sometimes interim, guidance on discrete topics.

Each institution giving guidance must know its role

Three. A scheme needs to have a clear notion of the division of labour as between its institutions. As has been seen in the discussion of the statutory scheme in England and Wales, broad principles in conjunction with other measures such as maximum sentences and requirements to consider or prohibitions on imposing particular sentence types operate to constrain the sentencer's discretion. This constraint, though vague on any view, places important limitations on sentencers and crucially provides the CACD and the Sentencing Council with the outline of the scheme. From there, the CACD and the Sentencing Council can provide further guidance. In a scheme where both an appellate court and a guidelines body share responsibility for adding to the outline of the scheme provided by the legislature, it is vital that there is a clear delineation of responsibility between the two. This will be for a particular jurisdiction to determine, however, the foregoing analysis has demonstrated that: (i) a guidelines body is better suited than an appellate court to providing wide-ranging sentencing guidance as the important elements of the English guidelines system (including its unique constitutional position, availability of resources and ability to conduct research and consult with interested parties and legal professionals) appear to be well fulfilled by an institution separate to an appellate court; and (ii) an appellate court is better suited to providing interim or *ad hoc* guidance on discrete topics either where the guidelines body has not provided guidance or further guidance on the guidelines is needed, due to its ability to react quickly and clearly and its inability to conduct research, and consult on proposed guidance.

It is obvious that it is necessary for the institutions understand their respective role and has the tools to be able to provide clear and accurate guidance on the relevant principles. Where a principle is unclear, for instance the principle of totality in England and Wales, efforts must be concentrated on establishing a clearer explanation of the principle, for this is where hard work in other areas can be undone. Conceive of this as a bucket of water, with vague principles with little or no substantive guidance represented by holes in the bucket. The remainder of the bucket is intact, maintaining the integrity of the vessel, yet there is water egression through the weaker parts of the bucket. Weaker/vaguer guidance allows for egression.

Combining limiting and guiding measures

Four. It appears to be important that the difference between limiting and guiding measures is appreciated, along with the general rule that (i) limiting measures are blunt tools which risk inconsistency (particularly the use of minimum and mandatory sentences) and (ii) guiding measures can be more nuanced, but require more effort to clearly identify the underlying principle to enable sentencers to better interpret the measure to achieve its desired result. Almost inevitably, a combination of both is required, but the balance between the two will be the subject of debate and dependent upon the desires of the scheme in question. No 'hard and fast rules' can be identified.

Combining offence-specific and overarching guidance

Five. Whether by guideline judgment or sentencing guideline, to best promote consistency, a combination of offence-specific guidance and overarching guidance is needed. It is well accepted that the principle of retributive proportionality is vague, and so in systems that have that at their heart, offence-specific guidelines, with detailed guidance on achieving a proportionate sentence, are necessary. But that is likely to be so for other principles too; any principle at the heart of a scheme is almost inevitably going to be vague so as not to unduly constrict sentencing courts in individual cases. Thus, clear, nuanced guidance on the quantum of a sentence is necessary. Similarly, overarching guidance is likely to bring about more consistency. Guidance on particular features of a sentencing scheme, or aspects of sentencing such as the nature of the sentence (community vs custodial, determinate vs indeterminate and so on) is likely to reduce other areas of inconsistency.

Consistency of approach and consistency of outcome

Six. Guidance must be principally directed towards consistency of approach, however, there must be an appreciation of the need for a degree of consistency of outcome. As developed in the early parts of this work, consistency of approach is important, not least to achieve some transparency and fairness and to afford a sentencing court with flexibility to do justice to difference, however, an important component of consistency in sentencing is the similarity of outcome. It is insufficient, theoretically as well as normatively, for sentencers to adopt the same process but arrive at wildly different conclusions in the case of identical circumstances. Thus, the guidance must promote consistency of approach and outcome, in accordance with the definition arrived at in Chapter 2.

A cautious use of language

Seven. In identifying the aspects of sentencing which require guidance, care must be exercised in the use of language. That applies equally to the legislature as it does to an appellate court or guidelines body. The foregoing discussion has illustrated that the language used in statute and guidelines has required the appellate court in England and Wales to step in and either correct any misapprehensions regarding the language used, or to provide additional guidance as a result of the vague language employed by the other institutions. Lawyers will always find something to argue about, however, where possible, clarity of meaning through language should be achieved, which will reduce inconsistent application.

Constraint is not the enemy of discretion, inappropriate constraint is

Eight. It is important that a balance between constraint and discretion is achieved. Constraint is not the enemy of discretion; discretion is to do through law what is just and constraint (whether limiting or guiding) is designed to assist in that endeavour. Guiding measures therefore 'push' the sentencer in the right direction, a gentle hand on the shoulder, rather than a straightjacket or harness. Limiting measures, naturally, have harder edges, but they operate to prevent a court from doing what would be unjust. The combination of the two is to achieve a sentencing outcome which is consistent with the principle(s) underlying the scheme. It is important that the limiting measures are used sparingly and the guiding measures are used effectively.

Guidance must be substantive

Nine. Guidance provided must be substantive; merely providing constraint will be insufficient. For limiting measures, this is less of a concern because of the likelihood that such measures will be smaller in number than guiding measures and of course the absence of the need for the sentencer to interpret the limiting measure (rather, they just need to apply it). For guiding measures, however, there needs to be something beyond a mere description of the principle of a particular measure; the guidance needs to provide the sentencer with assistance as to the application of the principle etc so as to provide material assistance in understanding its purpose and the way in which it is to be implemented.

With those points firmly in mind, it is respectfully suggested that a scheme that desires consistency in sentencing will have the foundations to develop a suitable sentencing system, whatever its dominant principle(s).

Bibliography

Advisory Council on the Penal System, *Sentences of Imprisonment: A Review of Maximum Penalties* (Home Office 1978)

Allen R, *The Sentencing Council for England and Wales: Brake or Accelerator on the Use of Prison?* (Transform Justice 2016)

Anthony T, Bartels L, and Hopkins A, 'Lessons Lost in Sentencing: Welding Individualised Justice to Indigenous Justice' (2015) 39(47) Melbourne University Law Review 47–76

Ashworth A, *Sentencing and Penal Policy* (Weidenfeld and Nicholson 1983)

Ashworth A, *Sentencing in the Crown Court: Report of an Exploratory Study, Occasional Paper No. 10* (Centre for Criminological Research 1984)

Ashworth A, 'Disentangling Disparity' in Pennington DC and Lloyd-Bostock S (eds), *The Psychology of Sentencing: Approaches to Consistency and Disparity* (Centre for Socio-Legal Studies 1987)

Ashworth A, 'Responsibilities, Rights and Restorative Justice' (2002) 42 British Journal of Criminology 578–595

Ashworth A, 'Criminal Justice Act 2003: The Sentencing Provisions' (2005) 68(5) Modern Law Review 822–38

Ashworth A, 'Rehabilitation' in von Hirsch A, Ashworth A, and Roberts JV (eds), *Principled Sentencing: Readings on Theory and Policy* (3rd edn, Hart 2009)

Ashworth A, 'Structuring Sentencing Discretion' in von Hirsch A, Ashworth A, and Roberts JV (eds), *Principled Sentencing: Readings on Theory and Policy* (3rd edn, Hart 2009)

Ashworth A, 'Coroners and Justice Act 2009: Sentencing Guidelines and the Sentencing Council' (2010) 5 Criminal Law Review 389–401

Ashworth A, 'The Evolution of Sentencing Policy and Practice in England and Wales, 2003–2015' (2016) 45(1) Crime and Justice 307–58

Ashworth A, 'The Evolution of English Sentencing Guidance in 2016' (2017) 7 Criminal Law Review 507

Ashworth A and Kelly R, *Sentencing and Criminal Justice* (7th edn, Bloomsbury 2021)

Ashworth A and Player E, 'Sentencing, Equal Treatment and the Impact of Sanctions' in Ashworth A and Wasik M (eds), *Fundamentals of Sentencing Theory* (OUP 1998)

Ashworth A and Roberts JV, 'The Origins and Nature of the Sentencing Guidelines in England and Wales' in Ashworth A and Roberts JV (eds), *Sentencing Guidelines: Exploring the English Model* (OUP 2013)

Bagaric M 'Proportionality in Sentencing: Its Justification, Meaning and Role' (2000) 12(2) Current Issues in Criminal Justice, 143–65

Bagaric M and Pathinayake A, 'The Paradox of Parity in Sentencing in Australia: The Pursuit of Equal Justice that Highlights the Futility of Consistency in Sentencing' (2013) 77(5) Journal of Criminal Law 399–416

Bagaric M, Edney R, and Alexander T, *Sentencing in Australia* (Thomson Reuters 2017)
Bailey D and Norbury L, *Bennion on Statutory Interpretation* (7th edn, Lexis Nexis 2019)
Beldam A and Holdham S, *Court of Appeal Criminal Division: A Practitioners' Guide* (2nd edn, Sweet and Maxwell 2018)
Bingham T, 'The Discretion of the Judge' (1990) 5(1) Denning Law Journal 27–43
Bontrager S, Barrick K, and Stupi E, 'Gender and Sentencing: A Meta-analysis of Contemporary Research' (2013) 16(2) The Journal of Gender, Race, and Justice, 349–72
Bottom, AE, 'Five Puzzles in von Hirsch's Theory of Punishment' in Ashworth A and Wasik M (eds), *Fundamentals of Sentencing Theory: Essays in Honour of Andrew von Hirsch* (Clarendon 1998)
Bottoms AE and Parsons AR, 'The Sentencing Council in 2017: A Report on Research to Advise on How the Sentencing Council Can Best Exercise its Statutory Functions' (Office of the Sentencing Council 2017)
Brand P and Getzler J, *Judges and Judging in the History of the Common Law and Civil Law: From Antiquity to Modern Times* (CUP 2012)
Brantingham PL, 'Sentencing Disparity: An Analysis of Judicial Consistency' [1985] Journal of Quantitative Criminology 1(3) 281
British Library, Victorian Prisons and Punishments, 14 October 2009 <https://www.bl.uk/victorian-britain/articles/victorian-prisons-and-punishments>
Brunton-Smith I, Pina-Sanchez J, and Li G, 'Re-assessing the Consistency Of Sentencing Decisions in Cases of Assault: Allowing for Within Court Inconsistencies' (2020) 60(6) British Journal of Criminology 1438–59.
Canadian Sentencing Commission, *Sentencing Reform: A Canadian Approach* (Minister of Supply and Services Canada 1986)
Carroll L, *Alice in Wonderland* (Macmillan and Co 1866)
Carter P, *Managing Offenders, Reducing Crime: A New Approach* (Home Office 2003)
Corston J, *A Report by Baroness Jean Corston of A Review of Women with Particular Vulnerabilities in the Criminal Justice System* (Home Office 2007)
Criminal Law Commissioners, *Seventh Report* (W. Clowes and Sons 1843)
Crown Prosecution Service, 'The Prosecutor's Role In Sentencing, CPS Legal Guidance' <https://www.cps.gov.uk/publications/code_for_crown_prosecutors/role.html>
Crown Prosecution Service, 'Misconduct in Public Office' <https://www.cps.gov.uk/legal-guidance/misconduct-public-office>
Crown Prosecution Service, 'Public Justice Offences Incorporating the Charging Standard, CPS Legal Guidance' <https://www.cps.gov.uk/legal-guidance/public-justice-offences-incorporating-charging-standard>
Davies M and Tyrer J, '"Filling in the Gaps"—A Study of Judicial Culture: Views of Judges in England and Wales on Sentencing Domestic Burglars Contrasted with the Recommendations of the Sentencing Advisory Panel and the Court of Appeal Guidelines' [2003] Criminal Law Review 243–65
The Defence Brief, Sentences, 6 February 2013 <http://defencebrief.blogspot.com/2013/02/sentences.html>

Dictionary.com, 'discretion' <http://www.dictionary.com/browse/discretion>
Dhami MK, 'Sentencing Guidelines in England and Wales: A Missed Opportunity?' (2013) (76) Law and Contemporary Problems 289–307
Doerner JK and Demuth S, 'Gender and Sentencing in the Federal Courts: Are Women Treated More Leniently?' (2014) 25(2) Criminal Justice Policy Review 242–69
Doob AN and Brodeur JP, 'Achieving Accountability in Sentencing' in Stenning PC (ed), *Accountability for Criminal Justice: Selected Essays* (University of Toronto Press 1995)
Doob AN and Webster CM, 'Sentence Severity and Crime: Accepting the Null Hypothesis' (2003) 30 Crime and Justice 143–195
van Duyne PC, 'Simple Decision Making' in Pennington DC and Lloyd-Bostock S (eds), *The Psychology of Sentencing: Approaches to Consistency and Disparity* (Centre for Socio-Legal Studies 1987)
van Duyne PC, 'Backgrounds of Disparity in the Administration of Criminal Law' in *European Committee on Crime Problems, Disparities in Sentencing: Causes and Solutions* (Council of Europe 1989)
Dworkin R, 'Judicial Discretion' (1963) 60(21) The Journal of Philosophy 624–38
Dworkin R, 'The Model of Rules' (1967) 35 University of Chicago Law Review 14–46
Easton S, 'Dangerous Waters: Taking Account of Impact in Sentencing' (2008) (2) Criminal Law Review 105–20
Endicott TAO, *Vagueness in Law* (OUP 2000)
Etienne M, 'Parity, Disparity and Adversariality: First Principles of Sentencing' (2005–2006) 58 Stanford Law Review 309–22
Farmer C, Parsons I, and Bagaric M, 'Inconsistencies in Sentencing of Theft Offenders in Victoria: Implications for the "Instinctive Synthesis"' (2017) 44 Australian Bar Review 318–37
Farrell A, Ward G, and Rousseau D, 'Intersections of Gender and Race in Federal Sentencing: Examining Court Contexts and the Effects of Representative Court Authorities' (2010) 14 Journal of Gender, Race & Justice 85–126
Farrell S, Burke N, and Hay C, 'Revisiting Margaret Thatcher's Law and Order Agenda: The Slow-Burning Fuse of Punitiveness' (2016) 11(2) British Politics 205–31
Frankel ME, 'Lawlessness in Sentencing' (1972) 41 University of Cincinnati Law Review 4–24
Frankel ME, *Criminal Sentences: Law Without Order* (Hill and Wang 1973)
Frase RS, 'Sentencing Principles in Theory and Practice' (1997) 22 Crime & Justice 363
Frase RS, 'Limiting Retributivism' in von Hirsch A, Ashworth A, and Roberts JV, *Principled Sentencing: Readings on Theory and Policy* (3rd edn, Hart 2009)
Frase RS, 'Norval Morris's Contributions to Sentencing Structures, Theory, and Practice' (2009) 21(4) *Federal Sentencing Reporter* 254–60
Frase RS, *Just Sentencing: Principles and Procedures for a Workable System* (OUP 2012)
Frase RS, 'Theories of Proportionality and Desert' in Petersilia J and Reitz KR (eds), *The Oxford Handbook of Sentencing and Corrections* (OUP 2012)
Freiberg A and Krasnostein S, 'Statistics, Damn Statistics and Sentencing' (2011) 21 Journal of Judicial Administration 73–92
Galligan D, *Discretionary Powers: A Legal Study of Official Discretion* (Clarendon 1986)

Gardener J, 'Ashworth on Principles' in Zedner L and Roberts JV, *Principles and Values in Criminal Law and Criminal Justice: Essays in Honour of Andrew Ashworth* (OUP 2012)

Gaudet FJ, *Individual Differences in the Sentencing Tendencies of Judges* (Archives of Psychology 1938)

Greenberg D, *Craies on Legislation* (11th edn, Sweet and Maxwell 2018)

Halliday J, *Making Punishments Work: Report of a Review of the Sentencing Framework for England and Wales* (Home Office 2001)

Handler P, 'The Court for Crown Cases Reserved 1848–1908' 29(1) Law and History Review 259–88

Hannah-Moffat K, 'Algorithmic Risk Governance: Big Data Analytics, Race and Information Activism in Criminal Justice Debates' (2018) 23(4) Theoretical Criminology 1–18

Hall Williams JE, 'Statutes: The First Offenders Act 1958' (1959) 1 The Modern Law Review 41–44

Harris L, 'The Role of the Prosecutor at Sentencing' University of Oxford Faculty of Law Blog, 4 March 2016 <https://www.law.ox.ac.uk/centres-institutes/centre-criminology/blog/2016/03/role-prosecutor-sentencing>

Harris L, *Thomas' Sentencing Referencer 2022* (Sweet and Maxwell 2021)

Harris L and Walker S, 'Difficulties with Dangerousness: The Timing of the Assessment of Risk—Part 1' (2018) 9 Criminal Law Review 695–710

Harris L and Walker S, 'Difficulties with Dangerousness: Determining the Appropriate Sentence—Part 2' (2018) 10 Criminal Law Review 782–807

Harris L and Walker S, *Current Sentencing Practice* (Sweet and Maxwell 2021)

Harris L and Walker S, *Sentencing Principles, Procedure and Practice* (2nd edn, Sweet and Maxwell 2021)

Harris L, Kelly R, Roberts JV, and Tai L, 'A Response to Scottish Sentencing Council's Consultation on the Principles and Purposes of Sentencing Draft Guideline' (2017) 3 Sentencing News 9–13

Harris L, Ashworth A, du Bois-Pedain A, Hough M, Jacobson J, Lightowlers C, Manson A, Padfield N, Player E, Quirk H, and Stark F, 'Academic Response to Sentencing Council's Consultation Paper on the Imposition of Custody and Community Sentences' (2016) 1 Sentencing News 12–17

Hart HLA, 'Discretion' (2013) 127 Harvard Law Review 652–65

Hawkins K, 'The Uses of Legal Discretion: Perspectives from Law and Social Science' in Hawkins K (ed), *The Uses of Discretion* (Clarendon Press 1992)

Hedderman C, 'Government Policy on Women Offenders: Labour's Legacy and the Coalition's Challenge' (2010) 12(4) Punishment and Society 485–500

Heidensohn F and Silvestri M, 'Gender and Crime' in Maguire M, Morgan R, and Reiner R (eds), *The Oxford Handbook of Criminology* (5th edn, OUP 2012)

Herbert A, 'Mode of Trial and the Influence of Local Justice' (2004) 43(1) The Howard Journal 65–78

Hill A, 'Judges given free rein by "pitifully loose" sentencing law' *The Guardian*, 5 April 2010, <https://www.theguardian.com/uk/2010/apr/05/judges-sentencing-andrew-ashworth>

von Hirsch A, *Doing Justice* (Hill and Wang 1976)

von Hirsch A, *Past or Future Crimes: Deservedness and Dangerousness in the Sentencing of Criminals* (Manchester University Press 1986)
von Hirsch A, 'Proportionality in the Philosophy of Punishment' (1996) 16 Crime and Justice
von Hirsch A, 'Proportionate Sentences' in von Hirsch A, Ashworth A, and Roberts JV, *Principled Sentencing: Readings on Theory and Policy* (3rd edn, Hart 2009)
von Hirsch A, *Deserved Criminal Sentences* (Hart 2017)
Hofer PJ, Blackwell KR, and Ruback RB, 'Effect of the Federal Sentencing Guidelines on Inter-judge Sentencing Disparity' (1999) 90(1) Journal of Criminal Law and Criminology 239–306
Hogarth J, *Sentencing as a Human Process* (University of Toronto Press 1971)
Home Office, *Making Punishments Work: Report of a Review of the Sentencing Framework for England and Wales* (Home Office 2001)
Home Office, *Making Sentencing Clearer: A Consultation and Report of a Review by the Home Secretary, Lord Chancellor and Attorney General* (Home Office 2006)
Home Office, and Ministry of Justice, *Integrated Offender Management: Key Principles: February 2015* (Home Office and Ministry of Justice, 2015) <https://www.gov.uk/government/uploads/system/uploads/attachment_data/file/406865/HO_IOM_Key_Principles_document_Final.pdf>
Hood R, *Sentencing in Magistrates' Courts: A Study of Variations of Policy* (Stevens and Sons 1962)
Hood R, *Race and Sentencing* (OUP 1992)
Hopkins K, Uhrig N, and Colahan M, 'Associations between Ethnic Background and Being Sentenced to Prison in the Crown Court in England and Wales in 2015' (Ministry of Justice 2016)
Hough M and Jacobson J, 'Personal Mitigation: An Empirical Analysis in England and Wales' in Roberts JV (ed), *Mitigation and Aggravation at Sentencing* (CUP 2012)
House of Commons Justice Committee, Oral Evidence on The Annual Report of the Sentencing Council, 13 January 2012 (2010–2012) HC 1711 I
Hudson B, 'Discrimination and Disparity: The Influence of Race on Sentencing' (1989) 16(1) Journal of Ethnic and Migration Studies, 23–34
Hutton N, 'Sentencing as a Social Practice' in Armstrong S and McAra L (eds), *Perspectives of Punishment: The Contours of Control* (OUP 2006)
Hutton N, 'Visible and Invisible Sentencing' in Hondeghem A, Rousseaux X, and Schoenaers F (eds), *Modernization of the Criminal Justice Chain and the Judicial System* (Springer 2016)
Hutton N and Tata C, *Patterns of Custodial Sentencing in the Sheriff Court* (The Scottish Office Central Research Unit 1995)
Husak DN, 'The Seriousness of Drug Offences' in Ashworth A and Wasik M (eds), *Fundamentals of Sentencing Theory* (OUP 1998)
Jareborg N, 'Why Bulk Discounts in Sentencing?' in Ashworth A and Wasik M (eds), *Fundamentals of Sentencing Theory: Essays in Honour of Andrew von Hirsch* (Clarendon Press 1998)
Hall Williams, JE, 'The Advisory Council Report: Sentences of Imprisonment' (1978) 18(4) British Journal of Criminology 396–400

Jacobson J and Hough M, *Mitigation: The Role of Personal Factors in Sentencing* (Prison Reform Trust 2007) <http://www.prisonreformtrust.org.uk/uploads/documents/FINALFINALmitigation%20-%20small.pdf>

Judiciary of England and Wales, *The Lord Chief Justice's Report 2016* (Judicial Office 2016)

Justice Committee, *Sixth Report Sentencing Guidelines and Parliament: Building a Bridge* HC 2008-2009 (The Stationary Office 2009)

Kelly R, 'Reforming Maximum Sentences and Respecting Ordinal Proportionality' (2018) 6 Criminal Law Review 450–61

Kelly R and Ashworth A, 'State Responses to Criminal Offences in England and Wales' in Dyson M and Vogel B (eds), *The Limits of Criminal Law: Anglo-German Concepts and Principles* (Intersentia 2018)

Krasnostein S, 'Pursuing Consistency: The effect of different reforms on unjustified disparity in individualised sentencing frameworks' (PhD thesis, Monash University 2015)

Freiberg A and Krasnostein S, 'Pursuing Consistency in an Individualistic Sentencing Framework: If You Know Where You're Going, How Do You Know When You've Got There?' (2013) 76 Law and Contemporary Problems 265–88

Lammy D, 'The Lammy Review: An Independent Review into the Treatment of, and Outcomes for, Black, Asian and Minority Ethnic Individuals in the Criminal Justice System' (Ministry of Justice 2017)

Law Commission of England and Wales, *Sentencing Law in England and Wales—Legislation Currently in Force* (Law Commission 2015)

Leverick F, 'Sentence Discounting for Guilty Pleas: An Argument for Certainty over Discretion' (2014) (5) Criminal Law Review 338–49

Leveson B, The Parmoor Lecture: Achieving Consistency in Sentencing, 24 October 2013 <https://www.judiciary.gov.uk/wp-content/uploads/JCO/Documents/Speeches/leveson-parmoor-lecture-20131031.pdf>

Lightowlers C, 'Drunk and Doubly Deviant? The Role of Gender and Intoxication in Sentencing Assault Offences' (2018) 59(3) British Journal of Criminology 693–717

Lucraft, M (ed), *Archbold Criminal Pleading, Evidence and Practice 2022* (Sweet and Maxwell 2021)

Mason T, de Silva N, Sharma N, Brown D, and Harper G, *Local Variation in Sentencing in England and Wales* (Ministry of Justice 2007)

Mawhinney G, 'Sentencing Murders Done for Gain: The Court of Appeal and Schedule 21' (2015) 3 Sentencing News 8–11

Ministry of Justice, Restorative Justice https://www.gov.uk/government/collections/restorative-justice-action-plan (2013)

Ministry of Justice, *Breaking the Cycle: Effective Punishment, Rehabilitation and Sentencing of Offenders: Evidence Report* (Ministry of Justice 2010)

Ministry of Justice, *Breaking the Cycle: Government Response* Cm 8070 (The Stationary Office 2010)

Ministry of Justice, *Black, Asian and Minority Ethnic Disproportionality in the Criminal Justice System in England and Wales* (Ministry of Justice 2016)

Ministry of Justice, *Statistics on Women and the Criminal Justice System 2017: A Ministry of Justice Publication under Section 95 of the Criminal Justice Act 1991* (Ministry of Justice 2018)

BIBLIOGRAPHY 307

Ministry of Justice, Female Offenders Strategy, Cm 9642 (Ministry of Justice 2018)
Mitchell B, 'Identifying and Punishing the More Serious Murders' (2016) 7 Criminal Law Review 467–77
Moore LD and Padavic I, 'Risk Assessment Tools and Racial/Ethnic Disparities in the Juvenile Justice System' (2011) 5(10) Sociology Compass 850–58
Morris N, *Punishment, Desert and Rehabilitation in Equal Justice Under the Law* (US Government Printing Office 1977)
Morris N, 'Towards Principled Sentencing' (1977) 37 Maryland Law Review 267–85
Morris N, *Madness and the Criminal Law* (University of Chicago Press 1982)
Munro C, 'Judicial Independence and Judicial Functions' in Munro C and Wasik M (eds), *Sentencing, Judicial Discretion and Training* (Sweet and Maxwell 1992)
Northern Ireland Assembly, 'Sentencing Guidelines Mechanisms in Other Jurisdictions: Research Paper' (79/16) (Northern Ireland Assembly Research and Information Service 2016)
Ofsted, 'Learning and Skills for Offenders Serving Short Custodial Sentences' January 2009, <http://dera.ioe.ac.uk/338/1/Learning%20and%20skills%20for%20offenders%20serving%20short%20custodial%20sentences.pdf>
The Open University, 'George Edalji' <http://www.open.ac.uk/researchprojects/makingbritain/content/george-edalji>
O'Malley T, 'Living without Guidelines' in Ashworth A and Roberts JV (eds), *Sentencing Guidelines: Exploring the English Model* (OUP 2013)
O'Malley T, 'Judgment and Calculation in the Selection of Sentence' (2017) 28(3) Criminal Law Forum 361–89
Padfield N, 'Time to Bury the Custody Threshold?' (2011) 8 Criminal Law Review 593–612
Padfield N, 'Intoxication as a Sentencing Factor: Aggravation or Mitigation?' in Roberts JV (ed), *Mitigation and Aggravation at Sentencing* (CUP 2011), 81–101
Palys TS and Divorski S, 'Explaining Sentence Disparity' (1986) 28 Canadian Journal of Criminology 347–62
Pattenden R, *English Criminal Appeals 1844–1944: Appeals against Conviction and Sentence in England and Wales* (Clarendon Press 1996)
Pina-Sanchez J and Linacre R, 'Sentencing Consistency in England and Wales: Evidence from the Crown Court Sentencing Survey' (2013) 53(6) British Journal of Criminology 1118–38
Pina-Sanchez J and Linacre R, 'Enhancing Consistency in Sentencing: Exploring the Effects of Guidelines in England and Wales' (2014) 30(4) Journal of Quantitative Criminology 731–48
Pina-Sanchez J and Linacre R, 'Refining the Measurement of Consistency in Sentencing: A Methodological Review' (2016) 44 International Journal of Law, Crime and Justice 68–87
Pina-Sanchez J and Linacre R, 'Sentencing Gender? Investigating the Presence of Gender Disparities in Crown Court Sentences' (2020) 1 Criminal Law Review 3–28
Pina-Sanchez J, Roberts JV, and Sferopoulos D, 'Does the Crown Court Discriminate Against Muslim-Named Offenders? A Novel Investigation Based on Text Mining Techniques' (2019) 59(3) British Journal of Criminology 718–36
Piper C, 'Should Impact Constitute Mitigation?: Structured Discretion versus Mercy' [2007] Criminal Law Review 141–55

Potter H, *Intersectionality and Criminology: Disrupting and Revolutionizing Studies of Crime* (Routledge 2015)

Radzinowicz L and Hood R, 'Judicial Discretion and Sentencing Standards: Victorian Attempts to Solve a Perennial Problem' (1979) 127(5) University of Pennsylvania Law Review 1288–349

Raine JW and Dunstan E, 'How Well do Sentencing Guidelines Work?: Equity, Proportionality and Consistency in the Determination of Fine Levels in the Magistrates' Courts of England and Wales' (2009) 48(1) The Howard Journal 13–36

Raz J, 'Legal Principles and the Limits of the Law' (1972) 81 The Yale Law Journal 823–54

Rehavi MM and Starr SB, 'Racial Disparity in Federal Criminal Sentences' (2014) 122(6) Journal of Political Economy, 1320–54

Reiner R, 'Law-and-order Politics' *The Guardian*, 22 December 2008 <https://www.theguardian.com/commentisfree/2008/dec/22/police-conservatives>

Richardson PJ (ed), *Archbold Criminal Pleading, Evidence and Practice 2018* (Sweet and Maxwell 2017)

Roberts JV, 'Sentencing Guidelines in England and Wales: A Review of Recent Developments' (2010) 82 Centre for Crime and Justice Studies 41–42

Roberts JV, 'Punishing, More or Less: Exploring Aggravation and Mitigation at Sentencing' in Roberts JV (ed), *Mitigation and Aggravation at Sentencing* (CUP 2011)

Roberts JV, 'Addressing the Problems of the Prison Estate: The Role of Sentencing Policy' (2017) 231 Prison Service Journal 8–14

Roberts JV and Ashworth A, 'The Evolution of Sentencing Policy and Practice in England and Wales, 2003–2015' (2016) 45(1) Crime and Justice 307–58

Roberts JV and Bradford B, 'Sentence Reductions for a Guilty Plea in England and Wales: Exploring New Empirical Trends' (2015) 12(2) Journal of Empirical Legal Studies, 187–210

Roberts JV and Harris L, 'Reconceptualising the Custody Threshold in England and Wales' (2017) 28(3) Criminal Law Forum 477–99

Roberts JV and de Keiser JW, 'Democratising Punishment: Sentencing, Community Views and Values' (2014) 16(4) Punishment and Society 474–498

Roberts JV and Rafferty A, 'Sentencing Guidelines in England and Wales: Exploring the New Format' (2011) 9 Criminal Law Review 681–89

Roberts JV, Hough M, and Ashworth A, 'Personal Mitigation, Public Opinion and Sentencing Guidelines in England and Wales' (2011) 7 Criminal Law Review 524–30

Roberts JV, Harris L, and Pei W, 'Structuring Judicial Discretion in China: Exploring the 2014 Sentencing Guidelines' (2016) 27 Criminal Law Forum 3–33

Roberts JV, Ryberg J, and de Keiser JW, 'Sentencing the Multiple Offender: Setting the Stage' in Roberts JV, Ryberg J, and de Keiser JW (eds), *Sentencing Multiple Crimes* (OUP 2017)

Robinson P, 'The A.L.I.'s Proposed Distributive Principle of "Limiting Retributivism": Does It Mean in Practice Anything Other than Pure Desert?' (2003) 7(3) Buffalo Criminal Law Review 3–15

Samuels A, 'Consistency in Sentencing' in Pennington DC and Lloyd-Bostock S (eds), *The Psychology of Sentencing: Approaches to Consistency and Disparity* (Centre for Socio-Legal Studies 1987)

Schneider CE, 'Discretion and Rules' in Hawkins K (ed), *The Uses of Discretion* (Clarendon 1992)
Scottish Sentencing Council, 'About Sentencing' <https://www.scottishsentencing council.org.uk/about-sentencing/>
Scottish Sentencing Council, *Definitive Guideline on Principles and Purposes of Sentencing* (Scottish Sentencing Council 2018)
Sentencing Advisory Council, *Sentencing Guidance in Victoria: Report* (Sentencing Advisory Council 2016)
The Sentencing Commission for Scotland, *The Scope to Improve Consistency in Sentencing—Report 2006*
Sentencing Commission Working Group, *Sentencing Guidelines in England and Wales: An Evolutionary Approach* (Ministry of Justice 2008)
Sentencing Council, Our work, <https://www.sentencingcouncil.org.uk/sentencing-and-the-council/>
Sentencing Council, Sentencing: How it works, <https://www.cps.gov.uk/legal-guidance/sentencing-overview-general-principles-and-mandatory-custodial-sentences>
Sentencing Council, *Sentencing guidelines and the Sentencing Council* <https://www.sentencingcouncil.org.uk/wp-content/uploads/Presentation_-_for_researchers_and_academics.pdf>
Sentencing Council, *Minutes of Meeting of the Sentencing Council, 22–23 April 2010*, <https://www.sentencingcouncil.org.uk/wp-content/uploads/web_22_23-04-2010.pdf>
Sentencing Council, *Assault Offences Definitive Guideline* (Office of the Sentencing Council 2011)
Sentencing Council, *Crown Court Sentencing Survey Experimental Statistics* (Office of the Sentencing Council 2011)
Sentencing Council, *Offences Taken into Consideration and Totality Guideline* (Office of the Sentencing Council 2012)
Sentencing Council, *Robbery Guideline: Consultation* (Office of the Sentencing Council 2014)
Sentencing Council, *Sexual Offences: Response to Consultation* (Office of the Sentencing Council 2014)
Sentencing Council, *Allocation Definitive Guideline (2016)* (Office of the Sentencing Council 2016)
Sentencing Council, *Children and Young Persons Definitive Guideline (2017)* (Office of the Sentencing Council 2017)
Sentencing Council, *Imposition of Community and Custodial Sentences Definitive Guideline* (Office of the Sentencing Council 2017)
Sentencing Council, *Reduction in Sentence for a Guilty Plea Definitive Guideline* (Office of the Sentencing Council 2017)
Sentencing Council, *Chairman's letter to sentencers on imposition of community and custodial sentences*, 24 April 2018, <https://www.sentencingcouncil.org.uk/news/item/chairmans-letter-to-sentencers-on-imposition-of-community-and-custodial-sentences/>
Sentencing Council, *Domestic Abuse Definitive Guideline (2018)* (Office of the Sentencing Council 2018)

Sentencing Council, *General Guideline: Overarching Principles* (Office of the Sentencing Council 2019)

Sentencing Council, *Theft Offences Guideline Assessment* (Office of the Sentencing Council 2019)

Sentencing Council, *Investigating the Association between an Offender's Sex and Ethnicity and the Sentence Imposed at the Crown Court for Drug Offences* (Office of the Sentencing Council 2020)

Sentencing Council, *A Review of Consistency in Sentencing* (Office of the Sentencing Council 2021)

Sentencing Council, *The Impact of Three Guidelines on Consistency in Sentencing* (Office of the Sentencing Council 2021)

Sentencing Guidelines Council, *Overarching Principles: Seriousness Definitive Guideline* (Sentencing Guidelines Council 2004)

Shapiro S, 'The Hart–Dworkin Debate: A Short Guide for the Perplexed' (2007) (77) Public Law and Legal Theory Working Paper Series, University of Michigan Law School 1–54

Shaw GC, 'HLA Hart's Lost Essay' (2013) 127 Harvard Law Review 666–727

Shiner R, 'Hart on Judicial Discretion' (2011) 5 Problemas 341–62

Silverman R and Dixon H, 'Lawyer Who Called 13-Year-Old "Predatory" Is Barred from Sex Offence Cases' *The Telegraph*, 7 August 2013 <https://www.telegraph.co.uk/news/uknews/crime/10228621/Lawyer-who-called-13-year-old-predatory-is-barred-from-sex-offence-cases.html>

Slobogin C, 'Plea Bargaining and the Substantive and Procedural Goals of Criminal Justice: From Retribution and Adversarialism to Preventive Justice and Hybrid-Inquisitorialism' (2015) 57(4) William & Mary Law Review 1505–1547

Spencer JR, *Jackson's Machinery of Justice* (8th edn, CUP 1989)

Spigelman J, 'Consistency and Sentencing' (2008) 82 Australian Law Journal 450–60

Spigelman J, Chief Justice of NSW, 'Consistency and Sentencing: Keynote speech to the National Judicial College of Australia' Canberra, 8 February 2008

Spohn C, 'Thirty Years of Sentencing Reform: The Quest for a Racially Neutral Sentencing Process' (US Department of Justice 2000)

Spohn C, *How Do Judges Decide? The Search for Fairness and Justice in Punishment* (Sage 2009)

Spohn C, 'Racial Disparities in Prosecution, Sentencing, and Punishment' in Bucerius S and Tonry M (eds), *The Oxford Handbook of Ethnicity, Crime, and Immigration* (OUP 2014)

Starr SB and Rehavi MM, 'Mandatory Sentencing and Racial Disparity: Assessing the Role of Prosecutors and the Effects of Booker' (2013) 123(1) The Yale Law Journal, 2–80

Steffensmeir D, Kramer J, and Streifel C, 'Gender and Imprisonment Decisions' (1993) 31(3) Criminology 411–46

Stolzenberg L and D'Alessio SJ, 'Sentencing and Unwarranted Disparity: An Empirical Assessment of the Long-Term Impact Sentencing Guidelines in Minnesota' (1994) 32(2) Criminology 301–10

Tarling R, *Sentencing Practice in Magistrates' Courts: A Home Office Research Unit Report* (Home Office 1979)

Tarling R, 'Sentencing Practice in Magistrates' Courts Revisited' (2006) 45(1) The Howard Journal 29–41

Tata C, 'Sentencing as Craftwork and the Binary Epistemologies of the Discretionary Decision Process' (2007) 16(2) Social and Legal Studies 425–47

Tata C, and Hutton N, 'What "Rules" in Sentencing? Consistency and Disparity in the Absence of "Rules"' (1998) 26 International Journal of the Sociology of Law 339–64

Tata C, Burns N, and Halliday S, 'Assisting and Advising the Sentencing Decision Process: The Pursuit of "Quality" in Pre-Sentence Reports' (2008) 48 British Journal of Criminology 835–55

Thomas D, *Principles of Sentencing* (Heinemann 1970)

Thomas D, *Constraints on judgment: The search for structured discretion in sentencing, 1860-1910: Institute of Criminology Occasional Series No 4* (University of Cambridge Institute of Criminology 1979)

Thomas D, 'Detention and Training Orders' (2000) 4 Sentencing News 7

Thomas D, 'Judicial Discretion' in Gelsthorpe L and Padfield N (eds), *Exercising Discretion Decision Making in the Criminal Justice System and Beyond* (Routledge 2011)

Tonry M, 'Punishment Policies and Patterns in Western Countries' in Tonry M and Frase RF (eds), *Sentencing and Sanctions in Western Countries* (OUP 2001)

Tonry M, *Punishment and Politics: Evidence and Emulation in the Making of English Crime Control Policy* (Willan 2004)

Tonry M, 'Individualizing Punishments' in von Hirsch A, Ashworth A, and Roberts JV (eds), *Principled Sentencing: Readings on Theory and Policy* (3rd edn, Hart 2009)

Treacy C, 'Letter to the Editor' (2016) 7 Criminal Law Review 489–490

Visher CA, 'Gender, Police Arrest Decisions, and Notions of Chivalry' (1983) 21(1) Criminology 5–28

Wandall RH, 'Resisting Risk Assessment? Pre-Sentence Reports and Individualized Sentencing in Denmark' (2010) 12(3) Punishment & Society 329–47

Warner K, 'Theories of Sentencing: Punishment and the Deterrent Value of Sentencing, Sentencing: From Theory to Practice', Canberra, 8–9 February 2014, 5.

Wasik M, 'Time to Repeal the Firearms Minimum Sentence Provision' (2017) 3 Criminal Law Review 203–212

Wasik M and von Hirsch A, 'Non-Custodial Penalties and the Principles of Desert' [1988] Criminal Law Review 555–572

Wasik M and Pease K, 'Discretion and Sentencing Reform: The Alternative' in Wasik M and Pease K (eds), *Sentencing Reform: Guidance or Guidelines?* (Manchester University Press 1987)

Willis J, Some Aspects of the Prosecutor's Role at Sentencing, Conference paper, 'Prosecuting Justice Conference' Australian Institute of Criminology in Melbourne, 18–19 April 1996

Wintour P, Stratton A, and Travis A, 'Ken Clarke Forced to Abandon 50% Sentence Cuts for Guilty Pleas' *The Guardian*, 21 June 2011 <https://www.theguardian.com/law/2011/jun/20/ken-clarke-abandon-sentence-cuts>

Woolf H, Jowell QC, JL, Donnelly C, Hare QC, I, and Bell J, *De Smith's Judicial Review* (8th edn, Sweet and Maxwell 2021)

Young W and King A, 'Addressing Problematic Sentencing Factors in the Development of Guidelines' in Roberts JV (ed), *Mitigation and Aggravation at Sentencing* (CUP 2012)

Young W, 'The Origins and Evolution of Sentencing Guidelines: A Comparison of England and Wales and New Zealand' in Ashworth A and Roberts JV (eds), *Sentencing Guidelines* (OUP 2013)

Index

For the benefit of digital users, indexed terms that span two pages (e.g., 52–53) may, on occasion, appear on only one of those pages.

assisting the prosecution
  statutory methods of
    structure 175–76

chivalry theory 63–64
consistency
  approach
    Sentencing Council definition 27
    England and Wales 26–27
  approach or outcome? 25–34
  benefits 14–15
  conclusions 34–41
  conclusions 281–300
  definition 18–22
  disparity 18–22
  England and Wales
    lessons to be learned 292–95
  existing accounts 16
  fairness 1
  general 4, 13–41
  importance of 13–15, 16
  and individualised justice 77–107
  lack of clarity 13–14, 16
  lessons for other
    jurisdictions 295–300
  methods of structure 13–14
  natural justice 1
  need for flexibility 29
  outcome 30
    uniformity 31
    criticism 31–32
  principled sentencing 21–22
  procedural device 29–30, 32–33
  procedural or substantive? 32–34
  range of permissible sentences 21–22
  revised definition 38–41
  substantive 33

summary of conclusions 18
treating like cases alike 22–25
Corston Report 62–67
Court of Appeal
  limits on the court's ability to provide
    structure 228–31
  structuring discretion 189–233
    conclusions 231–33
    guideline judgment 213–15
    history 190–95
    interpreting Sentencing Council
      guideline 215–19
    interpreting statute 219–26
    offences: approach 203–6
    principles 200–3
    reviewing specific cases 206–13
    sentencing procedure 226–28
    types of guidance 195–228

discretion 2
  importance of 44
  disparity 8

empirical evidence 43–76
  chivalry theory 63–64
  conclusions 75–76
  Corston report 62–67
  evil women theory 65–66
  examination of
    approach 44–45
  Frankel 43, 77
  gender 62–67
  geographical differences 51–57
  Halliday Report 52–53
  Hogarth, John 59–60
  human element 57–62
  hypothetical cases 49–50

empirical evidence (cont.)
　intersectionality 73–75
　introduction 46–75
　local justice 51–57
　methodological challenges 48–51
　　multiple offences 50–51
　personal penal philosophy 57–62
　race/ethnicity 68–73
　real cases 49–50
　sentencing guidelines 274–77
　sex 62–67
　sex/gender
　　mixed theory 66
　　summary 67
　Tarling, Roger 53–54
England and Wales 3–5
　non-retributive factors 8–9
　parsimony 8–9
　proportionality 2, 6, 9
　　lack of clarity 7
　retributivism 3, 5
　　limiting retributivism 7
ethnicity/race 68–73
　Hood, Roger 69–70
　Hudson 69
evil women theory 65–66

gender/sex 62–67
guidelines see Sentencing Council
　constraint 268–74
　empirical literature 274–77
　guilty plea 176–77
　offence range vs category range 273–74

Halliday Report 52–53, 150
　personal penal philosophy 58

individualised justice
　case law 93
　conclusions 107
　consequentialist 88
　culpability 87–88
　deterrence 90–91
　generally 77–107
　importance 78–80
　judicial discretion 96–99
　Krasnostein and Freiberg 97
　limiting retributivism 87–88
　offence or offender? 80–84
　rehabilitation 88–89
　structure 85–96
　tension 104–7
　the basic concept 78–80
introduction 1–2

judicial discretion
　conclusions 141
　Dworkin 112–15
　exercise of 124–31
　guidelines see Sentencing Council:
　　constraint
　Hart 112–15
　identifying judicial
　　discretion 116–24
　individualised justice 96–99
　methods of structure
　　limiting 137–39
　　guiding 139–41
　Raz 112–15
　statutory methods of structure see
　　statutory methods of structuring
　　discretion
　structure 109–41
　summary of argument 115
　what is judicial discretion? 110–32

mandatory sentences 183–86
minimum and mandatory
　sentences 179–86
　mandatory sentences 183–86
　minimum sentences 179–83
minimum sentences 179–83
Morris, Norval
　range of permissible sentences 22
multiple offences 177–79

parsimony 8–9
penal philosophies 26, 57–62
permissible range of sentences 21–22
　individualised justice 99–104
previous convictions 251
proportionality 6
　harm 3
　retributive proportionality 2

purposes of sentencing
England and Wales 155
lack of clarity 7

race/ethnicity 68–73

Sentencing Council
constraint on sentencers 268–74
content of sentencing
guideline 238–42
empirical literature 274–77
guideline development
process 237
guidelines
Step 2 250–51
history 236–38
offence-specific guidelines 242–58
interpretation of 247–53
overarching guidelines 258–68
interpretation of 261–62
guilty plea guideline 262–68
robbery guideline 253–58
structure
extent to which guidelines limit
discretion 268–74
conclusions 277–79
structure through
guidelines 235–79
substantive guidance 268
the need for guidance on
principles 258–60
sex/gender 62–67

statutory methods of structuring
discretion 143–88
assisting the prosecution 175–76
conclusions 186–88
Criminal Law Commissioners 145
England and Wales
Advisory Council 162
aggravation and
mitigation 170–74
available sentences 158–70
general provisions 151–58
maximum sentences 159–63
principles 151–58
purposes of sentencing 155
the extent to which discretion
is structured by
Parliament 186–87
guilty plea 176–77
minimum and mandatory
sentences 179–86
Parliament's role 144–51
politics 148–49
history 148
Royal Commission 147
totality 177–79

Tarling, Roger 53–54
theory v practice 9–10
totality 177–79
treating like cases alike 22–25

weight of guideline factors 250–51